The Making of Northeast Asia

Studies in Asian Security

A SERIES SPONSORED BY THE EAST-WEST CENTER

Muthiah Alagappa, Chief Editor
Distinguished Senior Fellow, East-West Center

The *Studies in Asian Security* book series promotes analysis, understanding, and explanation of the dynamics of domestic, transnational, and international security challenges in Asia. The peer-reviewed publications in the Series analyze contemporary security issues and problems to clarify debates in the scholarly community, provide new insights and perspectives, and identify new research and policy directions. Security is defined broadly to include the traditional political and military dimensions as well as nontraditional dimensions that affect the survival and well being of political communities. Asia, too, is defined broadly to include Northeast, Southeast, South, and Central Asia.

Designed to encourage original and rigorous scholarship, books in the *Studies in Asian Security* series seek to engage scholars, educators, and practitioners. Wide-ranging in scope and method, the Series is receptive to all paradigms, programs, and traditions, and to an extensive array of methodologies now employed in the social sciences.

★   ★   ★

The East-West Center promotes better relations and understanding among the people and nations of the United States, Asia, and the Pacific through cooperative study, research, and dialogue. Established by the U.S. Congress in 1960, the Center serves as a resource for information and analysis on critical issues of common concern, bringing people together to exchange views, build expertise, and develop policy options. The Center is an independent, public, nonprofit organization with funding from the U.S. government, and additional support provided by private agencies, individuals, foundations, corporations, and governments in the region.

The Making of Northeast Asia

Kent Calder and Min Ye

SPONSORED BY THE EAST-WEST CENTER
Stanford University Press • *Stanford, California*

Published in the East-West Center sponsored Series in Asian Security
under the auspices of the John Hopkins University,
SAIS Reischauer Center for East Asian Studies

Stanford University Press
Stanford, California

Printed in the United States of America

Library of Congress Cataloging-in-Publication Data

Calder, Kent E.
    The making of Northeast Asia / Kent Calder and Min Ye.
        p. cm. — (Studies in Asian security)
    Includes bibliographical references and index.
    ISBN 978-0-8047-6921-1 (cloth : alk. paper)—
    ISBN 978-0-8047-6922-8 (pbk : alk. paper)
        1. Regionalism—East Asia. 2. East Asia—Politics and government. 3. East Asia—
Economic integration. 4. East Asian cooperation. I. Ye, Min. II. Title. III. Series:
Studies in Asian security.
    JQ1499.A38R43235 2010
    320.951—dc22   2009049773

This book is printed on acid-free, archival-quality paper.

Typeset at Stanford University Press in 10/13.5 Bembo

To XIA AIYU
and
to the memory of
ROSE EYRING CALDER

Contents

9 Japan's Dilemma and the Making of Northeast Asia 204

Japan's Tangled Continental Ties, 205 Fukuzawa's Dilemma Revisited, 208
A Mixed History: Japan and Region-Building, 210 Regionalism and the
Emerging Profile of Japanese Domestic Political Interests, 212 Bureaucracy
and Regionalism, 215 Country-Specific Interests, 217 The Key Role of
Japanese Business, 220 Opponents of Closer Regional Ties, 221
In Conclusion, 222

10 The United States and Northeast Asian Regionalism 225

Northeast Asia's Importance to the United States, 226 America's Early
Absence from Northeast Asia, 229 Key Traits of the Classic San Francisco
System, 231 America's Changing Geopolitical Stakes, 232 America's Own
Transformation, 236 Deepening Corporate Stakes in Stable Trans-Pacific
Relations, 241 The Overall Profile of American Interests and Northeast
Asia's Future, 243 In Conclusion, 245

In Conclusion

11 Summing Up 251

Northeast Asia's Quiet Yet Fateful Transformation, 252 The Political
Dimension, 256 What Is New in This Analysis, 258 Implications for the
Broader World, 265

Notes 273

Bibliography 313

Index 325

Tables and Figures

Tables

Figures

Preface

The evolution of social, economic, and political ties among China, Japan, and Korea has fateful importance for global affairs in the twenty-first century. Japan and China are the largest economies on earth, apart from the United States, and together hold well over half of the world's foreign-exchange reserves. South Korea is an advanced nation in its own right. The Korean peninsula's internal uncertainties—particularly North Korea's nuclear and missile programs—could impact both Sino-Japanese relations and the broader world. Japan, China, and Korea are all technological powers of consequence in different political-economic spheres.

If the Northeast Asian trio actively collaborate, they could become the catalyst for a new global order—one of the few potential challenges to U.S. global hegemony. If the trio finds itself in conflict, its struggles could destabilize Asia, and perhaps the world. Northeast Asia holds, in short, a potential to reshape the world as we know it that is matched only by uncertainties in the Middle East.

Northeast Asia and its future have fascinated both of us throughout most of our careers. One coauthor has lived eleven years in Japan, taught at Seoul National University in Korea, and traveled more than 150 times across the Pacific, to all three countries of this region, over half a century. The younger co-author was born and raised in China, graduated from Beijing University, and has lived and traveled in Korea and Japan also. Together we have interviewed leaders, conducted seminars, and visited locations across the region—ranging from Korea's North-South railway station near Kaesong to Chiang Kai-shek's birthplace on the Chinese mainland—that bear powerful evidence to the historic transformations now underway.

This book has been close to a decade in the making—a decade over which we have seen our early premonitions—once intensely controversial—increasingly vindicated. The imagination of the senior coauthor was piqued first by the geopolitical changes set in motion by the historic Pyongyang summit of June, 2000, about which he wrote ("The New Face of Northeast Asia") for the Winter, 2001 issue of *Foreign Affairs*. Research at the East-West Center as a Pohang Fellow during the summer and fall of 2001 allowed him to deepen these conceptions further.

We began working as a team in the spring of 2002, just as the junior author, Min Ye, arrived in Princeton. Our first collaboration, as faculty advisor and graduate student, came in the fall of 2002, when we did a readings course on comparative regionalism together. This led to a joint paper on critical junctures and East Asian regionalism, which was published in *The Journal of East Asian Studies* (2004), and a decision to write this book together. In that connection, Min spent close to a year in residence at the SAIS Reischauer Center, where she completed first drafts of Chapters 5, 6, and 7. She has also done critical quantitative research and graphic presentation throughout. Cooperative research work in Korea and China, as well as a seminar that Kent taught at Seoul National University in the summer of 2007, were also important in the development of the ideas presented here. Seminars at Beijing University, East West Center, Fudan University, Harvard University, the Japanese Institute of Developing Economies, Korea University, SAIS, Sejeong Institute, Seoul National University, Stanford University, UC Berkeley, Waseda University, and Yonsei University, as well as panels at the American Political Science Association, the Association of Asian Studies, the International Political Science Association, and the International Studies Association also gave us important feedback.

Over the course of such a long and complex project, we have many people and institutions to thank. First and foremost are our spouses and our families, whose understanding we particularly appreciate. The Reischauer Center for East Asian Studies at SAIS has provided important financial support, and this book is written under its auspices. We also warmly thank the East-West Center for its support— both through the Pohang Fellowship Program, and through generous publication support. Boston University and the Princeton-Harvard China and the World Program also contributed to the book's production. Valued research assistance has come from Mariko de Freytas, Sato Momoko, Yoshikawa Yukie, Wang Yanan, and Zhang Qin. We are also grateful to Muthiah Alagappa, who introduced us to his fine series at Stanford University Press, and gave insightful advice throughout. Geoffrey Burns and John Feneron at the Press have also been most helpful. We are likewise grateful to numerous academic colleagues, including Amitav Acharya,

Vinod Aggarwal, Cho Lee-jae, Choo Yong-shik, Thomas Christensen, Chung Jae-ho, Bruce Cumings, Joseph Fewsmith, Fukushima Kiyohiko, Francis Fukuyama, Bill Grimes, Guo Dingping, Stephan Haggard, Han Seung-soo, Hyun In-taek, Karl Jackson, Peter Katzenstein, Kim Choong-nam, Atul Kohli, David Lampton, Haillie Lee, Lee Sook-jong, Moon Chung-in, Charles Morrison, Paik Jin-hyun, T. J. Pempel, Qin Yaqing, John Ravenhill, Gil Rozman, Bob Scalapino, Urata Shujiro, Wang Jisi, Lynn White, Yabushita Shiro, Yamazawa Ippei, Yoon Young-kwan, Zha Daojiong, and Zhang Yunling, among others, for their advice and comments along the way. Responsibility for facts and conclusions, however, must lie with us alone.

Both of us, having grown up in very different worlds, and having seen our own respective worlds change radically in recent years, cannot help but have a special interest in understanding political-economic change, both theoretically and practically. There is no higher task, for both scholarship and policy, as we see it, than understanding the forces that drive the future, in a manageable empirical context. Northeast Asia is such a context, and the forces at work there are fatefully reshaping our world, as a decade of research has shown us, and as the reader will hopefully come to see in the pages to come.

May, 2010   *Kent E. Calder*
                                                              Washington, D.C.

                                                                   Min Ye
                                                       Boston, Massachusetts

A Note on Conventions

Japanese, Korean, and Chinese personal names throughout the text are presented in their countries' conventional forms—that is, with the surname followed by the given name, in reversal of standard Western practice. We also follow the varied local conventions of Northeast Asia regarding the spelling and punctuation of given names. Regarding Korean and Taiwanese names, a hyphen is used between the characters of given names. In the case of mainland Chinese names, however, hyphens are not used. We also employ different romanization systems for Taiwanese and mainland Chinese expressions. In the Taiwanese case, we use the Wades-Giles system, commonly used in Taiwan. In the mainland Chinese case, we use the pinyin system, commonly employed in the PRC. The Ministry of Culture (MC) system of romanization is used for Korean expressions. Japanese expressions and book titles are rendered without macrons. Korea refers to the Republic of Korea, otherwise known as South Korea, unless otherwise specified.

Flashback

A Simple Journey

The ferry left Shimonoseki's pier promptly at 9:00 P.M., after dinner, on an overnight voyage traversing the Tsushima Straits to Pusan. The fare was Y3.55. Arriving on the Korean shores at first light, and after a brief tour of Pusan, the sightseeing group proceeded to Seoul by train. There they visited Kyongbok Palace, Nanzan Park, and the Botanic Garden.

Overnighting in Seoul, and following a morning excursion to the ancient Chinese settlement at Incheon, the group boarded a night train northbound. Arriving at Pyongyang at breakfast time, for a Seoul–Pyongyang fare of Y5, they spent the morning sightseeing, and enjoyed lunch, before once again boarding the Mukden train. After crossing the Yalu at Antung, passengers adjusted their watches by an hour, breezed through perfunctory Chinese customs, and continued on the South Manchurian Railway to Mukden itself, arriving around 9:30 P.M, after a pleasant, leisurely dinner onboard, offering optional Western or Japanese cuisine, for Y1.50. The next day they hired a horse carriage for a leisurely city tour, including the old city, the new city, and the Manchurian Medical College.

The year was 1928. The group had freely explored distinctive parts of Japan, Korea, and China's Northeast, in five days. Counting accommodations, rail, and ferry fare, the cost had been less than Y50, or around US$12.00, at prevailing exchange rates. The political complications had been minimal.[1]

The human profile of Northeast Asia, needless to say, has changed. Yet the geography has not. And economic interdependence across the region is rising. How and when might the easy interchange that prevailed in earlier years reassert itself? And what would a more unified Northeast Asia mean for the broader world?

Abbreviations

ABMI	Asian Bond Market Initiative
ADB	Asian Development Bank
AFC	Asian Financial Crisis
AMF	Asian Monetary Fund
ANEAN	Association of Northeast Asian Nations
APEC	Asia Pacific Economic Cooperation
APSC	Asia Pacific Sphere of Cooperation
APT	ASEAN Plus Three
ARATS	Association for Relations across the Taiwan Strait
ARF	ASEAN Regional Forum
ASEAN	Association of Southeast Asian Nations
ASPAC	Asian and Pacific Council
BESETO	Beijing-Seoul-Tokyo Corridor
BFA	Boao Forum for Asia
BYS	Bohai-Yellow Sea area
CASS	Chinese Academy of Social Sciences
CCP	Chinese Communist Party
CEPA	Closer Economic Partnership Arrangement
CFC	Combined Forces Command
CJ	critical juncture
CMI	Chiang Mai Initiative
CSCAP	Council for Security Cooperation in the Asia-Pacific

DMZ	demilitarized zone
DPJ	Democratic Party of Japan
DPP	Democratic Progressive Party of Taiwan
DPRK	Democratic People's Republic of Korea
EAC	East Asian Community
EAEG	East Asian Economic Grouping
EAFTA	East Asian Free Trade Area
EAS	East Asia Summit
EASG	East Asian Study Group
EAVG	East Asian Vision Group
EC/EU	European Community
ECAFE	UN Economic Commission for Asia and the Far East
ECFA	Economic Cooperation Framework Agreement
EEC	European Economic Community
FDI	foreign direct investment
FSA	financial supervisory agency (Japan)
FSS	financial supervisory service (Korea)
FTA	free trade agreement
GM	General Motors
GND/GDP	gross national (domestic) product
GSDF	Ground Self-Defense Force
HEU	highly enriched uranium
IMF	International Monetary Fund
IT	information technologies
JERC	Japan Economic Research Center
JETRO	Japan External Trade Organization
JSP	Japan Socialist Party
KEDO	Korean Peninsula Energy Development Organization
KIEP	Korean Institute for Economic Policy
KMT	Nationalist Party of Taiwan
KORUS	Korea-U.S.
KRIHS	Korea Research Institute for Human Settlement
LDP	Liberal Democratic Party
LNG	liquefied natural gas
LWR	light water reactor

MCEDSEA	Ministerial Conference on Economic Development in Southeast Asia
METI	Japanese Ministry of Economics, Trade, and Industry
MIA	missing in action
MOF	Japan's Ministry of Finance
MOFA	Japan's Ministry of Foreign Affairs
MSDF	Maritime Self Defense Force
NAFTA	North America Free Trade Agreement
NATO	North Atlantic Treaty Organization
NDFL	National Defense Foreign Language Program
NEADB	Northeast Asian Development Bank
NEAEF	Northeast Asia Economic Forum
NEAT	Network of East Asian Think Tanks
NER	Northeastern Rejuvenation Program (China)
NET	natural economic territories
NGO	nongovernmental organization
NIRA	National Institute for Research Advancement (Japan)
NPC	Chinese Communist Party National Party Congress
NPT	non-proliferation treaty
PAFTA	Pacific Free Trade Area
PAFTAD	Pacific Trade and Development
PBEC	Pacific Basin Economic Council
PECC	Pacific Economic Cooperation Conference
PLA	People's Liberation Army (China)
PRC	People's Republic of China
PRD	Pearl River Delta (China)
ROK	Republic of Korea
RTA	regional treaty agreement
SAR	Special Administrative Region
SCO	Shanghai Cooperation Organization
SEATO	Southeast Asia Treaty Organization
SED	strategic and economic dialogue
SEF	Straits Exchange Foundation
SOP	standard operating procedures
TCOG	Trilateral Coordination and Oversight Group

TEMM	Tripartite Environmental Ministers' Meeting
TRADP	Tumen River Area Development Project
UNDP	UN Development Program
VW	Volkswagen
WTO	World Trade Organization
YRD	Yellow River Delta (China)

PART I

INTRODUCTION AND THEORY

1

Northeast Asia in Global Perspective

Northeast Asia, where the interests of three major nuclear powers and the world's three largest economies converge around the unstable pivot of the Korean peninsula, is a region rife with political-economic paradox. It ranks today among the most dangerous areas on earth, plagued by security problems of global importance, including nuclear and missile proliferation. Despite its insecurity, the region has continued to be the most rapidly growing on earth for more than five decades. In 1960, the Northeast Asian economy—including Japan, Mainland China, Taiwan, and Korea—accounted for only 4 percent of world GDP, compared with 37 percent for the United States, Canada, and Mexico. By 2008 its GDP, as a proportion of the world total, had reached 17.7 percent, compared with 22.4 percent for the European Union (EU) and 27.6 percent for the North American free trade agreement (NAFTA).

This globally consequential share of world output is concentrated in a remarkably compact and densely populated area. As Figure 1.1 suggests, the heart of Northeast Asia's political economy centers around the East China Sea, now plausibly called the Shanghai Circle: major cities in Japan and Korea, Hong Kong, Taiwan, Mainland China, and Macao, within three hours' flying time of Shanghai. Within that circle, roughly the size of the United States east of the Mississippi River, live more than 1.3 billion people, who generate nearly one-fifth of global economic production.

Using purchasing power parity indicators, for many purposes a more accurate measure of economic significance than nominal GDP, Northeast Asia looms as

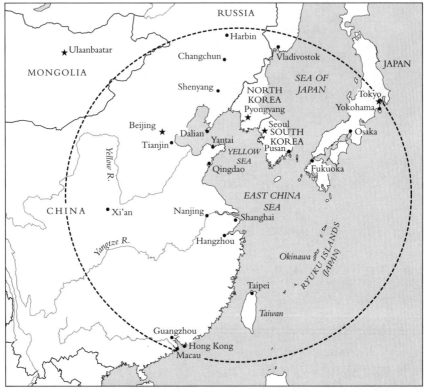

FIG. 1.1. The "Shanghai Circle": Economic Heart of Northeast Asia. The "Shanghai Circle" denotes areas within three hours' flying time from Shanghai by commercial aircraft. Virtually all areas are in China, Japan, and Korea. Direct Daily Flight Information, as of 2009: (1) Shanghai–Seoul: 2 hours, 11 flights per day; (2) Shanghai–Tokyo: 3 hours, 13 flights per day; (3) Tokyo–Seoul: 2.5 hours, 20 flights per day; (4) Shanghai–Beijing: 2 hours, 22 flights per day; (5) Shanghai–Hong Kong, 2.5 hours: 13 flights per day; (6) Shanghai–Taipei, 1.5 hours: 3 flights per day.

an even more substantial entity in global economic affairs. In 2008, as indicated in Table 1.1, this area's GDP on a purchasing-power parity (PPP) basis was $14.9 trillion, compared with $17.5 trillion for NAFTA and $15.1 trillion for the EU. Northeast Asia's share of global total GDP in PPP terms was thus 21 percent, comparable to 24.7 percent for NAFTA and 21.3 percent for the EU.

Northeast Asia has also become the world's second largest trading region, with its share of global trade, at 18.3 percent, conspicuously ahead of NAFTA's share at 15.7 percent and the EU's share, at 11.1 percent. The region's trade/ GDP ratio is also much higher than that of either NAFTA or the EU, sug-

TABLE I.I

The Northeast Asian Region in Comparative Perspective

	Population	GDP (trillion $ PPP)	GDP/ World PPP (%)	GDP (trillion $)	GDP/ World (%)	Trade/ GDP (%)	Trade/ World (%)
Northeast Asia	1.51 billion	14.9	21	10.7	17.7	58.7	18.3
European Union	313.9 million	15.1	21.3	13.5	22.4	29.3	11.1
NAFTA	430 million	17.5	24.7	16.7	27.6	31.7	15.7
World	6.4 billion	70.9		60.6	—	59.5	

SOURCE: World Bank, www.worldbank.org; and CIA, *World Factbook*, 2010. https://www.cia.gov/library/publications/the-world-factbook/index.html.
NOTES: Northeast Asia refers to the aggregate of Japan, China, South Korea, Hong Kong, and Taiwan. The data are current as of 2008.

gesting that trade has been an important policy determinant for the countries involved. The growing importance of intraregional trade since the 1997 Asian financial crisis and recent challenges from the global economic downturn have thus influenced and will continue to significantly impact regional integration in Northeast Asia.

Why Not a Broader Asian Calculus?

Much scholarly attention has been given to the broader geographical concept of "East Asia."[1] Why then the significantly narrower Northeast Asian focus that is adopted here? We take this approach because the nations of Northeast Asia are by an overwhelming margin the largest economically and the most potent militarily and technologically in the entire East Asian region, which stretches from Burma in the Southwest to Hokkaido in the Northeast.

As noted in Figure 1.2, Northeast Asia generates more than 80 percent of the total gross national product of that sprawling region, and supplies more than 70 percent of its military manpower. The Association of Southeast Asian Nations (ASEAN), although by no means insignificant, is much smaller, economically and politically, even in aggregate, than the Northeast Asian region. ASEAN has thus far played a remarkably substantial role in regional integration for its size, as we shall see. Yet its heretofore salient role is an embedded Cold War artifact, with a geopolitical logic now receding, that obscures momentous subregional developments elsewhere. ASEAN has steadily been eclipsed of late by the increasingly

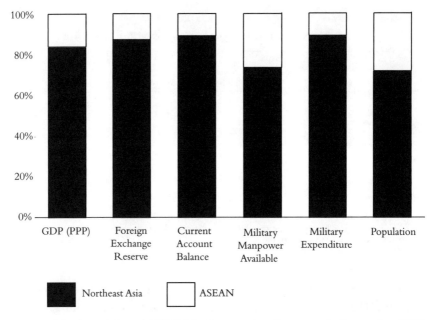

FIG. I.2. Northeast Asia and ASEAN in Comparative Geoeconomic Perspective. GDP (ppp), foreign exchange reserve, and current account balance data are for 2008. Military expenditure data is from 2004 reporting. Military manpower and population statistics are from 2009 estimates. Source: Original data are from Central Intelligence Agency, *CIA World Factbook*, 2009. www.cia.org. .

cohesive Northern powers, in a subtle evolution vested with fateful long-term global significance, that remains inadequately understood.

A second reason for our focus on Northeast Asia, related to the first, is that the resolution of these nations' delicate mutual relationships, however difficult, has profound implications for global war and peace, because of the sheer scale, technological sophistication, and complementarity of the parties involved. Their estrangement from one another became a commonplace of international affairs, from World War II through the Cold War and beyond, quietly leveraging America's dominance in Asia. Yet it can no longer be taken for granted.

If China, Japan, and Korea can find a peaceful, collaborative resolution to their historically rooted differences and their geopolitically driven dilemmas,[2] the region will become a locus of global political, military, and financial power to an unprecedented degree. If, conversely, Northeast Asians cannot resolve their differences, vicious cycles of political-military rivalry that threaten global stability may well be unleashed. The future of this Northeast Asian triangle, in short, is a major critical uncertainty for the United States, and indeed for the world as a whole, giving much greater long-term geopolitical significance to the nuances of conflict and cooperation among them than is generally understood.

A third reason for our focus on Northeast Asia is that intraregional linkages have deepened sharply and dynamically over the past decade.[3] Mutual interdependence has reached an unprecedented level among the Northeast Asian economies, even as reliance on the United States has slowly begun to decline. Social interactions among Japan, Korea, and Greater China have also come to greatly outnumber those between the subregion and other parts of Asia, making Northeast Asia an increasingly coherent and connected entity. And the deepening interaction is not purely social. Policy networks, linking top-level politicians, local governments, epistemic communities, and corporate elites to an unprecedented degree are actively engaging their counterparts across national boundaries in Northeast Asia. These diverse multilevel networks not only produce ideas for Northeast Asian cooperation but also generate concrete proposals for common action. Thus, although Southeast Asia still appears salient in many formal dimensions of East Asian integration, as an embedded consequence of Cold War struggles dating from the Vietnam War and the invasion of Cambodia, behind the scenes, Northeast Asian nations increasingly set the agenda and parameters for Asian regionalism more generally, in addition to pursuing closer trilateral cooperation among themselves. Since December 2008 they have been routinely holding full-fledged trilateral summits, independent of ASEAN.

A fourth reason for our Northeast Asian focus, in preference to a broader East Asian treatment, is that Northeast Asia stands uniquely on the cusp of historic geopolitical change, as Southeast Asia did in the 1970s. Change in Northeast Asia's subregional alignments could sharply alter the anomalous estrangement that has prevailed there since World War II. The dimensions and possible immediacy of Northeast Asia's fateful impending transformation urgently need to be appreciated, since intraregional commonalities and complementarities are so deep. Dramatic breakthroughs are occurring across long-frozen lines of Cold War cleavage, not least across the Taiwan Straits, allowing deep underlying complementarities to be realized for the first time in well over half a century.

Why Not Just China?

The pronounced recent transnational dynamism and deepening integration of Northeast Asia, particularly across the East China Sea and the Taiwan Straits, are becoming increasingly clear. This deepening integration is a complex, synergistic phenomenon involving the interaction of three large, proud, and suspicious—yet highly complementary and increasingly interdependent—countries. Many nevertheless ascribe the remarkable transformation of Asia in recent years largely to China alone, or to a "China Circle" of Sinic affiliates with a southern bias.[4]

Our analytical orientation is decidedly different. Without denying the dynamism of China itself, or the historic character of the recent detente across the Taiwan Straits, we highlight the transnational production networks, financial markets, security dialogues, and economic-policy consultations that are developing much more broadly, and the new transnational synergies among long-standing adversaries that are emerging as traditional political barriers fall across the dynamic expanse from Hokkaido, Manchuria, and the two Koreas southward to Taipei and the Vietnamese borderlands. Northeast Asia overall, we argue, is far more than the sum of its parts, with Japan and Korea, as well as the various components of China, having key roles in the emerging overall regional political-economic equation. And those roles subtly enhance one another, pulling the locus of Asian dynamism ineluctably northward from its earlier ASEAN focus, as historical suspicions in the Northeast gradually fade and common interests steadily rise.

To be sure, country-specific thinking—about China, Japan, or Korea—for many years made perfect sense as the central focus of political-economic analysis. The dark shadow of history distorted the political economy of Northeast Asia, dividing individual countries into separate, fiercely distinctive units, making potentially promising intraregional dialogue or steps toward policy coordination difficult even among nominal allies. Japan and South Korea, for example, could not even bring themselves to establish diplomatic relations with each other until 1965—twenty years after the end of World War II, despite parallel and intimate alliance relations that both enjoyed separately with the United States. China was aloof, suspicious, and poorly integrated with the others. Japan did not normalize relations with China until 1972, and South Korea not until two decades after that. China also loomed large on the Cold War stage, as a tacit strategic partner of the United States.

China continues to be important, of course—indeed, increasingly so, from a global perspective. Yet it has grown quietly interdependent with its neighbors, as well as politically conciliatory, in new ways that have not yet been adequately presented in most previous analyses. It is to capture that new reality—the broader regional context in which a rising China is increasingly embedded, that we cast a wider net.

Northeast Asian Fusion

Beginning in the early 1990s, Northeast Asia began to grow steadily more interdependent, connected, and cohesive in socioeconomic terms, its bitter historical and geopolitical differences of that period notwithstanding. Between 1990 and 2004, intraregional commerce among Japan, South Korea, and China doubled, to 12 percent of those nations' total world trade, while transactions with the United States accounted for only 18 percent of their collective global total. The importance of trans-Pacific trade continued to decline. In 2008, the trade with the U.S accounted for less than 13 percent of the three countries' global commerce, while trade among themselves was 11 percent. Historic post–Cold War developments in trade and investment also in turn began to drive sociopolitical reconciliation forward. Intraregional economic ties then further deepened and began to broaden, generating new economic interests that in turn transformed political affairs, as was clearly evident, for example, in cross-Straits and Sino-Japanese relations.

Adding Hong Kong and Taiwan to the trade equation, intraregional commerce has already vastly surpassed trans-Pacific commerce. In 2008, total trade among Japan, China, South Korea, Hong Kong, and Taiwan reached $1.25 trillion, while their aggregate trade with the United States was only $780 billion. The share of intraregional trade within Northeast Asia, with Hong Kong and Taiwan included, was almost 20 percent of the partners' collective total in 2008, while the share of trans-Pacific trade was slightly over 12 percent of the total.[5]

At the country level, combined trade with Northeast Asian neighbors surpassed transactions with the United States for each of these three countries during 2003.[6] China surpassed the United States as South Korea's largest export market during 2004, and Japan's in 2006.[7] Meanwhile, U.S.-Japan trade was actually contracting in absolute terms from 2000 to 2004. Since then, bilateral trans-Pacific trade has modestly rebounded, yet remains significantly smaller than Japan's intraregional trade with China and South Korea.

Corporate production networks are also deepening substantially across Northeast Asia, capitalizing on economic complementarities, as well as the remarkable concentration of industry within the compact physical space that constitutes the core of the region. Nowhere are production networks more dynamic today than across the Taiwan Straits, with Taiwanese investment on the Mainland exceeding $100 billion in 2005, and rising substantially since then.[8] Those growing cross-Straits activities are intensifying regionwide competitive pressures that compel Korean and Japanese firms to expand cross-border production activities also, with a catalytic impact on regional integration. They are also making cross-Straits political rapprochement easier, creating a virtuous political-economic cycle of declining tensions.

East-central China, with its rapidly growing consumer market, together with its expanding manufacturing and trading capacities, is steadily emerging as the center of gravity for these regional production networks. These networks converge especially—due to geographical proximity, organizational efficiency, and resource complementarity—on Shanghai, giving birth to the Shanghai Circle described above. They have important financial, technology, and marketing linkages, however, that connect them with far-distant parts of the world as well.

The strategic focus of major Japanese, Korean, and overseas Chinese companies that have established long-term investment sites in China is assembly and processing. Canon, for example, built its largest factory anywhere in the world at Suzhou, China, during 2001. By 2004, Canon had also established operation centers in Beijing, Shanghai, Guangzhou, and Dalian—at the heart of China's four major economic regions. Mitsui, meanwhile, concluded more than 110 joint ventures in China. Matsushita runs about fifty factories and is adding more. The auto giants Honda and Toyota are both likewise becoming major manufacturers and marketers in China, giving their leaders new stakes in the reduction of regional political tensions.[9]

"Korea, Inc." is investing even more aggressively in China than is Japan. Leading South Korean firms such as LG, Samsung, and Hyundai have made rapid progress recently in the People's Republic of China (PRC), although they were late entrants into the Chinese market, long inhibited by Cold War political barriers and tensions that are now largely dissipated. Hyundai-made passenger cars, for example, entered the Chinese market only in 2003 but soon gained the lion's share of Beijing's taxi business, accounting for more than half of all new taxis commissioned during Beijing's preparation for the 2008 Olympics.[10] Small, efficient Hyundai autos have also penetrated taxi markets in other major Chinese cities.[11]

In electronics, LG did $10 billion in China business during 2004, a level that even the most prominent Japanese brands have rarely reached. In 2005, Samsung employed 50,000 Chinese workers at its twenty-nine Chinese affiliates. In that year, China became the third largest Samsung market worldwide. The company strategically positioned China not only as a major market but also as a key production site for its global operations.[12] Many small and medium-size Korean electronics companies have also moved manufacturing to the PRC, cooperating with Chinese companies in marketing, technology alliances, and manufacturing, in efforts to make inroads there.[13]

Direct investment flows within Northeast Asia, traditionally dominated by Japanese multinationals, are growing increasingly multilateral and balanced, with Chinese firms becoming active even inside Japan itself. Chinese companies have established numerous strategic partnerships with Japanese firms since 2000, beginning to offset the heavy converse flow of Japanese capital to China. The Shanghai Electric Group, for example, in 2002 acquired Akiyama, a bankrupt Japanese manufacturer of high-tech printers, and then also purchased the long-established machine tool maker Ikegai in 2004.[14] In 2006 China's Haier, which had announced a comprehensive alliance with Japan's Sanyo four years earlier, took over Sanyo's refrigerator production, which had long been unprofitable.[15] Sanyo, in turn, focused its investment on complementary research and development, in an innovative new Northeast Asian division of labor.[16]

Other Chinese firms hire Japanese talent, reciprocating ongoing Japanese initiatives in China. Skyworth, a leading Chinese consumer electronics company, for example, hired one of Matsushita's most senior engineers, together with several of his research colleagues.[17] Huawei, a top Chinese telecom equipment manufacturer, recently established joint ventures with both NEC and Matsushita, pursuing advanced new third-generation (3G) mobile-phone technology.[18]

Increasingly symmetrical patterns of networking and cultural exchange are also emerging across Northeast Asia, helping to erode deep historical suspicions and to forge common new identities. Personal contact—ranging from intraregional telephone and mail communication to shipping and aviation, tourism, and television broadcast, as well as both legal and illegal migration—has risen rapidly in a variety of forms, political tensions notwithstanding. More than 4 million Japanese and Korean tourists visit each other's country every year, over 4 million travel between China and Japan, and more than 3 million people move annually between China and Korea.[19] Virtually all the personal-contact figures along the dynamic Northeast Asian triangle are much higher than a decade ago.

Some of the increased contact has marked political significance. Intergovernmental exchanges, including those among once bitter military adversaries, are rapidly rising, as are contacts among scholars. In May 2005, after three years of effort, for example, scholars in Japan, China, and Korea produced a joint history textbook, published in all three languages, that has sold well over 250,000 copies regionwide.[20]

Because of intensified investment and trade between China and Japan, Shanghai alone now has more than 40,000 Japanese residents. Japanese schools are operating in such major cities as Beijing, Shenzhen, and Shanghai. Statistics show that around 460,000 Chinese visited Japan and that over 3.45 million Japanese went to China in 2008.[21] For Hong Kong youngsters, Japan has consistently remained their favorite travel spot.[22] And even Kim Jong-il's eldest son has apparently visited Tokyo Disneyland.[23]

Popular culture in Asia has also recently shown a strong regionalization trend. For nearly two decades, Japanese movies and television dramas have been enthusiastically received in China. According to one recent survey, 75 percent of audiences in Mainland China have watched the Japanese TV drama *Akai Giwaku* [Blood Suspect], while 73 percent have seen NHK's *Oshin*. To Chinese viewers,

Japanese drama has become a vivid symbol of stylish and modern urban culture. Meanwhile, in Taiwan, more than 80 percent of families currently receive Japanese TV channels by satellite, while 70 percent of audiences there watch Japanese shows at least four days per week.[24]

Japanese movies and television programs have also become popular in Korea, especially since former president Kim Dae-jung relaxed long-standing restrictions on Japanese programs following the Asian financial crisis. In 1998, when the movie *Rabu Letah* [*Love Letter*] was first shown in Korea, more than 1.45 million Koreans made a point of seeing it.[25] Japanese music gained further visibility during 2000, when the South Korean government lifted restrictions on the local sale of Japanese pop, provided that the lyrics were not in Japanese.

In recent years, the Korean pop culture industry has steadily expanded its hold over East Asia. *Hanryu*, literally "Korean Wave," has swept triumphantly across both China and Japan.[26] In Mainland China, almost all forms of mass media broadcast Korean entertainment shows regularly, while many TV stations set up special channels to broadcast Korean dramas. South Korean programs now account for more than all other foreign programs combined in the PRC, including those from the United States and Japan.[27]

Korean pop culture is also the rage in Japan. In 2001, when the Korean movie *Ghost* first opened, more than 1.2 million Japanese moviegoers saw it.[28] The Korean program *Winter Sonata*, a love story starring Bae Yong-jun and Choi Ji-woo, took Japanese audiences by storm, becoming the local media sensation of the year during 2004. The Korean actor and singer Rain was another pan-Asian heartthrob. Ever since his debut in 2002, Rain, whose real name is Jung Ji-hoon, has been riding the Korean Wave. Through his leading roles in soap operas and his music, Rain has become the personification of *hanryu*, which some see as a high-quality regional alternative to American cultural dominance. In 2005, Rain sold out arenas across Korea, China, and Japan, playing to more than 40,000 in Beijing and 20,000 at the Budokan in Tokyo.[29]

Chinese pop stars from Hong Kong and Taiwan, such as Teresa Teng, have captivated audiences in both Japan and South Korea for years. Recently, pop stars from Mainland China have also become quite visible across Northeast Asia. Chinese films and cultural shows are regularly broadcast in both Japan and Korea. Zhang Ziyi, for example, has played major roles in two Korean movies and one Japanese film. Her role, together with that of Chinese compatriot Gong Li, was memorable in the Hollywood-directed but Japan-based *Memoirs of a Geisha*. Indeed, a new, well-justified phrase is emerging across the region to describe these transnational entertainers: "Pan-Asia Stars." And they are almost invariably from Northeast Asia, where the markets and the recording studios are predominantly located.[30]

Rising Interdependence in Northeast Asia Puts
Pressure on the "Organization Gap"

Cultural confidence-building has a unique contemporary political-economic, and even geopolitical, importance in Northeast Asia, because of the embedded bitterness and estrangement among neighboring countries—even strategic allies such as Japan and South Korea—that so long prevailed. Such conciliatory efforts create a common base of understanding and contact, allowing natural communities of interest to begin to express themselves. They thus help to neutralize the perverse impact of a pronounced "organization gap," distinctive in comparative perspective, that has long prevailed in the region. Before 2000, for example, among the thirty largest economies in the world, twenty-five were already members of regional free-trade agreements or customs unions. The remaining five nonparticipant outliers were all located in Northeast Asia: China, Japan, South Korea, Taiwan, and Hong Kong.[31]

Thanks to the rapidly evolving multilateral frameworks in East Asia that emerged following the financial crisis of 1997, Northeast Asian economies joined in a number of "North-South" free trade agreements with nations elsewhere in East Asia. Japan established free trade agreement (FTAs), for example, with Singapore (2002), Malaysia (2003), Thailand (2007), the Philippines (2008), and Indonesia (2008). Korea formed an FTA with Singapore in 2006. China signed FTA treaties with ASEAN (2004, 2008), and with Singapore in March 2009. With Hong Kong and Macao, China also formed closer economic partnerships during 2003, following their reversion to Chinese administration a few years previously.

Nevertheless, the organization gap long persisted in Northeast Asia itself, where economic and social ties are most intimate, and the functional need for multilateral coordination correspondingly severe. According to the 2009 regional treaty agreement (RTA) dataset of the World Trade Organization, there were thirty-three RTAs in Europe. In Africa, South America, and the Middle East, where regional trade interdependence is far shallower than in Northeast Asia, the comparable RTA figures in 2009 were seven, three, and one, respectively.[32] Yet Northeast Asia had no RTAs at all.

There are clearly strong pressures for change—for the closing of the organization gap—as economic interdependence rises, intraregional competition grows more intense, and divisive historical memories grow more distant. Some progress is being made, yet in the face of deepening transnational trade and investment relations worldwide, Northeast Asia will face serious future collective-action problems unless its fabric of local regional organizations grows even more robust. The Asian financial crisis of 1997–98, during which the lack of regional cooperative mechanisms both exacerbated a serious regional crisis and impeded its resolution, clearly showed the dangers of such a gap. So has the continuing—and deepening—environmental crisis confronting the region.

Northeast Asian countries also face serious and unique developmental challenges that would make a deeper and richer local network of regional organizations mutually advantageous. For example, Japan, Korea, and China all suffer from a severe shortage of readily accessible domestic energy reserves. Apart from Manchuria's Daqing and Shengli fields, both well past their prime, none of these nations boasts a single major onshore oil or gas field.

Sustained economic development, meanwhile, has generated explosive energy-demand growth across the region, leading to huge and rising energy-trade deficits with the broader world. Until late 1993, China was a net exporter of oil. Yet, a mere decade later, it had become the third largest importer in the world. Over the period from 2000 to 2004, China alone contributed nearly 40 percent of total global growth in oil demand. This pattern is likely to persist for the foreseeable future, as the prospects for sustained GDP growth in China appear strong, global financial volatility notwithstanding.[33]

Japan and South Korea are both long-time and large-scale energy importers. In 2000, the energy-import dependence ratio for Korea was 97.2 percent, and for Japan 81.2 percent. Japan has consistently been the second largest oil importer on earth, after the United States, while South Korea is the fourth largest oil importer and second largest importer of LNG in the world. Primary energy consumption composition is similar for the two countries: half of the total is petroleum, making their dependence on unstable Middle East oil supplies especially perilous.[34]

To compound Northeast Asian uncertainties, energy imports are less diversified than in many regions, with heavy local dependence on Middle Eastern oil and gas supplies. For instance, around 80 percent of Northeast Asia's oil imports are from the Middle East, while the United States obtains only 23 percent of its oil from that volatile region. Asian oil-import dependence—and reliance on Middle Eastern supply in particular—are projected to grow rapidly over the coming decade, as alternative sources in areas such as Indonesia and Manchuria are progressively exhausted. For each of the Northeast Asian countries, national dependence on Middle Eastern sources is likely to grow as well.[35]

Among the catalysts that intensify Asian energy insecurity are Middle East instabilities, transport vulnerability, and lack of alternative supplies. Northeast Asian countries rely heavily on Middle Eastern oil, despite that region's dubious standing as the only part of the world more volatile than Northeast Asia itself. Some major Middle Eastern supplier countries, such as Iran, also face Western economic sanctions and embargoes. For Japan, Korea, and especially for China, oil transport from the Middle East to Northeast Asia likewise poses unsettling maritime security issues.

Especially sensitive to its own vulnerability, as a non-ally of an American "hyperpower" that dominates the sea lanes, China has grown quite active in seeking alternative energy supplies in Africa, Latin America, and even Canada.[36] It thereby reduced its Middle East dependence by 2004 to 45 percent, compared with 72 percent for South Korea and 81 percent for Japan.[37] In the process, China's energy diplomacy has stepped on a few sensitive toes in the United States, either by undermining U.S. sanctions against "rogue nations" such as Sudan, or by dealing with Yankee-baiters close to U.S. shores, such as Hugo Chavez of Venezuela.

As in the case of energy, the financial system of Northeast Asia also harbors severe potential challenges for the region that make institutions for collective regional action desirable. First, the prevailing bank-based indirect-capital system could well trigger twin crises, either simultaneous or sequential, in the banking and currency areas—if provoked by external pressure.[38] Second, Northeast Asian capital-flow patterns are extremely unbalanced, creating the danger of sudden, destabilizing shifts. The countries of the region hold huge U.S. dollar–denominated foreign exchange reserves yielding relatively low returns, while the region simultaneously acquires internally needed capital at much higher rates from international markets. Among the top five foreign exchange reserve holders in the world, four are located in Northeast Asia—China, Japan, Russia, and Taiwan. China and Japan hold the top two positions, with $2.4 trillion and $1.02 trillion, respectively, as of December 2009. South Korea, although strained by the 2008 global financial crisis, still took the sixth position with $270.9 billion. Hong Kong also managed to be the eighth largest foreign exchange holder in the world, with $240 billion.[39]

This massive U.S. dollar horde, concentrated increasingly in greater China, gives the region insurance against future financial crises of the 1997 variety. This new stability manifested itself clearly during the sharp global turbulence of 2008–9. Northeast Asia's huge dollar stockpile also renders the region vulnerable, however, to potential long-term dollar decline, in the face of ambitious recent U.S. stimulus measures and persistent current-account deficits. Depreciation of the U.S. dollar would not only devalue the massive local foreign exchange reserves of Northeast Asia but could also severely harm the trans-Pacific exports of the region, and seriously reduce potential national economic growth.[40] Dollar decline, which began to occur in a serious way shortly after 2000, could also, however, ultimately strengthen the mutual reliance of Northeast Asian nations.

As Figure 1.3 suggests, the dollar has declined against all three major currencies in Northeast Asia since 2001. The Chinese renminbi's appreciation against the

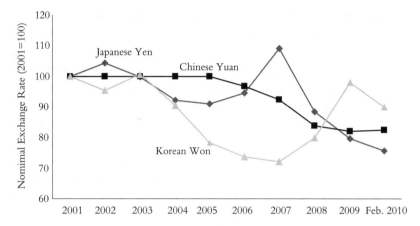

FIG. 1.3. The U.S. Dollar's Decline against Northeast Asian Currencies (2001–10). For each year, exchange rates are calculated as of June 1. Exchange rates typically vary during the year. China used fixed exchange rates until June 2006, after which it gradually began to widen the parameters of permitted fluctuation of the Chinese yuan. Source: IMF financial data, at: www.imf.org. Exchange Reserve Archives.

dollar has been most persistent, sharply depreciating the local value of the PRC's foreign exchange holdings of more than $2 trillion. The Japanese yen has also appreciated steadily against the dollar, albeit it with an aberration in 2007. The Korean won, suffering severely from the 2008/9 crisis, fell against the dollar during 2008 and early 2009, making the South Korean government especially anxious to find regional support in the face of global volatility induced by U.S. economic problems. By the fall of 2009, however, as the global crisis waned, the won had stabilized and begun to resume its upward long-term course.

The Waning of Constraints in History and Geopolitics

As ancient enmities wane, Northeast Asia is becoming a more coherent unit in its own right. Sino-Japanese and Japanese-Korean rapprochement are proceeding more actively than at any time in well over a century, while China and South Korea, deadly adversaries in the Korean War, are taking unprecedented steps in military confidence-building. The numerous recent state visits among the leaders of these three nations since late 2006—not to mention the constructive working-level dialogues now in progress across the East China Sea—all reflect deepening political ties between Tokyo and Beijing that have a solid economic basis. Relations between Tokyo and Seoul are also markedly improving, with moderate governments driven by economic logic and sensitive to regional solidarity issues prevailing in both countries.

Textbooks were a flashpoint between Japan and its continental neighbors for many years. Even as late as 2001 and 2005, the Japanese Ministry of Education's approval of a single conservative text as an option for Japanese schools triggered massive protests in both China and Korea, even though the ultimate adoption rate reached only 0.03 percent. In April 2009, however, when the same textbook was approved once again, the reaction was distinctly muted.[41]

Another traditional security flashpoint, the cross-Taiwan Straits relationship, has also been evolving rapidly since early 2007. Indeed, deepening rapprochement between the two long-time adversaries in the Chinese civil war, and the economic possibilities unleashed by that easing of tensions, have suddenly become major drivers of Northeast Asian integration as a whole. With Democratic Progressive Party (DPP) leader Chen Shui-bian stepping down in May 2008 as the president of Taiwan, the newly elected Nationalist Party (KMT) candidate Ma Ying-jeou restored political understanding with the Mainland, driven by socioeconomic dynamics outlined elsewhere in this volume. Since then, passenger flights have been regularized between major cities across the Straits, including Taipei, Kaohsiung, Beijing, Shanghai, and Guangzhou, as well as Hefei, Harbin, Nanchang, Guiyang, Ningbo, and Jinan. The weekly number of cross-Strait passenger return flights, both regular and chartered, reached 292 as of January 2010.[42] And the operations of major Taiwanese firms like Acer and Taiwan Semiconductor have grown rapidly on both sides of the Straits, accelerating a historic cycle of deregulation and rising interdependence.

The number of Mainland visitors to Taiwan surged rapidly in late 2008, as restrictions on tourism began to ease. Between July 2008 and February 2009 alone, more than 91,000 Mainlanders visited Taiwan.[43] Chinese premier Wen Jiabao even expressed his own strong personal interest in a sightseeing tour of scenic spots in Taiwan during a major Beijing press conference.[44] In mid-2009, daily tourist arrivals from the Mainland were averaging over 2,300 a day. And the numbers were steadily rising.[45] During 2009, as a whole, more than 600,000 mainlanders visited Taiwan.[46] In Taiwan, during the 2009 spring festival, thousands of local citizens flocked to see the two pandas especially dispatched from the Mainland,[47] despite the politically delicate fact that the two creatures' names together suggest reunion in Chinese (*tuanyuan*).

Policy coordination across the Taiwan Straits, like people-to-people relations, also revived and expanded substantially from the spring of 2008. In June of that year, only a week after being invited, the chairman of Taiwan's Straits Exchange Foundation (SEF), Chiang Pin-kung, was in Beijing, actively negotiating new agreements on charter flights across the Straits. Five months later, in November 2008, the PRC's return delegation, headed by former State Council Taiwan Office director Chen Yunlin, arrived in Taipei.[48] There, four agreements were reached, finalizing the three long-awaited "direct links" (postal services, sea shipping, and air travel), while also coordinating trans-Straits policy on food safety.[49]

When Chen and Chiang met for the third time in Nanjing during April 2009, they signed three additional agreements: (1) an amendment to the previous understanding on air travel, increasing weekly flights from 107 weekly to 270 and adding more lines for direct flights; (2) a cross-Straits cooperative financial framework; and (3) an agreement to fight crime jointly and to undertake judicial cooperation. In addition, Chen and Chiang made joint declarations supporting Mainland investment in Taiwan.[50] Since then, Beijing has outlined plans for encouraging Mainland Chinese businesses to expand their investments in Taiwan, and has scheduled several purchasing missions to buy food and consumer products.[51]

Northeast Asian governmental bodies will find it difficult to accommodate the status of Taiwan formally. Yet informal and semiformal policy coordination, as well as rapidly developing socioeconomic exchanges across the Straits, is becoming ever more feasible, increasing the vested stakes in peace and prosperity on all sides, while making armed conflict ever more difficult. And declining prospects for armed confrontation, despite the formidable array of weaponry deployed, should in turn facilitate confidence and trust across the region, whose fragility for three generations has been a principal roadblock to the Making of Northeast Asia in political terms.

Many steps clearly remain to be taken along the road to peace and economic interdependence on the Korean peninsula. North-South rapprochement seems much further off than limited reconciliation between Taiwan and the PRC, which is already proceeding so dynamically. Yet there is no denying the massive potential consequences of change along the demilitarized zone (DMZ) in Korea, as a catalyst for deepened ties within continental Northeast Asia, or the significant long-term prospect that historic change in Korea will actually occur.

South Korea as it currently stands is, after all, a geostrategic island—cut off from the Asian continent by the dark, economically subterranean expanse of North Korea. Should North-South relations substantially improve, or reunification actually take place, the ties of all Korea, and possibly Japan, with China and Far Eastern Russia could obviously grow much more dynamic. The more central location of Taiwan in the region, however, almost directly opposite booming Shanghai, probably makes cross-Straits rapprochement more central to economic growth in Northeast Asia under almost any scenario than parallel developments in Korea.

The future of North Korea, and its regional orientation, at this writing, is difficult to predict. Despite its relatively moderate stance during the 2007–8 period, in the spring of 2009 Pyongyang tested a new Taepodong II missile, as well as a nuclear device, and resumed plutonium production at Yongbyon.[52] A few months later it sent a conciliatory high-level delegation to Kim Dae-jung's funeral in Seoul. The North also appears to be intensifying its economic ties with the PRC.[53] No doubt an amicable resolution to the Democratic People's Republic of Korea's (DPRK's) tortured relations with its neighbors would accelerate Northeast Asian integration. Yet the steadily deepening ties among Japan, China, and South Korea are not critically dependent on Pyongyang's cooperation, or, indeed, on any substantial opening of North Korea. They run, as we shall see, on a very different, more cooperative track. Indeed, persistent tensions of all parties with North Korea have over the past decade actually been a crucial catalyst for regional cohesion, by encouraging neighbors to collaborate in countering its provocative behavior, much as tensions with the Soviet Union helped to animate Western European integration during the 1950s. China and South Korea, for example, established a hotline between their air force headquarters in 2006, precisely to minimize dangers of accidental conflict between themselves provoked by North Korea.

Deepening Trilateral Policy Dialogue

Each of the Northeast Asian countries, as we have seen, confronts two pressing domestic developmental challenges—energy insecurities and financial vulnerability. Both of these challenges, emerging in the context of rising regional interdependence, generate a need, and a corresponding demand, for regional coordination. Yet the persistent organization gap within the region, inherited from a century of military conflict and ensuing mutual sociopolitical estrangement, makes it institutionally difficult to satisfy that demand. Other common regional problems, such as infrastructural development and environmental degradation, intensify still further the all-too-often unmet need for collective action. What then are the prospects for ultimately satisfying these urgent needs through regional institution-building?

The raw number of transnational institutions in East Asia as a whole has increased notably over the past decade, to be sure. Across the entire four-decade period from 1950 to 1989, the year that the Berlin Wall fell, only seven new regional institutions were established, while in the short fifteen years from 1990 to 2005, the number nearly tripled to twenty. The most active period for institution-building was from 1989 to 1997, with most of the new entities emerging in Southeast Asia. Recently, some conspicuous, albeit largely formalistic, regionwide bodies such as the East Asia Summit have been created. Yet an even more striking, novel, and efficacious phenomenon has been the widespread emergence of systematic Northeast Asian trilateral cooperation, often bilateral and inter-regional

FIG 1.4. The Evolution of Northeast Asian Trilateral Dialogue, 2000–2009

Trilateral Meeting	2000	2001	2002	2003	2004	2005	2006	2007	2008	2009
Environment Ministers' meeting (TEMM)	1	1	1	1	1	1	1	1	1	1
Finance Ministers' meeting	1		1	1	1	1	1	1	1	1
Policy Dialogue meeting among SIPO, JPO, KPO[a]		1	1	1	1	1	1	1	1	1
Economic & Trade Ministers' meeting			1	1	1	1	1	1	1	1
IT Ministers' meeting		1	1	1	1	1	1	1	1	1
Heads of Personnel Authorities meeting						1	1	1	1	1
Personnel Director-Generals' meeting						1	1	1	1	1
Consultation for the Improvement of the Business Environment					1	1	1	1	1	1
Three-party Committee[b]					1	1		1		
Energy Ministers' meeting							1		1	1
Tourism Ministers' meeting							1	1	1	1
Latin American & Caribbean Director-Generals' meeting							1	1		1
Foreign Ministers' meeting								1	1	1
Customs Heads' meeting								1	1	1
Ministerial Conference on Transportation and Logistics								1	1	1
Health Ministers'								1	1	1
Culture Ministers' meeting								1	1	
Science & Technology Ministers' meeting								1		1
Trilateral Summit[c]									1	1
Central Bankers' Dialogue										1
Natural Disaster Relief Ministerial Meeting										1
Trilateral Cooperation Cyber-Secretariat (TCCS)										1
Trilateral Cooperation Forum										1
Youngsters' Friendship Meeting										1
Future Leaders' Forum										1

[a] SIPO, State Intellectual Property Office of the PRC; JPO, Japan Patent Office; KIPO, Korean Intellectual Property Office;

[b] The Three Party Committee originally consisted by the foreign ministers from China, Japan, and South Korea and served as a high-level coordinating body. Due to Sino-Japanese relations' downturn, it did not convene in 2006. Starting in 2007, however, the new foreign ministers of the countries established an annual convention and superseded the Three Party Committee.

[c] The Trilateral Summit, starting in 2008, spun off various policy dialogue mechanisms such a natural disaster relief ministerial meeting, TCCS, and others. In 2009, it also coordinated trilateral positions on climate change before the coming Copenhagen Conference, thus the Director-Generals' Policy Dialogue on Climate Change did not take place in that year.

in form, although the organization gap still continues to prevail much more markedly there than in the Southeastern quadrant of Asia.

At the subnational level, local, corporate, and epistemic linkages among Northeast Asian partners have continued to grow, even when political complications at the national and regional levels complicated formal diplomatic ties. Indeed, such subnational ties have often intensified, as in cross-Straits relations before 2007, or North-South relations in Korea at certain intervals, or in local ties between Hokkaido and Russia's Sakhalin, precisely because higher-level ties were so complicated. Local government networks deepened, and multinational corporations intensified their transnational operations, both in spite of and sometimes because of political uncertainties. Transborder interaction within epistemic communities was also vibrant, with meetings customarily held in major cities of Northeast Asia, particularly Beijing, Shanghai, Tokyo, and Seoul. Semigovernmental institutions developed rapidly. The Boao and Jeju forums, headquartered in China and South Korea, respectively, regularly brought together politicians, bureaucrats, corporate representatives, and think tanks, with the explicit aim of expanding cooperation in various functional areas.

Northeast Asian subregional interactions are thus quite dynamic, and continuously evolving. More formal trilateral institutions are also rapidly emerging, despite the general perception that such bodies are overwhelmingly Asia-wide. At the national level, summits among top political leaders and senior bureaucrats of Japan, China, and South Korea have grown increasingly frequent. As suggested in Fig. 1.4, at many governmental levels trilateral gatherings remained frequent and productive from 2002 to 2005, even though trilateral summits in Northeast Asia were suspended because of Japanese prime minister Koizumi's Yasukuni Shrine visits. Since 2006, major breakthroughs have been achieved in top level Sino-Japanese and Japanese-Korean bilateral relations as well. With new leadership in South Korea and Taiwan during 2008, and in Japan late in 2009, regional tensions have significantly declined, and cooperation across the region has gained even greater momentum.

During the critical year of 2008 itself, trilateral interaction and policy coordination rapidly deepened, propelled by the financial crisis. In May, the East Asian Foreign Exchange Reserve Bank expanded its reserves to $80 billion, with Japan, China, and South Korea contributing 80 percent of the increase.[54] In November, the finance ministers of the three nations met in Washington DC, on the sidelines of the IMF annual meetings, to broaden their bilateral currency-swap mechanisms with one another.[55] They also regularized their trilateral central bankers' dialogue in December.[56] Thus, when the heads of government of the three countries convened in Fukuoka, on December 13, 2008, they credibly declared an intention "to promote the trilateral summit as a platform for the future," substantiated by several new, concrete initiatives previously realized at lower bureaucratic levels.[57] The leaders of these countries met once again in Beijing nine months later, pursuing these initiatives further, while reviving serious consideration of a trilateral FTA agreement, and a cross-investment accord.[58]

Prevailing Academic Pessimism about Northeast Asian Regionalism

Existing literature on Asian regionalism has generally emphasized Southeast Asian or Asia-wide institutions; it has largely overlooked the historic new regionalization trends in Northeast Asia that are outlined above.[59] The conventional wisdom has long been markedly pessimistic about prospects for multilateral cooperation among China, Japan, and Korea, or across the Taiwan Straits, reflecting the deep-seated tensions of the past.[60] Structural, institutional, and cultural features in the conflict-ridden Northeast, haunted by memories of a bitter history of conflict, are simply not conducive to regional cooperation, this literature maintained.[61]

It has been argued, for example, that power disparities are too pronounced to support equitable and cooperative international relations within Northeast Asia.[62] China, it is alleged, is simply too much larger than the rest of Asia, in terms of demography and military strength, to make balanced mutuality possible. Economically speaking, Japan is likewise much more substantial and sophisticated than the second largest economy in Asia, China.[63] To make matters even more difficult, it is argued, Asia as a whole lacks a common heritage of "community," with the peculiar structure of state-society relations in key nations sadly hindering even today the emergence of a coherent formal regional framework.[64] Cultural, linguistic, and religious differences further complicate regionalist development in Asia, the pessimists argue.

The picture of Northeast Asian comity presented in the prevailing literature is even gloomier than that prognosticated for Asia as a whole. Each of the main countries of the Northeast Asian subregion—China, Korea, and Japan—conversely appears to privilege its relationship with the United States above intraregional ties. The U.S.-Japan alliance relationship appears formidable to many, allegedly intensifying Sino-Japanese tensions.[65] Even China attaches preeminent strategic and economic importance to its bilateral ties with the United States, it is argued. Indeed, Beijing opened an ambitious new strategic dialogue with Washington in the summer of 2005 with no precedent in its previous relations with other Asian states. This bilateral Sino-U.S. dialogue has continued, in slightly different guise, into the Obama years.

Despite divisions on matters of detail, the U.S.-Korea military relationship likewise seems resilient, with the ROK providing the largest non–Anglo Saxon military contingent in Iraq for several years. Seoul, in June 2007, also formally concluded a free trade agreement with Washington, although its ratification was substantially delayed. Furthermore, anti-Japanese nationalist outbursts in China and Korea, such as those in the spring of 2006, long appeared to justify gloomy projections for the future Northeast Asian relationship, as did persistent uncertainties surrounding the future of North Korea and the cross-Straits relationship.

An Alternative View

This book takes account of these conflictual intra-Asian patterns and cooperative trans-Pacific interactions. Yet it departs from the conventional pessimism about Northeast Asian regionalism to document a more dynamic, if still only dimly perceived, new reality. That is the Making of Northeast Asia: initially a socioeconomic, yet increasingly a political and diplomatic, phenomenon replete with long-term strategic implications.

We first provide an alternative explanation for the organization gap in Asia from the end of World War II to the 1997 Asian financial crisis, using a critical-juncture analysis. The critical juncture of the Korean War, as will later be demonstrated, gave birth to a distinctive and fateful "hub-and-spokes" relationship between the United States and its allies in Japan and Korea, with China to join later, as a curious de facto member. The Asian partners of the United States were locked, albeit often benignly, into this hierarchical system for four long decades, carrying on their intraregional relations with one another largely through the Washington hub of the system. "Spokes to spokes" relations were both limited and fragile, especially in Northeast Asia, where bitter, long-standing historical memories often compounded Cold War estrangement among the Northeast Asian states.

In Southeast Asia, fledgling regional organizations, such as SEATO and ASEAN, did begin to emerge, inspired by Cold War tensions. The Vietnam War, and then determination to contain Vietnam following the fall of Saigon in 1975 and Hanoi's subsequent 1978 invasion of Cambodia, helped ASEAN to flourish, and to occupy a central role in regional affairs that transcended the political-economic strength of its members. Meanwhile, deep historical tensions, and the lack of a geopolitical rationale for cohesion, inhibited ties further north, despite substantial and deepening socioeconomic complementarities among China, Japan, and Korea.

Economic development and transnational economic relationships within Asia itself, we argue, increasingly challenged this "hub-and-spokes" system. Trans-

Pacific trade ties confronted growing mutual irritants, beginning in the 1970s. Increasing difficulties in sustaining the U.S.-centric Asian financial framework, through which many local currencies were unrealistically dollar-pegged, eventually exploded in the 1997 Asian financial crisis.

The crisis represented another critical juncture for East Asian regional integration, comprehensively discussed in Chapter 4. For the first time in half a century, crisis-savaged Asian countries came together to confront a common economic challenge. Shared grievances against the International Monetary Fund, together with the World Bank's insensitive handling of the Asian crisis, united all the countries of the region, with Northeast Asian powers—especially Japan and China—taking the principal initiative. In stimulating their mutual cooperation, the 1997 crisis helped to fuse new policy networks. Those in turn helped overcome historic isolation and estrangement, which were especially salient between Japan and the closest neighbors, thus hastening the Making of Northeast Asia in later years, as we shall see.

In the following two chapters, we find that the nascent subregional integrating mechanism, born in the wake of the Asian financial crisis, goes far beyond the broad Chiang Mai agreement. It involves at its core an increasing economic and psychological connectedness within Northeast Asia that is ultimately replete with political implications. Visions of a common Northeast Asian identity, with positive historical roots obscured by bitter memories of war and colonialism, have re-emerged, after lying dormant for more than half a century. Epitomized in the thought of Sun Yat-sen, those visions gained renewed life and credibility following the 1997–98 financial crisis, which left the northeastern quadrant of Asia relatively more vigorous than its southeastern counterpart—and headed toward greater cohesion, even as it paid lip service to broader regional conceptions in a multitiered international system.

Beyond these general themes, we also engage in detailed country-specific analysis, concentrated in Chapters 7–10. Regional policies in China, South Korea, and to a lesser degree Japan have evolved substantially over the past two decades, most notably since the Asian financial crisis, helping each nation to transcend long-standing estrangement with its immediate periphery, and exploit latent mutual complementarity. The domestic politics of regionalism have changed substantially in each nation, as bitter memories fade and interdependence rises, with "regionalizing coalitions" giving new momentum to old ties with near neighbors. New local economic development policies are also promoting broader regional integration, especially in China. By examining these recent changes in both policy and political economy, we seek to explain the rising cohesion of Northeast Asia, sensitive to domestic factors, the external environment they confront, and the critical junctures that are bringing Mainland China, Taiwan, Japan, and the two Koreas closer once again.

The book closes by reviewing America's historic approach to Northeast Asia, its changing political-economic ties with the region, and the implications thereof for policy. The U.S.—a neighboring power to Northeast Asia in geographic terms, has of course long been an indispensable regional actor—a "resident power," in the words of U.S. Secretary of Defense Robert Gates[66]— with deep political-military roots in the western Pacific ever since World War II. Both Japan and South Korea have mutual security treaties with the United States, host American bases, and find the United States to be a substantial export market. Mainland China and Taiwan feel the economic attraction of the United States also.

Yet we find that America, despite its immense embedded leverage within the region, remains remarkably naïve about Northeast Asia's emerging internal political-economic trends. Many scholars and politicians in Washington know little of the subtly emerging cohesiveness and connectedness in Northeast Asian economic relationships, and remain persistently suspicious of such Asian integration as they perceive. These views, even when they perceive plausible dangers, generally entail no cohesive response strategy, and neglect the economic rationale for a more integrated Asia. They also overlook potential American cooperative stakes in the increasingly cohesive Northeast Asia that is steadily and perhaps inevitably emerging, whether the United States likes it or not.

Our Contribution

Publications on East Asian regionalism have proliferated in recent years. We thus need to differentiate our work from that of other publications, and we can do so in several respects.

First, this book is consciously oriented toward theory-building, in contrast to a prevailing tendency, with some notable exceptions, toward descriptive or prescriptive treatments. We attempt to offer a more general theory for Asian institution-building, using the dynamic framework of critical-juncture analysis. In this formulation, three catalytic factors are argued to be important preconditions for regionalist development in Northeast Asia: (1) changing geostrategic context; (2) political leadership; and (3) crises, real or perceived. Asian decision-making tends to be reactive, we argue, with institutional innovation hence heavily reliant on leadership initiatives. Political-economic crisis, however, tends to greatly stimulate policy innovation, policy-network development, and initial determination of the policy initiatives that ultimately emerge, even though implementation itself may follow the crisis in question at a significant interval.[67]

This book is also distinctive in that it focuses analytically on prospects for *Northeast Asian* cooperation, rather than that of Asia more generally. It does, to be sure, discuss broader developments in East Asian regionalism to some degree, particularly when Northeast Asia has taken special initiative. It also touches on the broad Asia-Pacific regional relationship as a whole, in the course of considering narrower Northeast Asian regionalist tendencies, and Northeast Asia's deepening leadership role in the broad Asian regionalist advances that do occur. Because of the relatively smooth progress for many years of multilateral regionalism relating to ASEAN, much of the current literature is naturally biased toward examining the "ASEAN Way."[68] Yet that approach, while once important and functional, is less and less relevant to emerging political-economic realities, especially those unfolding over the past decade, as the locus of both economic growth and political-military uncertainty in Asia has moved further to the northeast.

Northeast Asia is not substantial only in geoeconomic terms. Just as important, it is increasingly becoming an identifiable economic, political, and strategic region in its own right—a globally significant yet little-recognized new development. Since 2001 the two principal economic "networks" of the region (overseas Chinese and Japanese production chains) have converged and transfused with each other on the Chinese Mainland, especially in the Shanghai area and China's Northeast. Politically and strategically, the North Korean nuclear question, East China Sea energy disputes, and the Taiwan Straits issue are all intensely engaging the Northeast Asian countries. These controversies clearly have dangerous conflictual dimensions. Yet they also offer opportunities and incentives—precisely because of their danger—for network-building, and for cooperative attempts at resolution. Counterintuitively, yet consistent with the analytical framework developed here, tensions do appear to be nourishing a remarkably dynamic, if still subtle, institution-building process—replete with fateful global implications.

Third and finally, this book offers a detailed analysis of the domestic politics of regionalism in the three major nations of Northeast Asia (China, Japan, and Korea), as well as in the most important external actor, the United States. Employing comparative and historical methods, these country-specific assessments show how both politics and policies are evolving within each key nation, ultimately to enhance the prospects for closer cooperation among these key nations as a group. The book also inquires into how intellectuals and officials in these key countries regard regionalism in Asia more generally, and how their thinking resonates with civil society. Overall, it accents the remarkable parallelism that, interactive with economic trends, is quietly yet ineluctably bringing a new, more cohesive, and increasingly self-confident Northeast Asia into being.

Theories of Asian Institutional Development
Changing Context and Critical Junctures

Northeast Asia is paradoxically configured: on the one hand, the region enjoys sustained long-term growth and steadily increasing economic interdependence. Yet on the other, it is plagued by a fractious regional politics that all too often confounds potential cooperation. Despite the region's demonstrable macro-economic success, its collective economic management has been disappointing. Indeed, Northeast Asia has chronically failed to coordinate its own regional trade, financial, and environmental affairs in coherent fashion, or to protect itself from turbulence intruding from the broader world.

Northeast Asia's distinctive "organization gap" has traditionally stood at the heart of these multiple difficulties, and has seriously impeded their resolution.[1] Seen in comparative regional perspective, Northeast Asia long had the most pronounced formal organization gap of any such area on earth, amid a growing inadequacy of long-standing informal alternatives. In contrast to Western Europe, Southeast Asia, the South Pacific, or even the Middle East, Northeast Asia has never had a formal regionwide multilateral security structure, despite the manifest dangers of its situation. Until the late 1990s it was virtually devoid of regional economic or environmental organization as well. Even the Middle East, East Africa, and the Mediterranean Basin were more organized.[2]

Why did Northeast Asia for so many years lack formal regional institutions, despite the manifest need for coordination? What accounts for the important changes that have recently taken place, especially since the mid-1990s? This chapter presents a parsimonious answer to the contradictions of Northeast Asian regional organization, introducing and operationalizing the concept of "critical junctures" and incorporating changing political-economic context as well as the catalytic role of crises in the overall analysis.

Before developing the critical juncture (CJ) notion and exploring its utility, it is important to understand the explanatory gap that needs to be filled. Prevailing literature on Northeast Asia's regional-institutional environment was long based on comparison with European integration, and thus frequently overlooked parallel dynamics in other regions of the world. Causal mechanisms deduced solely from European experience are inadequate either to explain Northeast Asia's organization gap or to predict future institutional trajectories of the region, but they do provide some useful intellectual benchmarks. Before turning to the critical-juncture model and its analytical utility, we will therefore briefly review regional institutional developments throughout the world, exploring both the mechanisms that created these institutions and the nature of the resulting institutional framework. A comparative understanding of regional institutions facilitates a better understanding both of the institutional gap in Northeast Asia and of the potential alternatives for addressing that gap.

Among the regions of the world, we select Europe, North America, and South America to illustrate the nature and processes of regional institution-building from a comparative perspective. All three regions have achieved an impressive degree of institutional development, with varying levels of intraregional political cohesiveness. There is also a significant body of scholarly literature that seriously examines regional institutions in those parts of the world, and that undertakes serious cross-regional comparison.[3] A comparative review of such transnational organizations can help explain the original intellectual context for regionalism, while also providing insights into the functioning of the actual institutions themselves.

The Explanatory Gap in Current Literature

Serious attempts to explain Northeast Asia's organization gap have often been based on European experience, flowing from two streams of thought: the realist paradigm and institutionalist frameworks.[4] The realist tradition stresses the role of geostrategy in creating the gap. The contrasting institutionalist tradition explains the organization gap in terms of established norms and culture.[5] Within the realist tradition, one group has focused on the bilateral distrusts among nations in the region, and the other has emphasized the inhibiting role of the United States, as an unwilling hegemon. The institutional approach can be further broken down into one focusing on regime types and state-society relations, and another stressing cultural legacies and intellectual influences.

According to realists, power distribution among nations determines the profile of regional institutions. Power distribution in Europe, for example, has traditionally been quite even among major powers. All the bids for control by a single country have failed, because no country in Europe has had sufficient strength to prevail over all others in the region. Stability on that continent has been preserved by artful manipulation of the balance of power. Informed by European experience, realists see great-power balance as a precondition for regional institution-building more generally.[6]

In Asia, by contrast, China is considerably larger and more centrally located than the other countries, making that region ostensibly "hegemony-prone."[7] A European-style balance of power system has, to be sure, struggled futilely to emerge in Asia. Given China's long shadow and America's countervailing power, this hegemony bias persistently inhibits the emergence of serious regional cooperation—both in Asia and more generally, it is argued.[8]

Is the presence of a global hegemon necessarily subversive of regional organization? Contrary to classical realist assumptions, a hegemon with the power to decisively shape regional arrangements may choose institutions over direct suasion in managing a region; a constitutional global order predicated on rule-based organizations arguably has its own intrinsic value for both governor and governed.[9] Walter Mattli even goes so far as to argue that successful regional integration requires the presence of a dominant member who can serve as a focal point in the coordination of rules, regulations, and policies, while also easing distributional tension through side payments.[10] Indeed, after World War II the United States was the dominant power in both Europe and Asia. Its seemingly divergent strategies for managing the two continents show that a dominant hegemon can and did promote regional institutions, as manifest in the European case, although it raises the paradoxical question of why U.S. approaches to local regionalism appear to have been less supportive in Asia.[11]

From a different perspective, Gil Rozman suggests that the precondition for formal institutions is great-power balance. Such balance, he argues, has never been enduringly present in Northeast Asia, because of the complicated geopolitical relationships among Russia, China, Japan, and the United States.[12] Such lack of balance leads to an absence of Northeast Asian regional organization, Rozman contends.

This argument cannot avoid considering the marked and deepening economic complementarities that prevail in Northeast Asia. Among the major powers of the region, Russia holds huge reserves of energy, including nearly one-third of the proven natural gas reserves on earth, relatively close to major industrial and population centers of China, Korea, and Japan.[13] China has potentially the largest market in the world, and Japan the largest pool of national savings anywhere. South Korea can play, and is playing, a proactive, catalytic broker's role.

Clearly, the four countries, including Russia, all have enormous potential to gain from regional cooperation. The various product-cycle theorists have demonstrated the shaping and conditioning effects of economic forces on Northeast Asian systems, especially those of Japan, South Korea, and Taiwan.[14] In fact, all three of these distinctive political economies have assumed remarkably similar political-economic and industrial structures over the past two decades.[15]

Intraregional cooperation is made ever easier, especially at the corporate level, by the emergence of so-called transnational production networks. Such production systems, which are becoming especially common within Northeast Asia, are arrangements that link a multitude of producing units in different countries that provide components, materials, and management for the assembly of a particular product.[16] They are rapidly becoming pervasive in the Asian textile, electronics, automotive, and precision-machinery sectors, because of the particular efficiencies and complementarities operating within the region, particularly in the production of precision subassemblies such as motors, computer peripherals, and machine tools.[17] The manufacturing firms in question, however, often have markets outside the region or headquarters there. Global and subregional linkages, either formal or informal, thus clearly help to reduce the potential costs to third parties of any regionalist configuration—a nesting phenomenon that Rozman fails to recognize. It helps to make rising regional interdependence more likely than he suggests, especially among Mainland China, Taiwan, Japan, and South Korea.

Scholars in the historical-institutional tradition stress path dependence in institution building: there are many outcomes and many paths to political development, with each route leading to a distinctive outcome.[18] For such scholars, the forms and scope of prevailing organizations are the "unintended spillover" of preexisting institutional settings. And the future development of new social bodies is largely constrained by their existing configuration at any given point in time. As a consequence, institutional development is typically an evolution from existing institutions, rather than a product of individuals freely interacting with one another and their broader environment.

Peter Katzenstein and Takashi Shiraishi (1997) present a widely cited institutional framework for explaining the organization gap in Asia.[19] In *Network Power*, Katzenstein argues that two distinctive features of Asian countries contribute to the lack of formal institutions in the region: (1) hierarchic state-society relationships; and (2) peculiar state structures. He contends that in Asia the concept of community, especially horizontal and associational community, is underdeveloped: "The Western concept of community is often associated with organized and institutional structures, but there is no equivalent Chinese translation for this concept," he contends.[20]

On the other hand, Katzenstein simultaneously argues that "[s]ome state structures are better suited than others to deal with public law and formal institutions as the preferred vehicle for regional integration." These states, in his view, are "highly rationalized forms of bureaucratic and legal rule-Weberian states." In Asia, by contrast, he suggests that "nations are shaped by the legacy of universal empires, regional kingdoms, and sub-continental empires."[21]

Western Europe, Southeast Asia, Latin America, and North America, to be concrete, had cultural attributes distinct to their member countries, yet still achieved impressive intraregional associational growth. Southeast Asia, whose domestic structures parallel those in Northeast Asia, has nevertheless developed far more advanced regional institutions than its counterpart subregion farther north. The culture-determinant explanation, as historical institutionalism sometimes emphasizes, does not travel well.

Katzenstein's and Shiraishi's 2006 edited volume *Beyond Japan: The Dynamics of East Asian Regionalism* clearly notes this complex reality, and advances the concept of "hybrid-regionalism" to explain it.[22] As Katzenstein observes in the volume, the ongoing evolution of identities in East Asia has been influenced by various national paradigms. The result has been a hybrid of Japanization, Americanization, and, to a lesser extent, Sinicization. Ultimately, he suggests, it is impossible to untangle the three.[23] The 2006 volume, like their 1997 volume emphasizing national norms and institutions, is, however, more sensitive to transnational actors and processes. Indeed, Katzenstein readily admits in this later book that there are various discrete processes of regionalism in East Asia, each led by different sets of actors.[24] His observations are similar to those expressed in T. J. Pempel's 2005 edited volume *Remapping East Asia*. Pempel argues that looking beyond national governments, East Asia has become "considerably more interdependent, connected, and cohesive, ... largely driven by developments in non-governmental areas."[25]

Pempel further contends that "more than one path—not simply state actions—can lead to the development of greater regional cohesiveness," and he emphasizes three drivers—governments, corporations, and ad hoc problem-oriented coalitions—in the process of East Asian regionalism. His volume, as a whole, views these processes or drivers as products of evolutionary developments in East Asia, rather than abrupt transformations. Although the book notes that cross-border cohesiveness developed rapidly after the Asian financial crisis, it does not consider in detail how the Asian financial crisis (AFC) actually affected institutional development in the region. Most important, it overlooks entirely the subtle and multifaceted emergence of an increasingly coherent Northeast Asia, although that phenomenon was clearly not as well developed in 2005, when his book was published, as it has since become.

The next section of this volume undertakes a comparative examination of regionalism in Europe, North America, and South America. It does so to demonstrate that institutional development there has followed a junctured evolutionary process, rather than the smooth trajectory that functionalist and constructivist theories implicitly suggest. Even in Europe, traditional culture and norms provided mainly a context for institutions, rather than a clear determinant of their profiles. Market mechanisms and social-economic interdependence helped to make that region more cohesive. Catalytic events then precipitated discontinuous jumps in institution-building. Regionalism in both North and South America manifests a similarly junctured dynamic, the constraints of growing economic interdependence notwithstanding.

Regionalism in Comparative Perspective

Regional integration has clearly proceeded furthest in Europe. The Single European Act, ratified in 1986–87, set the goal of a single European market for goods, labor, and capital by 1992. It also streamlined collective decision-making by allowing for a qualified majority to pass some EC legislation, without the previously required consensus. From November 1993, the implementation of the Maastricht Treaty transformed the European Community into a tighter European Union, while strengthening cooperation on foreign and security affairs, justice, and police matters. It also broadened the reach of the European Commission in industrial policy, consumer affairs, health, and education.

A close examination of European integration trends reveals that market globalization, geopolitical logic, and the convergence of interests induced by globalization were the principal catalysts for European integration, rather than abstract principles or norms.[26] Simply put, closer union was driven by a felicitous balance of demand for regionalism, largely the result of economic forces, and a judicious supply, through collective political action.[27] Integration has involved an interplay between market pressures and the ability and willingness of political systems to respond. Together with the nineteenth-century Zollvereign,[28] European integration since the 1950s provides one of history's best examples of systematic rationalist response to the endemic dilemmas of coordination in international affairs.[29]

Common purpose, no doubt coupled with American hegemonic support, helped in the beginning. Stabilizing economic relations among Christian Democratic allies of the United States in Western Europe was, after all, a central objective of the 1957 Treaty of Rome. Over the following three decades, there was little further strengthening, however, of supranational regulatory mechanisms, despite growing movement of goods, services, labor, and capital among the partner nations. During the mid and late 1980s, however, European organizational development did achieve fundamental breakthroughs in a relatively short period, epitomized by the Single European Act of 1987, the Single Integrated Market (achieved in 1991), and the Maastricht Treaty of 1992. European integration has thus followed a discontinuous path that norms alone cannot explain.

Students of European regional integration have offered various explanations for this historic progress during the late 1980s, ranging from intergovernmental bargaining based on shared interest,[30] to the operation of a global market mechanism,[31] and to multidimension and multiactor processes of regionalization.[32] Stefan Schirm, for example, detailed changes in the global market during the early 1980s, which in turn influenced domestic politics within key European and Latin American countries. Globalization, he argued, led to inward-looking interventionist policies. Those in turn triggered domestic or regional financial crises, as affected nations were torn between domestic political and global market imperatives.

Walter Mattli similarly took as his point of departure the historic technological changes of the 1970s and 1980s that "shrunk" distances and "put pressure on governments to adjust the scale of political and economic organization to the level implied by the new technologies."[33] These changes generated economic pressures that gave birth to influential transnational business lobbies within Europe, such as the Round Table of European Industrialists (ERT). Such groups, through their powerful political-economic networks, pressed their case for regionalism with national political leaders, who were—he concurred with Schirm—seriously pressed to respond to the turbulence and stagflation of the times.[34]

Regionalism became an attractive alternative halfway house to obviate this pervasive turmoil and competitive pressure from globalization—not only in Europe, but elsewhere in the world as well. Nationalist proponents of regionalism, such as Mahathir Mohammed of Malaysia, showed concretely, as during the 1997 AFC, how regionalism might curb the volatility of global forces, thereby both enhancing domestic economies and stabilizing local regimes. This interactive process—crisis, interest, and instrument—was clearly evident in France and Germany during the late 1980s and the early 1990s, as in Brazil and Argentina also.[35]

The establishment of the Mercado Comun del sur, or Southern Common Market (MERCOSUR) in 1991 was a dramatic organizational achievement for South America, given that the two initiating members of the new body, Brazil and Argentina, had been bitter rivals until the beginning of the 1980s. In contrast to previous regional organizations, MERCOSUR was a clear response to globalization, whose tailwinds rose to galelike force during the 1980s. Within MERCOSUR, both Brazil and Argentina rejected their traditionally protectionist developmental strategies, and deepened mutual cooperation based on free-market reforms, driven by a shared need to be competitive in world markets.[36] Crises, such as the financial traumas of 1991, when the Southern Cone nations found themselves nearly destitute, as a result of the inefficiency of their industries as well as their heavy debt burden, clearly played important roles in the establishment and consolidation of MERCOSUR, which aided local impulses to cooperate regionally in restructuring.

Despite sporadic intraregional frictions, MERCOSUR transformed South America into a fundamentally different, and more integrated, region from anything conceivable before. Dramatic changes in the relationship between Argentina and Brazil were institutionalized, not only within the framework of MERCOSUR but also through a wide range of other agreements and confidence-building measures. Indeed, by the mid-1990s it was clear that a major break had taken place in the historic rivalry between these two large, jealous Latin powers, a rivalry that had at one earlier stage led them both toward the acquisition of nuclear weapons. The two countries were instead enmeshed in an increasingly dense process of institutionalized cooperation.[37] Customs barriers were dismantled, and tariffs fell sharply within MERCOSUR. Policies regarding foreign direct investment, trade, public procurement, and services were also harmonized.[38]

Further to the north, the idea of the North American Free Trade Agreement (NAFTA) was accepted by the Mexican government, also as an offspring of crisis. The Mexican government had been reluctant to enter a free trade agreement with the United States and Canada. This sea-change in its policy symbolized a major, counterintuitive liberalizing shift in Mexican policy toward Washington. It was particularly remarkable in that Mexico had lost half of its territory to the United States in 1848, becoming obsessed for well over a century thereafter with preserving autonomy from further Yankee inroads.

The dramatic shift in attitude toward the "Colossus of the North," epitomized in Mexican support for NAFTA, was not an isolated action. Indeed, it flowed from a clear, neoliberal shift in Mexico's economic-policy orientation, related to the rise of an internationalist, market-oriented middle class in Mexico itself, together with a converse decline in the strength of local public-service unions under President Carlos Salinas. Free market rules gradually yet decisively replaced the traditional statist and protectionist developmental model, which had prevailed since the revolution of 1910.[39]

The impact of global markets on Mexico was similar to that operating in

Argentina and Brazil. The heavy burden of foreign debt, together with the crisis that it precipitated in the early 1980s, and the specter of crisis that it threatened once again a decade later, all exerted strong pressures for change in the local economic-policy paradigm. These were intensified by domestic sociopolitical changes within the countries in question. The emergence of global markets provoked crisis-inducing volatility in the financial realm, which threatened both local entrepreneurs and the emerging middle class. Markets thus exerted powerful pressure on the economic situation, and through it on domestic interest-group coalitions, as well as on the Latin American technocratic search for more effective economic policy instruments. Ultimately, financial crises gave birth in Latin America to a profound, shared sense of the need for regional cooperation in ensuring smooth and economically efficient adjustment to the powerful global forces bearing down on local political economies.

The United States, of course, did not experience nearly as acute a set of crises as did Mexico, because of America's key-currency status, its preeminent global geopolitical role, and its long-standing economic openness. Yet America was nevertheless seriously affected by globalization during the 1980s and 1990s, with its heartland industrial base suffering, even as consumers, together with the financial and agricultural sectors, generally benefited. NAFTA, to be sure, was viewed as a useful instrument by both the Clinton administration and American private-sector groups. Indeed, it was clearly seen as efficient in facilitating and securing U.S. corporate access to production sites in Mexico.[40] Yet many labor groups and other supporters of liberal social and environmental agendas were nevertheless critical of the establishment of NAFTA, both in the early 1990s and thereafter, because of the deindustrialization that it precipitated.

Cross-Regional Commonalities

To sum up, the experience of regionalism in Europe, South America, and North America, as expressed in the form of the European Community (EU), MERCOSUR, and NAFTA, respectively, varied considerably, as external and internal environments in the three regions were different. Despite these variations, however, four general concluding observations can be made regarding the process of regional institution-building across the major areas of the world.

First, regardless of whether countries in a given region share cultural heritage or institutional norms, changes in both domestic and regional political-economic contexts are critical to their choice of regional cooperation, rather than a more unilateral approach, as a vehicle for pursuing national interests. Members of the EU undoubtedly share values more comprehensively with one another than do members of MERCOSUR or NAFTA. Yet fundamental breakthroughs in regional institution-building were immediately driven, even in Europe, primarily by changes in the global political-economic environment, interacting with domestic context, rather than by changes in values. As Mattli argued, the critical precondition was a balance between demand for and supply of regional institutions.[41]

Second, power disparity among nations does not necessarily impede the emergence of cooperative regional institutions. Indeed, the presence in a region of major powers that hold disproportionate influence often spurs institutional cooperation in solving what Mattli terms the "Coordination Dilemma."[42] History does not, however, suggest that there necessarily needs to be a single hegemon, or undisputed leader. In both the EU and MERCOSUR, for example, a pair of rival nations had historically vied for regional hegemony: France versus Germany in Europe, and Brazil versus Argentina in South America. These traditional rivalries ultimately did not inhibit the emergence of a more cooperative local regionalism, contrary to the assumption of some theorists.[43] As we shall see, transnational networks, business lobbies, and the exigencies of critical juncture can serve as a partial functional substitute for hegemony, or even single-power leadership, in promoting regional integration. This more complex equation prevailed in MERCOSUR, and seems to be emerging in Northeast Asia as well.

Indeed, competition for regional leadership actually appears to promote active regional institution-building when the nations in question are economically interdependent and have well-developed transnational political-economic networks that can help coordinate through relations with one another. Regional institutions, once established, can also help to neutralize regional rivalry, by mitigating zero-sum relationships. Such rivalry can be especially dangerous where the competitors are all-important to one another, generating potential zero-sum relationships. Regional integration thus helped to stabilize the relationship of heavily indebted Brazil and Argentina with global capital markets in the early 1990s, by offering both of them fertile new markets within which to expand.

Third, although political leadership is ultimately critical to regional institution-building, business elites and the private sector also serve as important agenda-setting drivers for regional integration, particularly when they are threatened by economic uncertainty, as during global financial crises. Domestic coalition politics strongly influence national leaders' decisions to cooperate within their region, especially when cosmopolitan business and the middle class are important members. Business interests often mobilize resourceful multinational corporations to lobby both their home and host-nation governments to establish regional institutions, as was clear in the process of creating both MERCOSUR and NAFTA.

Fourth, and most important, crises can be major catalysts for regional institution-building, because they sharply intensify both the economic demand for stabilizing institutions, and also facilitate the political supply of those institutions. Crises bring out weaknesses in existing domestic institutional structure. They also can encourage the perception among national leaders that regional institutions are an economically efficient and politically acceptable solution to such crises. It is no coincidence that a more forceful movement toward regionalist solutions occurs during crises than on other occasions, especially in developing nations, as the examples of Argentina in 1991, Mexico in 1995, and East Asia in 1997 all suggest.

The foregoing cross-regional review also indicates that regional cooperation can assume varied institutional forms. Patterns of regional integration vary in terms of the exclusivity of membership, stringency of institutional binding, breadth of issue areas considered, cross-regional policy orientation, and stance toward fully global cooperation. Regional organizations are more likely to be sustained when memberships have a clear geographic focus, although membership expansion to more diverse constituencies is quite conceivable later in an institution's evolution, as in the case of the European Community. The three regional organizations outside of Asia that are considered here involved countries within clearly defined geographic regions. Yet membership expanded steadily over time, as new nations expressed a desire to join these pre-existing organizational frameworks.

In terms of regional institutionalization, the EU has the highest level of legalization of any such body in the world. Agreements reached there also tend to shape local behavior more uniformly than in the other two regional contexts considered. MERCOSUR and NAFTA have lower levels of legalization, and the issue areas subject to supranational regulation are decidedly more limited than in the EU. Yet the establishment of these supranational bodies in North and South America has indeed transformed political and economic relations within their respective regions. Their precedent provides some reason to be optimistic about regional cooperation even where EU-style integration cannot be rapidly or readily achieved.

The three major existing regional organizations outside Asia also differ in their relationship to globalization. MERCOSUR members, for instance, have been more regionally defensive than the others, placing greater priority on economic "deepening" among their own members than on "broadening" toward outside economies.[44] The EU, by contrast, is more open to global trading partners, although its member states still enjoy considerably higher levels of openness and standardization with one another than they do with the world market in general. NAFTA lies in between. Varying relationships with the United States play a significant role in explaining these differences, with the MERCOSUR case, in particular, showing that U.S. hegemonic influence is not uniformly dominant in shaping profiles of regionalism.

The Critical-Juncture Framework

As we have seen in the previous section, there is considerable variation in the salience of regional organization in major global regions, and also in the profile of regional organization within those regions. Transcendent concepts such as "hegemony" or "norms" do not provide sufficient explanation for the variety that we actually observe. And neither "globalization" nor "market forces" fully explain causality. All of these notions are underpredictive.

The critical equation is indeed, as Mattli points out, the demand for and the supply of regional institutions.[45] Under conditions of interdependence and rapid technological change, demand tends to be there, albeit often unarticulated. There is nothing automatic, however, about supply.

In the following section, we introduce the *critical-juncture framework* as a key explanatory variable in regional institution-building, which both intensifies demand for regional institutions and helps provide as well as configure supply. We argue that individual decision-making at pivotal historical turning points is thus crucial in determining the ultimate institutional product. In particular, we focus on the crucial role of critical junctures in determining the configuration of new regional organizations, of broader frameworks for regional cooperation—or indeed, if such mechanisms emerge at all.

This analysis stresses the dynamic interaction among individual decision-makers at a critical decision point. In formulating it, we synthesize insights from both historical-institutionalist and rational-choice models. Historical institutionalists have directed our attention to persistent legacies from the past. New rules of the game, however, can and do emerge from strategic bargains among individuals at given points in time, especially in periods of crisis and uncertainty. The eclectic critical-junctures framework captures the key insights of both approaches.

Yet the rational choice approach, which captures the significance of individual decision-making, too easily falls into the trap of assuming that individual bargaining over new arrangements occurs on a so-called tabula rasa, without regard to entrenched understanding and institutional context.[46] In introducing the concept of critical juncture, we describe and conceptualize the process by which rational actors alter their goals and perceptions in response to uncertainty, and by which they bargain in dynamic ways, often producing outcomes at substantial variance from the embedded historical-institutional context. We hope, in testing this concept, simultaneously to gain deeper insight into the Northeast Asian organization gap and into regionalism and political development more generally.

Beyond postulating the crisis-driven CJ model, we argue that changes in structural profiles such as transnational political-economic networks can also be important conditions for institutional development. Highly developed transnational networks lead to institution-building in two ways. On the one hand, tensions between changed political-economic context and obsolete institutions often engender crises, as has occurred recently on the Korean peninsula. On the other, crises also intensify interactions among transnational actors, and existentially provoke new shared identities, as through the Six-Party Talks process, giving rise to enduring transnational policy networks. Through this network-building dynamic, crises also gradually transform the political-economic environment, and foster conflict-resolution networks as well as other institutions across a given region, even when they do not definitively resolve the crises they formally confront. Manifestations of this counterintuitive stabilizing dynamic have been clearly visible across the years in such disparate locales as Kashmir, the Golan Heights, the Taiwan Straits, and Cold War Berlin. Crises and transnational policy networks thus work in tandem to facilitate the birth and deepening of regional institutions.

The Critical-Juncture Framework: Theoretical Background

Scholars of regionalism seldom employ the critical-juncture framework. Yet a variant of this concept has been frequently and productively applied to explain domestic institution-building. In particular, many seminal works on nation-building find national policies and leaders' choices at critical decision points crucial in determining both the form and function of political-economic institutions that later emerge.[47]

In studying national response to crises, Sidney Verba recognized that political development tends to follow a branching-tree pattern, which conceives such development as a sequence of choice points. At any given point, there may be alternative next stages. But the choice of any one of them forecloses alternatives. Here Verba stresses the opportunistic element at each decision point—and as a result, in the subsequent overall pattern of political evolution.[48]

Stephen Krasner offers a "punctuated equilibrium" paradigm for conceptualizing the state-building process.[49] Punctuated equilibrium corresponds nicely to the idea of a branching tree. It suggests that institutional change is episodic and dramatic rather than continuous and incremental. Crises, in this formulation, are of central importance. During a crisis, the choice made regarding which path to pursue forecloses other routes, including potentially the paths that are most appropriate in functional terms to solving a problem. Using the idea of so-called punctuated equilibrium, Krasner suggests not only the constraints on institutional adjustments but also the converse opportunities for institutional innovation: at each juncture, there is a chance for self-correction and choice of alternative political directions.

Similarly, Stephen Skowronek emphasizes the significance of political crisis, defined as "a sporadic, disruptive event that suddenly challenges a state's capacity to maintain control and alters the boundaries defining the legitimate use of coercion." He observes that "[c]risis situations tend to become the watersheds in a state's institutional development. Actions taken to meet the challenge often lead to the establishment of new institutional forms, powers, and precedents."[50] Skowronek's underlying causal argument is that the outcome of institution-building during any particular periods of crisis is a function of both contemporaneous environmental factors and existing institutional structures. In other words, the on-the-spot interplay between events and the parameters that shape the meaning of those events to decision-makers at a critical juncture has important causal impact on the institutional configuration that emerges from a crisis. Pre-existing institutions alone cannot determine this outcome.

Crises reduce incongruence between state structures and the domestic environment, by ushering in structural change responsive to that environment. Yet during subsequent periods institutions created to resolve the original incongruence take on a life of their own. Bureaucracies and political parties, for example, reproduce themselves without necessarily matching societal changes, leading to increased tensions. These in turn eventually precipitate further crises. This dualism of change and continuity is crucial in understanding the significance of crisis-generated critical junctures in political development.

Some clear illustrations of political development utilizing the branching-tree model are presented in Lipset's and Rokkan's study of European party systems.[51] In that book, they see three crucial historical junctures: reformation, democratic revolution, and industrial revolution. At each of these critical junctures the elite that controlled the state machinery had diverse political alliance options. Once a particular alliance was chosen, it set the institutional form and scope for future party development. In their work the hybrid mix of *continuity and change* presented simultaneously by a critical juncture is strongly emphasized.

Peter Gourevitch explored the relationship between crisis and the state, finding that crises both reflect what is happening within states and also in turn shape those states themselves. He appreciated historical contingency, arguing that "in each crisis countries 'choose' a policy or a sequence of policies . . . but frequently in decision making, we find neither consciousness nor coherence."[52]

Kent Calder has also applied the notion of crisis in explaining public policy profiles. In a formulation approaching that of the critical juncture, he describes the periods surrounding a major political crisis as "climactic periods, when long-established patterns are suddenly called into question, and new, unusually enduring relationships are forged."[53] He notes that an explanation for policy change sufficiently predictive to suggest the direction of change needs to combine structural and historical approaches. Calder's study, focusing on Japan's post–World War II politics of public policy formation in comparative perspective, shows that in years of turbulence—that is, periods when old relationships crumble and new ones are forged—long-standing and often routinized circles of compensation are also recast. The new institutions and policy patterns fashioned during those short periods of flux often persist long after the original pressures that forged them have died away. Hence, he argues, detailed historical examination of both pre-existing social structure and newly arising pressures for change during periods of crisis is crucial. Public policy analysis thus becomes, for Calder, a form of political archeology.

The above theoretical inquiries highlight a striking aspect of political development: *crisis and individual response at a critical juncture.* In the terminology of the branching-tree model, every critical juncture serves as a node from which different branches lead in varied directions. Decision-makers, given their opportunities and constraints, inevitably make choices regarding which branch to pursue at these individual nodes.

Transcending this simplified paradigm, we see subdivisions within the tree model. After a choice is made at a given decision node, there comes another decision node and separating branches down the road. Decision-makers—potentially different from those active at the previous node—are given new opportunities and constraints, and make choices as to which branch to approach. The direction of the previous decision may be revised or even may be contradictory to the former choice. Hence, a more appropriate path foreclosed by the previous decision may reopen for additional subsequent political evolution.

This branching-tree model contrasts sharply with the realist paradigm, and also with historical institutionalism. Diverging from the realist paradigm, the tree model captures the dynamics in negotiations and interactions at a critical juncture. Power distribution and position in the international system, though important, do not control the payoff structure and bargaining routes of an interactive game at any level.

As a critical juncture contains a time-pressure constraint, leaders of small countries that can afford to wait often enjoy considerable leverage over traditionally dominant powers with responsibilities for system-maintenance in actual negotiations. The dominant power is forced to accept a satisficing outcome in preference to a more ideal result, given its own distinctive, asymmetrical need to conclude bargaining in a timely fashion, so as to preserve system stability. As a result, the dominant power cannot always get what it prefers at a critical juncture, even when alternatives are fully open for future development.

The branching-tree model also differs from the historical-institutionalist approach. The latter stresses determinacy in institution-building, while the former captures the profound contingency on events that is characteristic of critical junctures. While historical institutionalism focuses on the structural context of decision-making, the branching-tree model recognizes the relative autonomy of individual volition, especially the interaction among individual policy-makers.

Again, existing institutions are important contextual elements of a critical juncture. Yet because of the distinctive, indeterminate nature of such potential turning points, as elaborated in the following section, institutions by definition cannot determine the outcome of such a critical juncture. To the contrary, outcomes are usually contingent on individual decision-making—and the process through which individual preferences are determined and aggregated, even though that process tends to be spontaneously haphazard, as Allison has pointed out.[54]

Critical Junctures and Regional Institution-Building

Despite the clear utility of a critical-juncture framework in intranational political development, as demonstrated in a wide range of previous studies, there is an unwarranted lack of scholarly attention to the critical-juncture mechanism in the study of regional political development.[55] There is, as we have seen, a potentially catalytic link between the demand for regional organization, flowing from either market pressures or security challenges, on the one hand, and their political supply. Coordination dilemmas make it easier for leaders to concur on new frameworks during critical junctures than at other times—and also more imperative.

Clear logical parallels can be drawn between national and regional institution-building, especially when the units in a given region are highly interdependent, as in Europe, Latin America, North America, or East Asia. If the evolution of sociopolitical organization at the national level does not follow the path specified theoretically by historical institutionalism, there is no particular reason to believe that at a regional level, established precedents should necessarily determine future direction. If national institution-building follows the crisis and sequence pattern, as the above scholarship suggests, then similar logic may be working at a regional level as well, especially when the constituent units of the region are highly interdependent.

Indeed, the profile of regional institution-building could be particularly responsive to crisis, given the fragility of institutions at the transnational level, the complex cross-pressures confronting regionalism, which only crisis can resolve, and the systemic imperative of coping with crisis when it actually emerges. This pattern could be particularly pronounced, as suggested later, in regions of the world that are especially prone to political-economic crisis, such as Northeast Asia. These crises can in turn be a crucial catalyst for policy innovation.

Without rejecting alternative formulations, the critical-juncture framework explains many dynamics and consequences of regional political evolution. Domestic institutions are the product of interactions among interest groups, organizations, administrative branches, and even individual leaders, in an effort to tackle common crises. Regional cooperation is therefore the product of dynamic interactions among countries with different interests and resources, seeking to solve emergent common problems or to fill a power vacuum.

Common goals, institutional environment, and case-specific factors—international power position, domestic coalition profile, and leadership beliefs—offer a broad context within which policy interactions take place. Policy-makers, however, have various means and resources with which to modify context and seek better payoffs; their convergence on bilateral or multilateral approaches, for example, is fatefully shaped by the process of interaction at a critical juncture. If policy-makers choose to create new institutions, they must decide on the specific characteristics of those bodies or systems of rules, including the strength, nature, and scope of the arrangements in question.[56] The structural product of this critical-juncture interaction is stabilized, codified, and in turn itself shapes the future profile of cooperation in a given region. The form and scope of regional cooperation are thus both perpetuated until another crisis occurs at a subsequent critical juncture.

Given the foregoing, the study of regionalism should thus find its roots in the understanding of critical junctures. Yet we do not claim that critical junctures fully explain regional development profiles. Certainly we recognize that historical and institutional factors all contribute to the interactions among nations at critical junctures, by shaping the context of decision itself. To use another analogy, if pre-existing institutions provide a repertoire of policy options for decision-makers, the crisis-induced critical junctures can (1) contract the repertoire, limiting available choices; (2) change the repertoire, ranking preferences differently; and (3) expand the repertoire, making visible fresh options that were invisible prior to the crisis. CJs can influence the decision-making processes of hegemonic nations just as profoundly as they do the policy profiles of smaller powers, if not more so, rendering CJs ultimately more fundamental to understanding policy outcomes, in many cases, than the power structure of domestic or international affairs.

TABLE 2.1

Critical Juncture vis-à-vis Historical Institutionalism

	Historical Institutionalism	Critical Juncture
Research focus	Institutional context	Individual interaction
Temporal emphasis	Time sequence	Time pressure
Historical perspective	Lasting path-dependence	Discontinuous critical junctures
General arguments	New institutions are by-products of existing institutions	New institutions are products of leaders' creativity and innovations
Commonality	Both approaches see the importance of entrenched institutions and the process of political development Both pay attention to crises and significant events, considering those as important reference periods Both have a strong sense of temporality Both rely heavily on case studies and documentary analysis	

We stress here that at a historical critical juncture, states may have multiple responses to regional crises, and they choose one of them based on two-level game interactions with domestic interest groups and foreign counterparts. Institutional development at critical junctures has inevitable discontinuity from a historical perspective—both in domestic and in transnational decision-making. To better illustrate the critical-juncture framework, Table 2.1 contrasts the differences between historical institutionalism and the alternative framework that we propose.

The impact of critical juncture is not limited to the immediate handling of a crisis. More important, we argue, the policy networks established to deal with the crisis in question endure after the turbulence has subsided. Even when these actors fail to establish formal procedures or regulatory bodies to govern their own future relations, they build processes for interactions and coordination among the countries in question.

Individual actors involved centrally in the policy networks tend to be prominent political leaders, specialists, and other influential figures in their own countries. In the process of dealing with crisis, they establish and solidify ties to actors from other countries. These relationships serve as communication channels for information, and springboards for contemplating collective action in the future. After crises subside, these actors often continue making cooperative proposals for addressing further issues that arise, using their new crisis-established transnational networks. In post-AFC Asia, for example, such networks helped crucially in establishing a multilayered institutional environment across that region.

Critical Juncture: The Model Specified

What is a critical juncture? How should we define one in a fashion that best helps us to understand transnational governance structures? Can we recognize a critical juncture when we see one?

Here we define a critical juncture as a historical decision point at which there are clear alternative paths to the future. Specifically, for a decision point to be a critical juncture, certain defining features are both necessary and sufficient:

A. There usually exists a crisis that calls the legitimacy of current arrangements into serious question, no matter whether those arrangements are formal, informal, institutional, or hegemonic; and no matter whether the crisis involves a swift change of power distribution within a system, or collapse of authority, or wars and other forms of violence. In another words, crisis significantly alters the pre-existing bargaining context, and opens windows of opportunity for change. It thus generates new demand for institutions. It also creates an initial impetus for interaction and signals the beginning of a critical juncture. Crises can be strategic, economic, or a mixture of the two: the 1962 Cuban missile crisis; the 1971 breakdown of the Bretton Woods system; the oil shocks of 1973 and 1979; the 1989 collapse of Soviet satellites in Eastern Europe; the 1991 collapse of the Soviet Union itself; and the 1997 Asian financial crisis all qualify.

B. Crisis breeds stimulus for change. Yet it also generates a parallel need for collective action to address a common problem, thus catalyzing the process of institutional supply. Initial impetus typically creates differing incentives for policy-makers, who have diverse preferences and leverage, defined by "states' international capabilities, domestic coalitional stability, and elite beliefs and ideologies."[57] The actors, however, may or may not have the necessary capacity to solve the problem in question. If the states in a given region lack the capacity to address the pressing problem and to generate new institutional innovations, then the crisis persists—with no decision made and no option chosen—until the crisis develops to the point where some actors capable of innovating to solve the collective problem emerge.

C. There is intense time pressure on the parties involved. Time pressure is a crucial element in a critical juncture, which also affects institutional supply, and constrains its contours. Time pressure makes interactions hard to routinize, and constrains time to search out options. As a result, decision-making is conducted under severely bounded rationality. As the concept of the "fog of war" suggests, decision-makers are forced into sudden, high-stakes decisions, often with fateful institutional implications, under extreme circumstances. They may be forced to do so with remarkably little information, given the often serious consequences of their actions.[58] The parties involved are pressured to interact to produce a solution within a sharply defined and limited period, beyond which the opportunity for change presented by a critical juncture may be lost. Especially when the political agenda of individual policy-makers and their limited power shadow on a given issue are taken into consideration, the pressure for them to negotiate a workable framework overrides the pursuit of an optimum outcome. As a result, the form of the resulting institutions is usually not their best or optimal configuration; compromises and negotiations are therefore typically central elements of a critical juncture.

While all critical junctures share the foregoing three generic traits, they vary, to some degree, in their relationship to the political-economic systems within which they are embedded. There are two basic varieties of CJ: security related and financially induced. The former is typically provoked by war or other military action, is relatively short, mobilizes top national leadership to produce resolution, and often provokes major institutional changes. The Korean War, examined in Chapter 3, is a good case in point. The latter type of CJ, increasingly common in the globalized world that has emerged since the 1980s, is often more extended chronologically, involves technical specialists and transnational epistemic networks more extensively in institution-building, and produces new institutional outcomes more slowly. Examples include the 1997 AFC and the 2008–9 global financial crisis.

At national, regional, and systemic levels, critical junctures are all central in institution-building and institutional change. In each case, crisis is pivotal in pushing through institutional innovations—the supply of new organization—especially when prevailing decision-making is highly bureaucratized. Crisis, together with the powerful time constraints and imperatives for collective action and leadership that critical junctures in their entirety provide, becomes a catalyst that disrupts routines and provides the sense of urgency that provokes real change.

There are two main operational processes, we argue, in the building and maintenance of almost all institutions. They correspond to two distinct types of decision-making: routinized and crisis-driven. In most circumstances, institutions, be they government bureaucracies, political parties, or softer variants, operate according to routine. Their distinct organizational procedures and culture prevail, with most policy outputs being nothing more than "the result of normal people behaving in normal ways in normal organizations."[59] The salience of standard-operating procedures (SOPs)[60] makes creative, systematic institution-building under routine circumstances very difficult.

Yet crisis-driven decision-making—often dramatic and discontinuous—does, of course, occur, in a fashion very different from that of routinized processes. Under crisis conditions, an organization's culture can be so shocked (or discredited) that operational objectives, missions, and special capacities are redefined, creating a new, intrainstitutional dynamic. Confronted with an undeniable failure of procedures and repertoires, what had seemed predetermined becomes a blank slate: authorities outside the organization may demand change; existing personnel are less resistant to change; and key members of the organization are replaced by individuals committed to change.[61]

Individual leaders, in the process of crisis-driven institutional innovation, can trigger alternate programs within a repertoire, redefine existing organizational routines in a new context, or introduce distinct programs for multiple organizations simultaneously. Crisis thus gives birth to a different type of decision-making, often with different actors, different incentives, and dramatically different prospective outcomes.

The contrasting forms of decision-making that we observe can usefully be presented as contrasting types of governmental games. Graham Allison, for example, distinguishes between "action-channel" games and "action-politics" games.[62] The former, fundamentally a struggle among agencies over jurisdictions, are a regularized means of taking government action on a specific kind of issue. Typically, issues are recognized and resolved within an established bureaucratic channel for action. In the game of action-politics, however, decisions flow from leaders' preferences. Players pull and haul with the power at their command to achieve outcomes that will advance their conception of national, organizational, group, or personal interests.[63]

Certainly Allison's distinctions among varieties of governmental games do not apply only to crisis/normal situations. In the action-politics games, Allison notes the stimulus provided by unusual events and the ways in which such events sharpen individual rationality and utility-oriented decision-making. The utility involved can be national, jurisdictional, or personal interest. The game of action-politics that Allison outlines resembles the decision process that we observe at critical junctures. That process provides insights into both why critical junctures are important and how they actually operate.

As Allison has noted, the environment in which a game is played during a crisis—the inordinate uncertainty about what must be done, the necessity that something be done, and the weighty consequences of whatever is done—forces responsible leaders to become active players. The transcendent laws of the game— that he who hesitates loses his chance to play at that point, and that he who vacillates about his recommendation is overpowered by others who are sure—pressures

players to come down categorically and play with conviction. The reward of successfully playing the game is effectiveness.

At a critical juncture, decision-makers are clearly faced with enormous uncertainty, and simultaneous time pressure to decide. The players are forced to take
stands; failing to do so leads to lost opportunity to affect future changes. Crisis
necessitates decisions and actions, and time pressure alters the contours of agenda
setting, in turn decisively shaping the profile and resolution of issues. Interactions
among individual leaders after a crisis are conspicuously different from normal,
routinized interactions.

The two types of decision-making processes considered above are further
explicated by considering the logic of bureaucratic initiatives. As James March and
Herbert Simon note, two potential logics of action exist in bureaucratic behavior:
a logic of *consequences*, and a contrasting logic of *appropriateness*. Under the logic
of consequences, bureaucrats choose actions by evaluating the probable consequences for the preferences of the actor. This process operates principally through
a selective, heuristic search among alternatives, evaluating each option in terms of
its adequacy as it is found.

The second, alternative logic of action contrasts with the first logic in that
the latter involves little analysis of case-by-case principles, deliberation of action
alternatives, or selection based on specific consequences. Instead, the logic directs
individuals to match existing rules to a situation in question, and to treat situations
as familiar and frequently encountered types, to which rules are then applied.[64]
Bureaucrats generally operate in terms of this second logic, seeking appropriateness and conformity to established rules and procedures. As Jack Levy observes,
"[R]outines and organizational logic are a powerful and independent variable in
a complex interaction of influences on key officials, pulling them toward a logic
of appropriateness of programmed responses, and away from the logic of consequences."[65]

During crisis situations, however, bureaucrats are called on to analyze problems using their own individual intuition, expert knowledge, and experience.
Bureaucratic initiatives can clearly result from the first logic of action, which
entails ranking preferences, finding alternatives, and making choices by considering consequences.

Who, then, are the players at a critical juncture, and what determines their
preferences? As Graham Allison suggested in *Essence of Decision*, players of governmental policy games tend to be defined by their positions. "The governmental
actor is neither a unitary agent nor a conglomerate of organizations, but rather a
number of individual players. . . . Players are individuals in jobs."[66]

Players at critical junctures are the individual leaders that are in charge of problem-solving during, and in the immediate wake of, crises. They can be either the top political leaders, such as presidents, or otherwise designated negotiators interacting with other key parties involved. In other words, the players at critical junctures are defined by the discretionary power that they wield in resolving issues at hand. Their source of influence includes either formal authority and responsibility, or actual control over resources necessary to carry out action.

When the Korean War erupted, for example, John Foster Dulles was the key player in negotiating with Japan and other countries to finalize a World War II peace settlement. Yet Prime Minister Yoshida Shigeru of Japan and President Syngman Rhee of Korea were also crucial actors at that critical juncture, leading to an enduring system of international relations in the Pacific that was to flow from such a settlement. In confronting the Asian financial crisis of 1997, by contrast, the respective heads of state of the ASEAN Plus Three countries, rather than their finance ministers, were the driving force in launching policy initiatives.[67] The locus of decision-making power, and of potential leadership, thus varies with prevailing circumstances. Yet leadership of some sort is crucial.

Why Critical Junctures Matter in Northeast Asia

Crises do not necessarily give birth to new or refurbished institutions, it is important to note. They generate demand, in Mattli's parlance, but not necessarily supply.[68] Sometimes, when interdependence is low, a sense of urgency is not broadly shared, and demand for change is limited. Sometimes the actors involved are too uncertain of the future, or too entrenched in the status quo, to commit to or supply a new set of standardized rules. Sometimes the lack of a blueprint, or the opposition of an outside power, or lack of information and interpersonal networks, such as the sort that flow through epistemic communities, frustrates what would otherwise be rational cooperation.

International cooperation suffers from international structural anarchy and national free-riding incentives.[69] Many forms of mutually beneficial cooperation are unrealizable because of lack of enforcement mechanisms. These features of cooperation under anarchy—the endemic state of international relations—confer special significance on critical junctures. Indeed, under crisis situations, the imperative for collective action forces free-riding nations to come together, and to devise binding commitments that can have fateful long-term significance.

Yet regardless of the exact empirical outcome, we argue, critical junctures profoundly shape the sort of regional organization that ultimately emerges from the crucible that they provide. The significance of crises in determining the profile of regional institution-building, however, is more compelling in Northeast Asia than

SECURITY CRISES

	Likely	Unlikely
	Northeast Asia	Southern Cone
Likely		Mexico
	Southeast Asia	W. Europe
Unlikely	Middle East	USA

(FINNCIAL CRISES, with Likely and Unlikely subdivisions on the vertical axis)

FIG. 2.1. Northeast Asia's High Concentration of Critical Junctures

in most parts of the world, for a variety of domestic and international reasons. On the domestic side, national policy-making in this region has an organizational culture and modus operandi, as Peter Katzenstein observes, that is not prone to institutional innovation or the rule of law.[70] Structurally, bureaucratic organization, with a bias toward routine, is pervasive, and often politically dominant.[71]

Thus, under business as usual, SOPs—a characteristic decision rule for bureaucrats[72]—dominate political decisions in Northeast Asia, and new institutions are not readily supplied. Even when individual leaders are attracted to alternative institutional forms, the organization responsible for decision-making is resistant to dramatic change. Crisis is needed, in such bureaucratized societies, as an agent of transformation, rendering the state "reactive" in international matters, as well as domestic.

Two deeper political-economic traits of Northeast Asia in its international context further enhance the unusual importance of critical junctures in defining the face of regional organization there. First of all, security pressures, including the danger of war, are unusually salient and potentially destructive. As noted earlier, this is an area comparable only to the Middle East in its potential for globally significant conflict. War—the Korean War in 1950, the Sino-Japanese War before that, and conflicts older still—has profoundly shaped the sociopolitical profile of this turbulent region.

Simultaneously, however, much of Northeast Asia traditionally exhibits a second trait, as a result of its strong growth prospects, that other security hotspots do not: financial leverage. Heavy corporate debt, coupled with high dependence on the global economy, profoundly influences state structure and profiles of regional integration in countries like South Korea, and potentially China.[73] Heavy government debt, relative to GDP, arguably also affects calculations of the Japanese Ministry of Finance.[74] Only in Northeast Asia, as suggested in Figure 2.1, does one find the ultimate recipe for crisis-driven critical junctures: security tensions combined with financial vulnerability.

For a combination of domestic and international reasons—highly bureau-cratized domestic decision-making structures, combined with strong security and financial pressures from outside—policy innovation in Northeast Asia is thus unusually dependent on critical junctures, which both intensify demand for change and encourage the supply of new alternatives. CJs are, as suggested earlier, of two somewhat different types—security and financial. The former tend to be shorter, and simpler politically. National authorities are dominant, and subna-tional actors are relatively inconsequential. In the presence of both varieties of CJ, assuming interdependence, institutional development of some kind is likely, given adequate leadership, even if the form remains indeterminate. In the absence of critical junctures, such innovation is much more difficult.[75]

Critical Junctures and Regional Evolution: An Agenda for Research

We have argued in the foregoing pages that critical junctures play a catalytic role in the evolution of institutions generally, and at the regional level in par-ticular. We maintain that in Northeast Asia, such turning points have an especially important catalytic role, because of two distinctive features of the region: (1) the unusually rigid nature of routine decision-making, which normally constrains supply of new alternatives; and (2) the unusual salience of distinctive security and financial dangers that also increases demand for and probability of nonroutine, crisis-driven decisions. Northeast Asia, we hypothesize, should thus exhibit a dis-tinctive "stop-and-go" profile of decision-making, whereby a high proportion of the overall sociopolitical profile is forged in crisis at critical-juncture intervals. CJs are a distinctive, catalytic moment when the supply of new options can poten-tially meet the demand for them.

To argue that critical junctures are a catalyst for regional organization in Northeast Asia raises a provocative research agenda, of course. This logic suggests that crisis is a crucial driver of institutional change. Yet it fails to establish either the utility of the concept to an explication of concrete cases of institution-build-ing within the region, or the heuristic value of this paradigm elsewhere in the world. How critical junctures concretely shape the content of actual policy out-comes also remains unclear.

We plan to explore these issues succinctly in coming chapters. In doing so, we first present three main illustrative cases of how critical junctures catalyzed Northeast Asian institutional change, in the security and the economic spheres, respectively. These three cases—involving regional responses to the Korean War, the 1997 Asian financial crisis, and the global financial crisis of 2008—have together shaped the contours of Northeast Asian regionalism more profoundly than any other single episodes in modern history.

The first critical juncture—the Korean War of 1950–53—catalyzed the Washington-based "hub-and-spokes" political-economic structure of the region, which initially isolated China and estranged many Northeast Asian neighbors, yet proved remarkably enduring over the ensuing decades. It was catalyzed by a security crisis, although it ultimately had major political-economic implications as well, such as the China trade embargo and large-scale U.S. development assistance to South Korea and Taiwan. The second critical juncture—the Asian financial crisis of 1997–98—began to reintegrate policy actors in the region and helped initiate regional multilateral cooperation that had never been realized before. A third major critical juncture—Northeast Asian response to the global financial crisis of 2008—substantially furthered this process, as did subcrises (1994–95 and 2002–9) relating to North Korean nuclear and missile-system development. The second and third major crises were mainly financial in character, provoking slower, more incremental, and more technical policy responses, involving a larger group of subnational actors than the security crises.

Several Asia-related events with major global import, such as the fall of Saigon, and the end of the Cold War, have paradoxically failed to produce comparable effects in Northeast Asia to the critical junctures described above. In individual countries, these latter events have at times significantly influenced the regional policy-making of particular countries, however, and are discussed more fully in those specific country chapters. The reasons for their more limited institutional impact, and their relationship to critical-juncture theory, will also be explored.

The critical-juncture framework presented here naturally stresses the importance of changing context in shaping regional institutions. Chapters 4, 5, and 6 examine, from various perspectives, major changes in Northeast Asia since the Asian financial crisis of 1997. Chapter 4 chronicles the two major financial crises—1997 and 2008—that have recently racked the region, and helped galvanize institutional change. Chapter 5 documents the deepening confidence within the region following the 1997 crisis, regarding the possibility and prospective terms of regional cooperation. Chapter 6 focuses on the evolution of transnational economic, social, and even political-military networks that have arisen in response to the critical junctures of more recent years. Arguably, these historic developments will substantially contribute to the Making of Northeast Asia.

Inasmuch as nation-states remain the main actors involved in Northeast Asian regional cooperation, where no supranational entities of the European type yet exist, we examine changes in the regional policies of the three major Northeast Asian countries, China, Japan, and South Korea, in accordance with the critical-juncture framework. The United States, although geographically an external power, is nevertheless a central actor in enabling or hindering regional cooperation. Its policies have also experienced dynamic fluctuations that will be reviewed here. From these North Pacific cases, and the broader comparative analyses that they evoke, we consider the forces likely to be driving the Making of Northeast Asia in future years.

PART II

HISTORICAL CONTEXT: CRITICAL JUNCTURES

The Organization Gap in Historical Perspective
War in Korea and the First Critical Juncture

As the previous chapter suggests, there has long been a pronounced yet para-doxical "organization gap" in Northeast Asia. Emerging from the dissolution of Japan's colonial empire after World War II, and intensified by the Cold War, that estrangement among neighbors within the region has had major implications for world affairs. Despite their strong economic complementarity and long-standing cultural ties, China, Japan, and Korea have found it remarkably hard for most of the past century to get along. And the fragmented halves of two of them—China and Korea—refused to speak to each other—even informally—or to let letters pass between them until a decade or so ago. Nations of the region have few bod-ies of their own to regulate regional affairs or to promote collective action, even in highly technical and normally apolitical spheres.

This organization gap becomes especially puzzling when one considers the high level of economic integration among the constituent countries of the region, and the apparent functional need for collective arrangements to counter both market failure and security perils. The two general theories—realism and histori-cal institutionalism—that are typically advanced to explain the organization gap and Asian regionalism do so in terms of power distribution and norms/institu-tions within the region. These two explanations, however, present a coherent causal explanation for neither the origin of the gap nor its enduring legacy. U.S. hegemony was relevant, but not a determinant. As the process tracing soon reveals, the Korean War changed U.S. policy preferences as well as the capability of the United States to determine the institutional framework in the Asia-Pacific region.

The critical-juncture model advanced in Chapter 2 has suggested an alterna-tive rationale. It did so by incorporating insights from both realism and historical institutionalism, while stressing the importance of individual decision making at crisis-driven critical junctures in determining the overall profile of Asian regionalism. The foregoing general analysis concluded that critical junctures are central in determining the profile of regional organization in Northeast Asia, given that the region is prone to both financial and security crises. Understanding exactly *how* those critical junctures shape outcomes, however, requires more detailed case study and process tracing.

In this chapter, we outline the turbulent circumstances under which the system of post–World War II international relations in the Pacific was initially forged. In the process, we drop into the black box of national decision-making to consider how the nations of the Pacific responded, and thus how Northeast Asia's distinctive profile of cautious regionalism, inhibited by bitter and intraregional estrangement, actually came to be. We learn that the region, contrary to conventional wisdom, did at one point in the early postwar period actually consider indigenous architecture, including multilateralist options, that the United States sympathetically considered also. Yet the crises of that era made operationalizing those options infeasible. In particular, we examine the two regionalist concepts to emerge after China's 1949 revolution, which were fatefully refashioned by the ensuing Korean War–initiated critical juncture: the Pacific Pact and the "San Francisco System." We also consider the important potential catalysts for intraregional cohesion that were omitted from these two political-economic equations.

The Pacific Pact concept was originally an Asian collective-action notion. It was first presented formally by Philippine foreign minister Carlos Romulo at the New Delhi conference on Indonesia in January 1949—conceived as a league of Asian nations, working to promote mutual economic as well as security interests under U.S. auspices, with a small permanent secretariat.[1] Indian prime minister Jawaharlal Nehru, however, opposed such a grouping. World opinion, he contended, could easily interpret the idea as anti-West.[2]

Later in 1949, following the establishment of the North Atlantic Treaty Organization (NATO), as the prospect of revolutionary triumph on the Chinese Mainland grew stronger and stronger, the Pacific Pact idea became a vehicle for containing China, rendering it inoperative as an instrument for enhancing overall Asian cohesion. The strongest early proponents were Asian allies of the United States, including the Philippines, South Korea, and Taiwan. The notion was of a multilateral military alliance, analogous to NATO, centering on the United States and directed toward containing a revolutionary and prospectively militant People's Republic.

The San Francisco System, which conceptualized Pacific security as a network of bilateral alliances, or "spokes" radiating from the hub of Washington, DC, was an alternative architecture for safeguarding the regional security of the United States and its Pacific allies.[3] Like the Pacific Pact notion, it emerged during 1950–51 in the wake of the fall of China. It gained particular currency as a second-best alternative to the Pacific Pact concept following China's late-1950 intervention into the Korean War, as a means of coping with practical political difficulties in realizing the Pacific Pact. It also served to incorporate a post-Occupation Japan stably into the Pacific order of international affairs, while simultaneously quarantining the newly communist China.

The San Francisco System idea abandoned multilateralism, and any pretension of building bridges across the deepening intraregional divide, created by the breakup of the Japanese Empire and the deepening Cold War. In this respect it contrasted sharply with the architectural design of the Pacific Pact. The system, as fashioned by U.S. diplomat John Foster Dulles, soon to become Eisenhower's secretary of state, had four basic traits:

1. A dense network of *formal bilateral security alliances*, including U.S. mutual security treaties with Australia–New Zealand (July 1951); the Philippines (August 1951); Japan (September 1951); and South Korea (November 1954);

2. U.S. *military basing rights* throughout the region;

3. Relatively *limited reconstruction aid*, compared with Western Europe; and

4. Gradual integration of allied economies, included the noncommunist portions of divided Korea and China on *preferential terms* into the bilateral-internationalist *trade and financial order* fostered by the United States.

In contrast to the Pacific Pact concept, the San Francisco System architecture thus included an explicit economic dimension.

As we shall see shortly, a single Korean War critical juncture played a central role in four fateful developments: (1) the failure of the Pacific Pact; (2) the establishment in its place of the "second-best" San Francisco System; (3) the bitter, intractable, armed truce along Korea's contentious Demilitarized Zone (DMZ); and (4) the rigidification of China's relations with the noncommunist Pacific, with the cross-Straits political-military standoff, and a related economic embargo of the People's Republic of China (PRC) being the central elements. These two last aspects introduced an omnipresent security dimension into Northeast Asian political divisions. Through these four developments, the contours of regional political-economic organization within the region were established and perpetuated for the balance of five decades, a fateful process that we will also want to explore in some detail. In examining the changing profile of Northeast Asian relationships, we can also test the theoretical framework, that of critical junctures, that we have thus far developed.

Before the Korean Conflict:
Still Fluid Patterns in Regional Relations

August 1945, of course, brought the end of World War II in the Pacific, and with it the collapse of the Japanese Co-Prosperity sphere. Globally the cessation of hostilities with the Axis powers led gradually into the Cold War, which compounded and rigidified regional divisions. In Asia, the evolution also took time, with the Korean War decisively estranging communist from noncommunist elements.

As Akira Iriye suggests, the early postwar transition initially produced what might be called a "Yalta system of international relations": a wary condominium of American and Soviet power,[4] established at the Yalta conference of February 1945 among the United States, Britain, and the Soviet Union. This new system, replacing a long period of Anglo-Japanese dominion in East Asia, divided the region into two spheres of influence, in which China's role was fundamentally ambiguous. Under the Yalta system China was to recover lands that it had lost to Japan, but would compromise its Manchurian sovereignty in favor of the Soviets. Japan would come under U.S. control, while Korea would be detached from Japan and placed under some sort of trusteeship. Meanwhile, Britain would try to regain and maintain a position of some preeminence in Southeast Asia.

In accordance with the Yalta understanding, Korea was divided between North and South at the 38th parallel, through an initially peaceful arrangement, while the Red Army moved into Manchuria, Sakhalin, and the Kuril Islands as well as North Korea. The United States occupied Japan, on an exclusive basis, and began there an ambitious effort at Wilsonian social transformation. The Japanese found themselves "embracing defeat" with surprising alacrity, considering the bitter, bloody war that they had just fought with their new occupier.[5]

Uncertainties, however, continued in China. There the bitter animosities between the Communists and Nationalists, which had begun with Chiang's sudden attack on the Chinese Communist Party (CCP) in 1927, persisted throughout World War II. Although cosmetically obscured until the spring of 1946 by George Marshall's mediation efforts, the tension escalated into full-scale civil war by the beginning of 1947.[6]

Toward the end of 1949, after an epic struggle, the People's Liberation Army was triumphant on the Chinese Mainland, sending shock waves across both Northeast Asia and the broader world. At the regional level, the Yalta system of fragile East-West entente in the Pacific, contrasting with still more confrontational politics in Europe, stood at a delicate crossroads. As Iriye points out, there were three possibilities: (1) a continuation of the Yalta framework, on the assumption that the newly communist China, whatever its ideological relationships with the Soviet Union, would function as an independent, sovereign power; (2) a consolidation of American influence in areas of U.S. preeminence, such as Japan, South Korea, and the western Pacific, to offset the new developments in China; and (3) American attempts to establish a new order in Asia, by extending U.S. power to areas not committed under the Yalta scheme, such as Southeast Asia.[7] The overall configuration of Pacific relations, not to mention prospects for peaceful accommodation within the region, once again hung precariously in the balance, as in 1945.

China itself rapidly foreclosed the first possibility: that of a neutral China in the global balance. For domestic reasons related to maintaining the revolution's momentum it was difficult for Mao Tse-tung,[8] as Chen Jian points out, to countenance the possibility of moderation toward the United States in China's early postrevolutionary international relations.[9]

This radical orientation soon manifested itself, with fateful long-term consequences for Northeast Asian regional comity. In June 1949, Mao proclaimed Communist China's special relationship with the Soviet Union. And in February 1950, after a complex negotiating process, China signed a formal alliance treaty with the Soviets.[10]

There were, to be sure, important differences between the Soviets and the Chinese communists from the very beginning. Yet these were not immediately visible to the outside world, including the United States and its Pacific allies. Crystal clear to the West, however, were the dramatic and apparently threatening geopolitical developments of the immediate past: the communist coup against a democratic Czech government in mid-1948, which precipitated the formation of NATO; the Berlin blockade of 1948–49; the Soviet explosion of an atomic bomb on August 29, 1949; the dramatic communist revolutionary triumph in China; and the prompt conclusion thereafter of a Sino-Soviet alliance treaty explicitly directed at Japan and the United States. Communism, it clearly seemed, was both unified and on the march.[11]

For the United States and its allies, there was, however, some vacillation as to the appropriate parameters of their future Cold War defense line, and uncertainty as to how total their estrangement and isolation from the Northeast Asian continent should ultimately be. U.S. secretary of state Dean Acheson, for example, famously omitted Korea from the clear American defense perimeter, in a fateful National Press Club statement that apparently convinced both Stalin and Kim Il-sung that a U.S. military response to a North Korean attack southward would be unlikely.[12] There was considerable diplomatic maneuvering on relations with China; Britain actually recognized the PRC, Japan wanted to do so, and American diplomats and politicians were divided. The Taiwan Straits, like Korea's 38th Parallel, lacked the symbolic and strategic significance that it was soon to gain. Yet the likelihood of escalating future tensions with China was a matter of broad agreement in the American foreign-policy community, the major question being the form that the U.S. response should take. The Pacific, in short, lay at the cusp of a critical juncture.

At this crucial turning point between the "fall of China" in late 1949 and major Chinese intervention in the Korean War a year later, many key decision-makers, in both the U.S. and allied Pacific nations, initially favored the concept of the multilateral Pacific Pact, as noted above. For the smaller allies, such as South Korea, the Philippines, and, of course, Chiang Kai-shek's Taiwan, who were among the earliest and most vociferous backers, a Pacific Pact afforded both assurance of American support against the newly emerging Chinese Communist colossus, and more leverage with the U.S. than a purely bilateral relationship might provide. For the United States itself, a Pacific Pact could potentially provide collective security at less cost than either unilateralism or bilateralism.

The Pacific Pact concept, as noted earlier, was first broached in January 1949 by Philippine foreign secretary Romulo in New Delhi, as a diffuse pan-Asian political-economic conception. On March 21, 1949, just three days after the text of the NATO treaty was released, Philippine president Quirino gave the Pacific Pact concept a more explicitly military dimension, in an effort to gain U.S. support. Citing NATO and American leadership in Europe as precedent, Quirino advocated a similar Pacific defense pact to fight communism in the Far East.[13] He did not attract immediate official U.S. backing, although several influential American commentators—including Harold Noble in the *Saturday Evening Post* and Daniel Poling in *Look* magazine—took up the cause.[14]

During the summer of 1949, as the People's Liberation Army surged across the Yangtze into South China and toward victory, there was a flurry of diplomatic activity in Asia, supportive of the pact. In July, Chiang Kai-shek met with Quirino of the Philippines to discuss it, and the Chinese Nationalist cabinet in Canton supported the concept,[15] immediately drawing a vitriolic response from Radio Beijing. Australia was also actively promoting the idea.[16] In August, Generalissimo Chiang flew to Chinhae, a naval base on the southern coast of Korea, for a meeting with President Syngmun Rhee, to discuss the pact. Nehru, although he opposed the pact, called for collective action in the form of a Marshall Plan for Asia.

During 1949 the United States government still pursued a wait-and-see approach to both the pact and to China policy, as epitomized in the State Department's white paper on China, published in August 1949. There was as yet no categorical embargo or other form of definitive, irrevocable separation between communist and noncommunist Asia. The political bitterness and estrangement behind the organization gap of later years had yet to appear. Yet as the new PRC government in Beijing adopted an increasingly anti-American stance, a converse U.S. interest in more formalized collective security and quarantine of China gradually began to intensify. In January 1950, for example, U.S. ambassador at large Philip Jessup gave assurances during a Manila visit of American sympathy for any efforts by the Philippines to organize a union of other Asian nations to "preserve the democratic way of life."[17] In April 1950, encouraged by this American show of support, the Philippines hosted six key nations to discuss regional cooperation, at the Baguio Conference.[18]

Within two months, however, the geostrategic context of Pacific Asia would be decisively transformed, as the Korean War exploded and U.S. military forces were drawn to the peninsula in response. To be sure, it is difficult to project the hypothetical fate of the multilateral Pacific Pact in the absence of that struggle. Yet the eruption of that conflict and the Chinese intervention in it fundamentally changed the strategic calculation of U.S. policy-makers, forcing new decisions regarding regional architecture upon them. The time pressure to stabilize Japan, whose domestic politics were seen to be growing more volatile and fluid amid the Korean War, enflamed by the lingering foreign occupation, was enormous. And the lengthy process of multilateral negotiations implicit in consideration of the Pacific Pact concept became increasingly unappetizing to U.S. policy-makers of the period. A bilateral, "hub-and-spokes" structure became more feasible and attractive U.S. policy, as the shadows of war deepened across Northeast Asia.

War in Korea: The Emergence of Critical Juncture

In June 1950, North Korean forces burst across the 38th parallel, drastically altering the Asian security equation and inaugurating a historic critical juncture for the region. From the beginning, President Harry Truman saw the conflict as serious from a global perspective, and feared that it might broaden. He secretly made plans for an atomic strike on the Soviet Union should the Red Army enter the conflict.[19]

The Pacific Pact notion initially held some plausibility as a possible organizing concept. Just as the Czech coup and the Berlin blockade catalyzed concern for collective security in Europe, leading to NATO, so did the fall of China and the North Korean attack southward stimulate parallel anxieties in the Pacific. From the fall of 1950, John Foster Dulles, special adviser to Secretary of State Dean Acheson, apparently had some interest in the Pacific Pact concept himself. Exploring its feasibility was a central objective of his extensive Pacific trip in January and February of 1951.

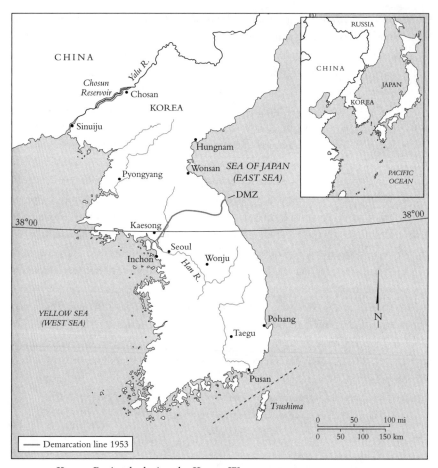

FIG. 3.1. Korean Peninsula during the Korean War

Within the U.S. government, a complete Pacific Pact was drafted in early 1951 and seriously discussed.[20] The United States stipulated in the draft that such a mul-tilateral security arrangement would be terminated only if: (1) the United Nations adequately covered the area; or (2) a broader, more formal framework was created into which the Pacific Pact could be merged.[21] Clearly the United States, less than two years after the formation of NATO in Europe, was groping for a viable Pacific collective-security concept as well. According to Dean Acheson, "[W]hen the question of security in the Pacific had been considered last year [1951], the United States Government had originally thought of having a single pact which would have included other countries in the area."[22]

The fateful Dulles Pacific trip was undertaken, however, at an extremely del-icate political-military juncture. Washington had just been traumatized by the sharp, sudden intervention of People's Liberation Army "volunteers" in Korea. This trapped more than 150,000 UN troops, many of them American, on the frozen battlefields of North Korea near the Yalu River, as indicated in Figure 3.1, ironically just after Thanksgiving, 1950.[23]

American politics and public opinion were especially fluid and intense during the period from 1949 to 1951, following Dewey's narrow and unexpected defeat in the 1948 presidential election. Although President Harry Truman had accumulated extensive foreign policy experience during five years in office, a deeply divided Congress was neither unified nor uniformly supportive of many of his policies in international affairs. McCarthyite sentiment blaming him for "the loss of China" was rampant. America's turbulent domestic political climate was hardly suited to support Northeast Asian institution-building, particularly across the sharp ideological divides and historical cleavages that characterized that—for America—still far-away region.

Polls in April 1950, even before the Korean War, showed that the president's overall personal popularity had dropped to its lowest level since his inauguration in 1945. Gallup poll analysts suggested that Truman's popularity drop might be the result of the increased international tensions and to "Communist gains in Asia."[24] There was a broad public perception in the United States that American policy toward the communist world generally called for a forceful shift—a feeling that deepened as the situation in Korea worsened during the fall of 1950. The intensity of domestic political frustrations about the war clearly enhanced the time pressure that U.S. decision-makers felt to make clear and rapid decisions. The Truman administration needed politically to bring a clear resolution to the dramatic yet frustratingly indeterminate developments on the Korean peninsula, and indeed throughout the North Pacific.

Truman's political vulnerability sharply intensified from November 1950 on. In the midterm elections of 1950, held in the first week of the month, 52 percent of the national vote went to the Republicans, with only 42 percent to Truman's Democrats.[25] The Democrats, to be sure, retained a narrow two-vote majority in the Senate. But Republican senator Arthur Vandenberg, on whom Truman relied heavily for bipartisan support on foreign policy, lay gravely ill.

On December 7, 1950—the ninth anniversary of Pearl Harbor, amid the desperate efforts to evacuate North Korea in the face of a Chinese onslaught—a Gallup poll revealed that 55 percent of the American people believed that World War III had already started.[26] Truman also reportedly saw the grim possibility—noted both privately in his diary and publicly at a national press conference on November 30—that the Korean conflict might actually escalate into nuclear war.[27] Republican leaders such as Governor Thomas Dewey of New York, the defeated

1948 presidential candidate, initially held their fire, stressing the need for national unity. Yet early in 1951 that reserve began to erode, especially among Republicans, who dominated the Congress.

Events moved very rapidly, intensifying the pressure for early and decisive decision. In the first week of December 1950, the Chinese PLA mauled the Second Infantry Division, inflicting some of the heaviest unit casualties in American military history, and nearly trapped the courageous First Marine Division near the Chosin Reservoir.[28] U.S. intelligence reported that between 231,000 and 400,000 Chinese troops were engaged against UN Command forces.[29]

On December 7, the CIA reported confidentially, inside the U.S. government, that the Soviets had promised China 300,000 Red Army troops, plus tactical support, in the event of a war with the US that many American analysts considered to be quite likely.[30] In mid-December President Truman proclaimed a state of national emergency, asking the Congress for an additional $16.8 billion to mobilize the country for a possible global war.[31] On December 24, the Marines completed evacuation of their Hungnam beachhead, and North Korea was completely returned to communist control. Little more than a week later, on January 3–4, 1951, Seoul itself was evacuated by UN Command forces, as PLA "volunteer" spearheads rolled across the Han, to Wonju and Chipyongni.[32]

The Korean War, in short, was moving toward a climax, at the heart of a historic critical juncture for the Pacific region as a whole. Within little more than a month, the war's complexion had totally changed. MacArthur's confident march toward victory on the Yalu—the resounding success that would "send the boys home by Christmas"—was beginning to look like one of the great military disasters in American history, with potentially grim political consequences for President Truman himself.

Added Complications in Japan

Meanwhile, ambivalence about the war was also rising in Japan, with its peace constitution, nuclear allergy, and bitter recent memories of its own concerning protracted land war in Asia. This ambivalence, combined with the formal constraints of Japan's "peace constitution," created virtually insurmountable barriers to active Japanese involvement in the only kind of regional institution-building that mattered at the time—collective security. Many Japanese feared being dragged more deeply into an apparently escalating conflict on their nation's doorstep. In the Japanese Diet, Prime Minister Yoshida came under intense socialist criticism from the very outset of the Korean conflict, even for allowing the United States to wage war from its bases in Japan, which the country was, of course, legally entitled to do.[33] More elaborate Japanese commitments to the war were politically out of the question, particularly given the absence of a formal peace treaty ending the Occupation.

When Chinese troops entered the fighting in the fall of 1950, there were even more intense calls for Japan to embrace neutralism and distance itself from the United States.[34] As U.S. policy-makers fully realized, opponents of the pro-American Yoshida conservatives were using Japan's formal lack of sovereignty as a vehicle for attacking the U.S.-Japanese relationship from both the Left and the Right. This situation made every escalation of the Korean War a more compelling reason for the United States to conclude an early peace treaty with Japan.

The increasingly critical Japanese sentiments were of particularly immediate concern to the United States because it had decided, in early September 1950, to begin negotiations with Japan on a peace treaty ending the Occupation.[35] Many American policy makers, including Secretary of State Dean Acheson and the Supreme Commander of the Allied Powers (SCAP) in Tokyo Douglas MacArthur, feared that Japanese attitudes would grow more critical, enflamed by the fighting in Korea, and that the United States could not afford to delay.[36] Most U.S. allies, including the British, also agreed on the importance of an early peace for their own reasons, including not least a desire to deal on Japanese matters with someone other than the imperious General MacArthur. Yet some major allies, such as South Korea and Taiwan, were unable for historical or political reasons to participate, and resented the proceedings themselves.

It was in this complex environment that Dulles embarked on his fateful January 1951 Pacific tour. He wanted, above all, a rapid resolution to the broad range of troubling geopolitical uncertainties across the region, ever more deeply inter-linked—and rendered more urgent—by dual challenges: the conflict in Korea, and the deepening imperative of formal peace with Japan. Both developments mandated immediate creation of a Pacific security framework. Time pressures were overwhelming, and profoundly shaped the institutional product that finally emerged full-blown in the wake of the Korean War.

The Urgency and Complexity of the Critical-Juncture Decision

The dual challenges of the Korean conflict—marked as it was by abrupt developments like the North Korean attack of June 1950 and the sudden Chinese intervention the following November, coupled with the Japanese peace treaty negotiations—constrained time available to search for an optimal institutional arrangement for regional security, and to coordinate fully to establish it. The peace-treaty talks established a clear and urgent need for some sort of security framework with which to contain and also stabilize the new Japan. Yet the Korean War radically transformed preference structures for both the United States and its Pacific allies, making institution-building more difficult. Under the pressure and urgency of the war, coupled with the imperative of shoring up ties with Japan through a peace treaty, and the historical animosities that limited cooperation, the allies could not readily concur on details of a broad, complex multilateral structure like the Pacific Pact.

Indeed, the United States itself was concerned about the diplomatic and political complications of a Pacific Pact. Should it include "non-white" Asian nations? If so, which ones?[37] Meanwhile, America's strongest ally, Great Britain, pushed hard to be included in a prospective Pacific Pact, an involvement that the United States was not ready to accept.[38] The Philippines was also eager to play an important part in any multilateral arrangement, while Britain resisted being relegated to a position comparable to that of what it considered to be a minor nation.[39] The limited, bilateral San Francisco System, involving more restricted international cooperation than the more ambitious multilateral pact concept, but firm security provisions, thus provided a "satisficing" solution for the United States and its allies that could consolidate trans-Pacific international relations generally, and U.S.-Japan relations, while avoiding broader diplomatic complications.

One single critical juncture—that of the Korean War—thus gave birth to multiple policy developments, which rigidified and clarified a Northeast Asian regional organization gap created by Japan's World War II defeat, that had previously been inchoate. First, the Chinese offensive across the Yalu effectively killed the Pacific Pact, by complicating Britain's prospective involvement and willingness to countenance the organization. The juncture also, as noted, stimulated emergence of the San Francisco System of "hub-and-spokes," as an alternative vehicle for simultaneously containing China and integrating Japan smoothly into the postwar system of international relations in the Pacific.

Apart from the Korean conflict's impact on international affairs, it also had fateful influence on the domestic politics of key nations—preeminently the United States, thus rendering the exigencies of CJ more central than hegemony itself in determining systemic outcomes.[40] Korea was clearly the critical juncture that provoked a "globalization of containment" of the Soviet Union—more the result of the circumstances under which the war began (surprise attack) than strategic calculations regarding the peninsula's intrinsic importance. Containment of the USSR involved large allied armies in Europe, the perception of a united Sino-Soviet bloc, the belief that limited wars anywhere were a major danger, and the emergence of large American defense budgets capable of generating a global U.S. security presence.[41]

The importance of the Korean War as a catalyst was graphically clear in the fate of National Security Council 68 (NSC 68), a momentous, hawkish Cold War document championing the militarization of the Western alliance against the Soviet threat. Issued in the spring of 1950, the document and its proposed expansion of American air, ground, and maritime strength, as well as air defense and civil defense programs, attracted significant domestic opposition, including skepticism from President Truman himself.[42] Yet in the fall of 1950, following the outbreak of the Korean War and Chinese intervention, NSC 68 was rapidly approved and implemented. It made both the rationale for robust bilateral security alliances across the Pacific, with Japan, Korea, and Taiwan—and the arguments against broader bridge-building with the communist parts of the region—much stronger than before.

The war also radically transformed China's relations with the world. To be sure, the revolution itself had already estranged the newly established PRC from the capitalist West to some degree. Yet in early 1950 American diplomats were still actively pursuing options for normalization with the PRC.[43] It was the Korean War, and particularly Chinese intervention in that conflict, which led to direct Sino-American confrontation and heavy U.S. casualties; to the sustained American efforts to keep China out of the United Nations; to intensified confrontation along the Taiwan Straits; and to the economic embargo against Beijing. Those events, taken together, estranged the two nations for two decades and more, and rigidified post-1945 divisions in Northeast Asia. The war also radicalized China internally, leading to sweeping purges, and retribution against those with previous foreign ties. Such a radicalization of Chinese domestic politics would have been much harder for Mao and his radical allies to orchestrate in the absence of the broad, emotional confrontation with the West that the Korean War provoked, both in China and across the region more generally.

Toward the San Francisco System

We have begun our detailed empirical examination of critical junctures and their consequences with a heuristic test: that of the historical origins of the Northeast Asian organization gap, in the chaos continuing from World War II into the tumultuous early Korean War era. This was the period in which the idea of the Pacific Pact failed, and the so-called San Francisco System of international relations in the Pacific, which isolated China through a Washington-centric "hub-and-spokes" framework, and privileged Japan, fitfully emerged. To a remarkable degree, that San Francisco System has persisted to this day, albeit with Chinese involvement since the 1970s.

The Korean War period clearly exhibits all the key hallmarks of a critical

TABLE 3.1

The Second-Best San Francisco System: Preference Structure amid the Korean War

US:	multilateralism > bilateralism> no treaty[a]
Australia:	multilateralism > bilateralism > no treaty
Taiwan:	multilateralism > bilateralism > no treaty
Britain:	bilateralism > multilateralism > no treaty
Japan:	multilateralism > bilateralism> no treaty
South Korea:	multilateralism > bilateralism> no treaty

[a] "No treaty" meant that military occupation of Japan would continue.

juncture as we conceive it. In tracing the historical evolution of the San Francisco System, with a special focus on critical junctures, we clearly see the salience of historical contingency and discontinuity at decisive intervals. During the pressured process of negotiating the San Francisco System, amid the deepening Korean conflict of early 1951, with a deadline for concluding the peace treaty with Japan impending, the preferences of nations shifted, transformed in the fiery crucible of critical juncture. Time pressure and incongruity of interests—particularly extreme during the excruciating ten months between Chinese intervention and the Japan peace treaty—made a preferred multilateral solution, the Pacific Pact, unachievable, and forced even the hegemonic United States toward a second-best alternative—a patchwork of bilateral arrangements.

Looking at the preferences of countries involved in the postwar negotiations on a peace settlement in Asia, we see that indeterminate prediction and bilateralism were decidedly not the best options for the parties involved, as suggested in Table 3.1.[44]

Between the Chinese Revolution of 1949, and the Chinese Korean War intervention late in 1950, as noted above, important actors in both the United States and Japan seem to have preferred a multilateral-security arrangement in East Asia to a narrowly bilateral one. Other important American allies in Asia likewise applauded the idea of a multilateral Pacific Pact, driven by the prospective regional dangers of simultaneous uncertainty regarding the political futures of both China and Japan.

Even though key State Department Asian specialists appear to have been serious about the Pacific Pact, at least until China's November 1950 intervention in the war, the U.S. military clearly accorded it lower priority. American military leaders were most immediately concerned about untrammeled U.S. access to bases in Japan. They saw a bilateral understanding with Japan on bases as a high priority, and were not convinced that a multilateral pact would be either necessary or sufficient to achieve it.

They were not convinced, for two basic reasons, of the intrinsic need for a broad, multilateral alliance in the Pacific, like NATO's in the Atlantic. Most important, the multilateral concept raised thorny collective-security issues that they wished to avoid, such as a prospective defense of Hong Kong against Mainland China. The sudden surge of 300,000 People's Volunteers across the Yalu, after all, had suddenly transformed that into a disturbingly real prospect. In addition, multilateralism in the Pacific offered few concrete military dividends, however attractive it might be diplomatically in reinforcing American political ties across Asia. The United Nations was already active in Korea, and there were no contingencies elsewhere in the region where the Pentagon seriously contemplated needing Allied support.

The British opposed the concept of U.S.-led Pacific multilateralism on many grounds. They were moved, most importantly, by the troubling prospect that an American-inspired Pacific Pact would exclude Hong Kong from security guarantees. Whitehall was understandably reluctant to see the emergence of a pact that either excluded the British or failed to provide such guarantees. The omission would undermine, they felt, the security of not just Hong Kong but also their other colonial possessions in the region, including Singapore, Malaya, and Sarawak/Brunei.[45]

As the process tracing presented here so clearly illustrates, the San Francisco System, with its enduring legacy of a Northeast Asian organization gap, and an isolation of communist Asia from regional political-economic affairs, was the product neither of geopolitical power alone nor of preexisting institutions. Process played a crucial role. To be sure, both power and institutional environment influenced the interests and preferences of the parties to negotiation—namely, the United States and its allies. Yet neither interests nor preferences alone decisively shaped the key actors' ultimate decisions. The interests and preferences of the key nations involved were ultimately refashioned in a critical juncture created by the Korean War, during which the structure and rules of the bargaining games among the United States, Japan, and other major nations in the Pacific were profoundly transformed.

The Korean War, Cross-Straits Confrontation, and the PRC's Economic Isolation

It was also at this juncture of the Korean War that the economic estrangement of newly communist China from its Northeast Asian neighbors became deep-rooted, creating the economic foundation for the organization gap that ultimately came to prevail in the region. The U.S. economic embargo against Mainland

China intensified sharply after the onset of the Korean War. In December 1950, shortly after the Chinese intervention, the United States applied a total ban on exports to the PRC. In May 1951, the UN General Assembly recommended that every state ban all shipments of strategic materials to Communist China.

Later in the same year, the U.S. Congress passed the Battle Act, denying aid to any country that failed to meet American standards of control over exports to communist countries.[46] This, of course, sharply inhibited Sino-Japanese trade. In 1950, for example, Japan imported around $39.6 million worth of goods from, and exported $19.6 million worth to, the PRC. By 1952, Japanese imports from China had fallen by two-thirds, to only $14.9 million, and exports had nosedived 95 percent to a little over half a million dollars.[47]

The collapse of Japanese exports to China was especially damaging, from the PRC's economic standpoint at the time, because promoting international trade, so as to secure valued foreign exchange, was an urgent priority of Chinese officials. In early 1950, on the heels of the revolution, the Chinese Ministry of Trade had drafted ambitious plans for expanding China's exports of tung oil, raw silk, and other goods enjoying high global demand at the time. The Communist Central Committee also admonished the whole nation "to try every possible way to increase exports first."[48]

After China's intervention in the Korean War, the United States tightened economic sanctions against the PRC. A December 1950 report by a Northern China regional foreign trade bureau warned that this American embargo was destroying China's foreign trade.[49] To compound the pain, Washington also closed the PRC's unofficial trading offices in both the United States and Japan, while freezing their assets.

The separation of Taiwan from the Mainland was also intensified and perpetuated by the Korean War. After two years of stalemate near the 38th parallel, the Korean War finally ground to a halt in July 1953. By then, however, as a result of the war, defending Taiwan had become a symbol of U.S. anticommunist resolve in Asia and around the world. China's efforts to recover the island thus became a direct challenge to the fundamental strategic interests of the United States and met forceful U.S. resistance.[50] In 1954, as Mao launched an attack in the Straits, hoping to deter the U.S. from including Taiwan in the Southeast Asia Treaty Organization (SEATO), he met firm resistance from the U.S. and provoked conclusion of a U.S.-Taiwan Mutual Security Treaty.[51] Mao's pressure thus backfired.[52] If anything, Mao's efforts to reclaim minor islets in the Straits offshore Taiwan strengthened America's commitment to defend Taiwan itself, as was later to be demonstrated in the 1958 siege of Quemoy and Matsu. The deadlock in the Straits and the Chinese-American confrontation related to it, together with the Vietnam War, prolonged both the American embargo and the U.S. determination to strengthen relations between Japan and Taiwan, and conversely impede those with the PRC, until the Nixon-Kissinger initiatives of the early 1970s.

Why the "Second-Best" Has Proven So Enduring

Although forged in the crucible of war, between the massive Chinese intervention of November 1950 and the peace treaty with Japan concluded ten months later, the San Francisco System proved remarkably durable. Indeed, its broad outlines—an organization gap in Northeast Asia, a "hub-and-spokes" security architecture, and broad, asymmetrical Asian access to U.S. markets—prevailed clearly until the 1997 Asian financial crisis, and remains prominent in its broad outlines even today, despite the impact of globalization—the only major change being the incorporation of China since the late 1970s. This architecture succeeded in imposing its imprint on Northeast Asia to a truly remarkable degree, although the isolation of communist Asia has gradually eroded amid broader globalization.

The *process* of the San Francisco System's formulation, we argue, had a critical impact on the *content* that ultimately emerged. The Pacific Pact failed and the San Francisco System succeeded, not because the hegemon of the period—the United States—wanted one and not the other, but because *events*—the profile of a critical juncture—dictated the outcome. The *timing* of the system's realization, together with its contents, and also its *durability*, were all profoundly shaped by the critical juncture of the Korean War.

The decisive importance of the Korean War critical juncture to the making of modern Northeast Asia is also illustrated by the frustrating subsequent history of institution-building in the region. For more than forty years (1953–97), virtually all new efforts to transform, or even build upon, the San Francisco "hub-and-spokes" bilateralist pattern ended in abject failure. Just as the presence of critical juncture led to innovation, its absence led to stasis—rising economic interdependence and functional imperatives notwithstanding.

Table 3.2 summarizes this long chronicle of futility and frustration for multilateral organizations in Asia, to which the sudden, historic bilateralist changes of the Korean War era—particularly mutual security and economic treaties with Japan, South Korea, and Taiwan—contrast so sharply. To be sure, John Foster Dulles succeeded in inaugurating SEATO in 1954, following the French defeat in the Indochina War. Yet the events of that period did not compel a cohesive organization. Indeed, SEATO was limited to Southeast Asia, and turned out to be a much more poorly institutionalized body than NATO, as Hemmer and Katzenstein point out.[53] The organization gap persisted in Northeast Asia, the most industri-

TABLE 3.2

Critical Junctures as a Catalyst for Regional Organization in East Asia (1950–Present)

Regional Organization	National Initiative	Pre-existing Conditions Geo-political rationale	Critical Juncture Crisis	Individual Leader-ship	Time pres-sure	Outcome[a]
Pacific Pact (1949–51)	Yes (U.S.)	Yes				Failure
San Francisco System (1951–54)	Yes (U.S.)	Yes	Yes (Korea)	Yes	Yes	Success
SEATO (1955)	Yes (U.S.)	Yes	Yes (Japan/China)	Yes	Yes	Initial Success
ASA[b] (1961)	Yes (Malaysia)	Yes				Failure
Maphilindo (1963)		Yes	Yes (Vietnam)			Failure
ADB (1965)	Yes (U.S./Japan)	Yes	Yes (Vietnam)	Yes	Yes	Success
ASPAC (1966)	Yes (ROK)	Yes (ROK)	Yes			Failure—defunct 1974—anti PRC
ASEAN (1967)	Yes (SEA)	Yes	Yes (Vietnam)	Yes	Yes	Success
APSC (1967)	Yes (Japan)	Yes (Japan)	Yes			Failure
PAFTA (1967)	Yes (Japan)	Yes (Japan)	Yes			Failure—defunct 1968
PBEC (1967)	Yes (U.S./Can Private sector)					Partial success (Track II)
PAFTAD (1968)	Yes		Yes			Partial success (consultative/nongov.)
PEC Concept (1960s)			Yes			Japanese Track II—no progress
PECC (1980)	Yes (Japan/Australia private sector)					Partial success (Track II)
APEC (1989)	Yes (Japan/Australia)	Yes		Yes		Partial success
EAEG (1990)	Yes (Malaysia)	Yes				Failure
NEAEF (1991)	Yes (Korea)	Yes				Partial success
TRADP (1991)	Yes (China)	Yes				Partial success
AFTA (1992)	Yes					Failure
EAEC (1993)	Yes (Malaysia)	Yes				Failure
NEADB (1993)	Yes (Korea)	Yes				Failure
ARF (1994)	Yes (Australia)	Yes				Partial success
KEDO (1995)	Yes	Yes	Yes		Yes	Initial success
AMF (1996)	Yes (Japan)	Yes				Failure
ANEAN (1999)	Yes (joint)	Yes	Yes	Yes	No	Failure
APT/Chiang Mai (2000)	Yes (joint)	Yes	Yes	Yes	Yes	Success
Six-Party Talks (2003)	Yes (China)	Yes	Yes	Yes	Yes	Initial success

alized and geopolitically significant part of the continent, leaving there only the "hub-and-spokes" that Dulles had fashioned during the critical juncture of the early 1950s.

The Asian Development Bank (ADB, 1965) and the Association of Southeast Asian Nations (ASEAN, 1967) were as close as the whole of Asia came for a generation thereafter to globally important innovations in regional organization. Both organizations emerged in the wake of strong geopolitical pressures accompanying the onset of the Vietnam War. Yet as a result of leadership failure and a paradoxical waning of crisis consciousness, these new institutions failed to provoke any major political-economic transformation of the region as a whole, despite their persistent visibility and diplomatic prominence, especially after Vietnam's 1978 invasion of Cambodia. Their impact on relations among Northeast Asian nations was minimal, although Japan has been supplying significant resources to the operation of ADB since its inception and has played an important leadership role there.

As Table 3.2 suggests, the record of the half-century following the San Francisco Peace Treaty was largely one of failure for East Asian regionalism, ASEAN and the ADB aside. The Vietnam War era gave birth to a series of regional initiatives—MCEDSEA, ASPAC, PAFTA, and PAFTAD, to name a few—that essentially went nowhere. Following the war, it was only unofficial Track II organizations, such as PEBC (1980) and PECC (1980), initiated by the private sector, that really achieved much of substance. The Asia Pacific Economic Cooperation (APEC), initiated by Australian prime minister Bob Hawke and Japanese prime minister Ohira Masayoshi in 1989, has been a mixed success. When that body has had clear leadership and astute intellectual advice, as was true early in the presidency of Bill Clinton, APEC has undertaken major new initiatives, at least in form. The Bogor Declaration of 1994, which proposed reducing tariffs across the Pacific Basin to zero among industrial members by 2010 and among less advanced counterparts by 2020, was a clear case in point. Yet these intellectually creative regional initiatives have lacked substantial institutional content. And none of them did much to bridge the lingering organization gap in Northeast Asia.

During the early 1990s, Malaysian prime minister Mohammed Mahathir insistently advocated a series of steps toward East Asian regional integration indepen-

NOTES TO TABLE 3.2:

a(1) "Success" is defined here as involving substantial institutional persistence over an extended period of time, and a substantial functional role in the political economy of the region. (2) "Partial success" involves both shorter institutional longevity and less functional significance. (3) In cases of "failure," the proposal in question was not adopted by the nations of the region at all.

b The Association of Southeast Asia (ASA) was formed by Malaysia, followed by the Philippines and Thailand in 1961. It lasted for only one year, however. In 1963, Maphilindo was formed to substitute for the AAS, comprising Malaysia, the Philippines, and Thailand, but unraveled soon thereafter, during the turmoil from the Vietnam War.

dent of the United States, that pointedly included China. In 1990, for example, he proposed the East Asian Economic Group (EAEG), and in 1993 the East Asian Economic Caucus (EAEC). Yet in the absence of compelling crisis or powerful leadership to drive new initiatives forward, these initiatives came to naught.

The paradox of East Asian failure in regional institution-building was compounded across the 1980s and early 1990s by the emerging reality of Asian economic power and intraregional interdependence. The paradox was most pronounced, of course, in the northeastern part of the region, where institutional stagnation was most acute, even as transnational production networks were becoming most sophisticated. In late 1951, when the San Francisco Peace Treaty was signed, Northeast Asia, including Japan, China, and Korea, accounted for only around 3 percent of global GDP. By the year 2001, just half a century later, that tiny initial fraction had grown sevenfold, to 21 percent, surpassing the global GDP share of the European Union.[54] Although Northeast Asia's global share declined slightly thereafter, because of fluctuating exchange rates, the region continued to rank as one of the three largest economic regions in the world, together with North America and the EU.[55]

Northeast Asia thus has grown steadily in economic terms, within the framework of a Washington-centric San Francisco System that did not afford it political standing commensurate with that rising economic role. Northeast Asia, for its part, found it most difficult to transform itself institutionally, and to move beyond the organization gap in the absence of critical junctures. Neither the emergence of new regionalist concepts nor the inception of vigorous nongovernmental organizations (NGOs) to promote them produced much change in this equation.

The evolution of the Northeast Asian Economic Forum (NEAEF) and the Tumen River Area Development Project (TRADP), both Track II initiatives emerging in 1991, are cases in point. NEAEF was originally proposed by South Korea, and has assembled officials, experts, and business representatives annually at the East-West Center in Hawaii for nearly two decades. Yet although TRADP was strongly supported by China, which valued that program's assistance in developing its northeastern provinces, the broader policy impact of these initiatives has been limited, and the Tumen project has attracted little foreign investment.

The ill-fated Northeast Asian Development Bank (NEADB) proposal, strongly supported by both of the NGOs described above for nearly two decades, likewise demonstrates the enduring legacy of the organization gap and the difficulty of overcoming it in the absence of critical juncture, even in the post–Cold War era. As early as 1993, the South Korean government, spearheaded by Prime Minister Nam Duck-woo, promoted the NEADB concept as a "regionally focused institution which would finance or arrange for financing of infrastructure and start-up projects" in Northeast Asia.[56] The NEADB was proposed to help develop underindustrialized yet resource-rich areas in the region, such as North Korea, Mongolia, Northeastern China, and the Russian Far East, drawing primarily on funds raised in the surplus nations of Northeast Asia itself. In the view of the initiators, the proposed development bank would both promote broad-based industrialization and also enhance regional stability in the region by bringing North Korea into multilateral cooperation.[57]

The timing, however, proved inauspicious. The World Bank's 1992 Wapenhans Report warned of inefficiencies in regional development-finance institutions, such as NEADB proposed to become. Even more important, the NEADB concept was resisted by the United States, which was wary of regional initiatives that openly focused on continental Northeast Asia. It was not well received by Japan either, on account of financial constraints Tokyo was facing at the time.[58] Absent a clear crisis in the early 1990s, it was hardly surprising that collective leadership capable of shouldering the cost of an NEADB did not emerge, despite strong South Korean advocacy.

In the wake of the 1997 Asian financial crisis (AFC), the NEADB concept resurfaced at the 1998 Northeast Asia Economic Forum in Yonago, Japan.[59] Supporters argued once again that an NEADB would enhance regional stability and security, as well as strengthen mutual economic, cultural, and political links of Northeast Asian nations. North Korean representatives at the forum showed strong interest in the concept. Stanley Katz of the East-West Center, formerly vice president of the Asian Development Bank, also argued that a Northeast Asian Development Bank is "the most feasible and effective means" to raise funds for regional infrastructure-building.[60] The South Korean government likewise showed strong support. Former commerce, industry, and energy minister Kim Young-ho stressed that an NEADB could help ameliorate the continuing financial crisis in Korea, while also reducing the risks of investing in North Korea.[61] In 2001, the Northeast Asia Economic Forum once again proposed an NEADB, with President Kim Dae-jung terming the notion "a timely proposal."[62]

These initiatives, however, required strong leadership from Japan, by far the largest economy and capital exporter of the region. Yet it declined, pleading budgetary constraints, in the wake of its massive commitments to Southeast Asia during the Asian financial crisis.[63] It was also unclear how the proposed NEADB would serve Japan's core interests, since the bank would most clearly benefit North Korean development, in which Japan had little interest in the absence of sweeping changes in the Democratic People's Republic of Korea's (DPRK's) behavior—and possibly its structure. Similar rationales also drove Japanese feelings about lending to China and Russia.

In recent years, there have been discussions of reviving the NEADB project. Money is no longer a critical, limiting factor, as the nations of the region—China, Japan, and South Korea—become substantially more liquid. Today, of course, they collectively maintain well over half the total foreign-exchange reserves on earth. Although the political future of North Korea remains critically uncertain, South Korea and China, in particular, would like to see the North Korean economy ultimately integrated into the regional framework.[64] In the event of a critical juncture on the Korean peninsula, possibly related to political turmoil or collapse in the DPRK, political leaders in the region would likely need to find a way to stabilize North Korea. Given such a critical juncture, the NEADB concept, in the context of broader multilateral cooperation, could well help close or narrow the organization gap in Northeast Asia, particularly if global institutions like the World Bank were unresponsive.

In Conclusion

To return to our theoretical discussion, the pre–Korean War power structure mandated that the United States should, by virtue of its hegemonic political-economic influence, be able to establish a collective-security arrangement, analogous to NATO and other multilateral agreements elsewhere, as realists have argued. Historical-institutionalist arguments explained the failure of the Pacific Pact in terms of norms and conventions. They contended that the institutional void in Northeast Asia following the collapse of the Japanese empire, coupled with the onset of Cold War tensions, was not conducive to multilateral collective-security arrangements. Yet such explanations clearly neglect the policy window opened after World War II, when major Asian countries were devastated by war and the region lay at the mercy of intense superpower rivalries. The central pre–World War II institutional attributes, including mechanisms for policy coordination between Japan and China, were not manifest in the early postwar years. It should have been possible to erect a coherent new multilateral order in the region, yet that did not emerge, although there were serious proposals for its configuration.

The preceding discussion makes clear that none of the classical variables—certainly neither power nor institutions—can fully explain either actual profiles of organization in Northeast Asia or the deep divisions between communist and noncommunist Asia that ultimately emerged. U.S. hegemony, in particular, is insufficient as an explanation, since American decision-makers themselves were uncertain about optimal courses of action, and they too were prisoners of events. Ultimately, it was the *process* of *critical juncture*—the time pressures, amid the sheer complexity of decision—that established definitive arrangements. The process, and the transformations that it wrought in both consciousness and decision-mak-ing structure, produced outcomes clearly different from what had been possible prior to the critical juncture itself.

The unexpected Korean War, and especially the intense, desperate weeks fol-lowing a sudden, traumatic Chinese intervention, are a prime example of the pro-found impact that critical junctures—in this case, a security-related juncture—can have. That short period rendered unviable one thoughtful, broadly supported proposal for regional architecture, while according an alternative, less ambitious formula formidable yet unexpected momentum, allowing it to determine the broad profile of Pacific political-economic affairs for half a century and more. The momentous developments of the Korean War years thus transformed the political landscape of Northeast Asia in remarkably enduring fashion. They created deep intraregional divisions, combined with strong dependence on Washington, until new catalysts nearly half a century later arose to reconfigure the region once again.

Overcoming the Organization Gap
Crises and Critical Junctures (1994–2008)

The critical juncture of the Korean War, despite its military character, crucially shaped the political-economic profile of Pacific relations across the post–World War II years. It created a "hub-and-spokes" framework, centering on Washington; a complementary network of economic ties; deep divisions between communist and noncommunist Asia; and an "organization gap" within Northeast Asia itself that persisted for a remarkably long time and contrasted to livelier subregional institutions farther south. Southeast Asia, challenged first by conflict in Vietnam (1951–75) and later by the task of quarantining Vietnamese expansion elsewhere in Indochina (1979–92), developed institutions, such as the Southeast Asia Treaty Organization (SEATO) and the Association of Southeast Asian Nations (ASEAN), supported by outside powers like the United States, which found those bodies useful from a global geopolitical standpoint. Only momentous developments at the global level in the 1980s and 1990s had any serious impact on the durable yet static "hub-and-spokes" structure in Northeast Asia, forged in the heat of crisis so many years before.

Three driving forces have supported regional integration around the globe in recent years. These mechanisms have included the following: (1) *Local economic pressures.* When trade and investment are regionalized to a significant degree, local businesses typically want responsive institutional mechanisms for stabilizing their mutual cooperation. (2) *Leverage seeking.* When countries grow frustrated with U.S. unilateralism and the market fundamentalism of institutions like the International Monetary Fund (IMF), they seek enhanced negotiating leverage through regionalist bodies. (3) *Counter-regionalism.* Developing economies, including those of Asia, have become eager to consolidate their own cohesion as a counterweight to the growing unity of both Europe and the Americas, and the possible trade diversion to other regional entities that might otherwise occur.[1]

Globalism savaged the Asian economy during the 1997 Asian financial crisis (AFC), in the view of many Asians, sharply increasing support for regionalist alternatives within Asia. A series of new initiatives, including the Chiang Mai financial-swap arrangement, emerged in the wake of the 1997 crisis, just as MERCOSUR had been catalyzed in South America by the financial earthquakes of the early 1990s there. Clearly, the 1997 AFC was a watershed in both the economic and the political evolution of the Asian region.

The 1997 crisis, in all its trauma, galvanized national governments into action. It provoked a dramatic change in thinking among both political and business leaders across Northeast Asia—impressing them with both their vulnerability and their growing economic power relative to a devastated Southeast Asia. The crisis also spurred a growing realization of the need for formal mechanisms to deal with similar crises in the future, so as to help sustain the economic growth of Asia as a whole.[2] The crisis provided, in short, a catalyst for major change, in both key nations and in the overall profile of the Asian region. Northeast Asian nations, with their powerful economies and advanced technology, were the natural spearheads for this change, especially since the factors giving Southeast Asia prominence in earlier years, such as the felt need during the 1980s to contain an expansionist Vietnam, were no longer central in regional affairs.

The significance of the 1997 financial crisis as a critical juncture can be clearly demonstrated through a brief survey of regionalism before that traumatic event. As the next section shows, Asia before 1997 was, at most, bound together in a rather loose, network-style, open regionalism, with ASEAN, for embedded historical reasons, an established linchpin. Alternative structures in Northeast Asia found it difficult to evolve. To be sure, there were efforts—many of them quite determined and persistent—to achieve greater intraregional cohesion, including cohesion independent of the United States. Yet most attempts to establish formal multilateral institutions in the region nevertheless failed.

One striking exception was the Asian Development Bank (ADB). Founded in 1966, it has since lent substantial sums to emerging nations throughout Asia, although its policy-related functions have been limited to economic consultation and coordination. Even that institution, however, was the product of unusual circumstances: a conducive regional and international environment (including close collaboration between Japan and the United States); and a critical juncture at the onset of the Vietnam War. Significantly, too, the ADB long excluded communist Asia, and thus failed to become a regional organization in the fullest sense.

Pre-Crisis Regionalism in Asia

Compared with the dynamic economic growth and market-oriented trading relations that prevail across most of Asia, the weakness of formal intraregional institutions is striking, and was especially so in the northeast quadrant of the continent before 1997. As Table 3.2 suggested, Asian regionalism over the last several decades has experienced a series of false starts. Only when critical junctures were present have regional institutions with substantial subsequent promise emerged.

During the 1950s the San Francisco System of asymmetric trans-Pacific political-economic relations, established as a result of the Korean War critical juncture, perpetuated "hub-and-spokes" relationships between the United States and its Asian allies, while simultaneously isolating communist Asia. Bilateralism prevailed, and multilateralist initiatives produced little more than "minimal open regionalism"—a shallow form of integration involving only limited institutional development. This pattern was epitomized in the Asia Pacific Economic Community (APEC).

Broadly speaking, the 1950s, 1960s, and 1970s were inauspicious for regional integration, especially that transcending traditional Cold War lines, and having a Northeast Asia focus. The only enduring Asian regional institutions to emerge during this period were the Asian Development Bank and ASEAN; both had a Southeast Asia focus.[3] Peter Katzenstein and Takashi Shiraishi, citing this sort of evidence, argue that hierarchical bureaucratic structure in Asian countries, together with lack of a public-law tradition and a strong sense of community, makes formal regional integration generally unlikely.[4] Stephan Haggard argues similarly that Asian states have a harder time reaching agreements on institutionalization than nations elsewhere, because of higher levels of political and economic diversity.[5] None of these authors consider the possibility of change in this "noninstitutionalized" pattern of Asian regionalism.

Systemic factors at the international level have also historically reinforced the difficulties of region-building in Asia. As Crone argues, U.S. hegemony in the region, in particular, has often frustrated such moves in the past.[6] Multilateral initiatives from Japan have confronted another difficulty: suspicion and mistrust on the part of other Asian countries, flowing from Japan's imperialistic role in the area prior to 1945. Such complications have been especially pronounced in Northeast Asia, around the periphery of Japan's home islands, where the experience of Japanese colonial rule was longest and, generally speaking, most bitter.

In the 1980s and 1990s, broad Asian regionalism did, to be sure, achieve some modest successes, albeit only those including the United States. In 1989, responding to an initiative from Australian prime minister Robert Hawke, APEC was created. This broad regional grouping brought together governmental and non-governmental representatives from Japan, the United States, Canada, the Republic of Korea, Australia, and New Zealand, as well as the six member states of ASEAN. The People's Republic of China (PRC), Taiwan, and Hong Kong all joined in 1992, Papua New Guinea and Mexico in 1993, and Chile in 1994.

With a budget of only $2 million and a small secretariat located in Singapore, however, APEC has distinctly limited administrative capacity, and relies mostly on technical working groups to conduct its substantive day-to-day operations. APEC remains a purely consultative forum bounded by the constraints of routine consensus decision, despite persistent business pressure for deeper integration.[7]

It has, to be sure, had larger aspirations at times.[8] In the years to come, however, APEC may well remain simply a forum for trade and investment liberalization, as well as transnational networking. It is unlikely to become a major driver for economic integration, unless it develops a more substantial support base in the major nations, including China, or is fatefully reshaped in the grip of a critical juncture.

It is noteworthy that proposals to establish smaller and more exclusively Asian organizations failed miserably on several occasions, during the decade prior to the 1997 Asian financial crisis. In the late 1980s, the East Asian Economic Grouping (EAEG), for example, was proposed by Prime Minister Mahathir Mohamad of Malaysia at the time of a seemingly faltering global Uruguay Trade Round. EAEG subsequently encountered persistently intense criticism, throughout the Pacific. Critics of the initiative argued that it threatened "to divide the Pacific down the middle," and was thus politically and economically counterproductive. After lengthy debates and intense exchanges between supporters and opponents, the proposal was later adopted, in a substantially reshaped, diluted, and renamed form, as the East Asian Economic Caucus (EAEC) within APEC. It has, in effect, been kept on the back burner in that form ever since.[9]

Thus, in the years before 1997, regional arrangements of an exclusive nature were not politically feasible in the Pacific. Strong U.S. opposition, Japanese hesitation, and lukewarm support from most Asian states demonstrated that the regional cohesion and political will necessary to implement controversial institutional proposals like EAEG were not present in Asia.[10]

In sharp contrast to Japan's 1991 hesitation at entertaining the EAEG idea, influentials in Tokyo conceived an even more ambitious and controversial regional proposal for an Asian Monetary Fund (AMF) shortly before the onset of the 1997 financial crisis.[11] The AMF was officially deliberated at the G-7 IMF meetings in Hong Kong in September 1997, before the full dimensions of the crisis were clear, with Japan offering to create a U.S.$100 billion fund to stabilize exchange rates in Asia. Japan differed sharply with U.S. neoliberal prescriptions for curtailing the financial crisis, reflecting its deep frustration with the IMF. If realized, Tokyo's AMF proposal would actually have allowed Japan to shape regional policy outcomes more effectively than the U.S./IMF alternative, in line with Japan's preferences for easy credit and looser conditionality in dealing with the financial crisis. Additionally, the AMF could have helped provide a greater headline figure for the multilateral bailout package, thus helping the financial authorities to calm markets and disburse funds more flexibly.

To U.S. policy-makers, such as Larry Summers, deputy secretary of the treasury, Japan's proposal appeared "out of the blue"—too suddenly presented, without consultation, excluding the United States, and devoid of an IMF link.[12] Furthermore, the timing was peculiar—by September 1997, both the Philippines and Indonesia had already floated their currencies, and the Asian financial crisis was increasingly showing signs of contagion.[13] Under such circumstances, a proposal of this scale naturally provoked enormous controversy, and was seen by many as gravely destabilizing.

The AMF in fact received a warm initial reception in virtually every Southeast Asian capital, with Taiwan and South Korea also favorably disposed.[14] The United States, however, strongly opposed the plan and lobbied China, which had similar reservations about Japan's regional leadership, to oppose it also. Significantly, Sino-Japanese interpersonal ties were still distant in the financial area, relative to Sino-American relations, complicating prospects for intra-Asian agreement.

The whole affair reached a climax at the Regional Finance Ministers' meeting on November 21 in Hong Kong, which the United States and the IMF attended as observers. While ASEAN and South Korea expressed support for the AMF proposal, Hong Kong and Australia remained neutral, and China voiced no opinion. Tokyo's AMF proposal thus was not adopted. In its place came a substantially downgraded "Manila Framework," which quietly dropped the AMF's most controversial features.

Tokyo's failure to deliver an Asia-based monetary fund, despite its massive financial resources, revealed much about the politics of Asian regionalism. Despite Japan's standing as the second largest economy in the world and the most influential economic power in the region, it was nevertheless unable to rally sufficient regional consensus to counter American opposition, because of underdeveloped network ties with the region—especially within Northeast Asia. The failure of the AMF, and the contrasting success three years later of the Chiang Mai Initiative, led by Japan, China, and South Korea, demonstrate nicely, in combination, a fundamental truth: crisis-driven critical junctures are crucial to overcoming collective action problems in Asia, broadening options for such joint action, and making formal regional cooperation possible.

In the following section, we recount how the crisis emerged, how it affected Asian countries, and how it forced them to act together in the common interest. Only through crisis, at a critical juncture in their development, were these nations able to achieve the cohesion to stabilize their region in the face of financial hurricanes gusting across the globe. And crisis, in particular, drew long-suspicious neighbors in Northeast Asia together seriously for the first time, just as earlier tensions regarding Vietnam and its role had drawn Southeast Asian neighbors together from the 1950s through the early 1990s.[15] Thereafter, periodic crises relating to North Korea helped emerging relationships among the Northeast Asian states to deepen.

Edging Closer to Crisis

Regional cohesion, as we have continually seen, does not come easily to East Asia, particularly the northeastern quadrant of the region. For half a century and more, much of the sprawling region, depicted in Figure 4.1, lay perched precariously around the rim of China, in the American shadow. Many of its key nations were integrally linked on a bilateral basis with Washington, but with remarkably few alternative intra-Asian regional ties. The bitter heritage of Japanese colonialism, World War II, and the Korean War, in particular, still complicated the development of neighborly relationships.

Economic interdependence within Asia has gradually deepened, and periodic initiatives toward regionalism have been made, particularly since the waning of the Cold War in the early 1990s. Those regionalist undertakings have had a plausible economic basis, especially given high and rising ratios of intraregional trade, and substantial local foreign-exchange reserves. Yet these overtures have foundered with remarkable consistency: on the shoals of intraregional conflict, as a result of opposition from across the Pacific, or both in tandem.

Despite such disagreement, a simultaneously quiet and revolutionary engine of change has been corroding the long-immutable Pacific status quo: the power of global finance. Two forces are at work. Finance itself has been changing profoundly. And Asia's role in that arcane but crucial world has been evolving as well.

Security crises have also at times contributed to innovation in regional architecture. America's 1965 intervention in Vietnam, for example, helped both the Asian Development Bank (1965), and also ASEAN (1967), to achieve the relative credibility that they have enjoyed. The Vietnamese invasion of Cambodia (1978) similarly helped enhance ASEAN's credibility still further.

More recently, a series of security crises relating to Korea—some of which might be considered subregional critical junctures—have measurably accelerated

FIG. 4.1. Northeast Asia in Broader Regional Context

the Making of Northeast Asia. In 1993, for example, North Korea withdrew from the non-proliferation treaty (NPT), provoking a severe crisis leading ultimately to creation of the minilateral Agreed Framework and the Korean Peninsula Energy Development Organization (KEDO).[16] In 1998, a North Korean missile shot, passing over Japan into the Pacific Ocean, led to the tripartite U.S.–Japan–South Korean TCOG process.[17] In 2002 North Korea's admission of a highly enriched uranium (HEU) program, and in 2006 its detonation of a nuclear device, gave birth to, and infused increased vigor into, multilateral processes for containing and dissuading the Democratic People's Republic of Korea (DPRK).[18] This soft-integration process was intensified once again by North Korea's missile tests and second nuclear test, in the spring of 2009.

What is crucially new in the world of finance, and important for political economy, is the emergence of what Alan Greenspan describes as "the new high-tech international finance system,"[19] based in part on dramatic advances in computer and telecommunications technology. In 1930, for example, a telephone call from New York to London cost $800 at today's prices. Today a short call costs less than a dollar, with the coming of the Internet reducing costs still further. International information-gathering and transaction costs among major financial centers have fallen to virtually zero, making it ever easier to deploy large amounts of capital rapidly across long distances.

The amount of money available for investment globally has also spiraled rapidly over the past decade. Flight capital from poorly managed or unstable economies—from Africa and Latin America to the former Soviet Union—has been one source. Another is the rapid swelling of pension funds in advanced nations, as the "baby-boom" generation moves steadily closer to retirement age.

Innovation in market structure and financial instruments also makes it easier to deploy capital strategically. Derivatives, for example, give investors—including speculators—amplified power to deploy capital at very specific times, and in magnitudes many times larger than the investment at risk, against very specific targets. Hedge funds provide the institutional vehicle to manage such tasks. Such often speculative funds, and more conventional investors, both have an increasing range of closely linked markets—including securities, bonds, and foreign exchange—in which to operate, increasing their leverage still further with officials intent on control and stability. Needless to say, such technically sophisticated and deeply integrated markets can be influenced profoundly by sudden national-security developments, such as wars or military demonstrations, as well as by economic considerations. Finance is becoming a key catalytic agent in provoking critical junctures, and hence in intensifying both supply and demand for regional organization.[20]

By 1997 as much as $2 trillion daily in transactions was surging across the financial markets of the world, exerting intense pressure on governments and corporations even under routine circumstances. The volatility of global financial flows had already provoked the Latin American debt crisis of 1982; the Indian financial crisis of 1991; the European exchange-rate crisis of 1992–93; and the Mexican foreign-debt crisis of 1994–95. Yet East Asia, until the summer of 1997, lay remarkably unscathed.

And there was ample room for optimism that things would remain that way. Indeed, nothing on the macroeconomic front forewarned of the troubles to come. Encouraged by the apparently benign economic environment, capital flowed in massive amounts into the Asian economies during the early and mid-1990s. Confident that the future looked bright, Asian firms borrowed heavily in risky dollar-denominated short-term capital markets, because interest rates were lower there.

In September 1997, for example, South Korea owed foreign banks more than $114 billion, of which nearly $78 billion was short-term debt. Korea's foreign exchange reserves were only $31 billion, or barely one-quarter of the total debt outstanding. And Indonesia and Thailand were in similar straits. Much of the dollar lending was to finance real estate and other projects denominated in local currency, exposing the borrowers to dangerous foreign-exchange risk should their nation's currency depreciate. And the regulatory structure within the region to monitor this accumulation of debt, and deal with its consequences, was, as soon became clear, perilously inadequate.

Reaping the Whirlwind: The Coming of Critical Juncture

Thailand's decision to float the baht on July 2, 1997, brought a storm in its wake that almost no one, even those most specialized in Asian finance, had anticipated. And it was one that swept far beyond Southeast Asia, to begin galvanizing new policy networks and regional consciousness far to the northeast, as well. On the first day of the float the baht plunged by a full 15 percent. Within a month it had lost 40 percent of its value, and in another sixty days it had plummeted a further 20 percent. Before long, all the Southeast Asian countries and Korea were in the throes of a historic international monetary crisis. As Figure 4.2 suggests, within a year, the exchange rates of Thailand, Indonesia, Korea, Malaysia, the Philippines, and Singapore had all dropped sharply against the U.S. dollar.

These sharp realignments made the weight of foreign debts, denominated in dollars against which local currencies were being devalued, painfully difficult to repay, and spurred fears of contagion among investors in heavily indebted countries across the region. Initially the United States did not intervene to stabilize the situation, leaving a lasting bitterness among the nations of the region that was to fuel regionalist initiatives excluding the U.S., as we shall see. To the $17.2 billion overall rescue package for Thailand, formalized in August 1997, Japan contributed $4 billion, while Australia, China, Hong Kong, Malaysia, and Singapore added $1 billion each.[21] Yet the United States, which had provided a massive $31 billion to support Mexico in its 1995 financial troubles, chipped in nothing whatever

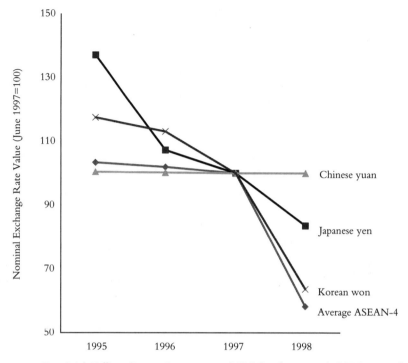

FIG. 4.2. East Asia's Falling Currencies, 1995–98 (U.S.$/local currency). ASEAN-4 refers to Singapore, Thailand, Malaysia, and Indonesia. The exchange value of China's yuan was fixed throughout the period 1995–98. Source: Original data from International Monetary Fund, *Exchange Rate Archive*, 1995–98.

for Thailand in its hour of need. The Clinton administration had badly depleted the Exchange Stabilization Fund in the Mexican debt crisis, and was politically unwilling to use significant political capital at home to over-ride opposition within the United States to replenishment.[22]

   The first target of speculators, in the wake of Thailand, was Indonesia. When that country was forced to devalue in August 1997, speculation moved to the Northeast, against Korea, whose banks were heavily invested in Indonesia, and which itself was heavily leveraged. The collapse of the Hanbo Group in February 1997—the first of eight of Korea's top thirty *chaebol* to fail by December 1998—and Korea's rising current account deficit together indicated that the ROK too might be vulnerable. And that raised deep concerns in neighboring China and Japan as well.

   Japan and China, although less directly touched by the crisis than their neighbors, also felt its trauma, and began for the first time a serious, cooperative financial dialogue, both with each other and with the broader region. Despite Japan's position as a long-standing U.S. ally, with the largest foreign-exchange reserves on earth and a GDP constituting 15 percent of the global total, it was lectured to summarily by American financial officials, and its proposal for an Asian Monetary Fund was rejected, as noted earlier. With Asia receiving 35 percent of its exports—significantly more than the United States—Japan also suffered economically from the macroeconomic downturn that followed the crisis.[23]

China, while siding with the U.S. in rebutting Japan's AMF initiative, also slowly began to see the substantial dangers of the emerging regional financial disaster, and the need for intra-regional cooperation. Indeed, its deepening propensity to collaborate with Northeast Asian neighbors in Japan and Korea was powerfully enhanced by this broader, unprecedented regional crisis. The PRC provided, for example, $1 billion to the Thai support package of August, 1997—$1 billion more than the United States—although the Chinese delegation was not able to announce its contribution until after the support-group meeting, following direct consultations with Beijing.[24] This was the first time that China had made a substantial contribution to a currency-crisis hit country, and in this sense represented its debut in international currency-crisis diplomacy.

Beijing's policies evolved further in the direction of intra-Asian financial cooperation during 1998. At the Hanoi ASEAN leaders' meeting that year, with the region still mired deep in the shadow of the financial crisis, China proposed that central bank governors, and the deputies of finance ministers throughout the region, should meet regularly to explore possibilities for further multilateral cooperation. At the Manila leaders' meeting in 1999, Prime Minister Zhu Rongji himself played a leading role, together with his Northeast Asian colleague, Japanese prime minister Obuchi Keizo, in finalizing the swap-quotas arrangement that led to the historic May 2000 Chiang Mai agreement.

The PRC's shift to support for intraregional initiatives in Asia was historic, and influenced heavily by both its perception of the Asian financial crisis and by substantive changes in Beijing's regional role that the crisis provoked. Its new responsibilities in Hong Kong, which had reverted to Chinese sovereignty on July 1, 1997, just as turbulence was beginning, also played a role. Hong Kong's broad exposure to Asia's economic difficulties, given its heavy trade and financial interdependence with the region, sensitized the PRC more to the broader volatility and potential danger of Asian monetary affairs than had ever previously been the case.

Hong Kong, additionally, had both political and economic significance in China's policy for dealing with Asian financial volatility. Politically, Mainland China was hoping to present Hong Kong as a showcase of its ability to govern a territory that was at once capitalist and democratic. With sustained Hong Kong "prosperity," China would have more leverage in resolving thorny cross-Straits issues, the government believed. Economically, the PRC relied on Hong Kong as a "laboratory" and "showcase" for implementing its own domestic corporate reforms, such as relieving the burden of bankrupt state-owned enterprises.[25] Deepening turmoil in Hong Kong would inevitably have political echo effects across China as a whole, reflecting inevitably upon the capabilities of top leadership in Beijing, even though the economic and political systems of Hong Kong and the Mainland remained still substantially separate from each other. And the sharp 9 percent fall in Hong Kong's Hang Seng index on October 20, coupled with the largest overnight point fall ever in the U.S. Dow Jones averages, convinced Beijing that the crisis could have potentially serious implications for both Hong Kong and the broader world, including even its own insulated domestic financial system.[26]

China's gingerly movement toward multilateralism, which ultimately fueled the Making of Northeast Asia, as we shall see, was driven by a complex mixture of four different motives, all related to the critical juncture of the Asian financial crisis:

1. A deepened sense of the danger to itself of international monetary developments. Between 1982 and 1997, Chinese foreign debt had risen fivefold, from $1.8 billion to $10 billion, excluding inflows to China (FDI) and bonds.[27] Although still low relative to exports, or to China's overall economic scale, China's debt was becoming substantial. In the PRC itself, there was extensive discussion of whether China would be the second Asian domino to fall, in the wake of Thailand. Although most outside scholars remained optimistic concerning China's economic prospects, the real worries were intense within China itself.[28] The unexpected difficulties that Thailand, Indonesia, and especially South Korea confronted during 1997–98— both economically and politically—convinced China both that it needed to insulate itself from such problems by retaining capital controls, and also that it should help neutralize them by playing a more cooperative international role. This sense of apprehension in Beijing for the region's stability persisted long after the initial crisis had waned, and fueled China's willingness to support intraregional financial cooperation within Asia.

2. A rising sense of its own long-term economic sustainability and diplomatic strength. By the latter part of 1998 it was clear that the Chinese economy had successfully weathered the crisis, although vulnerabilities remained in the region as a whole, and particularly in Southeast Asia. It was also clear that China's own emphasis on stimulative, countercyclical macroeconomic policies had been fundamentally correct. Both the PRC's continued vigorous economic growth—nearly 8 percent

annually in real terms, despite the regional crisis—and the support of prominent international economists for Chinese policies reinforced this perception.[29]
Beijing cannot also have helped observing how much its own relative position
had improved, both politically and economically, within a region where other
major nations were either decimated by crisis, like Indonesia and South Korea, or
enmeshed in stagnation, like Japan.

3. *Its perception of competitive dynamics within the region.* While Beijing undoubtedly felt empowered by the events of 1997–98, as suggested above, it also was
stirred by defensive impulses, in the face particularly of initiatives from Tokyo.
Beginning with the Asian Monetary Fund concept, first broached informally in
1996, and then formalized at the September 1997 IMF–World Bank meetings in
Hong Kong, Japan under its Ministry of Finance (MOF) vice minister for international affairs, Sakakibara Eisuke, was proactively promoting regional organization.
China must have been apprehensive that Japan would become a dominant player
on regional integration issues, if the PRC did not actively participate itself, interacting constructively with Tokyo in that process.[30] Meanwhile, Beijing was wary
of rising U.S. influence in the region as well.[31]

4. *Its deepening intraregional networks in international finance.* When Japanese
Ministry of Finance officials began actively developing the AMF concept in 1996–
97, they had few functioning "back-channels" for informal dialogue with China,
and engaged in little interaction with Chinese officials or think-tanks in developing the proposal. China's international financial dialogues were overwhelmingly
U.S.-centric: with the U.S. Treasury and Federal Reserve, as well as private investment banks. In the wake of the financial crisis, however, China actively began
to develop more extensive interpersonal networks of its own, especially within
Northeast Asia. Beijing developed these networks both intergovernmentally and
with semigovernmental think tanks such as Japan's National Institute for Research
Advancement (NIRA), and Korea's Institute for Economic Policy (KIEP).

Collectively, these four pressures, flowing from critical juncture, catalyzed a
major transformation in China's overall relationships with Asia, involving a particular deepening of Northeast Asian ties, which had been especially underdeveloped. Before the crisis Beijing had tended to pursue a narrow, detached, mercantilist definition of national economic interest, as manifest in the 1994 devaluation
of the renminbi. That evolved, in the crucible of financial crisis, into a broader
sense of responsibility not only for China's own growth but also for regional stability more generally.

By early 1999 Asia had begun to leave its financial crisis behind, with Northeast
Asia spearheading the recovery. In Korea, which helped lead Asia as a whole out of
stagnation, GDP growth surged to 10.9 percent in 1999, and 8.8 percent in 2000,

driven by both consumer spending and heavy new foreign investment.[32] Southeast Asia was slower to rebound. There the scars of the crisis remained—all the more traumatic for being unexpected and, in the view of many Asians, patently unjustified.

China was ultimately less affected by the crisis than any other major country in Asia, helping to shift the region's center of political-economic gravity northward from Southeast Asia. When the financial crisis erupted in July 1997, China's neighbors urged Beijing to keep its currency strong because of the possible contagion effect in their own markets, but they were unsure that it could do so. In response, China's political leaders promised to hold the line on the renminbi at least through 1999. Late 1999, at the penumbra of previous international agreements, was thus a moment of reckoning.

China's confidence was greatly enhanced by its success in weathering the financial crisis. In the PRC, foreign-exchange reserves more than doubled in the half-decade from 1997 to 2002,[33] to become second only to those of Japan,[34] which they then surpassed in 2007.[35] Hong Kong also steadily expanded its reserves. From $89 billion in 1998, those holdings steadily rose, to a total of $111.9 billion by 2002.[36]

Despite China's steadily improving balance of payments situation, however, as a result of in-bound capital flows, macroeconomic indicators did not pick up until well into 1999. The PRC's domestic market was weak, and exports remained stagnant.[37] China's GDP growth in 1999 was the lowest since the Tiananmen Square incident a decade earlier: only 7 percent, compared with 8.5 percent and 7.8 percent in 1997 and 1998, respectively. To contemporary outside observers, a renminbi devaluation seemed more and more likely, though the timing remained uncertain. There was thus a pronounced sense of economic deterioration within China, together with a strong belief in the need for policy change. Southeast Asia's slow pace of recovery compounded lingering regional pessimism. Indeed, Mohammed Mahathir of Malaysia, generally optimistic about Asia's prospects, still insisted in 1999 that "the Asian financial crisis is not over."[38]

The apprehension induced by these gloomy growth statistics and official pronouncements during 1998–99 was enhanced by the persistent fear across Asia of renminbi devaluation. Before the crisis, China was a major competitor of the Southeast Asian countries, in particular. This continuing sense of urgency and time pressure, flowing from the critical juncture of the 1997 financial crisis, yet persisting for at least two years thereafter, encouraged Asian collective action to build regionalist financial understandings. America's hesitance to act proactively itself, in the early stages of the crisis, made this Asian exclusivist determination all the stronger.

The Road to Chiang Mai

In November 1999, with the trauma of the AFC still fresh, the ASEAN Plus Three heads of government met in Manila and declared that monetary and financial cooperation had become priority areas of shared concern for them. The three Northeast Asian leaders, in their first trilateral "side summit" meeting independent of ASEAN—related, however, to the broader November 1999 ASEAN Summit—strongly concurred, and urged action. Working out the technical details took time, even after this top-level policy decision. Six months later, in May of 2000, however, the ASEAN Plus Three finance ministers gathered in Chiang Mai, Thailand, to establish a network of bilateral currency-swap agreements forestalling future currency crises such as they had so recently suffered during the 1997–98 crisis. Neither the United States nor Australia and New Zealand were included in the arrangements, and the International Monetary Fund did not endorse them until a year later.

The Chiang Mai agreement of 2000, set in motion many months earlier amid the AFC, although implementation took time, thus represented a substantial advance in East Asian regional cooperation—under Northeast Asian leadership—independent of both the United States and U.S.-influenced multilateral organizations such as the IMF. This regionalist innovation came in the wake of numerous futile attempts to advance such cooperation, as noted previously, including Mahathir's East Asian Economic Caucus (EAEC), and the East Asian Economic Group (EAEG) proposals, as well as Sakakibara's AMF initiative.[39]

The Chiang Mai model of regional policy innovation had seven distinctive characteristics that are especially noteworthy:

1. The *noninvolvement* of the United States and global multilateral institutions.

2. *An enhanced role for Northeast Asia*, which provided the overwhelming share of the swap guarantees.

3. The *sequence* through which deepened regional integration proceeds:

A. Significant trade interdependence.

B. A substantive regional-integration proposal (the AMF concept).

C. A critical juncture that opens a "policy window" of prospective innovation.

D. An indeterminate moment for leadership decision.

E. A concrete regional agreement.

F. International post facto acceptance.

4. The key role of *political leadership* in spurring policy innovation. It was the heads of government—Obuchi Keizo, Zhu Rongji, and Kim Dae-jung, in par-

ticular—who brought the Chiang Mai agreement to fruition, rather than the government ministries normally handling such technical issues as swap quotas.

5. The concentration of policy innovation in the *financial* area, where Northeast Asia is particularly dominant, because of its massive foreign-exchange reserves. In Europe, regional integration proceeded first in the trade area, with agreements such as the 1950 Treaty of Paris, which established the European Coal and Steel Community. Chiang Mai, one of the first substantive East Asian regional agreements, is thus distinctive, in that it links neighboring nations in the financial sphere first.

6. The *limited* nature of the constraints on national sovereignty. The swap quotas authorized under the Chiang Mai agreement do not constrain the prerogatives of national governments, in contrast, for example, to most steps toward regional integration in Europe.

7. The *limited* nature of the constraints on the established prerogatives of multilateral institutions. The Chiang Mai agreement, for example, has an explicit "IMF link." The borrower, in other words, must have completed, or be nearing completion on, an agreement with the IMF, as a condition for drawing "most of the funds" through swaps.[40]

The Chiang Mai agreement is an unusual case of formal regional policy innovation in Asia—a phenomenon in tension with the general view of Asian regionalism as informal and noninstitutionalized. It is clearly a case of Northeast Asian leadership, including the first-ever commitment by China in regional finance, although the problem addressed was significantly broader. It is also a case of policy innovation emerging in response to the manifest traumas of a critical juncture in international affairs. It was a forerunner, as we shall see, of deepening Northeast Asia–specific policy coordination, coupled with continued Asia-wide stabilization measures, in future years.

The 2008 Financial Crisis as Critical Juncture

Following the Asian financial crisis of 1997–98, East Asia as a whole—including particularly Northeast Asia—grew powerfully for a decade. China, in particular, expanded in double digits throughout most of that period, with South Korea coming close to matching that pace. Trade and financial interdependence between these two high-growth nations, and with Japan, steadily deepened. Despite ongoing military tensions, Taiwan also developed progressively closer economic ties and political-economic networks with Mainland China, to complement already established relations with Japan and the ROK. In 2000, for example, 250,000 Taiwanese were estimated to live and work on the Mainland.[41] By 2005, that number had quadrupled to over 1 million. Taiwanese companies were contributing major inputs for 40 to 80 percent of China's information and communication hardware exports.[42] Cross-Straits integration continued rapidly thereafter, especially following Ma Ying-jeou's election in early 2008.

In the wake of Koizumi Junichiro's September 2006 retirement, and the consequent disappearance of Yasukuni Shrine visits as a complicating factor in Northeast Asian relations, top-level trilateral political contacts among Japan, China, and Korea intensified also. The election of Lee Myung-bak measurably improved Japan-Korea ties, and the election of Ma Ying-jeou in Taiwan substantially improved cross-Straits relations as well.

By the spring of 2008, ties within the triangle were deepening all the way around. From May 6 to 10, 2008, Hu Jintao visited Japan, inaugurating Sino-Japanese Youth Exchange Year jointly with Prime Minister Fukuda Yasuo, and presenting substantial proposals for broadened policy coordination. The trip of "spring warming" concluded with proposals for seventy specific cooperation projects by Hu and Fukuda, respectively, devoted to intensifying exchanges and cooperation.[43] In its first year, more than 12,000 people participated in the youth program, China's largest bilateral exchange effort.[44]

Intergovernmental cooperation was also continuing to deepen. In May 2008 the East Asian Foreign Exchange Reserve Bank increased its reserves to $80 billion, with 80 percent of the contribution coming from Japan, China, and Korea. In June 2008, the foreign ministers of the three countries met in Tokyo, resolving to cooperate on disaster relief, Korean peninsula issues, food safety, aid to Africa, and the environment, while also agreeing to hold regular ministerial talks, rotating among their capitals.[45]

Although the socioeconomic foundations for the Making of Northeast Asia were quietly but steadily laid over the 1998–2008 decade, transnational institutions did not develop as rapidly. Northeast Asian leaders remained generally deferential to their Southeast Asian counterparts, who had formally led the regional-integration movement since the 1970s, despite the steady, quiet concentration of actual economic and military power in the Northeast. The United States, and often Japan, were also reluctant to see such Northeast Asia–centric ventures go forward. Such trilateral consultations as the Big Three of the Northeast chose to hold were strictly within the context of ASEAN-initiated bodies such as ASEAN Plus Three, or the East Asian Summit.

The fate of the creative yet premature ANEAN proposal, for an Association of *Northeast* Asian Nations (italics added), is an interesting case in point. This notion was vigorously discussed among intellectuals of the region during 1998–99,[46] and it attracted informal support from some major regional leaders, including Japan's prime minister Obuchi Keizo. Some feasibility meetings were held, but ultimately the idea was dropped by 2001.

At the working level, security tensions, in the form of an advancing North Korean nuclear program, did lead to some deepening policy coordination within Northeast Asia. This in turn generated policy networks with the potential for facilitating future integration, creating a virtuous cycle of soft institutionalization. This effort did get some tacit support from the United States. In October 2002, only a month after Japanese prime minister Koizumi's historic trip to Pyongyang, North Korea admitted to an HEU nuclear program. In 2003, the three Northeast Asian nations, together with the United States, Russia, and North Korea, began increasingly formalized Six-Party Talks, based in Beijing, to negotiate conditions for ending that program. In late 2006, North Korea conducted its first nuclear test. In April 2009 additional Taepodong II missile launches, followed by a second nuclear test in May 2009, gave increased urgency to these discussions, while also prompting enhanced regional cooperation. China and South Korea, for example, established an unprecedented hotline between their headquarters in late 2008, amidst certainties regarding North Korea's stability and strategic program.[47]

As economic interdependence among China, Japan, and Korea deepened during the mid-2000s, and as those nations became more formidable collectively in world finance, working-level trilateral consultations among central banks and ministries of finance began to deepen, in this case without the United States. These intra-Northeast Asian trilaterals began following the 1997 AFC. And they increased substantially as the U.S. subprime crisis began intensifying a decade later.

As in 1997–98, it was once again a turbulent critical juncture that produced really historic, discontinuous institutional developments in Northeast Asian finance. In May 2008, when finance ministers of the three countries met, amid quiet apprehension at the official level about America's subprime problems, the ministers agreed to set up a regional Asian fund of $80 billion to help provide emergency liquidity to financially troubled nations.[48] In October the long-submerged subprime financial crisis exploded publicly, leading to a catastrophic freeze in global financial markets; the bankruptcy and forced merger of many prominent global financial institutions, such as Lehman Brothers, AIG, and Merrill Lynch; strong deflationary pressures; and sharply rising unemployment worldwide. Mounting job losses reached far beyond the financial sector, into every corner of the global economy.[49] Northeast Asian nations, as the world's largest creditors, yet with a vulnerable Korea also in their midst, were galvanized into action.

Later in October 2008, when South Korean president Lee Myung-bak met

Japanese prime minister Aso Taro in Beijing, they both agreed to cooperate closely in combating the global financial crisis.[50] During the same month, Korea's Financial Services Commission chairman, Jun Kwang-woo, met with heads of China's major regulatory bodies and urgently discussed options for financial collaboration.[51] In November, finance ministers, supervisory authorities, and central bankers of the three countries met in Tokyo to prepare detailed measures for minimizing the impact of the global financial turmoil on Asian economies.[52] An Asian version of the Financial Stability Forum was inaugurated,[53] to discuss financial stability and internal monitoring of major financial institutions in the three countries.[54]

On November 14, 2008, the finance ministers of Japan, China, and South Korea met in Washington, DC, on the fringes of the G-20, to broaden trilateral currency-swap arrangements.[55] On December 10, the three countries established regular trilateral meetings of their central banks, while also expanding cooperation with East Asian nations more generally under the Chiang Mai agreement. In particular, the multilateral regional reserve pool was finalized, with the pool increasing from $80 billion to $120 billion, under Northeast Asian leadership. The Northeast Asian share was established at 80 percent, or four times Southeast Asia's share. As Figure 4.3 suggests, China and Japan were by far the two largest contributors to the regional pool, followed by South Korea. Malaysia, Indonesia, Singapore, and Thailand, the largest four contributors of ASEAN, were to provide $4.76 billion each, compared with more than $38 billion, respectively, for Japan and China.[56]

On December 13, Wen Jiabao, Aso Taro, and Lee Myung-bak—the three heads of government—met in Fukuoka, at the first trilateral Northeast Asian summit not tied to a broader multilateral meeting. The Fukuoka Summit, convened in the shadow of the deepest global financial crisis for at least three decades, was a landmark event. Their joint statement enunciated the rationale: "[O]ur economies are dynamic and deeply linked, our human relations are dense and deep, and we face the same opportunities and challenges . . . . [T]hus, we declare our intention to promote multilateral mechanisms in Asia, and to promote the trilateral summit as a platform for the future."[57] The three resolved to regularize the trilateral summit system, with the next gathering in fact being held in Beijing during October 2009, and its sequel on Jeju Island, off Korea's southern coast, the following spring.

At the Fukuoka Summit, the three leaders achieved substantive progress in three specific areas: financial coordination, cross-investment policy, and coordinated natural-disaster response. They agreed, most important, to expand their mutual currency-swap arrangements.[58] They also agreed to set up a ministerial-level meeting on natural-disaster relief, to be convened annually, with the first ses-

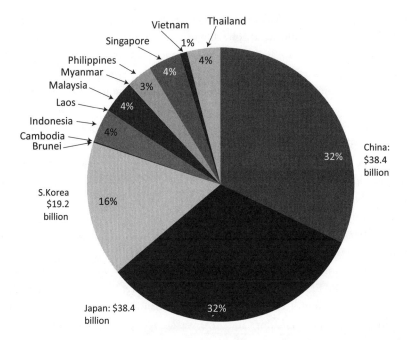

FIG. 4.3. Regional Foreign Exchange Reserve Pool under the Chiang Mai Framework (2008). Sources: Original data is from (1) "ASEAN Countries Agree on Individual Contribution to Regional Reserve Pool," Xinhua Net, April 9, 2009, http://news.xinhua-net.com/english/2009-04/09/content_11159564.htm; and (2) "China, Japan, and Korea Reached Agreement on Contribution Ratio of Regional Reserve Pool," Xinhua Net, May 3, 2009, http: //news.xinhuanet.com/english/2009-05/03/content_11302829.htm.

sion in Japan in October 2009.[59] They further resolved to have specialists explore the feasibility of a tripartite free-trade agreement.[60] Their summit, convened in the depths of financial crisis and critical juncture, thus clearly represented surprisingly concrete progress in the Making of Northeast Asia, as did the October 2009 Beijing Summit.

In Conclusion

As Mancur Olson observes, even when interests are congruent, there are two major obstacles to collective action.[61] One is the incentive to free ride, and the other is the limited stakes of individual participants in collective action. Within Asia, narrowly conceived, collective-action problems in many cases are further complicated by the influence and presence of the United States, itself a major "resident power" in the area.[62] The American interest may sometimes diverge from the narrower intra-Asian common interest, and occasionally, as in the Six-Party Talks, help consolidate it. The United States also has the power to apply selective disincentives, so as to abort autonomous collective action within the region.

As the foregoing evaluation of Asian regionalism in the pre–financial crisis has shown, over the first three decades following World War II, no common regional interest in securing an exclusively Asia-based organization was evident to the nations involved. Instead, most countries within the region deferred to the hegemonic role of the United States as a stabilizer, and placed priority on bilateral relationships with the U.S. in preference to intra-regional ties. This pattern was particularly pronounced in Japan and the Asian Newly Industrialized Economies (NIEs) (Korea, Taiwan, Hong Kong, and Singapore).

With the end of the Cold War, and emboldened by strong, sustained economic performance within the region, Asian leaders began proposing formal "Asia-only" institutional frameworks, epitomized in Mahathir's EAEG and Sakakibara's AMF. The appeal of EAEG to many Asian nations was clear. Yet the withering American attack on the notion of exclusionist Asian regionalism inhibited both Japan and ASEAN. In the end, Mahathir's initiative was temporarily subsumed into APEC, reflecting the strong inhibiting influence of the United States and the pressures of globalism.

The AMF had similar political momentum and resources as a result of Japan's direct involvement. The proposal clearly served the interests of many in the region, and might well have alleviated the 1997 financial crisis if put in place before it erupted. Yet U.S. opposition, once again, aborted the proposal, as had been true with EAEC nearly a decade earlier. China's hesitation at allying with the controversial Japanese initiative damaged its prospects for realization as well.

Although the United States has been consistently wary of "Asia-only" regionalism, it has also generally shown concern for the stability of the region, in which American interests are deeply engaged, and which constitutes such a large share of the overall global political economy. Washington has thus generally acquiesced in Asian cooperative actions ex post, both in economic and in security matters, with crisis thus rendering proactive Asian steps outside global institutions more acceptable than they would otherwise be.

The success of the Chiang Mai Initiative in the wake of the Asian financial crisis, sharply contrasting to the failure of the AMF proposal that preceded it, clearly demonstrates the potential importance of critical junctures as a mechanism for overcoming collective-action problems in Asia. The key decision to go forward was catalyzed by the crisis, although full implementation came later, as a result of bureaucratic inertia. The post-1997 period epitomized a new prospective mode of regional institution-building in Asia. In this sense, the interval was remarkably parallel to the Korean War critical juncture of 1950–51, even though the institutions created in the late 1990s were economic, while those born in the early 1950s were more geopolitical.[63]

The 2008 financial crisis, originating from the United States, catalyzed collective action within Northeast Asia directly. Policy networks developed among Japan, China, and South Korea in the post-AFC period facilitated more rapid policy coordination and institution-building than had been the case a decade earlier. The first Northeast Asian Trilateral Summit, dynamic new cross–Taiwan Straits relationships, intensified trilateral FTA discussions, and enhanced East Asian financial frameworks including efforts to conclude a trilateral investment agreement, all moved forward in the context of this 2008 financial crisis–induced critical juncture, thus consolidating trilateral relations in Northeast Asia, the protracted North Korean nuclear uncertainties notwithstanding.

PART III

REGIONAL DEVELOPMENT

5

Visions of a More Cohesive Regional Future

Northeast Asia, as we have seen, is quietly coming together, with its new cohesion spurred by the catalyst of financial and nuclear crisis, as well as the waning of older, long-disruptive historical memories. The deepening intra-Asian interactions now unfolding evoke the dynamic and cosmopolitan period a century ago, just before and after the Russo-Japanese War. Then Asian revolutionaries flocked to Tokyo, and pan-Asian intellectuals argued passionately in behalf of Asian integration for the sake of their national welfare. The locus of the interaction, especially in the early days, was centered on China, Japan, and Korea, although it ultimately diffused more broadly across Asia as a whole.

That period of vigorous intellectual comity is often forgotten today. It does, however, offer a provocative and surprisingly contemporary intellectual template for the contemporary Making of Northeast Asia—one that may well give it greater legitimacy, coherence, and momentum in future years.[1] This chapter revisits the history of pan-Asianism to ask: How did such sentiments emerge a century ago? What was their intellectual core? How and why have they varied so strikingly in their policy impact across the years? And what are their political implications today?

Apart from reviewing the classic story of pre–World War II Asianism, we also examine two recent periods of pan-Asianist ferment: one emerging during the 1980s and the second in the shadow of the 1997 Asian financial crisis. We address such questions as how pan-Asianist thought emerged, who its principal agents were, and how such ideas affected regional politics. We direct particular attention to the latest pan-Asianist movement—the ongoing community of thought

advocating Asian integration in the post-1997 era. The current pan-Asianist movement, especially the dialectic promoting Northeast Asian cohesion since late 2006,
embodies distinct characteristics and reflects different external and internal political-economic contexts than its forebears. These differences make the latest wave
of pan-Asianism potentially more enduring and influential as a unifying force than
its predecessors, we argue, and give it a particular relevance for Northeast Asia's
future that is replete with broader regional and global implications.

Optimistic Japan–Centric Origins

Northeast Asia has a long tradition of shared civilization, centering on China in
the premodern era and on Japan in more modern times. Reischauer and Fairbanks
half a century ago maintained that China, Japan, and Korea were clearly identifiable as the core of a distinct region—by geography, race, and, in particular, their
relationship to Sinic culture. East Asia, as they wrote,

> can be defined in three ways: in geographical terms as the area east of the great moun-
> tain and desert barrier that bisects Asia; in racial terms as the habitat of Mongoloid man;
> and in cultural terms as the domain of what we can call East Asian civilization. . . . The
> last definition is naturally the most important. . . . We concentrate on the histories of
> China, Japan, Korea, and to a lesser extent, Vietnam, the areas that derived much of their
> higher culture and their primary system of writing from ancient China.[2]

At the beginning of the twentieth century, particularly in the fateful decade
between the Russo-Japanese War and the outbreak of World War I (1905–14),
Asian intellectuals flocked to Meiji Japan. Such important and diverse Asian writ-
ers and activists as Sun Yat-sen, Okakura Tenshin, Liang Qichao, Nitobe Inazo,
and Rabindrath Tagore all explored the positive values, indigenous to Asia, that
could be presented to the broader world as universal. Vigorous intraregional dialogue during this period gave birth to a strong sense of mutual empathy among
Asian countries. Pan-Asianism was often proposed—first by Chinese, Japanese,
and South Korean intellectuals, and later by Indians and Southeast Asians also—as
a weapon for countering global imperialism, as well as a tool for promoting the
development of stable Asian nation-states.[3]

The idea of pan-Asianism was an attempt to preserve the traditional cultures
of Asia—Confucian first among them—in the face of an early-twentieth-century
Western imperialist onslaught. When intellectuals in Asian societies perceived a
threat from the West to their sense of cultural and political integrity, they similarly
felt a yearning to retain an idealized conception of the East as a psychological
counterweight to Western power and influence.[4] Stressing the value of pan-
Asianism was also a means of binding Asian countries together in their common

quest for independence and political modernization. The appeal of Asianism, as an intellectual weapon to both repel Western encroachment and simultaneously give meaning to locally defined nation-state contours, was particularly strong in China, Korea, and Southeast Asia, because of the vulnerable and often subordinate political status of those areas in regional and global affairs, at the high noon of Western imperialism.

During the late nineteenth century, however, it was Japanese thinkers who first explicated pan-Asianism.[5] Japan, it was argued, shared a common destiny with the rest of Asia. Japan's development was Asia's own, and Japan's progress, growing increasingly dynamic, ultimately required Asia's advancement also. Sugita Teiichi argued in his 1883 article "Koa Saku" ["Methods for Reconstructing Asia"] that Asian economic growth, and unified action to achieve it, was key to the survival of both Asia as a whole and of Japan individually. Japan needed to unite with other Asian countries—spiritually and even politically—in the face of Western onslaught, he contended.[6]

In 1891, Oi Kentaro and Tarui Tokichi organized the Asian Social Party, and soon thereafter published a long treatise, *Daito Gappo Ron* [*A Theory of Pan-Asian Federation*], advocating peaceful, selfless, and just approaches to rejuvenating Asia's regional power. This work came out originally in Chinese, curiously, although urging Japan to unite with both Korea and China. Oi and Tarui, together with Korean and Chinese activists, established the Asian Renaissance Association in Tokyo with its charter reading: "Asia has become the target of exploitation by the western countries. . . . Hence, Asian countries have to reunite and help each other to revive the weak position of Asia."[7] Tarui was later imprisoned for his socialist activism.

China and Japan were of the same written language and race, and hence should work closely together, the pan-Asianists persistently argued. Many liberals such as Miyazaki Toten participated directly in China's Kuomintang (KMT) revolution of 1911, emphasizing Asia's dependence on the survival of China. Naito Konan stressed that Sino-Japanese relations had to be peaceful and economically oriented, warning of the dangers of military confrontation between the two countries. Japanese scholars should pioneer new approaches to scholarship and establish an Asian knowledge system—namely, an "Asian Academy," he forcefully contended.[8]

Asian aesthetics, paralleling political thought, also experienced a renaissance in the early twentieth century. From 1902 to 1906, publications such as *Dream of Asia, Japan's Awakening; Asia's Awakening;* and *The Book of Tea* appealed passionately for a unified Asia. Okakura Tenshin, among the most representative scholars in this Asian cultural renaissance, defined Asian spirit as religious, harmonious, spiritual civilization, whose core values were love and peace. "It is the mission of Japan, as the great new power of Asia, to return to this spiritual civilization and to awaken old Asia," he argued, epitomizing the optimistic, hortatory, and often naive tone of many early Japanese pan-Asianist intellectuals.[9]

The Tortured Transwar Interlude

Amid World War I (1916), as Japan's geopolitical role on the Asian continent rapidly rose, with the rapacious, long-dominant European colonialists preoccupied with the bloody conflict in Europe, Odera Kenkichi elaborated the idea of Greater Asianism as a vehicle for establishing racial unity, so as to effectively confront the "white peril."[10] Royama Masamichi, Miki Kiyoshi, Takata Yasuma, Ozaki Hotsumi, and a number of other Japanese political thinkers thereafter comprehensively advanced the idea of Toa Kyodotai [East Asian Community] during the 1930s.[11] This notion gradually evolved into the grander concept of the Greater East Asia Co-Prosperity Sphere, increasingly popular among high-ranking Japanese military officers of the period.

In the context of the times, "Asia for Asiatics" was in practice synonymous with "Japan over Asia"—Japanese supremacy within Asia, to the exclusion of Western influence.[12] Japanese pan-Asianism in this sense was analogous to the regional exclusionism of the American "Monroe Doctrine" era. Such streams of thought justified Japan's invasion of Korea and China as an ultimately altruistic effort to safeguard Asian cultures and values from Western incursion. The 1937 Japanese attack on China, for example, was allegedly necessary to ensure the stability and survival of the failing Chinese state. The violent and militarist nature of this Japanese pan-Asianism, however, grievously complicated regional cooperation for generations into the future. Indeed, it compelled many Korean and Chinese scholars who had previously argued for solidarity with Tokyo ultimately to crusade against the newly aggressive Japan.[13]

Chinese Ambivalence

Pan-Asianism as a body of broadly accepted ideas was by no means limited to Japan, at least until Tokyo's military adventurism intensified during the 1930s. It also initially had strong intellectual advocates in China. Sun Yat-sen and Liang Qichao, for example, were very active in both promoting and elucidating pan-Asianism. Sun Yat-sen's philosophy was based on an antagonism of Right against Might that easily, in the context of the times, justified an alliance among Asian states against Western imperialism.

To Sun Yat-sen, China and Japan above all were racial and spiritual brothers, with a natural fraternal ability to work together. "Sino-Japanese relations must be based on mutual friendship and cooperation with a view to liberating the Far East from the domination of Western imperialism, and to finding a new order by which the Far East could be returned to the peoples of the Far East," argued Sun.[14] Observing the principles of pan-Asianism, the two countries could, for example, together develop the natural resources of the Pacific's western rim, and perform other momentous cooperative tasks, he contended.[15] When Japan defeated the Russian military in 1905, Sun regarded its victory clearly as "our own triumph," giving "a new hope to all Asiatic peoples."[16]

Sun, in particular, appealed directly to the Japanese people, with whom he was deeply familiar, seeking to move them to resist Western imperialism. "Japan today has become acquainted with the Western civilization of the rule of Might, but retains the characteristics of an Oriental civilization [which stresses] the rule of Right. Now the question remains whether Japan will be the hawk of Western civilization—of the rule of Might—or the tower of strength of the Orient."[17]

Sun stressed the importance of uniting Northeast Asia by applying the principles of reason and righteousness to achieve equitable yet enhanced integration among Japan, Manchuria, and China proper. Only by unifying the peoples of Asia on a foundation of benevolence and virtue could they become strong and powerful, Sun maintained. Should all Asiatic peoples thus unite together and present a united front against the Occidentals, they would win final victory, Sun further contended.[18]

Liang Qichao was another strong Chinese advocate of pan-Asianism, who saw Sino-Japanese relations as the linchpin. His central aspiration was "to create an East Asian academy in order to preserve Asian essence,"[19] and to serve as an intellectual defense against the aggressive West. Zhang Taiyan, another prominent Chinese revolutionary and philosopher in Japanese exile, in the face of Manchu oppression, made similar arguments. In February 1897, following continental Europe's controversial Triple Intervention against Japan,[20] he published "Asia Should Cooperate" in a progressive Chinese journal, *Shidai* [*Time*]. "China," he argued, "should rely on Japan, and Japan should rely on China. Mutual dependence can repel Russia and other imperial western powers from Asia." In April 1907, Zhang organized the cosmopolitan Asia Peace Association, with members from China, India, Japan, and Korea.[21]

Chinese intellectual support for Japanese pan-Asianism, initially strong, wavered when Japan began to wage aggressive wars in Asia. Sun, Liang, and Zhang—once principal intellectual advocates of pan-Asianism—became some of the most vocal critics of Japanese military aggression in China. Disillusioned with Japanese militarism, these intellectuals turned instead to the Soviet Union for inspiration, but conspicuously not toward Europe or the United States.[22]

Today, as we revisit these pan-Asianist ideas, now a century old, several conclusions emerge regarding this school of thought and its historical context. First, *crisis served as catalyst*. It was during periods of anxiety and transformation, such as the turbulent years between the Triple Intervention and the KMT Revolution (1895–1911), that Asian intellectuals and activists repeatedly came together and began envisioning Northeast Asia as a unit, rather than as a collection of separate countries. China's republican revolution of the early twentieth century, led by pan-Asianist intellectuals like Sun Yat-sen and Zhang Taiyan, with major practical backing from Japanese pan-Asianist supporters like Toyama Mitsuru, was a major case in point.

Second, pan-Asianism focused on establishing a collective, yet still nationalistic Asian defense against Western penetration. Indeed, in this formulation, *nationalism was the key to regionalism*—not its antithesis. The core nationalist aspiration was for autonomy vis-à-vis Western imperialist powers, achievable only through the solidarity of independent nations across the Asian region.

Third, prevailing concepts of regional cooperation required relatively *balanced distributions of power* for their practical realization. The principles of pan-Asianism were appealing to many in Northeast Asia a century ago. Yet China and Korea at that time were too unstable and weak to establish a truly equal union with Japan. As a result, the idea of "Asian unity" was hijacked by the Japanese military, destroying its broader regional credibility. Massive backlash on the Northeast Asian continent against Japan's so-called Greater East Asian Co-Prosperity Sphere, especially after the onset of war with China in 1937, made clear that regional cooperation, to be politically palatable, had to be based on equality and mutual interest.

From EAEC to AFC: Visions of Asia in the Early Post–Cold War Era

There were many competing ideas of, and proposals for, Northeast Asian regional integration during the Cold War, although none were ultimately realized. In 1984, Japanese scholars, for example, advanced a Northeast Asian economic-rim concept.[23] In 1987, Left-oriented Japanese economists suggested the establishment of an "economic circle of interdependence" surrounding the Japan Sea. In the same year, the South Korean government put forward a parallel, but Korea-centric, notion of an integrated Yellow-Bohai Sea economic area.

In Japan, the "new Asianism" of the 1980s was promoted more by economic elites than by political leaders. Kobayashi Yotaro, president of Fuji Xerox and a graduate of the Wharton School at the University of Pennsylvania, for example, encouraged his country to undergo "re-Asianization," and sent his own son to study in Shanghai.[24] Japan's Economic Planning Agency identified Japan, the NIEs, and also the Association of Southeast Asian Nations (ASEAN) as potential elements of one organic unit, and called for strengthened regional organization.[25] Under the Hashimoto cabinet (1996–98) the "ASEAN-Japan Multinational Cultural Mission" was established to promote contemporary Asian culture.[26]

As Watanabe Toshio, a prominent economist at the Tokyo Institute of Technology, maintained, "Japan's new nationalism is real, and it is intimately linked with Asianism."[27] That notion was initially Japan/ASEAN-centric, as epitomized in the intellectual collaboration of Ishihara Shintaro, governor of Tokyo, and Mahathir Mohammed, the Malaysian prime minister. They passionately contended that "[it] is possible for Asia to create a cultural region of unmatched historical greatness."[28] These leaders argued that Asia was "awakening to a new era, and there is no reason we cannot regain our former glory. If we preserve our distinctive values and cultures as we master modern technology, . . . Asia will again be great."[29] In this determined cooperative venture, Mahathir intently solicited the regional leadership of Japan.

Ishihara seconded Mahathir's appeal inside Japan itself, emphasizing that "Asia has a diverse and venerable civilization and culture, in contrast to a much shorter tradition in the U.S." He also contended that "it may be necessary" for governments in Asia to form "an anti-American Asian front on the issue of values." "Japan," he wrote, "is an Asian country of Asian people with Asian blood," and "it ought to realize that it exists for Asia rather than for America."[30] The assertive views of Mahathir and Ishihara enjoyed broad currency among the general population of Japan during the 1990s, as evidenced by Ishihara's successful election as governor of Tokyo in 1999, and subsequent re-elections in 2003 and 2007.[31]

Re-envisioning Northeast Asia after 1997

Since 1997, channels for intra-Asian policy dialogue have proliferated, especially in the Northeast quadrant of the region, facilitating conceptions of a common East Asian future once again. This Northeast Asia–centric revival follows two waves of broader pan-Asianism earlier in the century, as previously discussed.[32] The third wave followed the Asian financial crisis of 1997. As the East Asian Vision Group (EAVG) put it in 2002: "We should envision East Asia as evolving from a region of nations to a *bona fide* regional community, a community aimed at working toward peace, prosperity and progress."[33] Concretely, the Vision Group proposed: (1) establishing an "East Asian Free Trade Area" (EAFTA); (2) holding annual "East Asia Summits," bringing together leaders in the region; (3) working toward monetary integration; (4) setting up a regional cooperative organization; and (5) establishing the ultimate goal of building an "East Asian Community" (EAC).[34] This East Asia–wide vision progressed only slowly in succeeding years. A narrower focus on Northeast Asian integration has gained considerable momentum since 2006, however, as elaborated later, with waning consciousness of pre-1945 differences, deepening shared security concerns, and rising economic interdependence driving the process.

Chinese attitudes toward regionalism, in particular, have changed sharply since the mid-1990s, with a deepening sensitivity to immediate neighbors in Northeast Asia.[35] The prominent Chinese commentator Ma Licheng, chief editor of *Renmin Ribao* [*People's Daily*], was especially forceful in advocating cooperation among China, Japan, and South Korea, in particular. Commenting on Chinese premier Zhu Rongji's 2002 proposal for a China–Japan–South Korea free-trade area, Ma devoted a cover story in *Zhongguo Qiyejia* [*China's Entrepreneurs*] to the concept.[36] Also in 2002, addressing the rapidly evolving anti-Japanese sentiment in China, Ma argued that Japan's post–World War II economic miracle should be considered the pride of Asia. And China should employ new perspectives in thinking about Japan, and support Japan's pursuit of a normal statehood, Ma contended.[37]

Korean scholars have also recently suggested that pan-Asianism should take a fresh, more subregional approach, and have stressed Korea's mission, as the most centrally located nation of the region, to build a Northeast Asian community of cooperation. Lee Chang-Jae of the Korean Institute of International Economic Policy (KIEP), for example, proposed formation of a Council for Northeast Asian Economic Cooperation to discuss economic cooperation and other major economic issues among China, Japan, and Korea.[38] On November 27, 2000, President Kim Dae-jung himself suggested that the existing ASEAN Plus Three organization be transformed into an "East Asian Summit." The East Asian Summit, President Kim contended, could evolve into a viable and increasingly integrated community, leading ultimately to a coherent Northeast Asian economic unit.[39] Broad East Asian groupings could thus, in the view of Korean leaders and policy analysts, ultimately become the vehicle for producing much needed reconciliation at the fractious Northeastern core of the region—the delicate relationships among the two Koreas and the People's Republic of China (PRC).

The idea of an "East Asian Mediterranean" Free Trade Area, proposed originally by a Japanese scholar, Ogawa Yuhei of Seinan University, during the 1980s, has gained strong resonance among Chinese and Korean intellectuals since the 1997 Asian financial crisis, in a striking and important case of deepening Northeast Asian intellectual interaction.[40] As a first step to realizing this concept, Ogawa proposed minilateral cooperation at the local level, among cities and provinces/prefectures in Japan, China, and Korea. This grassroots cooperation was to be subsequently expanded in stages—first to involve Russia, North Korea, and Mongolia, and then to encompass the full East Asian Mediterranean area.[41] His related free trade agreement (FTA) proposal encompassed comparable regions surrounding the Japan Sea, Yellow Sea, and East China Sea, including three major economic regions: the Yellow Sea Economic Zone, the Japan Sea Economic Zone, and the Northern Altitude Economic Zone.[42]

Actual municipal collaboration within Northeast Asia has also intensified greatly since the 1997 Asian financial crisis, along the lines of Ogawa's prescriptions. Cities along the rim of the East Asian Mediterranean have signed agreements and held increasingly regular conferences on environmental, transportation, and economic-cooperation issues, including environment and technology transfers. By 2000, Kita Kyushu and Shimonoseki in Japan, Pusan and Incheon in South Korea, and Dalian and Qingdao in China had all become prominent in promoting the proposed economic-circle concept.[43] Two additional Chinese cities, Yantai and Tianjin, also joined in shortly after the original six.[44]

Northeast Asian functional cooperation in infrastructure, transportation, and energy has likewise been stressed by visionary intellectuals of the region, particularly since the historic Pyongyang Summit of June 2000, which made such projects appear suddenly more geopolitically feasible. Korea's president, Kim Dae-jung, enthusiastically supported this general concept of large-scale region-integrating transport architecture, which he termed the beginning of an "Iron Silk Road."[45] Shioya Takafusa, president of Japan's National Institute for Research Advancement (NIRA), likewise strongly promoted a "grand design for Northeast Asia," parallel to the Northeast Asia–centric conceptualization of Ma, Ogawa, and, in many respects, President Kim D. J. Shioya argued in 2004, for example, that a comprehensive development vision, stressing organic inter-relationships across the entire region, facilitated by ambitious new infrastructure, was essential to the sustainable joint development of Japan, China, Korea, and the Russian Far East.[46] His design is presented in Figure 5.1. The Northeast Asian community should be promoted, Shioya argued, not only through infrastructural development, as well as nongovernmental organizations (NGOs) and municipal cooperation, but also through official discussions at the national level.

Shioya, a former administrative vice minister of Japan's Economic Planning Agency, proposed an ambitious railway network—a "Big Loop" in his terminology—to connect central parts of Northeast Asia through a powerful, commerce-promoting central transportation artery. This major artery, in Shioya's vision, would start from Fukuoka and extend to Ulan Bator, Mongolia in the west and to Khabarovsk in the Russian Far East to the north, connecting Beijing, Shenyang,

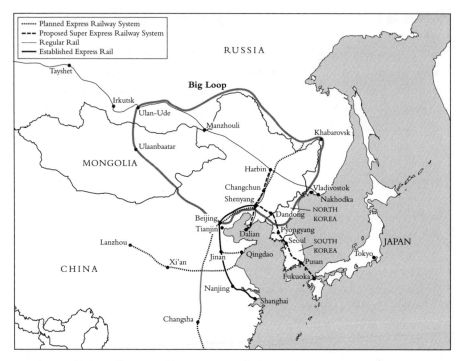

FIG. 5.1. The Grand Design of Northeast Asia

Harbin, Pyongyang, Seoul, and Tokyo. Other Japanese and South Korean analysts also repeatedly proposed a "Japan-Korea Undersea Tunnel" project. This venture, if realized, would "help Japan become a part of the Asian continent rather than an isolated island state," argued the enthusiastic former Japanese prime minister Mori Yoshiro.[47]

The 2005 Shenyang Declaration of the Northeast Asian Economic Forum augmented these early conceptual initiatives with concrete blueprints for regional cooperation, centering on energy and infrastructural development.[48] In 2007 Tianjin, another key Northeast Asian city located inside the rim of the "Shanghai Circle," hosted an important conference on China–Japan–South Korea trilateral TV programming. Experts at the conference pressed strongly for increased trilateral content exchange, on such cooperative themes as East Asian unity, and "the New Silk Road."[49]

Less ambitious, yet eminently practical proposals have also been advanced by pan-Asianist scholars in the three Northeast Asian nations. Zha Daojiong of Renmin University, a well-known energy specialist, contended in 2007, for example, that China, Japan, and Korea should collaborate on energy efficiency, bringing in governments and major firms from all three nations.[50] Gao Haihong, senior economist at the Chinese Academy of Social Sciences (CASS), argued that a consolidated regional financial institution, involving China, Japan, and South Korea, was critical to rectify the distorted financial relationship between the region's currencies and the U.S. dollar.[51]

Specialists suggested a multitude of projects, as we have seen: a Northeast Asian rail system, the Korea-Japan undersea tunnel, Northeast Asian gas and electricity pipelines, and China-Japan-Korea cooperation in the IT and high-tech industrial sectors.[52] Among China, Japan, and Korea, expanded cooperation in agriculture, oil exploration, energy efficiency, and environmental protection, not to mention trade, investment, financial collaboration, and social exchange, was both quite feasible and attractive, they suggested.[53] A creative vision of the Northeast Asian future thus emerged, distinct from broader pan-Asian notions, and more concrete, despite continuing political-economic obstacles to its actual implementation.

At the 2004 Three-Party Meeting among the leaders of China, Japan, and South Korea, Japanese foreign minister Machimura clearly stressed functional cooperation at the trilateral level, while respecting the traditionally proactive formal role played by ASEAN in regional matters.[54] Foreign Minister Li Zhaoxin of China and Foreign Minister Ban Ki-moon of South Korea concurred. They agreed that their countries should preserve their traditional ASEAN Plus Three configuration, while also fostering informal Northeast Asian ties.[55]

Expectations by some for a powerful Asia-wide framework were not realized at the inaugural East Asian Summit, held in Kuala Lumpur in late 2005. The complex relationships among China, Japan, South Korea, and the United States resulted in a final declaration that equivocated. First, at Japanese initiative and with U.S. encouragement, membership was expanded beyond the originally conceived ASEAN Plus Three framework by adding Australia, New Zealand, and India. Second, China, in response to such a transformed configuration, prevented the insertion of the East Asian Community concept in the final KL Declaration. The East Asia Summit (EAS) was thus formally demoted to being a regional institution parallel to the ASEAN Plus Three (APT), rather than replacing APT, as had been previously envisioned. Finally, despite their far greater economic scale, China and Japan nevertheless declared nominal support for ASEAN's leadership role in the EAS process.

Following the inconclusive outcome at Kuala Lumpur, however, Northeast Asian leaders, led by China, began focusing more explicitly on their own trilateral relationship. The retirement of Prime Minister Koizumi in Japan critically accelerated this process. Domestic political economic trends in all three nations also supported this new emphasis, as we shall see in Chapters 7, 8, and 9.

Chinese premier Wen Jiabao, Japanese prime minister Abe Shinzo, and Korean president Roh Moo-hyun pledged in their January 2007 ASEAN Plus Three trilateral summit side-meeting to actively promote deepening cooperation among their respective nations. "China, Japan, and the ROK are neighbors, and they are all important countries in East Asia, shouldering the common responsibility of promoting regional peace and development," Wen maintained. "This is the common aspiration of the peoples of all countries in the region, the common expectation of the international community, and accords with the developmental trends of the times." Both Abe and Roh concurred in Wen's cooperative sentiments.[56] Both leaders agreed to make positive efforts to establish a pattern of regional security, stability, and cooperation, also involving China.[57]

As the year proceeded, the trilateral Northeast Asian vision for mutual cooperation grew more concrete.[58] In May, senior foreign-affairs officials from South Korea, Japan, and China revived trilateral diplomatic cooperation with respect to economy, trade, energy, and the environment.[59] On June 3–4, 2007, the foreign ministers held exclusive trilateral talks on Jeju Island, South Korea. They not only discussed the ongoing North Korean nuclear crisis—a useful initial catalyst for deepening Northeast Asian policy dialogues—but also adopted the "Seoul Information Technology Declaration,"[60] calling for joint research in information technology and closing the digital divide between rich and poor within the region.[61] The general concept was adopted by Organization for Economic Cooperation and Development (OECD) members a year later.[62] Also at the Jeju Forum of June 2007, President Roh ambitiously proposed a Northeast Asian Economic Bloc, intended ultimately to emulate the European Union.[63]

The trilateral leadership vision appears to have been driven by two imperatives: peace in the region and accommodating the exigencies of economic growth. At the November 2007 APT Trilateral Summit, for example, Korean president Roh, Chinese premier Wen, and Japanese prime minister Fukuda Yasuo discussed the peace process on the Korean peninsula.[64] Premier Wen also presented proactive proposals for Northeast Asian regional cooperation. "We should increase our road, railway, airlines, and information telecommunications links to meet the demand of growing business ties," contended Wen.[65] For the newly inaugurated Fukuda, vigorous diplomacy in Asia was a clear linchpin of his foreign policy, as it was to be for his successors.

Korea's new president, Lee Myung-bak, later supplemented this vision of a practical, economically oriented reconciliation with his security-oriented "MB doctrine," exploring the concrete relevance to Northeast Asia of the multilateral confidence-building "Helsinki Process" of dialogue across long-standing Cold War barriers that had been successfully employed in Europe.[66]

Ideas for Northeast Asian cooperation developed rapidly during 2008, as the three countries confronted a new global financial crisis. They agreed not only to provide mutual assistance but also to coordinate external actions.[67] In October 2008, top financial policy-makers of China, Japan, and South Korea agreed to establish an emergency financial advisory body in order to "promote financial stability in Asia."[68] The South Korean government, confronted with an especially challenging external economic situation, yet flanked by the two nations with the largest foreign-exchange reserves on earth, was pushing especially hard for an Asian Monetary Fund.[69] This fund, once formed, would pool together $80 billion in liquidity, with the three Northeast Asian countries contributing 80 percent to ASEAN's 20 percent.[70]

These visionary efforts by politicians, experts, and business groups led to the historic Trilateral Summit in Fukuoka, Japan, on December 13, 2008, the first Trilateral Summit independent of broader East Asian dialogues. The Summit "opens a new chapter in the regional framework of Northeast Asia," contended South Korean foreign minister Yu Myung-hwan, Korean ambassador to Japan until February 2008.[71] At the summit, the participating leaders focused on collective measures to address the common challenges facing Northeast Asia. Yu further observed, amid the global financial crisis, that "[t]here is no sight more beautiful than a tableau of neighbors helping each other in times of difficulty."[72] Aside from the Fukuoka Summit, South Korea, driven by its own particular needs, and the massive resources of its neighbors, proposed to hold a "Korea-China-Japan Financial Summit," to address the global financial turbulence triggered by the United States through the subprime crisis, albeit within an explicitly regional context.[73] Japan's conservative *Daily Yomiuri,* among mass media, enthusiastically praised the summit, noting that "tripartite relations have entered a new stage."[74]

The deepening 2008–9 financial crisis thus proved to be a critical catalyst for the new trilateral grouping, focusing on Northeast Asia specifically, rather than on East Asia in general. China's *Renmin Ribao [People's Daily]*, with strong official connections, echoed the ROK's proposal: "With the global financial crisis deepening, economic powers of the East Asian region (China, Japan, and South Korea) should step up their regional strategic dialogue and policy coordination."[75]

As the financial crisis continued into the following year, a vision of Northeast Asian collaboration in finance gained further momentum. In April 2009, South Korea, China, and Japan agreed, at a "Trilateral Financial Supervisory Cooperation Seminar" in Seoul, to strengthen multilateral cooperation in dealing with problems caused by struggling global financial-service firms, by promoting information-sharing, and setting up standardized regulations in their financial sectors.[76] Representatives of the three countries jointly agreed that "[t]rilateral cooperation is essential to overcoming the financial crisis,"[77] and agreed to name working-level specialists to coordinate formation of a trilateral response.[78]

Stronger trilateral cultural ties were a final key element of the emerging cooperative vision. In December 2008, Chinese cultural minister Cai Wu; South Korean foreign minister Yu Myung-hwan; and Japan's Commissioner for Cultural Affairs, Aiko Tamotsu, discussed closer trilateral cooperation in the cultural-industry and heritage-promotion areas, as well as people-to-people exchanges, signing a joint declaration on South Korea's Jeju Island to promote these ends.[79] In March 2009, the Chinese minister of water resources, Chen Lei; Japan's senior vice minister of land, infrastructure, transport, and tourism, Kaneko Yasushi; and South Korea's vice minister of land, transport, and maritime affairs, Kwon Do-youp, also agreed to promote trilateral cooperation to combat common emerging water-supply challenges.[80]

Following the DPJ's August 2009 electoral victory in Japan, aspirations toward trilateral cooperation intensified still further. Prime Minister Hatoyama Yukio and DPJ Secretary General Ozawa Ichiro made early visits to both Beijing and Seoul, with Ozawa taking more than a quarter of the entire Diet to China's capital. At the October 2009 Beijing Summit, Hatoyama and his Chinese/Korean counterparts resolved to pursue early trilateral trade and investment agreements. In the resulting joint statement, the three parties also emphasized cooperation in green economy, technology sharing, clean energy, climate change, as well as management of water resources.[81]

Contending Asianist Visions

Asianist visions have acquired increasing coherence across China, Korea, and Japan over the past decade, in both intellectual and institutional dimensions, as demonstrated in this chapter and Chapter 6. Internal debates continue, however, as to the appropriate configuration of regional relations. There are three particular streams of Northeast Asian thinking on regionalism, each stressing different geographic configurations and prescriptions. The first school argues for a narrower and deeper grouping of Asian countries than heretofore, in order to counterbalance global (or U.S.) pressures, and to compete with coalitions from other regions. Adherents to this perspective prescribe a more geographically restrictive identity for Asia, and propose to establish organizations that privilege regional, as opposed to broader global, concerns.[82]

The second perspective is more liberal and cosmopolitan.[83] This school, like the first, recognizes that intraregional cooperation is important, since Asian countries face similar and distinctive developmental challenges in a steadily globalizing world. Proponents, however, argue that regional institutions should facilitate domestic reform in Asian countries, to help integrate the Asian regional economy into the global market. Regional cooperation, for these analysts, is more functional and limited than for the first group of specialists.[84]

The third regionalist perspective is incrementalist, and emphasizes breadth over depth. It stresses confidence-building measures, cultural exchanges, and the sort of comprehensive but porous regional cooperation that naturally flows from such measures, relying on spillover effects to drive integration forward.[85] Establishing a cooperative yet by no means exclusivist community of Asian countries is the ultimate goal. Subscribers to this perspective seek broader cooperation in politics and security among a wide range of Asian countries that involves few momentous, discontinuous political-economic steps.

The three schools of thought outlined above are present, to some degree, in all three Northeast Asian countries, indicating that internal debates within national borders are dynamic, and resonate transnationally. A close comparative examination of intellectual trends in these three countries also reveals, however, some important shades of difference in national conceptions of what Northeast Asia should and can potentially be. These divergent conceptions are rooted in the different historical paths that the three nations have followed, and often constrain their national approaches to envisioning Asia. In the following pages we outline these basic, country-specific differences in overall intellectual orientation regarding Northeast Asian subregionalism, and its relation to Asian regionalism more generally.

Japan's "Aimaisa": An Ambivalence in Clearly Bridging East and West

As the Japanese novelist and Nobel literature laureate Oe Kenzaburo noted in his 1994 Nobel lecture in Stockholm, entitled "Aimai-na Nihon no Watashi" ["Japan, the Ambiguous, and Myself"],[86] Japan is painfully torn between East and West, and has been since the early days of Meiji. It has a long-standing neo-Confucian heritage, but has classically needed Western technology, expertise, and political-economic connections to survive in a Euro-centric world.

Japanese people, such as Oe himself, with their Oriental heritage and Western intellectual aspirations, are existentially marked with the ambiguity of their historical circumstances. As its Northeast Asian neighbors, especially China, recover their classical power and affluence—for the first time since Perry's black ships arrived in 1854—the ambiguity grows more pronounced. Whether and how Japan bridges its two legacies—the East and West—will not only determine its own national self-perception but could ultimately also help shape the future trajectory of Asian integration itself.

In its current incarnation, the Japanese vision of Asia differs significantly from Chinese and to a lesser degree South Korean conceptions in its implicit value foundation. Although many other Asian countries urge Japan to be decisively aligned within Asia,[87] Japan is also emphatically a "Western" country. Japan's Western identity is rooted in the Meiji Restoration, which tore the country away from its feudal, neo-Confucian past and substituted European industrial prowess as a model to be emulated. That identity has been dynamically reinforced by democratic progress since World War II, as well as a strong bilateral defense alliance and deep economic ties with the United States.

For more than half a century, from the end of World War II until the very recent past, Japanese politics and foreign policy identified much more closely with counterparts in Western welfare states, especially the United States, than with Asian neighbors. Indeed, Japan has been among the most loyal allies of the U.S., both diplomatically and militarily. And its international political interaction with the G-7 advanced industrial democracies has been much more intense than that with Asia, although the priority on interaction with Asia has increased markedly since the September 2009 advent of DPJ rule.

As a consequence of Japan's persistent dual identity, it pushes for a broader and more porous regionalism than the versions propounded in China and to a lesser degree in Korea. Japan has repeatedly worked to incorporate democratic countries such as Australia, New Zealand, and India, far from East Asia's Confucian core, into regional bodies, as evidenced by its diplomatic approach to the December 2005 East Asian Summit. Clearly, shared democratic values, in part cloaking geopolitical considerations, have significantly shaped Japan's approach. Also, with countries such as India onboard, Japan is less fearful of isolation on issues relating to World War II history than if it were locked into narrower, China-centric regional arrangements like ASEAN Plus Three. Overall, Japan seeks a formula for Asian regionalism that allows Tokyo both to play a leading role and to marginally enhance its autonomy of the West without alienating its important American ally.[88]

China's Dilemma: How to Exert Rising Power

Beijing has strongly favored the new Asian regionalism since 1997, as represented by the ASEAN Plus Three framework and various narrower, Northeast Asia–centric processes, such as the Six-Party Talks and the recent trilateral Northeast Asian summits. These mechanisms both help stabilize the increasingly interdependent region and also enhance its autonomy of the West—a major long-term Chinese strategic objective. The PRC's own leadership within Asia, however, is greatly constrained by China's own hegemonic past as the "Middle Kingdom" in Asia before the arrival of the West, as well as by geopolitical unease in many corners of the world at rising Chinese military and economic power.

In contrast to Japanese efforts to conceptualize and lead a broad, open, globally oriented Asian regionalism, epitomized in the Asia Pacific Economic Cooperation (APEC) or the 2005 Kuala Lumpur East Asian Summit configuration,[89] China has pursued a deeper and narrower variant, focused on a more limited range of contiguous nations of political-economic importance to Beijing. Importantly, China's concerns for domestic development and the stability of its neighborhood, as cross-Straits relations undergo historic transformation, have led the government to focus increasingly on Northeast Asia—geographically, economically, and culturally the portion of the world most intimately connected to China. The intellectual and policy debates in Beijing surrounding the Sino-Japan relationship attest to this strategic vision.

In 2002, for example, Ma Licheng argued for a "new perspective toward Japan," amid rampant anti-Japanese nationalism in China, as we have noted. He emphatically maintained that China's grave challenges had domestic, not foreign, origins, and China's only correct policy toward Japan was "friendship."[90] Tang Shiping, a prominent scholar at CASS, shared similar views. Tang argued that China's uttermost diplomatic goal should be securing a peaceful external environment, with consolidating the Sino-Japan relationship as a central objective. Further, China should reorient its grand strategy to emphasize China-Japan-U.S. trilateral ties, rather than the previous focus on China-U.S. relations.[91] The leading scholar on China's grand strategy, Shi Yinhong, concurred, arguing that China should implement an innovative policy toward Japan to help promote Northeast Asian integration, and thus gain global leverage.[92]

Although Sino-Japanese bilateral ties worsened from 2003 to 2005, many Chinese scholars continued to advocate stronger relations with Japan, and deeper regional cooperation within Northeast Asia. Their arguments gradually came to influence official policies in China, particularly following the bilateral diplomatic crisis of 2005. The Sino-Japanese relationship improved dramatically during late 2006, after Koizumi left office, and scholarly opinion in the PRC grew even more enthusiastic about Sino-Japanese entente. In 2007, Shi Yinhong stressed again that China's peaceful rise could be ensured only by developing close ties with regional neighbors. China's rise would, in Shi's view, in turn strengthen regional stability and prosperity.[93]

In 2008, when the Trilateral Summit was held in Fukuoka, Chinese prime minister Wen Jiabao underlined the importance to the PRC of trilateral ties with

Japan and South Korea, putting forward concrete proposals for enhancing them. "China, Japan, and South Korea are countries of major influence in East Asia," said Wen, adding, "Developing peaceful and friendly relations is not only a common wish of the three nations, but a precondition for realizing regional stability and prosperity."[94]

Since the 1997 financial crisis, China has undertaken multiple regional initiatives, stimulating significant progress in broader East Asian cooperation. The PRC, for instance, negotiated an FTA with ASEAN in 2000, and helped establish the Shanghai Cooperation Organization (SCO), including both Russia and the major Central Asian states, in 2001. Meanwhile, the PRC's relationship with South Korea improved significantly also, culminating in a landmark visit by Roh Moo-hyun to Beijing in 2003. Since 2006, China has been clearly supportive of "a unified economic entity" in Northeast Asia, and has pursued domestic policies, such as its northeastern development scheme, that further enhance that prospect.[95]

Such policies, however, have stirred vigorous discussions worldwide about the revival of a China-led tributary system.[96] Although mainstream Chinese scholars and officials claim no intention of reasserting their country's traditional imperial dominance in the region, the "Middle Kingdom" mentality still clearly exists in some circles within both China and South Korea.[97] The actual operation of the SCO has been illustrative in this regard. At the 2006 SCO convention, for example, China bestowed lavish hospitality on, and advanced lucrative economic deals to, several visiting heads of other states in return for their deference, in the ancient tributary tradition.[98]

China's immediate neighbors in Asia, beginning with Japan, are understandably skeptical of the merits of reviving the classic tributary system.[99] South Korea and ASEAN, although receptive to Chinese overtures in past centuries, are now both resistant to any possible repeat of their bitter early-twentieth-century subordination to Japan, under the auspices of another Asian power.[100] As sovereign states for more than half a century, they are unlikely to accept anything not based on national equality as an organizing principle for broader regional relationships—the standard applied, after all, to relations within ASEAN. South Korea's 2005–6 disputes with China over the historical role of Koguryo, arguably Korea's ancestor state, suggest that the legacy of China's ancient tributary system continues to complicate the PRC's relationship with its smaller neighbors. In the course of the 2008 Olympic Torch Relay, for example, many Koreans similarly viewed xenophobic Chinese youths' behavior as an indication that "the ancient notion of China being the center of the world is re-emerging, both in the public psyche and in government policies."[101]

China clearly has rising political-economic leverage in Northeast Asia, flowing from its remarkable, sustained economic growth, and the gradual normalization of once-tense relations with its neighbors. The 2008–9 global economic crisis may have enhanced the PRC's leverage still further, by curtailing the economic capacity of the United States to mobilize geopolitically.[102] Beijing may also be benefiting from a historic relaxation of long-standing cross-Straits tensions. Yet a crucial precondition for China in realizing its new latent influence, and directing it concretely, needs to be the emergence of a future vision for its international relationships. That emerging vision appears to focus much more explicitly on Northeast Asia than has been true in the past, as a result of recent Taiwan-related developments, waning of history-related tensions, and economic considerations.

For Beijing, Taiwan has loomed large in China's domestic context ever since 1949, as an unfinished element of national unification. Recently it has gained enhanced significance for both domestic and regional foreign-policy reasons that in turn motivate the PRC to give unprecedented attention to relations with its Northeast Asian neighbors more generally. In the domestic context, the advent of the conciliatory Ma Ying-jeou administration in Taiwan may encourage Beijing to be optimistic about prospects for further deepening of its influence in Taiwan itself.

Precisely for that reason, neutralizing possible resistance to deepened Beijing-Taipei relations among Taiwan's neighbors—particularly Japan—becomes increasingly important for the PRC. This was a factor from 2006 to 2009 behind conciliatory Chinese policies toward Japanese conservatives traditionally close to Taiwan, such as Abe Shinzo and Aso Taro. Breaking the strength of Japan's Taiwan lobby could help substantially in paving the way for ultimate Chinese reunification, which may help to explain the appointment in 2008 of master PRC diplomat Wang Yi, vice minister of foreign affairs and ambassador to Tokyo during the critical 2004–8 period, as head of the Office of Taiwan Affairs.[103] Wang Yi, not coincidentally, is the first diplomat and the first Japan specialist ever to occupy that highly strategic position, relating centrally to China's reunification.

Conciliation continued and even intensified following the advent of Japan's DPJ administration in September 2009. China accorded both Prime Minister Hatoyama and DPJ leader Ozawa warm welcomes, with Ozawa bringing over 140 Diet members and around 500 business people to Beijing in December 2009.[104] In early 2010 the PRC appointed Cheng Yonghua, one of its most experienced Northeast Asia hands as ambassador to Tokyo. Previously ambassador to Seoul, Cheng had lived for 18 years in Japan, graduated from Soka University, and spoke impeccable Japanese, to complement his fluent Korean.

South Korea's Choice: Power Balancer or
Institutional Broker in Northeast Asia?

Sandwiched between the hesitant stances of Japan and China is the more balanced and assertive regionalism of South Korea. Small countries are usually big winners in the emergence of multilateral regional institutions, as the history of European, Latin American, and Southeast Asian regionalism also suggests.[105] Multilateral institutions tend, when middle-power mediation efforts operate effectively, to channel big-power confrontation in an orderly, nonthreatening fashion. Disputes among major powers can thus be resolved without resorting to military, political, or economic warfare. It is consequently in the interest of smaller nations to ensure that confrontation among major powers is reduced to innocuous levels: "When the whales fight, it is the shrimp that get hurt [*gorae saumae, saeoo tojinda*]," as the Korean saying goes.[106]

The evolution of Asian regionalism since 1997 suggests that relatively small powers such as South Korea and the nations of ASEAN can nevertheless play pivotal roles in determining the pace and scope of regional institution-building, provided that those smaller powers understand both the possibilities and the limits of their potentially pivotal roles. ASEAN Plus Three, for example, was jointly initiated by ASEAN and South Korea, later being also supported by China and Japan. President Kim Dae-jung was a particularly visionary, catalytic leader, who initiated three major regional advisory bodies—the East Asia Vision Group, the East Asia Study Group, and the Network of East Asian Think Tanks, amid the Asian financial crisis (AFC) critical juncture. The East Asia Vision Group final report, in which South Korea's aspirations for Asia's future were best epitomized, presented concrete visions for the Asian community and specific steps for achieving them. The idea of a high-level East Asian leaders' conclave, for example, which was ultimately realized in the December 2005 Kuala Lumpur East Asian Summit, originated in the EAVG report of 2002.

Smaller powers such as South Korea and ASEAN can also potentially play the systemically pivotal role of "power balancer" or "mediator." They can ally with one another to constrain big powers, or bandwagon with one substantial power to resist another by exploiting contradictions among larger nations. More constructively, the "shrimps" can use their nonthreatening profile to facilitate understanding and stable relationships among the "whales."

To be sure, ASEAN's strategic moves since the 1978 Vietnamese invasion of Cambodia demonstrate aspirations to this role of "power balancer."[107] South Korea, on the other hand, has been less active along these lines, except during the

Kim Young-sam and Roh Moo-hyun years (1993–98 and 2003–8). The ROK's more productive and more typical role since the 1990s has been that of mediator. Seoul has, for example, helped to incorporate China into regional dialogues. It also maintains extensive political-economic ties to Japan and the United States.

The ROK's ability to mediate coherently, however, is often constrained by populist pressures driven by its complex history with both Japan and America.[108] During Roh Moo-hyun's years (2003–8), South Korea, driven by nationalist pressures, often tried to pursue a "balancing" role in Northeast Asia.[109] Its potential as a strategic and visionary institution-builder in Northeast Asia, however, remains far from fulfilled. The Lee Myung-bak government since 2008 has advanced "pragmatic diplomacy," especially toward Japan. This new approach has borne significant fruit in promoting the Making of Northeast Asia, thanks also to proactive regionalist responses from Beijing and Tokyo. Successful in dealing with conservative leaders Fukuda and Aso, it also induced the more progressive Japanese leader Hatoyama to make his first international visits, as both party leader and prime minister, to Seoul.

Other Regional Actors

Mongolia and North Korea—two geographically Northeast Asian countries largely detached from the rest of the region—have traditionally played only marginal roles in regional integration. This pattern is gradually changing. Mongolia, for example, has expressed a strong desire to participate in Northeast Asian community activities, and even to play a catalytic role in regional integration, based on its wealth of raw materials, its central location between Russia and China, and its positive ties with both North and South Korea. Democratic political transition within Mongolia since the early 1990s has intensified that long-isolated nation's interest in playing an active regional role, so as to enhance its autonomy from two giant authoritarian capitalist neighbors.

As a consequence of changing regional and domestic-political dynamics, Ulan Bator has become a key intermediary between Pyongyang and the broader region. Mongolia is now also an observer in the SCO, and has proposed participating in ASEAN Plus Three. Its rail system and mining industry, especially strong in coal and nonferrous metals, are developing rapidly, capitalizing on both China's growing energy demand and Japan's infrastructure-building technology and financial assistance.

Both China and Japan also seem supportive of bringing Mongolia into a closer relationship with the rest of Northeast Asia. In China's view, Northeast Asian integration has not progressed rapidly enough, and adding Mongolia may accelerate this process, by geographically knitting the region together more closely.[110] Japan, which seeks more involvement on the Asian continent so as to balance China, likewise views Mongolia's new engagement with Northeast Asian regionalism favorably. So does South Korea, with which Mongolia has recently developed intimate ties.[111]

North Korea, whether it continues to exist in the future or collapses, could potentially become a focal point of Northeast Asian infrastructure-building and energy cooperation, should nuclear tensions with the broader region be reduced. Reconciliation between the two Koreas has already deepened remarkably since the June 2000 Pyongyang Summit. The northeastern provinces of China have been quietly investing since 1991 in special economic zones (SEZs) within the Democratic People's Republic of Korea (DPRK), such as Rajin, Chongjin, and Sonbong. In 2002, North Korea also established a special administrative region (SAR) at Sinuiju on the Chinese border, as well as an SEZ in Kaesong, ancient Korea's traditional capital, just north of the DMZ. In 2003, the Kaesong Industrial Complex was founded. By April 2009, more than one hundred South Korean companies were operating in Kaesong, and over 39,000 North Korean workers were employed there.[112] In light of military escalation in May 2009, North Korea disrupted the normal operation of the industrial park, while refraining from closing it, and resuming normal operations three months later.[113] The future of North Korea's position in the Making of Northeast Asia is thus critically uncertain. Its intermittently obstructionist steps, however, appear unlikely to disrupt the broader integration dynamic of Northeast Asia, which is driven strongly by cross-Straits and Sino-Japanese reconciliation. Indeed, North Korea's belligerence and unpredictability often help bring its neighbors closer to one another.

In Conclusion

Northeast Asian regional cooperation is now at a critical transition point. Since the 1997 Asian financial crisis, regional integration has been quietly proceeding, despite loud disagreements, especially between China and Japan, over matters such as Yasukuni Shrine visits. From late 2006, however, following the retirement of Koizumi Junichiro as Japanese prime minister, regional integration, supported by those deepening working-level policy networks, began to regain momentum more overtly, aided by the advent during 2008 of the Lee administration in South Korea, and the Ma administration in Taiwan. The three Northeast Asian countries do indeed have different preferences regarding regional integration. Yet a more consolidated Northeast Asia is nevertheless emerging, rooted in four structural and intellectual characteristics that differentiate the current pan-Asianism and its political expressions from their predecessors.

The new, Northeast Asia-oriented Asianism, first of all, is grounded in a more equitable distribution of power in the region than has traditionally prevailed. Japan remains the strongest economic power in East Asia, to be sure, but China and South Korea are rapidly catching up, while much of ASEAN is languishing. China, with a substantial nuclear-weapons capacity, and a broad range of conventional weapons, is no doubt formidable militarily. Yet its power-projection capabilities are constrained by U.S. bases in Japan and Korea, and also by Japan's own vastly underestimated high-tech military machine. Meanwhile, the U.S. security role in Northeast Asia, although important, is arguably less dominant than it was a decade ago, in part the result of American entanglements in the Middle East.

The new Northeast Asianism is also supported by the strong mutual interest of its adherents. This variant of regionalism was initially propelled by the financial crisis of 1997, and reinforced by the crisis of 2008. It is also strengthened by common developmental challenges that China, Japan, and Korea all confront. As Northeast Asian economies become more integrated into global markets, U.S. business interests in the region could also potentially grow. Without rejecting globalization, Northeast Asian regional cooperation can prospectively deliver substantial economic gains—not only for the region but for the United States as well. The region's vision could potentially grow more exclusivist, but this seems unlikely, because of persisting economic, social, and security ties across the Pacific. Northeast Asia's rising cohesion will take place within a multitiered global system, within which trans-Pacific ties will continue to represent one important layer.

The new Asianism, thirdly, is supported by increasingly global networks, which help allow Asianism and broader cosmopolitanism to coexist. The cross-border expansion of those networks is steady and proactive, allowing Northeast Asian nations to explore ideas for regional cooperation, to recommend regional policies to governments, and to engage the business communities of multiple nations. Regional networks have a Southeast Asian dimension, to be sure, but the Northeast Asian element, as China grows even as historical tensions with Japan subside, is increasingly dominant. The shared belief of the network members in a cooperative Asia, knowledgeable about economics, finance, and institutional design, with substantial cross-national connective capability, is also making regional networks themselves strong advocates for regional integration.

The new Asianism, finally, is also supported by an unprecedented intensification of interdependence within Northeast Asia in terms of trade, production networks, and social interactions. That interdependence is steadily deepening, even as tensions instilled by a bitter yet receding history gradually subside. This process of region-building we see unfolding before our eyes. In the country-specific chapters to follow, we chronicle its progress within the key nations of the region—China, Japan, and South Korea. And we likewise show how together the domestic politics of these nations increasingly foster a geopolitically important new political-economic reality that has already begun emerging at the intellectual level: the Making of Northeast Asia.

6

A Deepening Web of Regional Connectedness

The Asian financial crisis of 1997–98 was a clear critical juncture in Northeast Asian institution-building. Intraregional interactions since then have grown much more vigorous than before, with rising trade interdependence and deepening production networks clearly manifest. Regional epistemic networks forged during the 1997 financial crisis have since continued to expand, deepen, and assume a life of their own, playing increasingly significant roles in regional policy-making. Even military forces have begun developing ties with their counterparts, in unprecedented ways.

Despite the still complicated bilateral relationships across the region at the national level, burdened by history and geopolitics, local governments in China, Japan, and South Korea have begun to engage one another vigorously. Economic, social, and political interaction among the civil societies of the three countries is also steadily deepening. And even national leaders are growing increasingly reconciled with one another, transcending substantial differences among their respective nations in historical interpretation. Bottom-up regionalization trends, synergistic with reinvigorated top-down institution-building, are creating an ever more heavily networked Northeast Asia, with positive policy implications that the pessimistic conventional wisdom manifestly fails to appreciate.[1]

On the eve of the 1997 Asian financial crisis, Katzenstein and Shiraishi wrote generally about "network power," stressing the apolitical, static nature of interpersonal linkages across Asia.[2] The novel sociopolitical dynamic now emerging, which involves substantial intergovernmental cooperation and soft institution-building, is rather different from what they envisioned, with fateful long-term implications. Indeed, networks—profoundly political and social, as well as economic—are the cornerstone in the making of a much more cohesive, Northeast Asia than has ever before existed in the post–World War II era.

Deepening Trade Relations: A Key Basis for Networks

Northeast Asian economies, which surprised much of the world with their dynamic ability to overtake the West, have long been deeply enmeshed in the global trading system. Their trade strategy has forged deep and symbiotic links to global markets, as well as intimate and efficient production networks closer to home.[3] Intraregional trade within Northeast Asia has recently shown much stronger growth than have overall trade figures for the nations in question. Indeed, even China's regional trade has grown more rapidly, for nearly a decade, than its hitherto dynamic commerce with the United States.

Each of the three Northeast Asian countries has historically relied on the U.S. export market. Yet although exports to the United States remain important to their economic growth, reliance on the U.S. market, as a share of total exports, has been steadily declining in *all* three countries since 2002—*including* China. And in Japan and Korea that decline has been continuing, as suggested in Figure 6.1, since the late 1980s, when Japan's and Korea's exports to the U.S. occupied nearly 40 percent of their total exports to the world. Today neither country sends even half that ratio to the United States, and both export far more heavily to China.

In terms of trade volume, each of these three countries' regional trade within Northeast Asia has also recently *surpassed* its trade with the U.S.[4] For South Korea, such intra–Northeast Asian trade was roughly equal to trade with the United States in 1991, yet slowly surpassed the latter during 1992–97, as Figure 6.2 suggests. Today, South Korea's intraregional trade, with Japan and Greater China, is now more than twice as large as that with the U.S. Korea's trade with the People's Republic of China (PRC) alone now substantially exceeds its trade with the United States. In 2008, that Sino-Korean trade approached $200 billion, more than double trade with the United States ($83.6 billion). Korea's trade with Japan was also $10 billion larger than its trade with the U.S.

Japan's trade dependence on continental Northeast Asia has likewise deepened sharply since 1997. Indeed, as Figure 6.2 suggests, the 1997 Asian financial crisis (AFC) appears to have been a decisive watershed, with Japan's intra–Northeast Asian trade intensifying sharply thereafter. Prior to the AFC, Japan's trade with the U.S. was more than 50 percent larger than its combined trade with Chinese and Korean neighbors.[5] By 2003, however, Japan's total intraregional trade had outstripped that with America. In 2007 and 2008, Japan's trade with China alone surpassed that with the United States, by increasing margins.[6]

FIG. 6.1. Declining Export Dependence on the U.S. Market (percentage). Source: IMF, *Direction of Trade*, 1980–2009 editions. For data on Taiwan, the ROC Bureau of International Trade, Foreign Trade Statistics, http://cus93.trade.gov.tw/bftweb/english/ FSCE/FSC001 1E.ASP.

The PRC, ironically, is the Northeast Asian nation now most economically dependent on the U.S., despite persistent Sino-American geopolitical differences. Although China's trade with Japan and South Korea combined has been clearly larger than its trade with the United States, the PRC's gap between intraregional and trans-Pacific trade has recently been the smallest among the three Northeast Asian countries, because of extensive processing of components originating elsewhere in Northeast Asia, for ultimate consumption in the U.S. market. Over more than two decades, from the early 1980s, Japan was the largest trading partner of China, being surpassed only by the United States in 2003. Recently, however, the increase in intra–Northeast Asian trade has been faster than the increase with the U.S., even for China, as suggested in Figure 6.2. Korea's explosively growing trade with China has more than balanced the more subdued pace of Japan's traditionally larger transactions with the ROK.

The bilateral patterns of deepening intraregional trade within "Greater China," presented in Figure 6.3, are also instructive, and potentially indicative of broader geoeconomic transitions underway. Hong Kong's and Taiwan's regional economic relationships, with both each other and the Chinese Mainland, for example, are

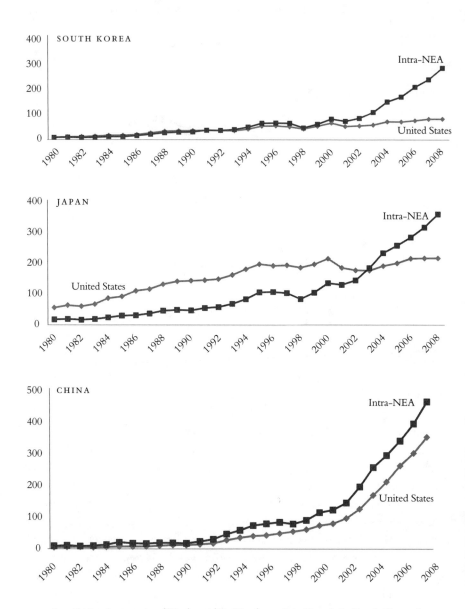

FIG. 6.2. Rising Intraregional Trade within Northeast Asia: Trends in South Korea, Japan, and China (1980–2008) ($ billion). Northeast Asia here refers to China, Japan, and South Korea. Source: International Monetary Fund, *Direction of Trade*, 1980–2009 editions.

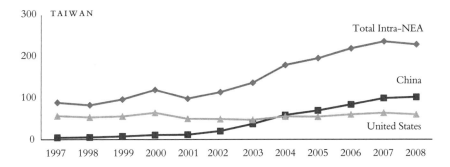

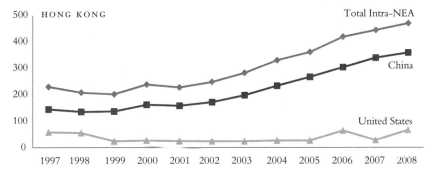

FIG. 6.3. Taiwan and Hong Kong's Rising Northeast Asia Reliance (U.S.$ billion). Note: Total intra-NEA includes Japan, South Korea, Mainland China, Taiwan, and Hong Kong. Source: Original data for Taiwan are derived from Republic of China Bureau of Foreign Trade statistics, and for Hong Kong from IMF, *Direction of Trade*, 1997–2009 editions.

rapidly intensifying. These trading patterns are also being reinforced by political developments.[7] Since KMT president Ma Ying-jeou came to office in March 2008, the three direct links (air, sea, and postal) were established across the Straits, and passenger flights have become regularized. By December 2009, the weekly number of cross-Straits passenger flights had reached 290. Before October, 2008, there were no regular flights at all.[8]

Taiwan's trade with Northeast Asia and especially Mainland China has been rising steadily for many years, while its trade dependence on the United States has conversely declined. As suggested in Figure 6.3, the U.S. was Taiwan's largest trading partner until 2003, when it was surpassed by Japan. In 2005, despite serious political tensions across the Taiwan Straits, the Mainland emerged as Taiwan's largest trading partner, and has since strongly consolidated that position. Japan has maintained its second position, and the U.S has declined to third. As recently as 1997, the Mainland did not even place among the top ten trading partners of Taiwan; indeed, it lagged even Malaysia as a Taiwanese trading partner. The return to KMT governance in March 2008 sharply enhanced Taiwan's economic relations with Mainland China, through the relaxation in travel and other long-standing restrictions that it set in motion.

Hong Kong's dependence on Mainland trade started earlier and has historically been much deeper than that of Taiwan. During the 1990s, Hong Kong's absolute trade with the United States remained static, but its Northeast Asian trade dependence nevertheless increased. The most dramatic shift in Hong Kong's external trade was naturally with the Mainland, especially following 1997 reversion. Indeed, mutual interdependence has intensified substantially since 2001, as Mainland Chinese growth has accelerated. In 1999, China was already the largest trading partner of Hong Kong. By 2005, however, the gap between Hong Kong's trade with the Mainland and dealings with other major partners had widened dramatically. As suggested in Figure 6.3, Hong Kong's trade with Mainland China in 2008 was well over five times as large as its trade with the United States.

To be sure, most of the growth in Taiwan's and Hong Kong's external trade occurred with the Mainland. Yet it is a larger economic story than that of "Greater China" alone. On the one hand, much of the gain in trading with the Mainland took place in the process of relocating labor-intensive manufacturing from other Northeast Asian economies to the PRC, taking advantage of the latter's abundant cheap labor. On the other, absolute trade volume between the two Chinese economies and Japan and South Korea to the north has also clearly grown. Between Taiwan and the ROK, for example, trade almost tripled between 1997 and 2008, from $7.8 billion to $22.7 billion. Between Taiwan and Japan, trade also increased, from $43 billion to $67 billion during the same period. Similarly, Hong Kong–ROK trade almost doubled in that decade, from $12 billion to $21 billion, while Hong Kong–Japan trade also gained, from $40 billion to $53 billion.[9]

Deepening Intrasectoral Linkages

Intraindustry trade within Northeast Asia has traditionally been quite low.[10] This pattern has, however, begun to change dramatically since 1997. Studies on the auto and electronics industries suggest a particular increase in intrasectoral trade among China, Japan, and South Korea in those sectors.[11]

The main export items produced by Korea and China, for example, are in similar areas—namely, electronics goods and machinery. Five of the ten principal Korean exports to China, and the ten main Chinese exports to Korea, substantially overlap in sectoral terms.[12] Intraindustry trade between Korea and Japan has also grown. Five of the 10 principal Korean exports to Japan overlapped in 1998, but seven products overlapped in 2003, together with the ten principal exports of Japan to Korea.[13]

Emerging Production Networks in Northeast Asia

Since the 1980s, particularly following the 1985 Plaza Accord, which led to a doubling in the value of the yen by December 1987, and a massive surge of Japanese direct investment into Asia, intra-Asian production networks have been central to the corporate business plans of such major Japanese firms as Canon and Matsushita Electric.[14] Investment flows have served as a key driver of economic integration across Asia. Japan has historically been a major source of foreign direct investment (FDI), and the majority of its investment traditionally went to the United States and Southeast Asia. In 1996, for example, Japanese FDI to the U.S. was almost five times the size of Japanese FDI to China ($11.1 billion versus $2.3 billion). And Japanese FDI flowing to the Association of Southeast Asian Nations (ASEAN) was almost double the scale of that to China.

These trends have sharply eroded since 1997, with Japanese investment increasing in Asia at the expense of the U.S. Within Japan's Asian investment, FDI to China has also been growing rapidly at the expense of that flowing toward ASEAN. In 2004, Japan committed $10.5 billion to Asia and only $7.6 billion to North America. By 2006, Japan's new Asian investment had risen to $17.2 billion compared with a little over $10 billion going to North America. And between China and the U.S., the shift was especially clear in those years. In 2003, Japan's new FDI in China totaled less than $4 billion, but increased to $5.9 billion just a year later. Conversely, Japanese investment in the U.S. was $10.7 billion in 2003, but declined to less than $7.6 billion during 2004.[15] Because of the massive anti-Japan demonstrations in the PRC during 2005, the shift has slowed down somewhat thereafter. With U.S economic recession and Sino-Japanese joint commitment to develop a green economy, as suggested at the October 2009 Beijing Trilateral Summit, Japan's investment in China is expected to grow steadily in the future.

There has also been a major shift in the locus of new Japanese investment from Southeast to Northeast Asia since 1997. Japan's investment in the ASEAN-4 nations, for example, declined continuously from 1997 to 2003. Conversely, Japan's investment into China steadily grew during this period. Since 2003, Japanese investment in ASEAN has revived somewhat, especially in Vietnam, but its primary Asian locus continues to be China. In 2005, however, new Japanese investments there were inhibited by massive anti-Japan demonstrations, with some investment bound for China shifting to Southeast Asia instead. With the improvement in bilateral Sino-Japanese political relations since late 2006, however, China has regained its preeminent position versus Southeast Asia with respect to Japanese overseas investment.

After the 1997 Asian financial crisis, the thrust of Korea's foreign direct invest-

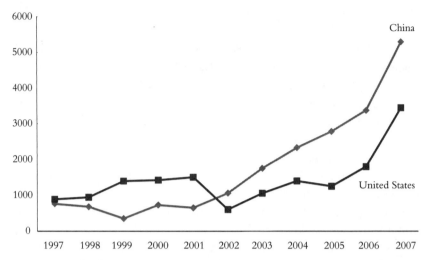

FIG. 6.4. Growth of Korean Investment in China since the Asian Financial Crisis (1997–2007). ($ million). Source: Korean Exim Bank, *Foreign Direct Investment Statistics*, 2007 edition, www.koreaexim.go.kr. Figures are for new investment flows.

ment also shifted from the United States to China. The reorientation has been dramatic, as suggested in Figure 6.4. In 1999, Korea's FDI in China was less than $366 million, while that in the United States was nearly six times larger. By 2002, the pattern had completely reversed, with Korea's new FDI in China rising to more than $1 billion, or nearly double new investment in the U.S. Between 2002 and 2006, Korea's investment flows to the U.S. revived to some degree, due in particular to the building of new automobile plants there. Yet in 2006, Korea's direct investment into China still remained nearly twice as large as that into the U.S., at $3.3 billion versus $1.8 billion.[16] Despite short-term fluctuations, this general orientation toward China rather than the U.S. has now continued for more than a decade.

Hong Kong's and Taiwan's direct investment in Mainland China has also expanded substantially since the Asian financial crisis. In 1998, for example, investment in Mainland China absorbed 40 percent of Hong Kong's total outward-direct capital flows. This share nearly doubled, to a massive 78 percent of Hong Kong's outbound investment, in 2000. By 2003, Taiwan's investment in China had grown to more than six times that of 1999, constituting over 75 percent of Taiwan's total overseas investment. The share of Taiwanese investment in Mainland China's own total direct capital inflows also nearly doubled, from 8 percent in 1993 to 14 percent a decade later. Although Taiwan's share declined during the Chen Shui-bian years, reaching only 3.4 percent in 2006, and 2.4 percent in 2008, by all indications it began to surge again following the election of Ma Ying-jeou. And even at the recent reduced levels, Taiwan's investments in China have been comparable quantitatively to FDI from the entire United States, which has roughly fifteen times Taiwan's population, and thirty-seven times its GDP.[17]

Increasing intraregional investment has produced an ever more integrated trading structure in Northeast Asia, with China becoming the center of both regional production and assembly. New trade triangles have emerged in which components are exported to China for processing and assembly, with finished products then being sold on world markets, displacing exports from other countries farther south.[18] Taiwan, in particular, is becoming an important producer of intermediate-level components and commodity semiconductors, which are highly complementary to the PRC's labor-intensive assembly potential for finished electronic goods. Improvements in Taiwan's political-economic relations with Mainland China, building on Taiwan's established ties with Japan and Korea, are thus accelerating the emergence and growth of broader regional production networks, especially in consumer electronics.[19]

With its own hierarchical division of labor, involving some outsourcing to Southeast Asia and elsewhere, Northeast Asia is clearly emerging as an integrated manufacturing complex, to supply the world as a whole. Korean and Taiwanese firms produce in Mainland China with capital equipment and raw materials drawn from their home bases. They then export finished products back home, to the United States as well as Japan, and to the broader world market. It is also typical for Japanese producers and assemblers to move their intermediate production to China and then export finished products back to Japan.[20]

How Northeast Asian Production Networks Operate

There are three key institutional vehicles for informal economic integration in Northeast Asia: (1) corporate industrial groups like Japanese *keiretsu* or Korean *chaebol*; (2) ethnic Chinese business networks, many based in Hong Kong and Taiwan; and (3) a variety of subregional economic zones, or natural economic territories (NETs).[21] These distinctive economic structures have helped promote phenomenal growth across Asia generally, while also integrating the northeast part of the region as a unit centrally into broader Asian trade and production networks. Any explanation for Asian political-economic development that focuses solely on individual countries cannot capture the complex transnational integration dynamics that are now vigorously underway, and that have a distinct geographic dimension, centering on the Shanghai Circle.

In the auto industry, production has also shown a pattern of regional integration based on national specialization. Major Japanese and Korean auto manufacturers, such as Toyota, Honda, and Hyundai, have established production facilities in China and Southeast Asia. Core components are generally produced in their home countries, while subsidiary components such as brakes, spark plugs, and windshield wipers are sourced locally. The local assembly plants for these companies in China then assemble parts and components into finished products for both the Chinese and global markets.

A similar pattern is emerging in the fashion industry. Pace-setting firms in Tokyo, Osaka, Seoul, and Hong Kong, such as Uniqlo and Giordano, work with designers and marketing strategists to conceive attractive new apparel. They fax or e-mail cutouts for new coats, suits, and blouses to affiliates in Harbin or Dalian in China for manufacture, simultaneously ordering upscale cloth by e-mail from South Korea. Weeks later the stylish new garment—the work of many hands in many nations—ends up on clothes racks from Shinagawa and Seoul to Salt Lake City.

In Eastern China surrounding Shanghai, Northeast Asian regional production networks are ubiquitous. Chen Feng, a textile-exporting company in Jiangsu Province, for example, imported thousands of technologies from Japan during the 1990s. Today it has a production capacity of 38 million pieces of apparel annually. For the most part, the company produces clothes to order for Japanese, American, and Korean companies, with designs and many specialized fabrics imported from elsewhere in the region. Japanese orders, in particular, fill more than half of Chen Feng's annual production inventory.[22]

South Korea and Northern China, including Shandong, have also developed vigorous transnational production networks with each other. The top products among Korea's imports from and exports to China have been electrical and mechanical equipment, often also including specialized Japanese components. The largest sector of Korea's investment in China is also electronics and manufacturing equipment.[23] Overall, around 75 percent of Korean direct investment in China is concentrated in manufacturing sectors, and most manufactured Chinese exports back to Korea are mediated by Korean firms.

Since China's 2001 accession to the World Trade Organization (WTO), in particular, Korean companies have begun substantial investments in the PRC. By 2004, Samsung, for example, had invested $2.7 billion in China, and by 2005 employed 50,000 Chinese workers at its twenty-nine factories in the PRC. Lucky Goldstar had invested $2 billion and was continuing to expand.[24] In 2003, Hyundai planned a total investment of $1.1 billion in Chinese auto manufacturing by 2010.[25]

Korean firms have also been making substantial investments in parts and components all across Northeast Asia. In particular, Korea's input share in China's final exports of parts has risen substantially over the past decade, tripling during the 1996 to 2003 period alone.[26] China's share in Korean exports of auto parts increased nearly tenfold over the four short years from 1999 to 2003, substantially faster than even Japan's significant expansion of exports from its Chinese production bases.[27]

This growth in auto-sector intraindustry trade has been driven largely by China's increasing demand for vehicles assembled by joint-ventures in which Japanese and Korean companies were participants—most notably Toyota, Honda, Nissan, and Hyundai. All of these Northeast Asian firms have increased their share of the Chinese market at the expense of the traditionally dominant Western players, VW and GM. In 2005, Hyundai/Kia emerged as the most successful automotive brand in China.[28] The competition has since become fierce, with all the major auto manufacturers churning out new models and opening new sales outlets, vying to capture a bigger share of the world's largest auto market, and one of the most rapidly growing.[29] As of 2009, Hyundai/Kia remained the third most popular brand there.

Xin Kai Digital, based in Dalian, Northeast China's largest port city, is a good case of the truly regional Northeast Asian production-network pattern discussed here.[30] Xin Kai was established in 1990, as a licensed dealer for Japanese-made Panasonic products in China. By 2005 it had expanded into diverse business operations, including manufacturing, research, and design, while acquiring 15 affiliates, 850 licensed stores, 3,000 chain stores, and 200 repair shops in major cities across China.

Regional production networks across Northeast Asia are the lifeline of Xin Kai's operation. Partnership with Japanese and Korean firms has provided the firm with more advanced product designs than its domestic competitors. Xin Kai, for example, remains one of the few Chinese manufacturers to produce color ink for printers. It was able to do so by forming a joint venture with Hanson of South Korea in the early 2000s. Xin Kai is also one of China's first movers in manufacturing LCDs, big-screen TVs, and multimedia TV screens. The core parts are typically sourced from Japan, with final assembly in China.

Xin Kai's R&D department also conducts research on contract for Japanese, Korean, and Taiwanese firms. Mitsui, for example, often places orders for concrete R&D tasks. When the results emerge from the Chinese firm's R&D center, Mitsui purchases the resultant output for resale in Japan. Xin Kai also purchases patents from Japan, manufacturing products, ranging from beer containers to fax machines, locally in Dalian while also selling its finished products to Mitsui, which in turn markets them in Japan.

Xin Kai's production networks operate as follows: (1) technology (or materials) from Japan; (2) component manufacturing in China; (3) marketing and specialized processing in Japan; and (4) export of finished products from China to the world. Xin Kai, for example, purchases patented materials from Japan to manufacture beer trays at the request of the Japanese Beer Association. Then that group sells the trays to Asahi Beer, which in turn exports its product to China and shelves it at Walmart stores in the PRC. The overall production and distribution processes, in short, are highly transnational, requiring well-organized, interactive business networks to match. A rapidly growing share of the production networks operating in China, Japan, and Korea, however, are Northeast Asia–based, the result of comparative advantage and market scale there.

The Geographical Dimension: Production Clusters

As Paul Krugman and others have pointed out, geography can have a powerful effect on both trading patterns and overall economic growth.[31] The truth of this insight is clearly manifest in Northeast Asia. Figure 6.5 enumerates some of the dynamic regional production networks in the Northeast Asian IT sector, illustrating the dynamic and increasingly transnational character of much business activity in China. Around the world, as Michael Porter notes, complexes that pit competitors in close proximity with one another can generate formidable growth and competitiveness, as in Silicon Valley, Germany's Mittelstand, and Italy's Po Valley.[32] Such appears to be true along the central Chinese coast, at the heart of the Shanghai Circle, with transnational and cross-Straits interaction lying at the heart of explosive growth in that area also.

There are three basic clusters of IT production networks in the PRC, within which major Asian companies are involved. In Northern China, these networks center on Beijing and its environs. In Eastern China, the concentration is around Shanghai. In Southern China, the cluster centers on Guangzhou and Shenzhen. All of these centers, but especially the second and third, benefit substantially from improved cross-Straits relations, since they are physically close to Taiwan, which cost-effectively produces major intermediate components for which Mainland factories can easily undertake final assembly.

Japanese companies are important players in all three clusters, interacting intensely with Taiwanese and Chinese counterparts in those dynamic industrial regions. Japanese business finds Eastern China's availability for outsourcing and electronic component production, in addition to cheap labor, to be the key reason that the PRC is a priority investment destination.[33] The seaboard clusters thus play a key role in attracting Japanese investment.

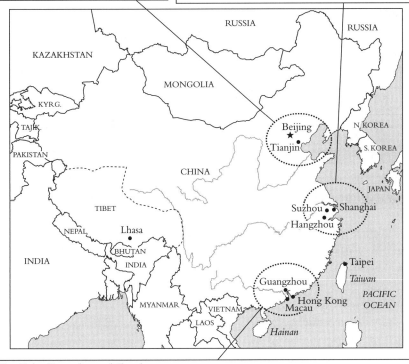

Bohai-Yellow Sea: Beijing and Tianjin

Japanese:	Sanyo, Matsushita, Sony, Panasonic, and Mitsubishi Electric
Korean:	Samsung, LG, Hynix (Hyundai Electronics)
Taiwanese:	Acer, Asus
Chinese:	Lenovo, Tsinghua Tungfang, Shouxin, Haixin, Haier, Langchao
Others:	Motorola, Ericson, Nokia, IBM, Dell

Yangtze River Delta: Shanghai, Suzhou, and Hangzhou

Japanese:	NEC, Toshiba, Sony, Matsushita, Hitachi, Mitsubishi Electric, and Panasonic
Korean:	Samsung, LG, Hynix
Others:	HP, Siemens, Motorola, Nokia, IBM, Dell
Taiwanese:	Acer, Compal, Jingying, Lantian, Benq, Quanta, Asus, Twinhead, Mitac, Daba, IBC, Arima, Datong, Quantier, Uniwill, Mio
Chinese:	TCI, Panda, Zhongxin, Dongxin, Bird

Pearl River Delta: Guangzhou and Shenzhen

Japanese:	NEC, Panasonic, Sony, Mitsubishi Electric, Sanyo, Toshiba, Hitachi, Matsushita
Korean:	Samsung, LG, Hynix
Taiwanese:	Skyworth, Lantian, Asus, Compal, Mio, Liteon, Msi, Gigabyte, Honghai, Huasheng, TK, Zhongshan, Mitae, Acer, and others
Chinese:	Great Wall, Xinghua Tongfang, Beida Foundation, TCI, Konka, Lenovo, Xiahua, Zhongqiao, Nanfang Gaoke, Qixi, and others
Others:	Nokia, IBM, Dell, Philips, Intel

FIG. 6.5. Transnational Information Technology Clusters in China. Source: Modified and updated from Chen Desheng, *jingji quanqiuhua yu taishan dalu touzi (Globalization and Taiwanese Investment on the Mainland)*, Taipei: Dianjin Wenhua Shiye Publisher, 2005.

A Deepening Taiwanese Role

Taiwanese companies also play a strategic role in intra–Northeast Asian (NEA), or even global, production networks, despite Taiwan's own ambiguous international standing, the result particularly of their formidable, if specialized, manufacturing capabilities. These established them as so-called "IC foundry" producers of commodity chips for Japanese electronic appliance makers during the 1990s. The typical computer produced in a Taiwanese-owned factory on the Mainland, for example, incorporates LCD display screens and memory chips sourced from South Korea or Taiwan, as well as hard drives from Japan, microprocessors made by Intel, and an operating system produced by Microsoft.[34] Taiwan's Quanta Computer, which makes roughly a third of the world's laptops, has shifted 90 percent of its production to a facility in Shanghai, employing more than 20,000 Chinese workers there.[35] And Quanta is only one of many Taiwanese companies, several of whom have already established Japanese and Korean ties, which are moving to the Mainland.

Acer, one of the world's largest producers of personal computers, is another important case of regional production networks in operation, using Northeast Asian transnational synergies to attain global competitive prominence. In 1994, Acer formed AA Soft International in Hong Kong to distribute educational and entertainment products. By 2000, Acer had three subsidiaries on the Mainland, including Acer Softech in Shanghai, as well as Acer Information Products, operating in Shenzhen and Zhongshan. Drawing on its regional production network, Acer has risen, amid the 2008–9 global financial crisis, to vie for standing as the second-largest producer of personal computers on earth.[36] The low production-cost structure and substantial market access that it enjoys, because of its deepening interdependence with Mainland China as political barriers across the Taiwan Straits steadily wane, are both fundamental elements of its international success.

Asus, Taiwan's largest IT hardware manufacturer, also produces components for Sony, Apple Inc., HP, Intel, and many others. It has a lower commercial profile than Acer but similar transnational production and marketing networks. Its main manufacturing facilities are also located on the Mainland, complementing extensive research and development facilities in Taiwan, its home base. Asus Hi-tech Park in Suzhou, just north of Shanghai, however, already covers 540,000 square meters, roughly the size of eighty-two soccer fields, and is rapidly expanding, as Asus also transfers research activities to the Mainland.

Japanese and Korean Production Networks in Greater China

Another significant change in the post-1997 Northeast Asian political economy is the deepening transnational integration in Mainland China, between overseas Chinese entrepreneurs and Japanese production networks. Such integration takes place in two directions. First, the PRC's own economic dependence on overseas Chinese business networks is declining, against the background of China's own rising involvement in broader Northeast Asian transnational production networks that transcend Greater China. Second, within the PRC itself, FDI from overseas Chinese, as well as Japanese and Korean investors, has become increasingly concentrated in the same locations. Investment from Hong Kong and Taiwan, previously concentrated in the Pearl River Delta of Southern China, has moved steadily northward along the coast over the past decade, reaching the Yangtze River Delta (YRD) and the Bohai–Yellow Sea (BYS) areas of Northeastern China. Investment from Japan and Korea, initially localized in northern coastal Shandong and Liaoning provinces, has simultaneously been spreading southward.

These two movements along the coast met and overlapped in the lower Yangtze provinces of Shanghai, Zhejiang, and southern Jiangsu, directly opposite Taiwan, and near the epicenter of the Shanghai Circle, aiding the creation of truly multinational production networks in those areas that are also synergistic with cross-Straits rapprochement. Shanghai and its environs—within three hours of virtually all the major industrial centers of Northeast Asia, and only half that distance from Taipei, Seoul, and Fukuoka—are thus becoming a breeding ground for the formation of fully transnational business networks, which are key sinews in the formation of a more integrated Northeast Asia.

By 2008, Shanghai itself was home to more than 33,000 Japanese and nearly 23,000 Koreans, making those groups the two largest agglomerations of foreign residents in China's megalopolis. Japanese alone constituted 22 percent of the total foreign residents in Shanghai, while Koreans made up 15 percent.[37] Shanghai was also the hottest overseas travel destination for Koreans. In 2006 Koreans made twice as many trips to China as to any other country, with Shanghai the focus. Korean "villages"—where South Korean citizens concentrate in China—are everywhere, although especially numerous from Shanghai to the northeast.

The Bohai–Yellow Sea region further north, still inside the Shanghai Circle, includes two major cities (Beijing and Tianjin) and three provinces (Hebei, Shandong, and Henan) in China, as well as the west coast of the two Koreas, and western Japan. This transnational economic area has both rich natural resources and a sound foundation for agriculture. Its ports, airports, and rail lines are also relatively developed, while the level of industrialization and quality of education likewise considerably exceed China's average. Not surprisingly, the Bohai–Yellow Sea area has become an increasingly dynamic hot spot for integrated Northeast Asian development, as well as a proliferation of intra-NEA transnational production networks.[38] In Beijing, for example, Hong Kong, Japan, and South Korea are the three largest investors, in combination holding more than 40 percent of total FDI there.[39]

The economic boom in the Yangtze River Delta and Bohai–Yellow Sea areas, as well as rejuvenation of the Manchurian "Rust Belt" in recent years, suggests clearly that the dynamic center of China's economy is moving steadily northeastward, following earlier growth spurts during the 1980s and 1990s in Guangdong and Fujian. The locus of Asian economic integration more generally has also migrated from Southeast Asia to Northeast Asia, driven by rising Japanese, Korean, and Taiwanese investment in Manchuria, Shandong, and the Shanghai region. Needless to say, this emerging pattern of East China–centric regional growth is being accelerated still further by the relaxation of geopolitical tensions along the Taiwan Straits. Parallel relaxation of tensions along the DMZ in Korea would no doubt further accelerate the process of regional integration, and stimulate another growth pole still further north.

In contrast to the rapidly deepening Northeast Asian intraregional economic interaction, Southeast Asia's involvement in China, also important to PRC growth during the 1980s and early 1990s, has been somewhat less dynamic since the Asian financial crisis, although it remains substantial. Investment from Southeast Asia into China declined steadily after 1997, inhibited both by the AFC, and by problems with projects inside China, such as Singapore's Suzhou venture. Singapore, for example, contributed 5.4 percent of total FDI in China during 1996. By 2004, however, its share of China's incoming FDI had fallen by two-fifths, to only 3.3 percent. Singapore's share has since increased somewhat since 2007, however.

Policy Networks

Bottom-up economic regionalization has led to the rapid emergence of Northeast Asian policy, as well as production, networks supporting further regional integration. Governmental agencies in the three Northeast Asian countries—China, Japan, and South Korea—all fostered such networks following the 1997 financial crisis. These policy networks have deepened substantially in recent years, complemented by the remarkable improvement since 2008 in cross-Straits relations. *Ministries* initiate policy discussions about regionalism into which they often systematically integrate private actors. The subsequent role of the committee members is to advise and disseminate information through their organizational and individual networks. *Think tanks* with ties to ministries are becoming intellectual centers for promoting regional trade agreements; the *business community* is also playing an active supporting role through both top-down and bottom-up mechanisms now in place, in order to engage the Asian region as a whole.

On a bilateral basis, the number of summits and exchanges among regional leaders has proliferated since the 1997 Asian financial crisis, with the leaders of Japan, China, and South Korea now meeting, on average, more than twice a year. Between China and Korea, in particular, bilateral exchanges have been deepening rapidly for more than a decade. In 1998, during President Kim Dae-jung's visit to China, for example, the two countries declared their intention to form a "cooperative partnership" (*hezuo huoban*) for the twenty-first century. Some modest yet concrete collaborative agreements were reached regarding criminal laws, visa regulations, and youth exchanges, as well as cooperation relating to railways. A further accord was struck in 2001 that expanded areas accessible to Korean fisherman, allowing them to increase their annual catch and income substantially.[40]

In 2000, Chinese premier Zhu Rongji visited South Korea and met top leadership in Seoul. Then in 2003 when President Roh Moo-hyun visited China, South Korea and the PRC established an augmented "all-around cooperative partnership" (*quanmian hezuo huoban*). Once again, the leaders signed major agreements on civil/corporate laws, standards, telecommunications, and related matters—this time more elaborate and ambitious than before.

In 2004 alone, Premier Wen Jiabao met President Roh twice, in addition to the summit between Roh and Chinese president Hu Jintao. In that year, a high-level Chinese delegation also visited South Korea, including top bureaucratic specialists on foreign affairs, commerce, finance, customs, aviation, science and technology, telecommunications, mass media, forestry, agriculture, and irrigation matters. Officials from the Chinese Supreme Court, the Women's Federation, the Party School, the CCP Youth League, and the Ministries of Education, Culture, and Athletics also engaged with South Korean counterparts. The reciprocal delegation from South Korea to China that followed was equally representative of leadership in the government, the business community, and major universities.[41]

Initially, even as networks between the PRC and the ROK deepened, top-level bilateral ties between China and Japan were inhibited by political tensions, because of Prime Minister Koizumi's persistent visits to the Yasukuni Shrine. Yet this crisis actually served as a quiet catalyst for deepening Sino-Japanese relationships, at a variety of levels. Between 2002 and 2006, top Chinese leaders actually held side-meetings at least twice annually with Koizumi himself at broader international gatherings, even though they held no formal bilateral summits.

Reciprocal midlevel diplomatic exchanges, including meetings of foreign ministers, also continued, albeit at a reduced level.

During 2005, despite Sino-Japanese political relations at their worst in years, two new top-level forums for bilateral communication opened—a political-military dialogue and an exchange of strategic views relating to the East China Sea. In 2006, the Sino-Japan ruling party dialogue mechanism (*zhizhengdang jiaoliu jizhi*) held its first meeting in Beijing. Five additional Japanese delegations, including economic bureaucrats, as well as representatives of semigovernmental organizations, opposition party leaders, and business groups, also visited Beijing, to a warm reception from top-level Chinese leadership.[42] Thus, beneath the top-level political impasse, policy networks were nevertheless on full display, helping to broker stable bilateral relations between China and Japan. In doing so these interactions laid the basis for even more dynamic interactions in late 2006, after Koizumi left office, which accelerated still further, when the Democratic Party of Japan took power in late 2009.

These bilateral dialogues between China and its Northeast Asian neighbors are much more extensive than interactions between any of these Northeast Asian nations and their Southeast Asian counterparts, with the partial exceptions of Vietnam and Singapore. They demonstrate that, although formal regional institutions usually cover East Asia in general, supplementary policy networks run deeply across Northeast Asia and knit the subregion into a much more cohesive entity than has been conventionally thought.

Emerging Institutional Manifestations

Asian multilateralism, meanwhile, has grown more vigorous and has developed three distinct layers: (1) formal governmental organizations, including ASEAN, the Asia Pacific Economic Cooperation (APEC), the ASEAN Regional Forum (ARF), ASEAN Plus Three, and the East Asia Summit; (2) various Track II channels for dialogue on economic, political, security, environmental, and other transnational issues, such as the Council for Security Cooperation in the Asia-Pacific (CSCAP) and the dynamic Boao Forum for Asia; and (3) civil society–based activity involving nongovernmental organizations (NGOs), regional advocacy groups, and professional and business associations, most notably the Network of Northeast Asian Think Tanks (NEAT).

In monetary and financial affairs, concrete steps toward institution-building have included the Miyazawa Initiative (October 1998); the Chiang Mai Initiative (May 2000); and the Manila Framework Group (2001).[43] An Asian bond market initiative (2003),[44] and Asian Development Bank feasibility studies regarding an East Asian currency basket (2006–7) have pushed integration still further. The

Chiang Mai Initiative, essentially bilateral, is now being converted into a multi-lateral reserve-pooling mechanism, with the Asian Bond Market also providing another broad-based and potentially valuable self-insurance mechanism for the region.[45] Northeast Asian countries now supply 80 percent of the reserves in the Chiang Mai Initiative (CMI) and are also stepping up collaborative currency-support mechanisms among themselves, independent of the CMI itself.[46]

On trade, ideas and proposals for regional agreement have been numerous. In addition to the series of bilateral free trade agreement (FTA) agreements between Northeast Asian countries and ASEAN members, intra-NEA arrangements have also been studied and proposed. Joint research on trilateral FTAs has been continuing since 1999, centering on the three government-affiliated think tanks of Northeast Asia: Japan's National Institute for Research Advancement (NIRA), South Korea's Institute of Economic Policy (KIEP), and the PRC's development research center of the State Council (DRC).[47] In 2002, Chinese premier Zhu Rongji promoted the trilateral FTA concept at the ASEAN Plus Three (APT) meeting that year. In 2003, the PRC concluded a Closer Economic Partnership Arrangement (CEPA) with Hong Kong. Although an intra-NEA trilateral FTA proved difficult to finalize at that time, because of domestic complications in South Korea and Japan as well as bilateral political difficulties, advocacy and proposals for trilateral economic cooperation have continued.[48] Indeed, the recent environment has grown more favorable, particularly since the late 2009 advent of a DPJ government in Japan, with pro-Asia inclinations and reformist ideas on critical agricultural issues. The relaxation of political tensions between Beijing and Taipei has triggered an active search for an even more comprehensive regional economic agreement, although political obstacles clearly remain.

On the security side, new intergovernmental mechanisms within Northeast Asia have evolved since the mid-1990s in an especially dynamic fashion, spurred by the continuing challenge of dealing with North Korea. This is particularly significant for Northeast Asia, given the long-standing heritage of estrangement, flowing from a bitter heritage of colonialism and war that prevails within that long-volatile region. New integrating mechanisms in the security sphere have included KEDO (1995–2005), the TCOG process (1998–2003), and the Six Party Talks (2003–). Parallel Track II frameworks include the Network of East Asian Think Tanks (NEAT), the Northeast Asian Security Dialogue, and the Three-Party Meeting among China, Japan, and South Korea. To acquire a better understanding of the deepening layers of policy networks in Northeast Asia, and their real-world implications, we focus in particular detail on (1) the ASEAN Plus Three mechanism; (2) the Boao Forum for Asia (BFA); and (3) subnational networks.[49]

The development of ASEAN Plus Three is one of several major Asian institutional innovations born of the 1997 financial crisis. APT, a summit grouping of the ten ASEAN nations plus the three major economies of Northeast Asia (Japan, China, and South Korea), emerged at the 1997 Kuala Lumpur Summit, and has involved annual meetings of heads of government, ministers of finance, trade, and foreign affairs, and assorted high-level advisors since then. It includes eleven institutional mechanisms for regional cooperation, operating through periodic meetings of national leaders, ministers, and other senior officials.

In the APT processes, which involve both Southeast and Northeast Asia, the Northeast has of late consistently been either setting the agenda or playing a central role in the dialogue. The APT Economic Ministers' Consultation, which has convened annually since 2000, is a case in point. It has produced (1) Cooperation toward Co-prosperity in East Asia (2007–11), proposed by Korea; (2) an APT website for customs information exchange, also proposed by Korea; (3) APT logistics cooperation for future trade facilitation, proposed by Japan; and (4) an agricultural technology and training program, proposed by China.[50] Furthermore, three of the four meetings of the expert feasibility study on an East Asian FTA, occurring between April 2005 and July 2006, were held in and chaired by Northeast Asian nations.

In addition, Japan spearheaded the APT Cooperation in International Comparable Statistics program, and the Biomass Asia Workshop focusing on agricultural research, while also playing a central role in the Asian Bond Market Initiative. China likewise strongly promoted the Nuclear Energy Safety Forum.[51] Although APT is administratively linked to the ASEAN secretariat, its senior officials' meetings on finance, energy, telecommunications, labor, social welfare, and many other topics are typically cochaired by one official from ASEAN and a second from Northeast Asia.[52] Thus the APT processes since the AFC have definitely helped to give the Northeast Asian nations a subtle yet important subregional identity, which has become ever more clearly manifest.

Independent of broader East Asian regionalism, Northeast Asian trilateral dialogue mechanisms have developed remarkably since 2000, as demonstrated in Figure 1.4. There have been more than two dozen ministerial meetings among China, Japan, and South Korea. Ministers of environment, finance, trade, intellectual property, and information technology have held continuous annual conferences since 2000–2002. From 2007 on, the three countries institutionalized more important ministerial conferences, including foreign ministers, customs heads, health ministers, and ministries in charge of transportation and logistics, with the 2009 addition of ministerial meetings on natural disaster relief.

Track II Innovations: The Boao and Jeju Forums

The Boao Forum for Asia (BFA) demonstrates clearly the pattern of intensified, policy-oriented conference networking that has begun emerging in Asia since 1997. BFA is nominally a nongovernmental and nonprofit international body, but one that informally involves many current and former Pacific Asian national leaders. On February 27, 2001, the BFA was formally established, when its declaration was adopted by delegates from twenty-six founding member countries. The first BFA annual conference was convened two years later, with the theme "New Century, New Challenge, A New Asia." More than 1,900 delegates from forty-eight countries attended, with Chinese premier Zhu Rongji keynoting the inaugural meeting.

Jiang Xiaosong, the son of a famous Chinese artist, initiated the idea of the BFA, which he conceived as an Asian counterpart to the Davos World Economic Forum, during a golf outing with former Australian prime minister Robert Hawke and some Japanese acquaintances. The BFA was to be held annually at Boao, a relaxed tropical resort on Hainan, off China's southeastern coast. Several top Asian political leaders outside China were immediately interested. Based on this initial high-level enthusiasm, Jiang also secured backing from Chinese vice president Hu Jintao and President Jiang Zemin.[53]

Although the BFA was not directly formed at Chinese government initiative, Beijing has played a de facto leading role in BFA ever since its inception. Top leaders, including Jiang Zemin, Zhu Rongji, Hu Jintao, and Wen Jiabao, have participated actively in BFA annual conferences every year since 2002. Major economic bureaucrats, including Deputy Commerce Minister Zhang Xiang and Vice Commerce Minister Long Yongtu, were either elected directors general or provided significant support for the organization's growth.[54] Since the BFA's inception, "Asia seeking common development through cooperation" has been the persistent featured theme of the forum.

Through the Boao Forum, the PRC has promoted regionalist ideas, introduced its major domestic and foreign policy agendas, and communicated with complex bilateral partners—Tokyo and Taipei in particular.[55] At the 2004 BFA annual conference, President Hu emphasized the mutual symbiosis between China's growth and Asian development. In 2006, Chinese vice president Zeng Qinhong spoke at BFA on China's currency policies and banking reforms. In 2007, Wu Banguo, the chairman of China's National People's Congress, came to urge cooperation in science and technology. With respect to all of these questions, relations with Northeast Asia were central.

The Boao Forum's April 2009 convention marked a major gathering of "Asian voices,"[56] offering "a platform for Asian leaders to seek 'Asian insights' in tackling the worst global economic turmoil in seven decades."[57] More than 1,600 political leaders, business people, and academic scholars from across the globe, including Chinese premier Wen Jiabao, former Japanese prime minister Fukuda Yasuo, and former Chinese vice premier Zeng Peiyan participated. Their discussions assessed the impact of the crisis on Asia and how the region might best weather its challenges.

China's support for a comprehensive regional economic institution complementary to global bodies like the WTO, yet not subject to clear Western domination, has been clearly signaled over the years at the forum. Since Boao's inauguration in 2002, an increasingly diverse group of governmental participants has joined the gathering. Korea, in particular, has been increasingly well represented. At the April 2007 conference, for example, the SK Group of Korea was the second largest among all the corporate donors.

Japan's official participation has not been quite as active. Japanese prime minister Koizumi did attend the first Boao Forum in 2002, but no sitting Japanese head of government participated during the following six years. In 2009, however, former Japanese prime minister Fukuda spoke, and also conferred with Chinese premier Wen on the sidelines of the forum.

Although bureaucrats and think tanks play important roles at Boao, private companies are the central participants, apart from Chinese leadership, in contrast to the patterns at most other regional policy assemblies in East Asia. The majority of participants at the Boao Forum have been from either private Asian firms or, interestingly, from Western multinationals such as IBM, Microsoft, BMW, and UPS International.[58] Major Chinese firms such as Haier and Lenovo, as well as state-owned giants like Shanghai Bao Steel, China Construction Bank, and China Life Insurance, also participate actively at Boao.

Northeast Asian integration is a pivotal concern of the forum, even though the BFA includes delegates from far beyond that core area. Japan-China-Korea economic cooperation and WTO negotiations are invariably major topics there, according to Yin Zhongyi, director of China's Development and Reform Council in Hainan, which has served as the brain behind BFA since 2003.[59] Overall, the forum seeks win-win solutions and a clear role for Asia in the global economy, with Northeast Asia as the fulcrum.[60]

South Korea is emulating the Boao pattern, with a similar objective of deepening Asian regional policy networks. In 2001, commemorating the first anniversary of the Pyongyang North-South Summit, President Kim Dae-jung inaugurated the Jeju Forum, a gathering of distinguished current and former policy-makers as well as business people, on the island of Jeju in the East China Sea, often called "Korea's

Hawaii." This gathering, which has assembled biannually ever since, has featured a particularly heavy concentration of high-level Northeast Asian policy-makers. Korean presidents Kim Dae-jung and Roh Moo-hyun, U.N. secretary general Ban Ki-moon, Chinese vice premier Qian Qichen, Japanese prime ministers Nakasone Yasuhiro, Kaifu Toshiki, and Murayama Tomoichi, as well as former Philippine president Fidel Ramos have all spoken at the forum.

Japan, consistently the least proactive of the Northeast Asian trio about regionalism, has no direct analogue to either Boao or the Jeju Forum. The *Nihon Keizai Shimbun,* however, has taken to holding an impressive Asian leaders' conference every June, involving heads of government throughout Asia, as well as a small number of Western representatives. The Japanese prime minister is also a regular participant.

Transnational Epistemic Communities: Bringing Regionalist Dreams to Earth

Cross-border epistemic communities have also been instrumental in deepening regional cooperation in Northeast Asia.[61] Indeed, establishment of formal intergovernmental organizations in the region has traditionally been preceded by cooperation among scholars, think tanks, and nonofficial activists.[62] In the shadow of the 1997 Asian financial crisis, for example, governmental initiatives for the establishment of regional organizations were numerous. Subsequently, epistemic, personal, and private networks have gotten involved directly in planning and implementing these initiatives, even where they have focused on public-policy questions. There is thus a clear evolution from bureaucratically inspired to more dynamic NGO-driven regional agenda-setting, in many important issue areas.[63]

Through deepening inter-regional interaction at the subglobalist level, Asian leaders, businessmen, and technocrats have moved subtly away from traditional U.S.-centric bilateralist perspectives and acquired an increasingly clear-cut Asian identity. The Asia-Pacific Institute of CASS, for example, had focused its research and publications during the 1990s on APEC and Sino-U.S. relations, as well as China's own economic reform and openness. Since 2000, however, research on East Asian regional cooperation has become far more prominent, with Northeast Asian topics gaining particular importance since 2003. In 2008, for example, the institute even published four articles in Korean, written by Korean economic specialists. In security and diplomacy, Northeast Asian issues have also dominated the Chinese Academy of Social Sciences (CASS) agenda since 2003.[64]

A variety of experts' groups have been established explicitly to promote East Asian integration, involving research institutes from key countries, meeting bilaterally and regionally, to investigate free-trade arrangements and other forms of enhanced cooperation. Think tanks in Northeast Asia, such as the Korean Institute for Economic Policy (KIEP); Japan's National Institute for Research Advancement (NIRA); the Nomura Research Institute (NRI); the METI Research Institute (RIETI); the Chinese Academy of Social Sciences (CASS); and the development research center of the State Council (DRC) under China's State Council, have stressed intra-Asian regionalism and the APT process as main agenda items. Korea's KIEP, Japan's NIRA, and China's DRC explicitly serve as a brain-trust for the annual trilateral summit meetings among Northeast Asian leaders, generating specific policy proposals for those summits through cooperative research and policy dialogue. Like so many Northeast Asian agenda-setting bodies, they have been filling this function, in increasingly sophisticated fashion, since shortly after the 1997–98 Asian financial crisis, and were actually galvanized into action by that cataclysm.

Within the Northeast Asian triangle, institutional vehicles for mutual interaction include governmental, nongovernmental, and epistemic cooperation, ranging from the Three-Party Committee, the Economic and Trade Ministers' Meeting, and the Economic Directors-General Consultation Meetings, to bilateral arrangements such as the China-Japan Economic Partnership Consultation, the Japan-Korea High-level Economic Consultation, and the Korea-China Joint Economic Committee Meeting. All these bodies have the common goal of creating an attractive environment for regional trade and investment, through the creation of soft, institutionalized transnational policy-coordination networks.

It is important to note that the transnational private-sector epistemic community in Northeast Asia and policy-makers in the respective governments are closely linked, enhancing the policy impact of the epistemic community. In September 2007, shortly after the KMT candidate Ma Ying-jeou won Taiwan's election, for example, the Center for Taiwan Affairs at Beijing University was commissioned by the State Council to organize a conference on "Cross-Straits Crisis: Prevention and Management." This conference was heavily attended by officials in charge of the PRC's Taiwan affairs.[65] Another major 2007 conference, held successively in Beijing and at Liaodong, near the North Korean frontier, dealing with "Nuclear North Korea, Security Dynamics and Regional Transition in the Future," was again attended by university scholars, think tank researchers, and government officials from China, Japan, South Korea, and the United States. Within such informal settings, expert opinion can quietly influence policy-making and orient officials toward more effective regional cooperation, an enterprise that disproportionately benefits Northeast Asian interaction, due to the endemic "organization gap" that has traditionally prevailed there.[66]

Military Exchanges and Dialogue:
Transcending a Complex History

Northeast Asia, as we have noted, is a region long haunted by a bitter history, of first Japanese colonialism and bloody intraregional conflict, followed by prolonged and intense Cold War. For most of the past century political-military tensions have been the most important single obstacle to integration in a region with enormous, innate economic complementarities. Yet now at last those once-chronic defense-related tensions are beginning to wane, with the advent of significant military-to-military dialogue.

The militaries of Japan and South Korea, both major allies of the United States, have had significant contact with one another for some time since the early 1990s. Yet until recently their interaction was distinctly limited and wary, reflecting the bitter heritage between them. In 2001, for example, as a means of protesting Japan's textbook treatment of historical issues, the South Korean government inhibited military exchanges with Japan. From 2005 to 2008, the South Korean government even considered "cutting military ties with Japan" over the disputed islet of Dokdo.[67] With the coming of the Lee Myung-bak administration in early 2008, however, the pace of bilateral military interaction and coordination between these wary neighbors has intensified, particularly following escalation of the North Korean nuclear crisis in the spring of 2009.

Shortly after Lee came to power in Seoul, South Korea, the United States and Japan discussed launching a trilateral military dialogue and small-scale field training exercises that could flexibly expand in intensity and scope.[68] During April 2009, South Korean defense minister Lee Sang-hee visited Japan, where he signed a letter of intent to substantially expand bilateral defense cooperation with Tokyo, including joint training and more extensive intelligence sharing.[69]

Perhaps the most dramatic recent changes in Northeast Asian military to military relations, however, and the most consequential so far for future regional integration prospects, have been those between China and Japan. Those two nations, after all, dominate East Asia geopolitically, and have been locked in conflict for more than a century. As many as 30 million people are said to have died in their fourteen years of military conflict between 1931 and 1945 alone.

Since 2006, however, Sino-Japanese military to military relations have dramatically improved.[70] This movement began just before the retirement of Japanese prime minister Koizumi Junichiro, with an unprecedented June 2006 visit of Japan Self-Defense Force officers to the PRC's South China Sea Fleet. It was followed the next year, in August 2007, with an official visit by China's defense minister Cao Gangchuan to Japan—the first such visit in almost a decade.[71] The visit, following Prime Minister Wen Jiabao's successful meetings with Prime Minister Abe Shinzo in April 2007, also proved to be highly productive. The two sides agreed on mutual missile-destroyer ship visits before the end of 2007, establishment of a military "hotline," and a return visit by the Japanese defense minister to China.

Defense relations continued deepening thereafter, supported by the positive relations of a series of Japanese post-Koizumi prime ministers with China. In September 2007, China for the first time invited Japanese observers to a People's Liberation Army (PLA) military drill. Two months later, in November 2007, the first Chinese naval vessel since the 1949 revolution, the missile destroyer *Shenzhen*, visited Japan, to commemorate the thirty-fifth anniversary of Sino-Japanese diplomatic normalization. In June 2008 the Japanese Marine Self-Defense Force (MSDF) destroyer *Sazanami* reciprocated, becoming the first Japanese naval vessel to visit China formally since World War II. On its historic voyage the *Sazanami* carried aid for China's earthquake-stricken Sichuan region, traversed the South China Sea, and visited some of China's most strategic naval bases, including Zhanjiang, in Guangdong Province, and Sanya, on Hainan Island.

Sino-Japanese military dialogue continued, and deepened rapidly, during 2009. In February, a dialogue between ground-force commanders began, when General Ge Zhenfeng, deputy chief of the General Staff of the PLA, visited Tokyo for talks with the Ground Self-Defense Force (GSDF) chief of staff, General Oriki Ryoichi. A month later, Japan's defense minister, Hamada Seiichi, visited China, inspecting a PLA military camp during his visit. In March, China and Japan agreed to cooperate and share information during their respective antipiracy naval campaigns off Somalia, and to hold a joint security conference in Tokyo before the end of the year. They also agreed to initiate communication among their respective military institutes and academies, with a first step being the visit of the president of Japan's National Defense Academy, Iokibe Makoto, to Beijing in June 2009.

China and South Korea two generations ago fought a bitter war, in which 392,600 Chinese, including Mao Tse-tung's eldest son, together with 984,400 South Koreans, ultimately perished.[72] Their conflict was followed by nearly forty years of Cold War. Over the past decade, however, relations between the Chinese and South Korean militaries have begun to improve rapidly. In 1999, as the military situation on the Korean peninsula was growing tense, Chinese and South Korean defense ministers held a historic meeting, redefining military relationships between the two countries, just before the summit between Zhu Rongji and Kim Dae-jung in Seoul that year.[73]

In 2000, China's defense minister, Chi Haotian, led a high-powered seventeen-member delegation from the PLA in a landmark visit to Seoul. The visit lasted for five days and reached consensus on joint military drills and reciprocal naval visits, opening new prospects for military cooperation between the two countries.[74] In October 2001, Korean naval vessels docked at Shanghai. In 2002, for the first time, the PRC's warships visited Incheon, on the ROK's west coast, carrying a combined crew of 438.[75] In 2005, China–South Korea military exchanges furthered expanded to the air force,[76] with exchanges expanding thereafter to defense academies (2008),[77] and to general-staff dialogue (2009).[78]

Operational links between the Chinese and South Korean militaries have also expanded to a remarkable degree, driven by a relaxation in bilateral tensions and a common concern about North Korea, especially after it began nuclear tests in 2006. During 2007 the two countries engaged in their first joint search and rescue exercise (SAREX), and agreed at the highest levels to establish a military hotline. In 2008, that agreement was actually implemented, despite a transition in Korean presidential administrations, with Sino-Korean naval and air force hotlines actually being established in November 2008.[79]

Across Northeast Asia, in short, personal relationships among national militaries that were once deadly foes are rapidly deepening. Networks are developing most vigorously at the ministerial level, but are broadening at the working level as well, driven by ship visits, military exchanges, and staff dialogue, as well as the establishment of hotlines. Mil-mil networks are emerging even among such long-standing adversaries and fundamental geopolitical rivals as Japan and China. Since the dark shadows of history and geopolitical rivalry have long stood as the fundamental constraints on regional integration, in the face of powerful economic complementarities, the recent deepening of military networks loosens one particularly significant and long-standing obstacle to the Making of Northeast Asia.

Emerging Subnational Networks in Northeast Asia: Quiet Transnational Integration

Often obscured in an analysis of Northeast Asian integration are substantively important subnational civilian networks quietly emerging within the region. Major cities are helping to link neighboring countries in a more intimate economic embrace than ever before. Prior to 1997, Tokyo, Hong Kong, and Singapore were the key centers linking Asia together economically. After the financial crisis, however, Shanghai also emerged as a fourth major Asian hub, measured by the volume of goods handled at container ports, the number of passenger arrivals at international airports, the volume of international phone calls, and capital-market transactions.[80] Rising PRC dealings with nearby Japan, Korea, and especially Taiwan, will doubtless enhance Shanghai's role still further, giving increased prominence to the "Shanghai Circle" at the core of an increasingly coherent Northeast Asia.

There is a parallel revolution going on at the local level across the region, fueled by shared economic and cultural interactions that transcend nationalist politics. Regional economic cooperation in Northeast Asia has received more concrete support from local governments than from national administrations, especially among the geographically adjacent localities in the three countries, such as those surrounding the East China Sea, an "Asian Mediterranean."[81] Indeed, the earliest form of policy-supported economic integration in the region came at the grassroots level, in the form of cross-border developmental zones, such as the Tumen River Development Area, the Japan Sea Rim Economic Zone, and the Bohai–Yellow Sea Rim Development project. Local governments are typically less affected by nationalist politics than their counterparts at the national level. China's proactive support policies since 2003 for its Northeastern provinces, and the relaxation since 2008 in cross-Straits relations also, have catalyzed unprecedented cooperation within Northeast Asia, much of it through "bottom-up" initiatives, as elaborated in Chapters 7 through 10.

Below the radar screen of nationalist animosity, transnational ties among local authorities have been steadily deepening. In 2003, there were 266 sister-city relationships between China and Japan. By 2005 that number had jumped by nearly 20 percent to 313, second only to the U.S. total of 434 with Japan, the much-publicized tensions over Yasukuni Shrine at the national level notwithstanding. Some 108 Japanese local authorities also had Korean affiliations in the latter year, while ten had Taiwanese counterparts. Substantially more Japanese prefectures also have ties with Chinese counterparts than with American (34 versus 24).[82] Between China and South Korea, local "friendship" ties have reached down even below the municipal level, capitalizing on the proliferation of grassroots NGO's in Korea, to enhance the Sino-Korean relationship. Districts within Beijing municipality, for example, have formed "friendly exchange networks" (youhao jiaoliu wang) with comparable districts in Seoul.[83] Governments in all three nations of Northeast Asia have thus been actively conducting cultural, educational, and developmental exchanges at a variety of levels, helping to bridge the yawning gaps in national relationships that well-worn historical controversies intermittently create. There is naturally conflict as well as cooperation, at times, among such transnational coalitions, but the net effect is emphatically positive for relations among China, Japan, and Korea at the national level, because national relations had been so distant and embittered before.

In Conclusion

Since the 1997 Asian financial crisis, Northeast Asia has returned to economic growth, and simultaneously expanded intraregional economic linkages to an unprecedented degree, despite well-publicized national political tensions. Improved political relations between China and Japan since the fall of 2006, and between Japan and South Korea since early 2008, not to mention rapidly improving cross-Straits relations since mid-2008, should help loosen lingering political obstacles to this rising economic interdependence, and aid the steady growth of institutions capable of managing it.

Through increasing trade and deepening production networks, Northeast Asia is thus becoming an identifiable and tightly knit economic region. Common developmental challenges inevitably flow from this interdependence, to be sure. Yet they also precipitate a struggle to develop cooperative institutions that have recorded numerous, if surprisingly unrecognized, recent successes.

Driven by deepening integration, epistemic communities and policy networks supportive of regional cooperation—civilian and even military—are expanding and deepening. Transnational networking forums like Boao, Jeju, and Nikkei, together with defense-related exchanges, are proliferating. Institutional cooperation has deepened between governmental agencies, while also linking important nongovernmental epistemic communities in an ever more intimate embrace, especially in issue areas where cooperation is functionally important for participants, such as the environment, energy, and finance. Less constrained by political complexity and the shadows of history than their national counterparts, local governments are also increasingly involved in social, cultural, and economic cooperative projects involving Chinese, Japanese, and South Korean collaboration.

Indeed, Northeast Asia has evolved into a vastly different and more cohesive entity than was true before 1997, with the pace of change accelerating in the wake of serious regional tensions during 2005–6, and the financial crisis of 2008–9. This new cooperative reality reflects quite different domestic interests and coalitions in each of the individual countries of the region. Paralleling economic interdependence and growing social interaction is an increasing regionalization of corporate interest in these traditionally competitive nations, the result of the rapid expansion of transnational production networks. As dominant coalitions in one country become intertwined transnationally with groups elsewhere in the region, domestic policy-making regarding regionalism has also grown progressively more coordinated and more cooperative, as elaborated in the following country chapters.

PART IV

NATIONAL TRANSFORMATION

The Making of Northeast Asia has many dimensions. Previous chapters have surveyed the profile of deepening integration at the regional level, and the following four chapters complement this by profiling the domestic forces now driving the constituent nations toward closer regional integration. To guide a systematic examination of national transformations in China, Japan, South Korea, and the United States, we present a single analytical framework for considering undergoing transformations in all four countries, based on the central notions of critical juncture and coalition politics. To elaborate the commonalities, we include this brief introduction to the country chapters.

Transnational factors—such as the catalytic role of private actors with multiple national affiliations, economic ties, and social interactions—clearly influence regional institution-building, through their impact on domestic actors. Ultimately, a state's propensity to promote (or inhibit) regional integration is profoundly influenced by the profile of the prevailing coalitions that dominate its domestic political economy. How individual leaders interact with their often contrasting domestic social bases and transnational policy networks crucially affects their ultimate decisions regarding regional cooperation as well.

Regional Policy-making and Domestic Politics

In most current academic literature, explanations for a country's regionalist policies emphasize changes in transnational factors. Functionalist scholars stress the "spillover" effect that existing institutions exert in replicating new ones.[1]

Other analysts focus on the spillover of domestic institutions within a regional or international context, in shaping the ultimate profile of regional institutions.[2] These perspectives, reviewed in Chapter 11, are insufficient, however, to account for regionalist configurations in general, or for Asian regionalism in particular.

Recent literature on regionalism contends that globalization helps promote regionalization worldwide, since globalization creates common challenges from which nations seek to shield themselves through regional organizations.[3] Common problems, in this conception, thus lead to concerted actions among neighboring countries. The process—globalization leads to common problems, which in turn lead to regional institution-building—does not take into account the dynamics within national boundaries, nor the impact of domestic politics on ultimate outcomes.

Neither in theory nor in practice, however, is the impact of transnational factors on regionalism automatic. There is no self-evident reason why globalization should lead to regionalization. To the contrary, economic globalization in theory ought to reduce region-preferential institution-building in favor of wider cooperation. Even when countries in a region do face common challenges generated by the globalization process, regional integration can be slow to emerge for two reasons. First, common interests may be imperceptible to decision-makers in different countries. Second, coordination among the nations in question, central to the creation of regional institutions, may be lacking.

Before the Asian financial crisis (AFC), Asian regionalism was slow to evolve, especially in Northeast Asia. Accidents of geography and politics separated the major economic center, island Japan, from massive, populous China on the continent. Business groups with major stakes in regional integration were slow to evolve, especially in the face of strong trans-Pacific counterincentives. The bitter heritage of history, including the lingering effects of the Cold War, clearly inhibited much potential cooperation also, despite numerous common developmental challenges in the face of global economic forces. And Asian decision-makers did not foresee a financial crisis mandating a regional collaborative mechanism.

Although Asian nations had substantial trade and investment ties, few intra-regional policy networks initially linked their decision-makers. As a result, even when regional mechanisms such as the Tokyo-inspired Asian Monetary Fund concept were conceived, they failed to receive broader collective support. Thus, we highlight the importance of critical junctures in this study. Regional institution-building, we argue, requires a crisis (actual or perceived) or other critical events as a catalyst, to dramatize common regional interests to decision-makers, and to inspire cross-regional collective action.

Critical junctures are also important, as our nation-specific chapters suggest,

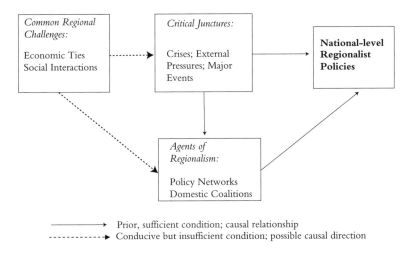

FIG. P4.1. Framework of Regionalist Decision-making.

in helping decision-makers mobilize domestic support within their respective countries for broader regional integration. Any institutional change naturally faces some resistance from entrenched interests; crisis typically weakens that resistance by generating urgency about change. Regional policy networks, born in critical junctures, interact with domestic social forces to finesse and co-opt potential resistance to regional integration.

The dynamic causal interaction between critical junctures and domestic coalition politics is suggested schematically in Figure P4.1. Common regional problems can potentially stimulate the formation of transnational policy networks within the region. These in turn bias the domestic policy processes toward regional integration, and shape their concrete profile. If no regional collective action occurs in such circumstances, unsolved common problems provoke a crisis. To cope with the crisis, regional policy networks are created or strengthened. These policy networks then positively influence the formation of subsequent regional-cooperation policies.

China, Japan, and Korea, as we have suggested, are the three principal regional actors in the Making of Northeast Asia. The United States—itself a major North Pacific power—is a critical uncertainty: the main potential inhibitor of their deepening interaction, but a prospective regional stabilizer as well. The following chapters examine concretely the domestic coalitions and policies formed in these four critical countries that are currently shaping the process of Northeast Asian regional integration, and indeed, East Asian integration more generally.

Relevant domestic actors include economic bureaucracies, political leaders, private firms, labor movements, mass media, and nongovernmental organizations (NGOs), including lobbyists. Which groups favor and oppose regional integration? And how cohesive are their positions? How do the positions of relevant actors evolve over time? How extensively do they collaborate with counterparts elsewhere in Northeast Asia?

The forthcoming chapters outline national profiles of demand for and supply of regionalist options, in comparative perspective, contrasting China, Korea, Japan, and the United States. These chapters also explain how critical junctures and changes in economic structure advantage some domestic groups and weaken others in each individual country, thus shaping their distinctive national approaches to regionalism. Overall, as we shall see, country-specific analysis demonstrates that growing economic integration, on the one hand, enhances demand for region-specific institutions. Cross-national, elite-network linkages established during critical junctures, conversely, also tend to enhance the supply of new policy options, thus propelling the Making of Northeast Asia.

The Transformation of China's Regional Policies

China has been at the heart of the "organization gap" in Northeast Asia ever since the revolution of 1949, and especially since the Korean War critical juncture. It was unable to trade with its neighbors for years, after its bitter confrontation with the United States during the Korean War. Then, when the People's Republic of China (PRC) finally established diplomatic ties with Japan and the United States during the 1970s, it conveniently adopted the bilateralism embodied in the San Francisco System. The 1997 Asian financial crisis, however, has transformed Beijing's stance toward regionalism.[1] More important, since 2003 the PRC has clearly embraced intra–Northeast Asian cooperation as a concept, with actual cooperative dealings with neighbors accelerating since late 2006. From a remarkably detached and isolated, albeit massive, nation, China has become a proactive and principal driver of regionalist initiatives, in both East Asia generally and within Northeast Asia in particular.

Behind the PRC's remarkable reorientation on regional matters are two powerful internal shifts that have also been reshaping China's domestic politics and foreign policies. There has been a strategic shift from Deng Xiaoping's principle of *taoguang yanghui* (hiding your strength and biding your time) to a more proactive and responsible foreign policy within the region. There has also been a shift from favorable treatment of coastal cities toward a more balanced development of the traditionally backward northeastern parts of China. These strategic and developmental shifts worked in tandem, and increasingly led the PRC's Northeast Asian regional policies toward multilateral institution-building. Since 2006, in particular, multilateral cooperative regionalism, with a strong Northeast Asian (NEA) element, has become a core component of China's foreign policies.

China's new thinking after 2003 motivated it to proactively support Northeast Asian regionalism. This subregion is fundamental to China's core economic interests, which include sustaining dense trade, investment, and social flows from Japan, South Korea, and Taiwan. It also poses an unusual concentration of serious security challenges for the PRC. After 2006, dramatic changes transpired in the PRC's relationships with Japan, and in 2008 and 2009, Beijing's relationship with Taipei also drastically improved. The PRC's ties with South Korea have simultaneously been even more steadily deepening, ever since the 1990s. Driven by both diplomatic considerations and fundamental domestic interests, China is contributing quietly but in historic fashion to the Making of Northeast Asia.

Wei Ji ["Crisis"] and the Transformation of China's Regional Policies

As China's ancient philosopher Laozhi famously noted, "With every disaster come good things [huo xi fu zhi suo yi]." The Chinese character for crisis, Wei Ji, expresses exactly such dual meanings. Wei (meaning "jeopardy") coexists with, or precedes, Ji (meaning "opportunity"). Almost all the major shifts in contemporary China's domestic and foreign policies have been driven by crises (perceived or real), of various scales and types. The Korean War estranged China from its capitalist Asian neighbors and led the PRC into a massive socialist mobilization. Crises during the socialist period, especially the Cultural Revolution, again realigned China's internal and external relations. Deng Xiaoping, in reaction against the Cultural Revolution, was able to lead China on a new path—a path that prioritized economic development and improved relations with the United States and capitalist Asian nations. The PRC's involvement in Asian regionalism was marginal in the beginning and evolved only gradually, until being driven by catalytic events toward much stronger and more proactive support.

1978 to 1997: Chinese Lack of Interest in Regionalism

From 1978 to 1989, China's regional involvement was quite restrained. Beijing lacked the capability to lead any multilateral initiatives in the region, and was wary of any potential infringement on its own sovereignty by supranational institutions. Beijing's foreign policies, including regional ones, were conveniently formulated in a "hub-and-spokes" bilateral structure centering on Washington, remarkably similar to those in Tokyo and Seoul.

The end of the Cold War sharply transformed the relationship between Beijing and Washington, as well as between the PRC and its Asian neighbors. As the Soviet Union collapsed, the security basis for Sino-U.S. cooperation disappeared.

The Tiananmen crisis of June 1989 seriously damaged the Sino-American bilateral relationship. Encouraged by the United States, Western countries imposed economic sanctions on China and restricted trade and investment flows to the PRC. It was at this juncture that Beijing's ties with its Asian regional neighbors, especially the developed, technologically sophisticated nations of Northeast Asia, began to intensify.

While the flow of new capital from the West declined, Japanese investment in China between 1989 and 1992 remained quite steady, and increased significantly in Guangdong and Shanghai, although aid was temporarily suspended in the immediate aftermath of the Tiananmen crisis.[2] A Japanese delegation visiting Beijing in December 1989 was the first official foreign group to arrive there after the crisis, a gesture greatly appreciated by the Chinese government. Deng Xiaoping personally welcomed the visiting Japan External Trade Organization (JETRO) delegation and praised Japan's "goodwill." In his words, "The visit represented true friendship."[3]

Sino–South Korean relations grew significantly also during the early 1990s. In 1991, when the Republic of Korea (ROK) hosted the Asia Pacific Economic Cooperation (APEC) Summit, China was invited to participate, and its delegation visited Seoul for the first time, with the two Northeast Asian nations starting their bilateral trading relationships soon after and establishing diplomatic ties in 1992. Sino-Korean trade rapidly expanded, to become Korea's fastest growing commercial relationship during the 1990s and Korea's largest overall trading tie by 2003.

Despite these dynamic interactions with Japan and Korea, China's official attitudes toward regionalism before 1997 were cautious at best. In this period, China's foreign strategy was paradoxical indeed. On the one hand, it abided by the "hiding strength, biding time" principle set by Deng Xiaoping, who was in charge of military affairs while President Jiang Zemin held the top nominal position in China. On the other, Chinese strategists, facing the collapse of the Soviet Union, argued for a "multipolar world" posture, ambitiously projecting China as one of the major power centers in global affairs, on a par with the United States.

Overall, however, Beijing was preoccupied with improving bilateral ties with the United States, which had become highly critical of Chinese domestic politics since the Tiananmen crisis and had conditioned its trade with China on humiliating annual reviews of the PRC's human rights record. Beijing's strategic policy-making continued to be influenced by hub-and-spokes bilateralism. Its interactions with ongoing Asia-Pacific institutions were largely driven by defensive concerns: a desire not to be left out, rather than by any clear impulse to proactively shape patterns of regional cooperation. It was uninterested in Malaysian prime minister Mahathir's proposal for an East Asian Economic Caucus in 1990. It joined hands with the United States in 1997 to kill the Asian Monetary Fund, proposed abruptly and inconveniently by Japan.

After 1998: China's Active Leadership in Formulating and Promoting Regionalism

The 1997–98 Asian financial crisis marked a critical juncture for the PRC's regional policy, transforming that massive nation from a passive—and at times obstructionist—participant into a proactive and consequential actor. The PRC responded positively to the ASEAN Plus Three framework in 1997, and since then has played a significant role in the ASEAN Plus Three (APT) process. Beginning in 1999, it participated actively in the APT-affiliated Trilateral Meetings with Japan and South Korea. For the first time, China also initiated several important regional frameworks on its own. In trade, Chinese premier Zhu Rongji proposed the China-ASEAN Free Trade Area (CAFTA) in 2000.[4] In February 2001, China also inaugurated the Boao Forum for Asia (BFA) in Hainan.

In the political and security-affairs area, the PRC first mended relations with Southeast Asia, before turning seriously to the Northeast. China signed the 2002 Declaration on the Conduct of the Parties in the South China Sea, acceded to the Association of Southeast Asian Nations' (ASEAN's) Treaty of Amity and Cooperation, and simultaneously signed a Joint Declaration on Strategic Partnership for Peace and Stability. And in central Asia, China promoted the Shanghai Cooperation Organization, which included Russia and four central Asian countries (Kyrgyzstan, Tajikistan, Kazakhstan, and Uzbekistan).

In late 2002, following North Korea's revelation that it had been pursuing a secret nuclear weapons program, Beijing proposed the Six-Party Talks with North Korea, an approach that recognized not only Chinese, U.S., and South Korean interests in North Korea but also Japanese interests as well. Within the Six-Party Talks, the PRC has been playing an important brokerage role. Many Chinese analysts are talking about consolidating the multilateral process into a permanent security regime, with or without North Korea's nuclear ambitions being resolved.[5]

China's regionalism has focused increasingly on Northeast Asia since the departure of Japanese prime minister Koizumi Junichiro in late 2006.[6] At the summit of Northeast Asian local governments in September 2006, China played a key role, for example, in developing ideas for a unified economic community in Northeast Asia.[7] At the second Northeast Asian Economic Cooperation Forum, also in September 2006, Chinese vice premier Wu Yi highlighted the importance of Northeast Asian economic ties and urged deepening cooperation in infrastructure, trade, and investment.[8] In 2007, China's State Council affirmed the PRC's commitment to a high-level Northeast Asian Economic-Trade Cooperative Forum, consisting of trade ministers from China, Japan, South Korea, North Korea, Russia, and Mongolia.[9]

Trilateral developments after 2006, culminating in Premier Wen Jiabao's participation at the 2008 Trilateral Summit, were truly remarkable, considering the tumultuous relationship between China and Japan before. From 2002 to 2005, after all, the PRC had refused to hold top-level summits with Japan, in protest against Prime Minister Koizumi's Yasukuni Shrine visits. During the spring of 2005, massive anti-Japan demonstrations and riots erupted in dozens of Chinese cities, many with tacit government approval. In May 2005, Chinese vice premier Wu Yi canceled a scheduled meeting with Japanese prime minister Koizumi, a serious slap in the face within Japan's protocol-sensitive society. In December 2005, when the first East Asia Summit convened in Kuala Lumpur, rivalry between the PRC and Japan was on full display, with the PRC pursuing a narrower East Asian grouping while Japan promoted an expanded membership to include India, Australia, and New Zealand.

Remarkably positive developments have also occurred in the cross-Straits relationship since 2008, sharply contrasting to the tense cross-Straits situation of 2002–5. Taiwanese president Chen Shui-bian pursued one quasi-independence maneuver after another, provoking the Mainland leadership to respond with harsh words and military threats. The situation spiraled further downward in 2005, when Chen used a referendum to promote a new independence constitution. Although it was unlikely that such a constitution, leading to Taiwan's de jure independence, could possibly pass, this move cornered Beijing into a chain of negative reactions, culminating in the adoption of a highly divisive antisecession law in March 2005.[10]

Matters changed sharply a couple of years later. After Chen Shui-bian was succeeded by KMT president Ma Ying-jeou in May 2008, cross-Straits relations improved greatly. What had been accomplished within a year and a half, between the two ruling parties and the two governing authorities, was more than the total of what had been achieved in the previous two decades. Between June 2008 and December 2009, the two sides restored and deepened the dialogue mechanism between the Association for Relations across-Taiwan Straits (ARATS) on the Mainland and the Strait Exchange Foundation (SEF) on Taiwan.[11] The chairmen of the two associations held four historic meetings: Beijing in June 2008, Taipei in November 2008, Nanjing in April 2009, and Taichung in December 2009. They also concluded twelve major agreements, including the three direct links—sea travel, air flights, and postal services—as well as permission for Mainland visitors and investors to enter Taiwan regularly. In the first year of détente, more than 750,000 Mainlanders visited Taiwan, with over 3,000 arriving on newly direct flights from the Mainland every day.[12] Even Chinese premier Wen Jiabao declared in March 2009 that if the opportunity to visit Taiwan arose, he would "crawl" to get there.[13]

Beijing has also shown an accommodating posture toward Taiwan's request for "international space." In President Hu Jintao's speech of December 31, 2008, he demonstrated rare flexibility toward Taiwan's aspirations, provided that its actions did not directly contradict the one-China principle. Hu's speech included three major proposals: a comprehensive economic agreement; political dialogue and accommodation of Taiwan's aspiration for "international space"; as well as dia-logue to consider a mechanism for enhancing mutual military trust.[14] The two sides have also begun considering an actual cross-Straits peace agreement, as well as working toward the signing of the economic cooperation framework agree-ment (ECFA) in the near future.[15]

To be sure, difficult negotiations remain ahead, and crises are also possible, as leaders on both sides of the Straits face serious domestic counter-pressures against these integrating trends. Factions of Taiwan's opposition DPP are mobilizing forces to oppose President Ma Ying-jeou's moderate line. Within China, some conservative forces, especially within the military, are concerned that President Hu's approach may unintentionally allow Taiwan to pursue complete indepen-dence from the Mainland. Yet precisely because of those domestic uncertainties on both sides of the Straits, people seeking to stabilize cross-Straits relations showed a desire to accelerate the pace, trying to get as much as possible done by 2012, with President Hu and President Ma both predictably in power.[16]

The Dual Drivers of China's Regionalist Transformation

The preceding account suggests that critical junctures have played an impor-tant role in China's transformation with respect to regionalism—from being the perpetuator of an "organization gap" to becoming a leading actor in promoting a viable multilateral framework for Northeast Asia. It was in the context of the Tiananmen crisis in 1989 that the PRC improved bilateral relations with its Northeast Asian neighbors: Japan and the Republic of Korea. Then, in the wake of the 1997/98 AFC, Beijing participated proactively and at times even led mul-tilateral regionalist efforts in East Asia. Yet it was because of the change of leader-ship in 2003, to Hu Jintao and Wen Jiabao, coupled with a nuclear crisis on the Korean peninsula and two protracted, mini crises between China and Japan and across the Taiwan Straits, that the PRC's regionalist momentum increased steadily and focused even more clearly on Northeast Asia.

The Strategic Driver: "Peaceful Rise" and "Harmonious East Asia"

Former president Jiang Zemin led the PRC from 1989 to 2002, facing a volatile and at times hostile external environment.[17] While Jiang spent a decade repairing the relationship with the United States, the PRC's ties to regional nations suffered, with the "China threat" perception broadly shared across East Asia. Following the 1997/98 AFC, Beijing seized the opportunity created by that critical juncture and markedly improved relations with many of its East Asian neighbors. The PRC's strategic vision regarding regionalism, however, remained unclear and nontransparent. When Premier Zhu Rongji proposed free trade agreements (FTAs) to ASEAN, Japan, and South Korea in 2000, he surprised even the State Council's own research institute—the development research center of the State Council (DRC). Although the PRC's ties to Southeast Asian nations, as well as to South Korea, improved significantly during this period, its relations with Japan and Taiwan remained distinctly troubled.

Hu Jintao and Wen Jiabao, who came to office in 2003, presented a different strategic vision from their predecessors—a vision that embraced cooperation with China's Northeast Asian neighbors and also conciliation toward Taiwan. In November 2003, the vice president of the Central Party School, Zheng Bijian, expounded a "peaceful rise" strategy in his landmark speech at the Boao Forum.[18] Zheng contended that in the new world then emerging, China's interests were served by developing peaceably and contributing actively to a peaceful international environment.[19] Regional stability was an integral, vital component of that strategy.

Zheng Bijian's remarks on "peaceful rise" were widely seen as a new Chinese strategic vision, inspired by President Hu Jintao himself. Zheng, after all, had been executive vice president of the Central Party School from 1997 to 2002, during a portion of the time (1993–2002) that Hu had been director. The two also shared long connections with China's former president Hu Yaobang (who served from 1982 to 1987). Zheng Bijian had served as Hu Yaobang's personal secretary from 1982 to 1987. Hu Jintao had been a good friend of Hu Yaobang's son. The two Hus, of different generations, became close also because they had both built their political careers through work in the CCP Youth League.

This close connection of the two Hus likely has had important implications for Hu Jintao's Japan policy. Former president Hu Yaobang was quite close to Japanese prime minister Nakasone, and it was during his tenure that Sino-Japan relations reached their best condition ever. Tragically, however, Hu Yaobang was removed from his leadership position partly because of his close ties to Nakasone, whose controversial visit to the Yasukuni Shrine in 1985 led to massive student demonstrations across China.

The "peaceful rise" strategy has potentially significant implications for Northeast Asia—especially for Sino-Japan relations, cross–Taiwan Straits interactions, and China's stance on the Korean peninsula. The ultimate goal of the strategy was to secure a peaceful and stable environment for China's domestic development; volatile relations with Japan and Taiwan, as well as deteriorating security on the Korean peninsula, had prospectively serious consequences for China. In a 2003 interview with *Shijie zhishi* [*World Affairs*], Chinese vice foreign minister and long-time Japan specialist Wang Yi explained, "The key is to identify our current developmental position and appropriate international role." He continued, "Our relations with our neighboring nations directly affect our political-economic security, and we have to enhance pragmatism and build trust with neighboring countries."[20]

Beijing's pragmatic shift in 2003 was preceded by sustained advocacy of change by influential scholars. As noted in Chapter 5, Ma Licheng and Shi Yinhong both publicized the idea of "new thinking" on Sino-Japan relations, inspiring heated foreign policy discussion within China. Scholars such as Yan Xuetong and Hu Angang also wrote widely during 2001–3, advocating better relations with Japan and Taiwan, as well as multilateral cooperation across Northeast Asia. Yan, a well-known professor at Tsinghua University, President Hu Jintao's alma mater, argued that China's main obstacle to global advancement was the cross-Straits relationship, because of the special ties between Taipei and Washington.[21] Hu Angang, also a professor at Tsinghua University, argued that Northeast Asian regional integration was clearly in line with China's appropriate grand strategy.[22] When Hu Jintao and Wen Jiabao came to power, their policies toward Taiwan, Japan, and North Korea reflected the more accommodating, patient, and confident voices of scholars cited here.[23]

In late 2002, North Korea admitted the existence of a secret nuclear weapons program, and the crisis in its relations with the broader world intensified early in 2003. The PRC's response was sharply different from that of the previous decade, when Beijing was protective of the Democratic People's Republic of Korea (DPRK). After all, the two socialist nations had been "lips and teeth" allies from the time of the Korean War. This time, when Pyongyang exacerbated the nuclear crisis on the Korean peninsula, Beijing proposed instead to host Six-Party Talks to deal with the nuclear crisis, bringing four other concerned parties in the region—the United States, Russia, Japan, and South Korea—into dialogue with the DPRK.

China's vice foreign minister, Wang Yi, a rising star among PRC diplomats, whose father-in-law had been the foreign-affairs secretary of Zhou Enlai, was placed in charge of the Six-Party Talks. Despite the myriad of thorny issues and parochial interests inherent in the format, Wang was able to bring the parties together and to keep the talks going. His performance elicited international praise for Beijing, reinforcing in turn the PRC's positive orientation toward multilateral regionalism in Northeast Asia.[24]

Meanwhile, Japanese prime minister Koizumi's repeated visits to the Yasukuni Shrine and Taiwanese president Chen Shui-bian's independence moves were exacerbating tensions in the region. They also created serious dilemmas for President Hu and his strategic team. Former president Jiang Zemin was still in charge of military affairs, and the military had been hawkish in its stance toward both Japan and Taiwan. The moderate message embodied in the "peaceful rise" strategy, together with the supporters of this new strategy themselves, were under challenge within China.[25] The opposition argued that a moderate approach toward either Japan or Taiwan not only failed to achieve results but also emboldened Japanese conservatives and the Taiwanese independence movement.[26] It was under these complicated circumstances that anti-Japan demonstrations spread across China, with the Mainland also passing an antisecession law legalizing the use of force against Taiwan.

Beneath the turbulence were concerted efforts to repair relations with Japan. In September 2004, Vice Foreign Minister Wang Yi was dispatched to Tokyo as the new ambassador. His appointment demonstrated the tremendous importance that Beijing attached to the Sino-Japan relationship. A college graduate in Japanese, he had served in the Department of Asian Affairs of the Foreign Affairs Ministry since 1982, the same year that Hu Jintao was transferred to Beijing to become the secretariat of the CCP Youth League. Wang was posted in Tokyo as a midlevel diplomat from 1989 to 1994, a propitious period in Sino-Japan relations, when Japan became the first G-7 nation to normalize with China following the Tiananmen incident.

Wang Yi was clearly inspired by the people-centered diplomacy of Zhou Enlai, who had normalized relations with Japan in 1972. Wang also understood Japanese politics and society very well. Shortly after arriving in Tokyo, he invited leaders of the seven major pro-China associations in Japan to a special reception to show his appreciation. Within a month, he had invited influential politicians, including nine of the eighteen cabinet members, five former prime ministers, and more than 200 Diet members to other inaugural receptions. He also held multiple press conferences, often in Japanese. Within two months, the new ambassador also sent personalized invitations to ordinary Japanese living near the Chinese embassy compound for "friendly visits."[27] These multifaceted efforts gradually paid off, breaking the ice between China and Japan and laying groundwork for the dramatic improvement in Sino-Japanese relations that took place after Koizumi left office.

Since 2005, China's regionalist strategy has become much more proactive and clearly focused than previously. In that year, President Hu Jintao personally introduced the "harmonious world" concept concerning the construction of a new regional and international order. In May 2006, Hu further advanced the idea of "harmonious Asia."[28] Hu's "harmonious world" concept was adopted as the PRC's official diplomatic goal at the 17th National Party Congress in 2007. These important, albeit vague notions were elucidated by Chinese premier Wen Jiabao, who explicated "harmonious East Asia" at the APT Summit of 2007. Wen contended that regional cooperation had become the core means to achieving Hu's "harmonious world" strategy, and that Beijing's involvement in regional institutions "fully demonstrated China's new diplomatic concept, and showcased the country's determination to follow the path of peace and development."[29]

Wang Yi successfully concluded his ambassadorial tour in Japan late in 2007. As a key Chinese architect of the new Northeast Asia, however, his work continued. Shortly after returning to Beijing, he was sent to South Korea, as a special PRC envoy. His four-day visit was intended to strengthen China's ties to South Korean president-elect Lee Myung-bak and to ask South Korea to continue the Sunshine Policy toward North Korea. In June 2008, Wang Yi was named director of the Taiwan Affairs Office (TAO) of the State Council, the first diplomat ever named to that strategic position.[30] Wang Yi's strong performance as ambassador to Japan from 2004 to 2007 was clearly a key reason for this appointment, since cross-Straits relations are of considerable concern to Japan, and relate intimately to its domestic politics.

As the director of TAO, Wang Yi quickly developed a vibrant, multidimensional, and multilevel policy network across the Taiwan Straits. His policy network includes key executives representing the major Taiwanese companies operating in China, as well as politicians, bureaucrats in charge of economic and cultural affairs, and Taiwanese researchers and scholars long involved in cross-Straits dialogues.[31] Local governments on the Mainland have been actively organizing social exchanges and business cooperation with Taiwan,[32] and accelerating their efforts since the relaxation of cross-Straits tensions. Wang Yi has been proactively engaged in many of these local efforts, demonstrating again his versatility as a diplomat—at both the domestic and international levels.

Commerce as a Driver: From Regionally Balanced Development
to Northeastern Rejuvenation

Economic integration in Northeast Asia involving China has been deepening rapidly since 1997, as detailed in Chapter 6. In 2005, at the lowest ebb of Sino-Japanese relations, China's trade with Japan and South Korea combined was

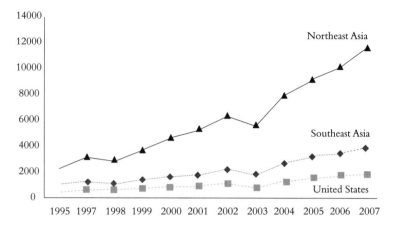

FIG. 7.1. Foreign Visitors to China, 1995–2007 (thousands). NEA visitors include visitors from Japan, South Korea, and Russia. SEA visitors include visitors from Malaysia, Philippines, Singapore, Thailand, and Indonesia. Source: *China Statistical Yearbook,* various issues.

approaching $300 billion. Actual combined capital flows from Japan and South Korea into China totaled almost $12 billion. Japan and South Korea were the second and third largest investors in China, surpassed only by Hong Kong, and much larger than the United States or Singapore, the largest Southeast Asian investor nation in the PRC.

Although the PRC's intra-NEA relations were difficult in 2005, half of the foreign visitors to China came from that region, including visitors from Japan, South Korea, and Russia. These visitors constituted nearly three-quarters of all those visiting from Asia as a whole. Americans also visited China in substantial numbers, but were fewer than half the number of Japanese and South Korean tourists visiting China during that year. As indicated in Figure 7.1, over the period from 1995 to 2007, the number of Northeast Asian visitors to China greatly exceeded the number of foreign visitors from either Southeast Asia or the United States—and by an increasing margin.

With such intensive socioeconomic exchanges between China and other nations in Northeast Asia, economic actors were zealously, although quietly, working to repair Sino-Japanese relations and cross–Taiwan Straits ties. The Chinese commerce minister, Bo Xilai, mayor of Dalian (1993–2000) and governor of Liaoning Province (2001–4) in northeastern China, came out in defense of the Sino-Japanese trade relationship during April 2005, at the height of anti-Japanese demonstrations in the PRC.[33] Meanwhile, Bo pushed for a deepening and acceleration of Sino–South Korea free trade negotiations, calling, in particular, for cooperation on retail, energy, and environmental protection issues, while asking for Korea's involvement in Beijing's high-priority northeastern rejuvenation program (NER).[34]

As seasoned observers of China have also recognized, a major shift occurred around 2003 in China's reform strategy.[35] In August 2003, Chinese premier Wen Jiabao formally advanced northeastern rejuvenation as a national policy goal (*guoce*). Two months later, the third plenum of the 16th Party Congress ratified the NER proposal as a major PRC policy priority. The ruling party also set up a Central Committee small leading group on NER, and premier Wen Jiabao served as group leader.[36] Under the NER plan, Beijing aimed to transform northeastern China—the PRC's most formidable rust belt—into a fourth engine of economic growth, after the Pearl River Delta, the Yangtze River Delta, and the Beijing-Tianjin Corridor. This ambitious new strategy had fateful implications for the Making of Northeast Asia, because China's northeastern provinces lie closest to Japan and Korea, both geographically and historically.[37]

Specific policies in the northeastern rejuvenation program also strengthen the potential for Northeast Asian regional cooperation. Unlike the western development project, also expounded by president Hu Jintao, in which the central government simply poured out money to improve infrastructure, the NER project offered local governments a free hand to solicit transnational business partners. Responsibility for revitalizing existing industry and expanding commerce was also placed mainly in the hands of local officials. These two aspects were similar to earlier liberalization programs in Guangdong and Shanghai; in all these cases, local governments consequently became major, proactive agents of external opening.[38]

To be sure, the NER was a major liberalization strategy, with an even bolder design than previous liberalization efforts in 1978, 1984, and 1992. Using both foreign and domestic private capital to reform state-owned enterprises and to transform existing heavy industry was explicitly encouraged. This unusual incentive strongly motivated both local governments and state-owned enterprises to seek foreign capital and become forces for external collaboration. Neighboring Japan and South Korea naturally became the main sources of capital and technology for northeastern China, particularly because their nearby location aided the creation of production networks for complex manufacturing. These Northeast Asian neighbors were also, to a greater extent than Hong Kong and Taiwan investors, globally competitive in machine building and heavy industry. Their underlying economic strength was synergistic with northeastern rejuvenation, and Japan's corporate world naturally showed immediate interest in China's NER proposals.

In early August 2003, JETRO's Beijing office organized a group of sixty Japanese executives to visit Liaoning Province, exploring investment and trade potential. In October, after the NER was officially inaugurated, Itochu, which has been involved in China since 1972, sent a top-level delegation to the PRC.[39] This group met leading local officials in the three northeastern provinces, and discussed a wide range of prospective investment projects. In Heilongjiang, Itochu aimed for raw materials; in Jilin, it contracted for substantial soy bean production, and a research center, while negotiating cooperation in automobiles.[40] In Liaoning, collaboration in heavy machinery was emphasized. Itochu was also well aware of infrastructure development opportunities under the NER program, strongly recommending the introduction of Japanese high-speed surface transportation maglev technology.[41]

The Northeast Rejuvenation project signaled more than a shift in Chinese economic planning. It also represented a profound change in local-central dynamics within China. President Hu Jintao harbored a profoundly different developmental vision for China than his predecessor, stemming from a different geographical power base. Former president Jiang Zemin has risen to the top through his work in Shanghai, with his main power base being the so-called Shanghai gang. Under his tenure, especially after 1995, when Jiang consolidated power, the PRC's developmental strategy strongly favored Shanghai and the surrounding Yangtze River Delta. President Hu Jintao, on the other hand, had spent most of his adult life inland. When he came to power, he was keen to develop areas that had been left behind during the previous reform period.

Northeastern China was precisely such a region. Before World War II, it had been one of the most developed industrial regions of the PRC, and one of the richest in raw materials and agricultural products. During the first three decades of the PRC's history, this region remained more advanced, and strategically more important, than other parts of China, supplying grains, raw materials, and heavy machinery to regions of the PRC. By the time President Hu Jintao came to power, however, northeastern China had fallen sharply behind the east, which had benefited greatly from the economic liberalization policies of the reform era.

Figure 7.2 presents the GDP performance of the three northeastern provinces in 1978 and 2008, compared with three eastern provinces, Guangdong, Zhejiang, and Jiangsu. Those three eastern provinces have a total population of 130 million, moderately larger than the northeastern three, with a total population of 107 million. In size, however, the eastern three combined are considerably smaller. With a total area of 201,000 square kilometres, the eastern three are roughly one-fourth the size of the three northeastern provinces combined. Furthermore, the northeastern region has rich natural resources, fertile agricultural land, and an advanced industrial base. In 1978, Liaoning Province generated a significantly larger GDP than either Guangdong or Zhejiang, two of the three selected eastern provinces. By

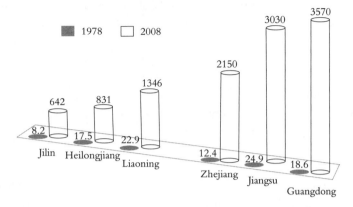

FIG. 7.2. GDP Growth Disparity between Eastern and Northeastern China, 1978 vs. 2008 (billion yuan). The northeastern three refer to Jilin, Heilongjiang, and Liaoning; the eastern three refer to Zhejiang, Guangdong, and Jiangsu. Source: China Dataonline. *Provincial Statistics*, 1978–2008.

2008, however, the eastern three had surpassed the northeastern three by a substantial margin. Guangdong's 2008 GDP alone was larger than the total for Liaoning, Jilin, and Heilongjiang. Zhejiang Province, whose 1978 GDP was about half of Liaoning's, generated over one-third more GDP than did Liaoning in 2008.

With the top leadership so positively inclined toward "regionally balanced" development after 2003, local officials in northeastern China seized their new opportunity and forcefully advocated northeastern rejuvenation. Through the implementation of NER, these local officials strengthened their network with top leaders and enhanced their own political power. The career path of Bo Xilai, former governor of Liaoning Province, is most illustrative of how northeastern development aided Chinese political careers, and why local officials in the Northeast pushed so strongly for Northeast Asian regional integration.

Bo Xilai was the son of former vice premier Bo Yibo, and spent most of his political career in northeastern China. Originally a low-ranking official in Dalian, he emerged in 1993 to become a legendary mayor of the city. During his tenure, Dalian was completely transformed, from a rather sleepy, old town to the "Hong Kong of northeastern China," as it was often called. Bo was also extremely open to foreign investment and trade. He led delegations to Hong Kong, Japan, Korea, and Europe to solicit new international opportunities. When Bo became governor of Liaoning in 2001, he lobbied China's central leadership aggressively to establish Liaoning as the center of the northeastern region,[42] and he has been a leading advocate for rejuvenation through interdependence with Northeast Asian neighbors ever since.[43]

The eventual adoption of NER as a state-prioritized developmental policy greatly enhanced Bo Xilai's political career. Although he had been born to a politically prominent family, Bo Xilai's political career had not always been smooth. In 1997, despite his strong political connections, solid performance as mayor of Dalian, and wide publicity in his behalf, he was refused a seat among the Liaoning provincial delegation to the 15th Party Congress.[44]

The adoption in 2003 of northeastern rejuvenation as national policy, however, was typically credited to Bo. In 2004 he became China's new commerce minister—a super minister with broad responsibilities for China's massive domestic and external trade. In 2007, Bo was named party boss of Chongqing—once capital of the wartime Republic of China, and one of China's four provincial-level municipalities, on a par with Beijing, Shanghai, and Tianjin.[45] This promotion was thanks to the credentials that he had established in northeastern China.

As an old industrial city in central China, however, Chongqing's economic development had lagged far behind the other provincial-level municipalities. The Hu Jintao-Wen Jiabao administration wanted to energize it through market liberalization, hoping that the city could play a central role in spreading Chinese economic growth further inland. Bo Xilai's role in northeastern rejuvenation was clearly a factor in his appointment to Chongqing. If Bo could bring about a transformation in Chongqing comparable to what he had achieved in northeastern China, his prospects for personal advancement at the national level would be further strengthened. Bo Xilai has been a standing member of the CCP Central Committee since 2007, on the strength of his previous successes, and could move still higher.

As the commerce minister in 2004–7 and the new boss of Chongqing from 2007, Bo Xilai kept strong connections to Japanese and Korean companies, as well as to northeastern China, his key political base. Within months of his appointment as commerce minister, Bo held meeting with South Korean business representatives to enhance the Sino-ROK trade relationship.[46] In 2005, at the height of anti-Japanese demonstrations, Bo Xilai similarly held a press conference to defend Sino-Japan economic relations.[47] In his meeting with his successor as Liaoning governor, Li Keqiang, Bo advised Li that the key to northeastern development was to open to foreign direct investment (FDI) and foreign trade, to build new ports, and to establish special economic zones.[48] That, of course, meant deeper ties, given Liaoning's geography, with Japan and Korea.

After arriving in Chongqing, Bo Xilai ambitiously set a target to develop Chongqing to the same level as Beijing, Tianjin, and Shanghai over the ensuing thirty years. And he did not hesitate to harness his networks with Japanese, South Korean, Hong Kong, and other sources of investment and trade to promote these goals. Within months, Bo received a delegation from JETRO to discuss Japanese investment in and trade with his new region. In response, JETRO organized a large group of Japanese business representatives to visit Chongqing. Thus, through Bo Xilai, Japanese business representatives that share strong personal ties to Bo expanded their activities to additional growth centers deep in China. Itochu, for example, opened three branch offices in northeastern China in 2004, and an additional two in central China during 2008.

Bo Xilai was not the only official to play a crucial role in promoting the PRC's northeastern rejuvenation strategy. Many other local officials in China's three northeastern provinces have also been proactive in seeking closer ties with Japan and South Korea. Many of those officials are also well connected in Beijing policymaking. Among them is the governor of Jilin, Hong Hu, son of Hong Xuezhi, a veteran revolutionary who had served as deputy secretary of the powerful Central Military Commission in the early Deng era. The deputy party secretary of Jilin, Lin Yanzhi, is the son of Lin Feng, who once headed the Central Party School and served as vice chair of the National People's Congress.[49] The current first-ranking vice premier of the PRC, Li Keqiang, was also once governor of Liaoning from 2004 to 2007, succeeding Bo Xilai.[50]

Li Keqiang is a strong candidate to be the next premier of the PRC, succeeding Wen Jiabao in 2012. Li has been President Hu Jintao's protégé since 1982, when Li became a member of the secretariat of the Communist Youth League under Hu's charge. Li also has a doctoral degree in economics from Beijing University. He clearly holds developmental views similar to Hu Jintao's. Before becoming governor of Liaoning in 2004, Li had served as governor of Henan since 1998. In Henan, Li pursued a balanced development approach, and improved the province's economic ranking in GDP output from 28th to 18th position in the PRC. Then in Liaoning, Li promoted the "five points to one line" project, connecting Dalian with Dandong and other Manchurian ports in a comprehensive infrastructural network. Because of his connections to the northeastern region and his support for "regionally balanced development," Li is likely to pursue vigorous northeastern Asian integration policies, should he advance to higher office, as seems likely.

Through the northeastern rejuvenation policy, rank-and-file officials in northeastern China became energetic proponents of broader transnational policy networks within Northeast Asia.[51] They actively organized industrial fairs, corporate conferences, and epistemic forums to promote regional cooperation.[52] They clearly recognized that Northeast Asia could be enormously helpful in the rebirth of their localities. Japan and South Korea, they understood, could provide more advanced technology, fresh capital, and advanced corporate management skills—all badly needed to restructure the massive yet mostly defunct state-owned enterprises and infrastructure in this rust belt area.[53]

Local officials in Liaoning, following the lead of former governor Bo Xilai, made concerted efforts to enhance economic ties with Japan and South Korea. The provincial government proposed to experiment with China–Japan–South Korea free trade zones in its two major cities, Shenyang and Dalian, while also establishing special zones for Japanese and Korean investors. At the 2008 CCP National Party Congress (NPC), the Dalian representative officially proposed to establish a Trilateral Free Trade Zone in the city in order to further stimulate northeastern rejuvenation and broader integration in Northeast Asia. Dandong, China's border city with North Korea, has been promoted as a pivotal economic link to the Korean peninsula, and has served as a commercial center for border trade with North Korea.[54] Jilin's border city with the DPRK and Russia, Wenchun, also boasts both a Korean industrial park and a Japanese biosphere park, each offering special incentives for Korean and Japanese investors respectively.

Jilin, another core province in northeastern China, has held annual Northeast Asian Investment and Trade Fairs since 2004. These have been customarily attended by central bureaucrats, corporate representatives, and local officials from throughout Northeast Asia.[55] Since 2006, the Jilin provincial government has actively promoted an ambitious Tumen River integration strategy, as a contribution to northeastern rejuvenation. Jilin's trade with Russia increased by 123 percent and 101 percent in 2006 and 2007, respectively.[56]

Local officials in northeastern China are not the only powerful local actors pushing for intra–Northeast Asian cooperation. The more developed areas of the Pearl River Delta, Yangtze River Delta, and Beijing-Tianjin Corridor all have formed significant socioeconomic ties to other Northeast Asian countries and regions. Table 7.1 captures Northeast Asia's shares of FDI in the major growth centers in the PRC: Dalian, Beijing, Shanghai, and Guangdong. Japanese and Korean investment, as indicated, has been especially important in Dalian, contributing more than 30 percent of total FDI. In Beijing also, these two countries constituted over 22 percent of the total. In Shanghai, where sources of FDI have been more diverse, Japan alone provided almost 12 percent, holding second place after only Hong Kong. In all these areas, as indicated in Table 7.1, Northeast Asian investment dwarfed that from the United States by huge margins. In Guangdong, farthest away, among major Chinese cities, from the Northeast Asian center of gravity, Hong Kong investment was predominant, at over 56 percent of the total.

The incoming FDI presented in Table 7.1 has been extremely important for local officials, as their political advancement within the PRC as a whole has typi-

TABLE 7.1

Northeast Asian Investment Shares in Major Chinese Growth Centers in China

(Percent)

External Investors	Dalian[a]	Beijing	Shanghai	Guangdong	All China Average
Hong Kong	22.8	19	19	56.3	32.1
Japan	18	14.8	11.6	2.3	7.3
Korea	12.2	7.8	1.6	0.5	6.2
Total of NEA	*58.1*	*41.6*	*36.6*	*61.6*	*49*
U.S	11.6	4.4	5.1	2	4.5

SOURCE: For national statistics, see *zhongguo tongji nianjian* [*China Statistics Yearbook*], 2007; for other local statistics, see *beijing tongji nianjian* [*Beijing Statistics Yearbook*], 2007; *shanghai tongji nianjian* [*Shanghai Statistics Yearbook*], 2007; *guangdong tongji nianjian* [*Guangdong Statistics Yearbook*], 2007; and *dalian tongji nianjian* [*Dalian Statistics Yearbook*] 2005.
[a]Dalian's data are for 2004. The rest are for 2006.

cally been based on ability to develop their local economies. FDI is a quick route to improving local conditions by helping to expand exports, build infrastructure, enhance the local tax base, and provide local employment. Local officials therefore have enormous incentives to preserve and expand ties to Japan, South Korea, Hong Kong, and Taiwan, all being sources of capital and technology. They thus have become powerful advocates for closer and better Northeast Asian relationships within the PRC's domestic politics. Southeast Asia, with the partial exception of Singapore, cannot provide a remotely comparable set of domestic political incentives to orient Chinese policies in its favor.

Local interests have recently further enhanced their influence on central policy-making in the PRC, as many top leaders are now being promoted upward from local positions, rather than rotated within Beijing. Some 19 percent of politburo members at the 17th Party Congress in 2007, for example, were promoted from provincial leadership, a sharp increase from the 10 percent of 1992.[57] Xi Jinping, the top contender for the next presidency, served previously as the party boss in Fujian, Zhejiang, and Shanghai, all at the very heart of the Shanghai Circle. Bo Xilai and Li Keqiang, two other rising political stars, have served as successive governors of Liaoning, as noted earlier.

Complex yet powerful policy networks within China, in short, are now driving Northeast Asian integration, despite lingering political and security shadows on the Korean peninsula. These domestic networks, which desire stability so that economic development can go predictably forward, appear to have helped shape Beijing's increasingly critical position toward North Korea's nuclear-weapons program. Although the PRC can rest assured that the DPRK's nuclear weapons would never target China, the possibility of an accelerating nuclear arms race in the region, with South Korea and Japan beginning to acquire countervailing weapons, could seriously affect business confidence in the region, and in turn the personal careers of China's upwardly mobile provincial leaders. Hu Jintao and Wen Jiabao, who have placed such strategic importance on developing China in a "regionally balanced" fashion, will be the top leaders until at least 2012. Yet their legacy would be tarnished if two of their major grand strategies—"peaceful rise" and "northeastern rejuvenation"—failed to succeed. Strategy, business, and pursuit of personal political power have thus converged in the Hu-Wen administration to lead China increasingly toward a proactive role in the Making of Northeast Asia.

In Conclusion

China's involvement in Asian regionalism came relatively late; the PRC began cautiously participating in cooperative ventures with its neighbors only during the 1990s. The transformation in its stance since then, however, has been sweeping and dramatic—from perpetuator of an "organization gap" to the role of a major catalyst for integration. The 1997/98 Asian financial crisis was the first critical juncture propelling China's regionalist shift. In the wake of the AFC, China began participating actively in the actual design of multilateral regional organizations, and the world came to understand and appreciate Beijing's conciliatory approach. Positive lessons were quickly learned. And China has begun, however hesitantly, to lead. Chinese strategists have begun to internalize regionalism, as a concept and a value. Their proposals regarding regionalism, and the practical refinements by skilled practitioners like Bo Xilai and Wang Yi, have been reflected particularly in the foreign policy of the Hu-Wen administration that came to power in 2003.

President Hu Jintao, on assuming office, faced a strategic environment quite different from that of his predecessor, Jiang Zemin. As Beijing's political-economic relationship with Seoul deepened following the AFC, Pyongyang's nuclear ambitions increasingly came to threaten regional stability and prosperity. While the PRC's relations with Southeast Asia, central Asian nations, and even the United States remained relatively stable, its ties with Japan and Taiwan were politically troubled. Japan and Taiwan, however, were meanwhile becoming increasingly important investors and trading partners of China, as regional production networks became more prominent. These contradictions underlay the complex and paradoxical political economy confronting Hu and Wen as they assumed leadership. Their administration found proactively constraining North Korea—while improving ties with Tokyo and Taipei—to serve China's fundamental long-term interests.

The strategic perceptions of Hu and Wen regarding Northeast Asian conciliation were further intensified by two mini-crises in 2005—between Japan and China, and across the Taiwan Straits. Within China's strategic circles, proponents of improved Sino-Japan and cross-Strait relations were strengthened politically. Bureaucrats with expertise on Northeast Asian relations, such as Wang Yi, Bo Xilai, and Li Keqiang, were promoted. Developments between China and Japan since 2006 and those across the Taiwan Straits since 2008 have further intensified Beijing's emphasis on intra-NEA cooperation, and strengthened the political networks that underlie it.

Strategic priorities and crisis, of course, have not been the only driving forces behind Chinese policy-making. Domestic business stakes in intra-NEA cooperation are also compelling. Japan and South Korea are two of the largest investors in and trading partners of the PRC, as the U.S. role in Northeast Asia slowly declines. The involvement of these two neighbors in China (Japan since 1972 and the ROK since 1992) has fostered strong connections with domestic Chinese interests, which in turn lobby for better political ties with the ROK and Japan when those ties are threatened. The northeastern rejuvenation strategy has been especially important in promoting intra-Northeast Asian cooperation, provoking a "virtuous cycle" of deepened human ties and rising regional leadership enthusiasm about regional integration. Local governments, state-owned enterprises, and private companies are eager to collaborate with their counterparts in neighboring Japan, Korea, and Taiwan, as their ability to attract outside collaboration is often vital for their own domestic political advancement or personal economic well-being.

The future naturally remains uncertain, as complex political and strategic difficulties persist in Northeast Asia—between the PRC and Japan, not to mention across the Taiwan Straits and on the Korean peninsula. Yet since Beijing's strategy and developmental priorities seem to align with closer and more cooperative ties to its Northeast Asian neighbors, the PRC is likely to seek mechanisms that can manage strategic complexities in the region. Beyond President Hu Jintao's tenure ending in 2012, his grand strategies—"peaceful rise" and "regionally balanced" development—will likely become embedded and continue, as they are based on a realistic assessment of China's current global position, as well as its domestic and external circumstances.

Political-military crises are certainly possible in the foreseeable future, especially on the Korean peninsula. Yet major developments in Chinese domestic and foreign policy-making have often been products of crises in the past, as the Chinese well understand the crisis philosophy that "underneath jeopardy lies opportunity."

Future crises may well decisively shape the landscape not only of China but also of the broader Asian region. Even in their absence, however, domestic political-economic transformation, and deepening political, local, and corporate networks across China's borders, are already contributing to the PRC's rising willingness to lead in the Making of Northeast Asia.

Catalysts
Korea and ASEAN in the Making of Northeast Asia

Smaller powers can at times have disproportionate influence in international affairs, counter to the general assumptions of realist theory, as students of both comparative and international politics point out from time to time.[1] The recent history of regional integration worldwide clearly illustrates this paradox. As the role of Benelux in Western Europe, Canada and Mexico in North America, and Uruguay in South America's Southern Cone suggest, smaller nations, especially when they have decisive leaders with broad personal networks that inspire international trust, can play decisive, catalytic roles in driving regional integration forward.[2]

East Asia clearly illustrates this common transnational pattern in action. Smaller states have played unusually catalytic roles in the Making of East Asia. They have done so, however, with a paradoxical twist. For many years, especially during the 1980s and most of the 1990s, it was the diminutive Association of Southeast Asian Nations (ASEAN), spearheaded by Malaysia's outspoken leader Mohamed Mahathir, that drove the integration of a region whose economic center of gravity actually lay much farther north.

The Rise and Fall of ASEAN as Early Catalyst

There were three major reasons for Southeast Asia's early leading role. First of all, it was, for historical reasons rooted in geopolitics, the only part of East Asia with a functioning subregional organizational infrastructure. The Southeast Asia Treaty Organization (SEATO), founded in 1954, just after the Indochina War, had been one of the earliest post–World War II Asian regional bodies. The Asian

Development Bank, founded in 1965, just as the Vietnam War was beginning, was located in Manila. ASEAN had been founded in 1966, amid the Vietnam War, to help reinforce regional solidarity in the face of communist challenge.

Northeast Asia, fractured in multiple ways by the Cold War—along the DMZ, across the Taiwan Straits, and by both the Yellow and East China seas—lacked the geographic cohesion to do the same. As a consequence of these pre-existing organizations, founded to arrest communist advances in Indochina during the 1950s and 1960s, Southeast Asia thus had the institutional base for broader initiatives in later years that Northeast Asia initially lacked. This embedded advantage lasted for well over three decades.

A second reason for ASEAN's long-standing primacy in regional integration was the diplomatic support that the United States, Japan, and ultimately China provided. All felt they should defer to ASEAN, following the fall of Saigon in 1975. During the late 1970s and the 1980s, that complex and often slow-moving body nevertheless proved to be a sturdy bulwark against Vietnamese expansion in Southeast Asia, because of strong outside support. Later on, especially after Hanoi itself joined ASEAN, it was perceived as balancing a rising China. With the geopolitical equation of Northeast Asia frozen by North Korea's recalcitrance and South Korea's lingering isolation, only the diplomatic chessboard of Southeast Asia was malleable, in any event.

A third factor dictating ASEAN regional leadership, even on Northeast Asia–specific matters, was the distinct preference of North Korea and China for this counterintuitive equation. Although the Democratic People's Republic of Korea (DPRK) remained on delicate terms with several of its neighbors, particularly conservative South Korea and former colonial master Japan, Pyongyang developed relatively relaxed and even friendly ties with several states in Southeast Asia, particularly Malaysia, Indonesia, and Thailand. Indeed, these ASEAN members were among only a relative handful of nations worldwide maintaining diplomatic relations with both North and South Korea. Pyongyang also viewed them as potentially important future markets for its exports.

A fourth factor dictating ASEAN's surprising pre-eminence as a regional catalyst was the proactive stance of Southeast Asian leaders, who reveled in their prominent regional role. Malaysian president Mohammed Mahathir, in particular, felt strongly that Western leadership in East Asia, which he saw as neocolonial, should be supplanted by an exclusivist Asian regionalism. And through his "Look East" policies, Mahathir cultivated Japanese, South Korean, and ultimately Chinese support for his controversial, confrontationist vision of global affairs.[3]

Mahathir took the agenda-setting lead for several years on issues of East Asian integration, as we have seen, with his provocative East Asian Economic Caucus

(EAEC) proposal. He was also instrumental in bringing the Chiang Mai financial-swap agreement and the East Asia Summit concept to fruition.[4] As the 1997–98 Asian financial crisis subsided, however, Mahathir's relative influence—and that of Southeast Asia more generally—gradually began to wane, particularly following his departure from the Malaysian presidency in 2003.

Southeast Asia's decline as a catalyst for Asian regional integration has occurred for many reasons that are the obverse of reasons for its rise.[5] The central geopolitical challenges in Asia, which so readily engage the major outside powers, have shifted northward, with Korea and the Taiwan Straits replacing Vietnam as Asia's principal flashpoints. Secondly, Southeast Asia's economic engine has sputtered since 1997, as a result of the lingering effects of the financial crisis, even as North Pacific economic relations with booming China, in particular, have deepened.[6] Thirdly, Southeast Asia–centric bodies such as the ASEAN Regional Forum (ARF) have proved ineffectual, as evidenced in East Timor. Meanwhile Northeast Asia, with its trilateral summits and think-tank dialogues, is conversely growing more institutionalized. Fourthly, Southeast Asia faces something of a leadership gap on regionalist issues. Mahathir retired in 2003, and no Southeast Asian leader has clearly moved to fill his long-standing ASEAN-centric regional leadership role.

Korea's Natural Catalytical Role

One glance at the map of Northeast Asia clarifies a crucial geopolitical reality: Korea lies literally at the heart of that region (see Figure 8.1). As a unified entity, it commands the strategic space between Russia and China to the north, and Japan to the southeast, serving as a potential bridge among them. As a divided country, however, Korea easily becomes a pawn among the Great Powers, with the North easily relegated to pariah status. And the South—marginalized from continental Asia—subsists instead for most purposes as a geostrategic island.

Korea's future evolution could also strongly shape East Asia's overall role in the broader world. A categorically divided Korea is a marginalized, weakened land, naturally inclined to dependence on outside powers, especially the United States, and relatively ineffective on matters of regionalism. South Korea, in particular, is divided from the central powers of the Asian continent, Russia and China, by the obstreperous darkness of North Korea, on which so little political-economic light traditionally shines. A divided Korea's complex circumstances, and the regional "hub-and-spokes" dynamics that they engender, tend to reinforce the traditional, dominant U.S. global role.

Conversely, a unified Korea—or one in which North and South were deeply engaged with each other—could be a more self-sufficient entity, and a mark-

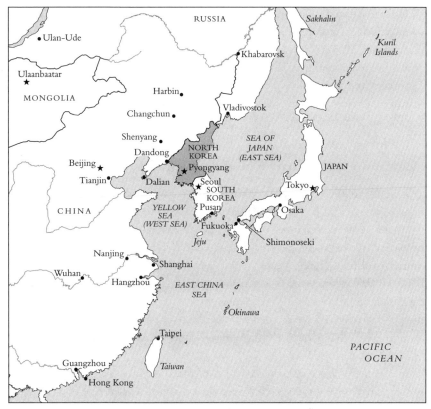

FIG. 8.1. Korea's Strategic Location. The map illustrates Korea's ideal location as a logistic hub in Northeast Asia. As indicated, five major cities with easy access to more than 700 million people are within a two-hour flight radius from Seoul. Another forty-three cities with more than a million people are located within a three-hour flight radius of Seoul.

edly more proactive force for East Asian regionalism.[7] Such a Korea could truly become a more major hub for the Northeast Asian subcontinent, around which regional affairs would more naturally revolve. A unified Korea's deeper interaction with Asia as a whole would in turn give the region more cohesion and autonomy in dealing with the broader world.

Korea has certain domestic structural qualities that enhance its ability to serve as a catalyst for regional integration, under any configuration of international circumstances. It is highly homogeneous, with a powerful socioeconomic center in Seoul. Its economy is quite centralized, with substantial market share and market power in the hands of the *chaebol*. And its political system is also centralized, with a powerful presidency and a unicameral national assembly. All these features aid Korea's maneuverability in the complex world of Northeast Asian affairs.

How is Korea in fact evolving between these internal poles of conflict and cooperation? What deeper forces have been shaping, and will in future determine, that tortured nation's role in East Asia, and in the world? In particular, how are domestic developments in Korea affecting prospects for a more interactive, inter-dependent, and ultimately cohesive Northeast Asia? These are the fateful questions that this chapter considers—issues all too often lost in the pessimistic analyses of regionalism's unclear prospects.

How Far Korea Has Come: A Historical Perspective

Korea's evolution from isolated pawn to proactive catalyst for Northeast Asian regional integration has not happened overnight, and remains clearly incomplete. Yet there has been a sharp transformation over the past two decades, as Korea has become an increasingly enthusiastic and effective advocate of regionalism. That shift from a trans-Pacific to an increasingly Northeast Asia–centric orientation has been driven by a potent interaction between political-economic crisis and economic opportunity, with presidential leadership helping to give the transition sharper definition. This clear change in Korea's stance on regionalism reveals much about the underlying forces within Korean politics that are supporting the Making of Northeast Asia itself.

Interestingly, classic Korean strategists of the late nineteenth-century, such as Hwang Jun-Hun and Queen Min, were playing regional balance of power politics well over a century ago, so as to secure the survival of the weak Chosun Dynasty. Their calculations appear to have been remarkably similar to those of many mod-ern Korean leaders since Roh Tae-woo.[8] After securing Japanese support to end Chinese suzerainty over Korea in 1895, these classic nineteenth-century strategists turned to Russia for support of Korean independence against the Japanese. Only with Japan's historic defeat of the Russians at Tsushima in 1905, followed by the Portsmouth Peace Treaty and the infamous Taft-Katsura agreement, did this deft balance of power manipulation by the Koreans end, forcing them into subservi-ence as a colony of Japan.[9]

Korea's bitter heritage of Japanese colonial rule is a matter of record. It began in 1905, with the declaration of a Japanese protectorate, and continued in 1910 with full annexation, and a fierce ensuing wave of local protest. The Japanese governor general and a major leader of Japan's Meiji Restoration, Ito Hirobumi, was assassinated at Harbin by a Korean patriot, An Jung-geun, in October 1909. Waves of nationalist demonstrations rolled across Korea throughout much of the first decade of Japanese rule, with 140,000 Koreans arrested during 1918 alone.[10] In March and April of 1919, inspired by Woodrow Wilson's promises of self-determination for oppressed people, half a million Koreans took part in mass demonstrations, followed by brutal Japanese suppression.[11]

For nearly two generations, use of the Korean language was forbidden in Korea's own schools, and Koreans were recognized, for legal purposes, only by Japanese names. Forty percent of the Korean adult population was uprooted from their place of birth and transferred either to unfamiliar provinces or overseas. By 1944, 11.6 percent of all Koreans were residing outside Korea, including nearly 2 million in Japan.[12] Indeed, by the end of World War II a full one-third of the industrial labor force in Japan was Korean, while between 100,000 and 200,000 Koreans had been forced into slavery as comfort women for the Japanese military.[13] Among the saddest statistics: more than 10,000 Koreans were annihilated at Hiroshima and Nagasaki—most of them forced laborers at the time in Japanese war industries.[14]

Given the bitter colonial heritage, it is not surprising that post–World War II Korea was long estranged, both diplomatically and economically, from Japan. South Korea's first president, Rhee Syng-man, was militantly anti-Japanese, and avoided all contact with his nation's former oppressor. Rhee's first powerful successor, Park Chung-hee, however, had Japanese military experience, as an officer in Manchuria during World War II, and was somewhat more pragmatic. Yet when Park normalized relations with Japan in April 1965, in return for grants of $300 million and loans of $200 million to his country, there were massive riots of protest all across Korea.[15] The Korean public was simply not prepared, given the bitter history, for easy reconciliation with Japan.

Early postwar South Korean relations with neighboring China and Russia were similarly tortured. More than 3 million Koreans lost their lives in the Korean War, a bitter conflict escalated by a Chinese intervention in which 700,000 PLA "volunteers," including Mao Tse-tung's eldest son, also died. Sino-Korean economic and political ties were virtually nonexistent until the late 1980s, long after both Tokyo and Washington had normalized their relations with Beijing. Ties with the Soviet Union were similarly dormant, save for angry interactions related to the downing of a Korean Airlines passenger plane by Soviet fighters southwest of Sakhalin in 1983.

Despite a bitterly conflictual early postwar history of relations with all its Asian neighbors, Korea has come to play a sharply different regional role since the late 1980s. At first, South Korea's interest in regional cooperation developed around the natural economic territories near the Tumen River, adjacent to North Korea and the Yellow Sea. The earliest players were private firms and local governments, like that of Incheon, which had special historical or economic links to the Northeast Asian continent.

The dramatic recent intensification of Korean interest in regionalism at the national level has been deeply related to historic changes in South Korean domestic politics. In June 1987, amid widespread rioting, President Roh Tae-woo announced democratic elections for the following December and soon thereafter removed controls on labor organizing.[16] During the June 1987–June 1988 period alone, unions increased their membership by nearly two-thirds, and labor unrest sharply escalated.[17]

Toward the Making of Northeast Asia: Deepening Korean Domestic Incentives

Democratization meant new influence in politics, not only for labor but also for small businesses, and not least for a rising middle class. It circumscribed above all the military. Democracy also intensified pressure on the Blue House for dramatic policy initiatives. New departures came most easily in the foreign-policy sphere—particularly across old Cold War boundaries in Northeast Asia that offered both political reconciliation and economic advantage.

The first major step in South Korea's Northern diplomacy came in March 1990, when Seoul established diplomatic relations with Mongolia. In June 1990, President Roh held a historic San Francisco summit meeting with Soviet president Mikhail Gorbachev. In September of that year, President Roh Tae-woo, in a historic U.N. General Assembly speech, first enunciated the concept of a six-nation consultative body for East Asian peace, which was to become a dynamic element of Northeast Asian affairs in future years. In November 1991, the Republic of Korea (ROK) mediated the simultaneous admission into the Asia Pacific Economic Cooperation (APEC) of the "three Chinas"—the People's Republic of China (PRC), Taiwan, and Hong Kong—demonstrating clearly its potentially catalytic regional role.[18]

South Korea's mediating role in Northeast Asia was leveraged further in 1992 by mutual diplomatic recognition between the ROK and China, and in 1993 by the simultaneous admission of the two Koreas to the United Nations. In the wake of these historic developments, the ROK finally had full diplomatic ties with all its neighbors, and at least potential informal contacts at the United Nations with North Korea as well. Seoul was at last in a strong diplomatic position to promote the multilateral frameworks and regional integration that the geopolitical logic of its central location in Northeast Asia so powerfully suggests.

Korean leaders began exploiting their expanding diplomatic ties to undertake regional-policy initiatives, with an increasing emphasis on Northeast Asian relationships. In May 1993, President Kim Young Sam underlined the importance of a multilateral security dialogue within the region in a historic speech at the APEC summit meeting. And in July 1994, amid darkening storm clouds on the Korean peninsula, Minister of Foreign Affairs Han Sung Joo proposed the launching of a Northeast Asia multilateral-security dialogue associated with the ASEAN Regional Forum.[19]

The North Korean nuclear crisis of 1994–95 also clearly accelerated Korea's interest in multilateralism, as a complement to U.S.-ROK bilateral security ties.[20] Indeed, it manifested many traits of a critical juncture, as noted in Chapters 2 and 4, in the development of Northeast Asian regional institutions. Following Jimmy Carter's July 1994 Pyongyang visit, and the subsequent October 1994 U.S.-DPRK agreement, the quadrilateral Korean Peninsula Energy Development Organization (KEDO) was founded among the United States, the ROK, and Japan, to provide two light-water reactors (LWRs) to North Korea. Emerging regional problems were simply becoming so complex, as the nuclear agreement recognized, that multilateralism was necessary in resolving them. Such approaches also helped to neutralize the marked and inveterate tendency of North Korea to gain advantage by playing its neighbors against one another, and encouraged the emergence of broader and deeper transnational networks.

Korea's mediating and agenda-setting role on matters of Asian regional integration expanded during the late 1990s. In 1997, the first ASEAN Plus Three Summit was held, with Korean support. In late 1999 in Manila, at the initiative of President Kim Dae-jung, the leaders of Korea, Japan, and China also held a precedent-setting trilateral dialogue for the first time, separately from their ASEAN colleagues, albeit convened at the same set of regional meetings. This marked another important step in the Making of Northeast Asia.

Kim Dae-jung played an especially fateful agenda-setting and policy-development role on many aspects of Asian regionalism, subtly striving to enhance Northeast Asia's role without alienating the Southeast Asians. At the ASEAN Plus Three Hanoi Summit of December 1998, he proposed an East Asia Vision Group (EAVG) to discuss long-term cooperation within the broad Asian region.[21] This body, launched with two members from each of the East Asian countries, drawn from both governmental and nongovernmental sectors, was given a mandate to submit a major report to the 2001 Brunei Summit of the ASEAN Plus Three.

The Vision Group was launched in Seoul during October 1999, with former Korean foreign minister Han Sung-joo as chairman, and held five sessions from the second half of 1999 to May 2001. It produced a set of original recommendations that gave added momentum to East Asian regionalism, including proposals for an East Asian Free Trade Area, and for an East Asia Summit. This latter idea was realized at Kuala Lumpur during December 2005.

Seoul's ability to play a central, proactive role on regional-integration issues has also been enhanced by its evolving ties with North Korea. Most dramatically expressed at the June 2000 Pyongyang Summit, Kim Dae-jung's Sunshine Policy enhanced Korea's leverage with China and Russia also, even as it broke the long-standing American monopoly on dialogue with North Korea.[22] Whatever complications it produced for U.S.-Korean relations—problems that became starkly clear at the Bush-Kim Washington Summit of March 2001—the Sunshine Policy clearly made Seoul a more dynamic player on Northeast Asian regional issues than it had ever been before, as a result of the geopolitically important prospect of intra-Korean rapprochement—however distant—that it portended.

Although the pragmatic Lee Myung-bak administration, taking office in February 2008, disapproved formally of the Sunshine Policy, it nevertheless built implicitly on the foundations of that earlier initiative. Lee made transition-period efforts to abolish South Korea's Unification Ministry, principal architect of the Sunshine Policy, but ultimately abandoned them, and was pragmatic toward North Korea in his inaugural address.[23] Even after the North Korean missile and nuclear tests of early 2009, Lee's administration permitted continued trade, food aid, and investment in the Kaesong industrial complex that had been virtually inconceivable only a decade before. Lee also proactively pursued positive relations with Japan, China, and Russia, as well as the United States, from his first day in office.[24]

Recent Korean policies have promoted Northeast Asian regionalism beyond North-South relations also, through both direct policy measures and support for Track II initiatives. Upon Roh Moo-hyun's inauguration in February 2003, his government launched its "peace and prosperity policy," with the Northeast Asian Initiative serving as the major vehicle through which that policy would be implemented. The initiative aimed to promote peace and mutual prosperity on the Korean peninsula and Northeast Asia through "trust, cooperation, and mutual gains."

President Roh established the Presidential Committee on the Northeast Asia Business Hub, oriented toward infrastructural issues, in April 2003. He broadened the focus a year later, creating the Presidential Committee on the Northeast Asian Cooperation Initiative as an advisory body for planning and implementing related projects.[25] This committee subsequently conducted substantial research, and supported more articulate Korean agenda-setting on regional issues.[26]

The presidential committee, reporting directly to President Roh, put particular emphasis on domestic projects to enhance Korea's capacities as a logistical and financial hub for the broader Northeast Asian region. It also promoted cooperative energy, transportation, environmental, and cultural projects, involving all the nations of the region. It defined Korea's role as catalytic in three respects: (1) as a "bridge nation," linking continental and maritime powers; (2) as a "hub nation," emerging as a center of ideas and intraregional networks; and (3) as a "cooperative nation," striving realistically to build a peaceful regional community.[27]

The Roh government also forged markedly improved ties with China, mirroring rapidly deepening economic relationships with the Middle Kingdom. Lee Myung-bak, while more conciliatory toward the United States and Japan than his predecessor Roh, also worked to preserve positive relations with the PRC. These deepened ties, plus concern over North Korea's nuclear program—especially in the wake of the 2006 and 2009 nuclear tests, also encouraged Beijing to place increased emphasis on the Six-Party Talks and other forms of Northeast Asian dialogue. With support from both Seoul and Beijing—and after 2006 from Tokyo as well—Northeast Asia–specific regionalism thus acquired both diplomatic and economic momentum, to Seoul's advantage, as the most geographically central of the three major Northeast Asian nations.

Korea as Catalyst: Why the Policy Shift?

From a historical perspective, the shift in Korean policies toward regional integration over the past two decades has been striking. Until the mid-1960s, Seoul had been totally estranged from all of its giant Northeast Asian neighbors. It did not normalize relations with Japan until 1965, and prior to the early 1990s lacked diplomatic ties with both Russia and China. It did not even talk to North Korea for nearly a decade after that. Regional interactions, as noted above, were largely at the local government or private sector level.

Today, however, Seoul has forged vigorously interactive relationships with all of its neighbors, and developed a deeper, albeit volatile, set of ties with North Korea. Located at the heart of the region, with an ideal logistical location, as is clear from Figure 8.1, Korea is playing a pivotal role in connecting the "spokes" of the Washington-centric "hub and-spokes" political economy of the Pacific. And through a catalytic mediating role among its neighbors—in many ways like that of the Benelux nations in the formation of the European community—South Korea is dynamically inspiring the Making of Northeast Asia, even though it is the smallest of the three major nations of the region.

The political-economic trends are striking. In 1979, for example, Korea's trade with China was only $19 million, diplomatic relations were nonexistent, and broad Korean images and opinions of the PRC, only three decades after the Korean War, were still markedly hostile. Now the PRC is by far South Korea's largest trading partner, as indicated in Figure 8.2, with PRC-ROK trade volume

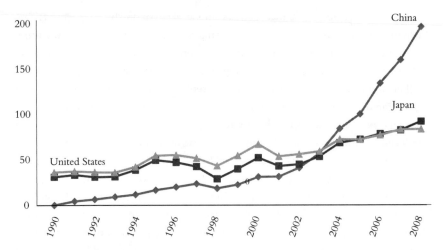

FIG. 8.2. Korea's Trade with China, Japan, and the U.S. Source: IMF, *Direction of Trade Statistics*, various issues.

exceeding U.S.-ROK trade by more than 30 percent. Bilateral trade between the ROK and China has risen well over two thousandfold from its meager origins, yielding a 2008 surplus for Korea of $14.5 billion.[28] China is likewise the largest recipient of Korean overseas-development assistance, and since 2002 has also been the most rapidly growing destination for Korean direct foreign investment. In 2008, trade with Japan also surpassed that with the United States, making Japan the second largest trading partner of the ROK.

Korean investment in China more than doubled during the 2002–5 period, to over 40 percent of Korea's global total on a flow basis. Korea's investment now accounts for well over 10 percent of total foreign direct investment in China, more than double the level of 2002. The number of Korean companies operating in China also jumped eightfold in little more than a decade, from 650 in 1992 to almost 5,000 by 2003, and has continued to rise steadily since then. Korea has also decisively overtaken Japan in total value of investments in China—a remarkable feat, in view of Korea's much more modest economic scale.[29] The ROK's deepening ties with the PRC have both stimulated Japanese competition in China and new Japanese overtures to Korea, thus helping once again to catalyze the Making of Northeast Asia.

Diplomatic and even political-military relations between China and South Korea have grown much closer in recent years, contrasting sharply to a long history of estrangement. Since the Hu-Roh bilateral summit of 2003, the two countries have entered a sanguine era of "all-around cooperation," which now extends even to extensive contact between their militaries. The two countries exchange ship visits and meetings of defense ministers, conduct military staff talks, engage in search and rescue exercises (since 2007), and even operate air and naval hotlines with each other.[30] They have pledged to coordinate policies in the judicial area, while `also accelerating interparliamentary, as well as party to party, relationships. South Korea's Fair Trade Commission is even providing technical aid to China regarding competition and antimonopoly policies.[31] To celebrate deepening political-economic ties between China and Korea, the year 2007 was designated in China as China-Korea Exchange Year.[32]

Sino-Korean cultural ties are also deepening, building both on a shared, if long suppressed, Confucian heritage in the PRC and the presence of more than 2 million ethnic Koreans with permanent, historic roots in China. In 2000, more than a million Koreans visited the PRC, of whom 60,000 were long-term residents, with an additional 13,000 temporarily studying there.[33] Since 2001 visitors to China have topped the rolls of Korean tourists abroad, with more than 1.67 million visiting the PRC in that single year.[34] One in four South Koreans traveling outside their country chose China as their destination in 2004, a third more than in 2002.[35] By 2006, 2.85 million South Koreans were visiting the PRC, with more than 850 flights operating between South Korea and China every week. In 2008, 60,000 Koreans studied there, while 34,000 Chinese also studied in the ROK.[36] To promote expanded tourism from the PRC, in 2008 the Federation of Korean Industry (FKI) even began promoting establishment of an elaborate Chinatown in Seoul.[37] More than 2 million ethnic Koreans living in China provide still another source of mutual emotional attachment, deepening support for amicable Northeast Asian continental ties in both nations.

South Korea is also rapidly consolidating its relations with Russia, further spurring the Making of Northeast Asia. Bilateral trade was relatively limited in the thirteen years following normalization, achieving an all-time high of $4.18 billion in 2003. That total rose sharply thereafter, however, to around $20 billion by 2008.[38] In Vladivostok and Khabarovsk, Korean consumer goods and automobiles are ubiquitous, as they also are in Irkustsk and Central Asia.

Russian-Korean ties appear destined to deepen substantially in the future, driven by natural complementarities between the largest energy exporter in the world, with more than a third of proven global gas reserves, and a manufacturing power that is simultaneously one of the world's ten largest energy importers.[39] Investment relations have likewise deepened. Despite normalization in the early 1990s, Korea's investment in Russia was initially low, totaling only $205.7 million in all the years up to 2003. In 2003 alone, however, Korean investment in Russia surged to $44.6 million, compared with only $3.6 million in the previous year, and it has since continued to expand.[40] By the end of 2008, the stock of Korean direct investment in Russia reached $1.66 billion, with major cooperative projects in energy, petrochemicals, and the automobile industry rapidly progressing.[41] Bilateral trade in 2007 was $15 billion, a huge jump from less than $10 billion in 2006. In 2008, Korea-Russia trade made another leap, to more than 18 billion.[42]

One important albeit little-known aspect of Korea's deepening integration with its Northeast Asian neighbors is its dynamic new relationship with Mongolia, formalized only in 1990. Korea is called "Solongos" in Mongolian, meaning "Land of Rainbows." Mongolians describe Korea as the "country of hope," and a "model country that they should emulate."[43] More than 34,000 Mongolians, or 1.2 percent of the entire population, live in Korea, including over 1,700 students, making Korea the biggest overseas educational destination for Mongolians.[44] Annual remittances from Mongolians working in Korea total more than $200 million annually. Apart from cultural and economic ties, Mongolia is important diplomatically to the ROK, as a listening post between Russia and China, and as one of the few nations that Seoul recognizes which also has an active North Korean diplomatic mission. It thus is capable of serving as a quiet venue for North-South talks of fateful consequence for the broader Northeast Asian region as a whole.

Korea has traditionally had delicate relations with Japan, reflecting forty years of bitter colonial subjugation. Korea and Japan did not even re-establish diplomatic ties until 1965. Yet economic relations quickly deepened thereafter, with the intensification of transnational production networks, especially in electronics and precision machinery. Today Japan is Korea's third largest trading partner, and the constituency in Korea for stable and realistic relations with Japan is growing, especially in the precision-machinery sector, as transnational production networks expand.[45]

Five Driving Forces

Five factors, a combination of international and domestic, have been at work since the late 1980s to produce the fateful intensification of Korea's support for regionalism—a transition of decisive long-term importance for the Making of Northeast Asia. Most important, in the international area, has been the waning of the Cold War. Until the Reykjavik Summit of 1986, at which U.S. president Ronald Reagan and Soviet Communist Party general secretary Mikhail Gorbachev made a historic move toward conciliation, strong U.S. opposition, and domestic repugnance within Korea to associating with the perpetrators of the Korean Air Line Incident of 1983,[46] made rapprochement with the Soviet Union politically impossible in the ROK. The subsequent waning of the Cold War, however, removed a crucial roadblock within Korea that could otherwise have rendered the shift toward a dynamic Northeast Asian regionalism impossible.

As these international and domestic constraints began to wane in the late 1980s, President Roh Tae-woo made a far-sighted overture to the Soviet Union, culminating in his dramatic summit meeting with Mikhail Gorbachev at San Francisco during the fall of 1990. That historic summit set in motion many of the geopolitical changes that led within a decade to dramatic transformations in the geoeconomic map of Northeast Asia, and to a steady shift in the locus of Asian regional integration toward the powerful Northeast quadrant of the continent.

The Korean business world, it is important to note, has been broadly and consistently supportive of its government's regionalist initiatives, especially those with Russia and China. Indeed, *chaebol* interest in rapprochement with the Asian continent long predates Roh Tae-woo's own diplomatic initiatives. As early as the mid-1970s, soon after the first Oil Shock, Korean companies, led by Hyundai, were investigating oil and natural-gas prospects in central Siberia, more than 4,000 kilometers north of Seoul.[47]

Korean *chaebol*, like their Japanese *keiretsu* cousins, integrated the activities of banks, trading companies, and industrial firms, creating business conglomerates capable of operating on minuscule margins across many sides of complex transactions, like those involved in resource development. The *chaebol* were also capable of barter trade and varied forms of risk management, giving them a comparative advantage in transactions with the nonmarket economies of continental Northeast Asia. Indeed, the unorthodox economic interests and capabilities of Korean firms have supplied the positive stimulus that has driven Korea's increasingly positive orientation toward Northeast Asian regional integration steadily forward. The Federation of Korean Industry (FKI) has also supported these efforts, by sponsoring and organizing periodic business summits and joint projects with both Japan and China.[48]

The Hyundai Group, in particular, has had strong interest in deepening ties with both China and Russia, as well as North Korea. Long-time Hyundai chairman Chung Ju-yung, himself born in North Korea, was a strong supporter of Korean "Northward Diplomacy" from its early inception. He stressed in particular the dividends to energy security that could rebound to Seoul through deeper political-economic relations with its giant continental neighbors. Chung served as president of the FKI for nearly a decade during the 1980s.

Also supportive was the entrepreneurial Daewoo Group—like Hyundai structurally configured to benefit from large-scale resource development projects. Thus, as implicit geopolitical constraints from Washington, D.C. relaxed, economic and diplomatic imperatives within Korea drove it toward an expanded role on the

Northeast Asian continent. This trend is being continued under President Lee Myung-bak, once a senior executive of the Hyundai Group, who was inaugurated in February 2008 and who also places explicit priority on energy diplomacy.[49]

Korea's regionalist shift, provoked by underlying economic logic and strong *chaebol* support, was clearly accelerated by *critical junctures*: both the Korean nuclear crisis of 1993–94, and the tumultuous Asian financial crisis of 1997–98. The nuclear crisis drove Seoul inevitably to coordinate with its regional neighbors in search of a resolution, in the hopes of adding their leverage with Pyongyang to its own.[50] It also led to the birth of a unique organization—the Korean Peninsula Energy Development Organization. KEDO fostered interpersonal policy and business networks among Seoul, Tokyo, and Pyongyang—and even a few with Washington—where virtually none had existed before. These new networks helped, over time, to deepen the confidence-building between North and South that ultimately led to the Pyongyang Summit of June 2000.

The Asian financial crisis had an incalculable shock impact on Korea, as we have seen. Surging in abruptly, like a sudden, uninvited hurricane, the political-economic tumult shattered sanguine regional expectations of both growth and prosperity, giving birth to a new and unsettling sentiment: distrust of global institutions. The International Monetary Fund was roundly condemned within Korea, as the bogeyman that had savaged Korean prosperity and unjustly opened the country to scavengers from abroad.[51] Many Koreans consequently began to believe more strongly than before in regionalism, as a buffer against the shocks conveyed by global institutions (and implicitly by market forces as well) that lacked sensitivity to Korea and its uniquely vulnerable circumstances.

The critical juncture of the Asian financial crisis clearly deepened Korean consciousness of the need for regional autonomy in finance. It also served, as is suggested earlier in this chapter, as a catalyst for concrete policy steps to limit the vulnerability displayed by the crisis. The Chiang Mai swap-quotas agreement of May 2000, and the Asian Bond Fund (ABF) initiative that followed in 2003, were but two manifestations. Both were strongly supported by Korea, as was the initiation in 1998 of an ASEAN Plus Three Finance Ministers' meeting, oriented toward coordination on concrete, technical problems, to parallel the annual top-leader summits.[52]

A third critically important driving force behind the ROK's "pro-Asia shift," and the corresponding migration in the locus of regional-integration efforts northward, were the changing politics within Korea of the reunification issue, and of intra-Korean relations. The politics within Korea of intra-Korean relations are deeply linked, of course, to those of regionalism. Korea's northern neighbors, after all—Russia and China—have deep strategic and economic interest in the pace and profile of North-South relations within South Korea itself. Steps toward reconciliation with those northern giants are simultaneously perceived by many within Korea as hastening the day of stable reunification—precisely the policies that Roh Tae-woo adopted in his Northern diplomacy of 1989–93. Until the late 1980s, of course, Korean reunification looked like an abstract, long-term question. Yet with the fall of the Berlin Wall, and the collapse of North Korea's main bene-factor, the Soviet Union, the question began to take on much more immediacy in Seoul.

This seismic shift in the international politics surrounding the Korean pen-insula, facilitating important new contacts with communist neighbors, coincided with a fateful transition in Korean domestic politics as well. In December 1987, South Korea conducted its first largely democratic election in twenty-five years, inaugurating a drift toward populism, and away from traditional elite dominance. That shift continued for two decades, led by the so-called 3-8-6 generation,[53] through the successive elections of presidents Roh Tae-woo, Kim Young-sam, Kim Dae-jung, and Roh Moo-hyun. Populist nongovernmental organizations (NGOs), left-of-center mass media, students, and labor unions likewise grew substantially stronger in Korean politics, as did depressed, traditionally nonfavored areas such as the Cholla region, the ancestral home of Kim Dae-jung. All tended to be more oriented toward Korean ethnic kin to the north, and to nearby China, than the previously dominant military and bureaucracy, with the new actors also often resentful of Korea's powerful ally of the previous half-century, based in Washington, DC. By the time the conservative Lee Myung-bak became president in February 2008, these sociopolitical changes of the preceding two decades had become embedded, helping to impart a more pronounced Northeast Asian bias to South Korean politics and regional policies than previously.

Political-economic crisis, it is important to note, has contributed significantly to this structural transformation in Korean politics, a dynamic that has in turn helped accelerate Seoul's shift toward Northeast Asia–centric regional policies. The Asian financial crisis, in particular, led to decisively new roles for labor and multinational firms in the Korean political economy, while the related left-ori-ented political bias of the 1998–2008 decade also aided NGOs. All these groups were less attached to Korea's traditional trans-Pacific ties than the previously dominant military, bureaucracy, and sociopolitical elite had been.

As the reunification issue began gaining more salience in Korean domestic politics across the 1990s, Korean leaders became more concerned with diplo-matic and political strategies to pursue it, or at least to cope with its perceived inevitability. Since the North itself was proving so belligerent and recalcitrant in its direct dealings with the South, leaders in Seoul from President Roh Tae-woo on decided to outflank Pyongyang with "Northern Diplomacy." This meant both better bilateral relations with Moscow and Beijing, perceived to have influence in Pyongyang, and also a new concern for the overall multilateral architecture of the Northeast Asian region. Both preoccupations, supported by heavy-industrial firms such as many of the Hyundai companies, helped to reinforce a gradual drift from alliance to regionalism in Seoul's hierarchy of priorities. Although Lee Myung-bak began moving during 2008 to a renewed emphasis on alliance with the United States, his revival of relations with Japan gave new overall momentum to Northeast Asian regional relationships also. And business interests, in the FKI and elsewhere, pressed him to deepen ties with Mainland China as well.[54]

The final, and in many ways the most important, catalyst in Korea's drift toward regionalism has been political leadership. The Korean presidency, as noted earlier, is institutionally strong, so presidents have substantial leverage with both the uni-cameral National Assembly and civil society, especially early in their single five-year term. Each of the past five Korean presidents has taken concrete initiatives in the interest of burnishing his historical legacy, either at the very beginning or the very end of their terms, that have intensified the shift in Seoul's priorities toward a higher estimate of regionalism. Many of those steps, especially the decisive moves by Kim Dae-jung, were driven by political-economic crisis, stronger regional ties offered a safer haven in the economic storm triggered by globalism than relations with the West alone could provide.

Underlying the policy moves toward regionalism, in many cases, have been economic interests, especially those with an energy linkage. Deepening energy ties with Russia are a case in point. Large-scale energy-development projects such as pipelines interest a broad range of Korean industrial firms, including steel, machinery, and construction companies, as well as banks. Yet it has been national leaders, in Korea's powerful presidential system, that have determined timing, and given concrete substance to these economically rational policy shifts.

President Roh Tae-woo's initial preoccupation seems to have been the Soviet Union, spurred by the interests and background of policy advisors like Kim Hak-joon, South Korea's foremost authority on the Russian Revolution.[55] Roh thus stressed the six-party process formula for Northeast Asian negotiations, privileging Russia, in his landmark 1989 General Assembly speech. He also pressed for, and realized, the 1990 Roh-Gorbachev San Francisco Summit, which was followed by the simultaneous admission of North and South Korea to the United Nations in 1991. Toward the end of his term, in August 1992, Roh also normalized relations with China.

President Kim Young-sam (1993–98) moved further to consolidate relations with China, and also to gain Seoul's admission to the United Nations. In this task, he again needed to deepen relations with the two erstwhile communist superpowers, both of which held a potential Security Council veto. In 1993, as noted earlier, both Seoul and Pyongyang were simultaneously admitted to the United Nations.

President Kim Dae-jung (1998–2003) took, together with President Roh Tae-woo, the most dramatic and substantive steps toward regionalism in recent Korean history. Many of these, such as Kim's 1998 acceptance of Japan's apology on historical issues, had landmark significance, and transcended the populist bias of recent Korean politics. Kim Dae-jung improved, in different ways, Seoul's relations with every one of its major neighbors, enhancing Korea's prospects for playing the central regional-brokerage role for which its location and size logically suit it, in place of a geographically far-removed ASEAN.

Kim Dae-jung, first of all, improved Korean relations with Japan, by accepting Prime Minister Obuchi's apology on historical issues early in Kim's state visit to Tokyo. He also strengthened ties with Washington, by supporting the so-called Trilateral Coordination and Oversight Group (TCOG) process of trilateral relations among Korea, Japan, and the United States, also established in 1998.[56] Finally, and most remarkably, Kim achieved a breakthrough summit with North Korea, through his historic visit to Pyongyang in June 2000. This combination of overtures, building on stable ties with both Moscow and Beijing, gave leverage to Korean diplomacy, and made it arguably easier for Seoul to gain Washington's acquiescence in continuing steps toward East Asian regionalism itself.

President Roh Moo-hyun, narrowly elected in late 2002 in a close three-way election campaign over two more conservative opponents, perpetuated and expanded the deepening regionalist bias of Korean foreign policy. As noted earlier, Roh established the Presidential Commission on Northeast Asia, to define an agenda for regionalism, and appointed well-known, proactive scholars, such as Moon Chung-in of Yonsei University, to head it. Roh also strengthened bilateral Korean ties with China. He likewise deepened Kim Dae-jung's heritage of rapprochement with North Korea, holding a bilateral summit with Kim Jong-il in late 2007, initiating the joint Kaesong Special Economic Zone, and reviving North-South road and railway travel.

Roh's East Asia policies, although influenced by long-term business logic, were also colored by his own distinctive populism. That included a healthy distrust both of Seoul's traditional domestic elites and of the United States, to which those elites have been historically aligned. It also led to periodic Japan-baiting, and investigation of prewar colonial-era collaborative ties between Japanese and Koreans. Combined with provocative Japanese gestures, such as the Yasukuni Shrine visits of Prime Minister Koizumi and the equivocation of his successor, Abe Shinzo, on the comfort women issue, the Roh administration's populism soured relations with Tokyo until Roh's own departure from office in early 2008.

The inauguration of conservative Lee Myung-bak as president in February 2008 showed promise of deepening some of Korea's regional ties still further, as suggested above. Lee, like Roh, enjoys positive ties with Beijing, and as a former Hyundai executive has a positive basis for relations with both North Korea and Russia, which had been pioneered by Hyundai's founding father, Chung Ju-yung. Additionally—in contrast to Roh—Lee enjoys positive relations with Japan, based in part on a political base within Korea that sees more virtue in cooperation than in conflict with Tokyo, and also on astute early personnel choices.[57] Lee's strong relations with Washington—which itself are much more enthusiastic since 2005 than previously about détente in Northeast Asia, provided that the North Korean nuclear issue is resolved—also facilitate this positive Northern diplomacy, enhancing the catalytic regional role that Korea's unique geographical and economic position affords it.

In Conclusion

Throughout the 1980s and most of the 1990s, ASEAN was the key catalyst in creating a broad, if shallow and often ineffective, Asian regionalism. That coun terintuitive, ASEAN-centric pattern, we have found, is rapidly changing, as Asia's locus of both economic and political gravity moves steadily northward. South Korea, because of its geographic centrality, and its relatively centralized decision-making, coupled with important shifts in both the regional geopolitical equation and Korean domestic politics, is rapidly emerging as the heart of a dynamic new Northeast Asia that is beginning to forge its own regional identity. Under President Lee Myung-bak, Korea is playing a dynamic role in promoting regional integration, the North Korean nuclear crisis notwithstanding.

Korea, as we have seen, has undergone a major "shift toward regionalism" over the past fifteen years, that has allowed it largely to displace ASEAN as the principal catalyst for Northeast Asian regional integration. Until the late 1980s, the ROK was continually suspicious of regionalist initiatives, as undermining the vital "hub-and-spokes" alliance with Washington. That attitude has radically shifted, as Korea has moved from military to left-oriented civilian rule, and back to a regionally sensitive conservatism. Under the Roh Moo-hyun administration (2003–8), in particular, Korea's foreign policy grew increasingly Northeast Asia–centric. Under Lee Myung-bak (2008–13), strong relations with neighboring Northeast Asian states apart from North Korea are continuing, while ties with Washington are more positive than under Roh.

Korea's proactive role in promoting regionalism, and the increasingly Northeast

Asia–focused nature of its efforts—within the context of a multitiered system where it retains positive ties to Washington, has been the product of both changing domestic politics and a changing global economy beyond its frontiers. Asia currently takes more than 60 percent of Korea's new foreign investment, compared with only 16 percent flowing to the United States.[58] China is South Korea's largest trading partner—by a decisive margin. And economic ties with Japan are deepening also, both in manufacturing and in technology development.

Within Korea, there is a supportive domestic coalition behind closer ties with the ROK's neighbors. Not surprisingly, Northeast Asia—especially China—has major attractions for the trading companies and banks that have traditionally been influential in Korean politics. It also has rising attraction, relative to the West, for a range of other Koreans too. The Asian financial crisis exposed the West in the eyes of many Koreans as insensitive to their unique national vulnerabilities with respect to energy, security, and finance, with the IMF taking the strongest criticism. The crisis also showed Korea's Northeast Asian neighbors to be more empathetic than their Western counterparts. The Korean nuclear crisis, strangely, has been reinforcing parallel ambivalence, exposing corresponding differences in assessment of North Korean attitudes and capabilities. Many of today's South Koreans, especially a younger generation newly activist in the wake of an energizing 2002 World Cup, in which Korea moved surprisingly to the semifinals, view the North as relatively weak and benign, while criticizing Americans for being too harsh toward it. Other Koreans urge conciliation with Pyongyang because of the grim Doomsday threat that its weaponry poses to Seoul, less than fifty miles from the DMZ—a challenge that they observe the West does not existentially understand. Both psychology, in the form of ambivalence toward U.S. policy, as well as economics, in the shape of rising dependence on China, and gradual reconciliation with Japan, thus combine to make Korea increasingly disposed to support—and indeed in many ways to lead—the Making of Northeast Asia.

9

Japan's Dilemma and the Making of Northeast Asia

More than a century ago, as Japan's industrialization began, the scholar Fukuzawa
Yukichi, founder of Keio University, argued that Japan had two choices in its relations with the broader world. It could either be part of the West, or part of Asia. It
could never be both.[1]

Fukuzawa opted decisively, in those days, for the industrially and militarily
powerful West. And for many years he appeared to have made a prescient choice,
as burgeoning Western military and industrial power came to dominate world
affairs. Yet in recent years, many analysts would contend, the tide of history has
been steadily shifting once again, reinforced by economic tectonics, back toward
Asia.

As we have seen, there are powerful winds on the continent of Asia, blowing
outward from China, toward a deeper and more coherent regionalism that is also
more explicitly Northeast Asia–focused than at any time in the past three generations. Trade interdependence within the Northeast quadrant of the continent is
rising, as increasingly elaborate transnational production networks are being fused
among Mainland China, Taiwan, South Korea, and Japan. Financial coordination
and intellectual exchange are also intensifying. Even the militaries, with long
histories of mutual antagonism, are talking to one another once again, with only
North Korea the outlier.

This steady movement toward Northeast Asian integration, driven by economics and facilitated by political-military normalization, has a rising momentum that
remains only poorly understood in the Western world. A relaxation of tensions
across the Taiwan Straits is already feeding this dynamic, and parallel developments

in Korea may well someday do so as well. Massive China and Russia have highly complementary factor endowments to crowded, energy-short, yet industrially sophisticated South Korea and Taiwan.

Japan's Tangled Continental Ties

Over the past decade, as this continental Asianism has been deepening, and growing more exclusive, Japan has been more ambivalent toward the new dynamic than its neighbors. In 1991, to be sure, Japan was the first of the G-7 nations to normalize relations with China after the Tiananmen Massacre. In 1992, the Japanese emperor, son of the alleged perpetrator of the Pacific War, visited both Beijing and Shanghai, greeted with a warm public reception. And in 1994, American pressure to support UN sanctions against North Korea helped provoke a major crisis in the Hata Cabinet, and the subsequent fall of that Japanese reformist regime.

The year 1995, the fiftieth anniversary of the end of World War II, was a watershed year in Japan's relations with continental Asia. Japanese prime minister Murayama Tomiichi, a socialist himself, with a strong antipathy to his own nation's wartime militarism, visited Beijing and tendered a heartfelt personal apology to China, as his predecessor Hosokawa Morihiro, relative of wartime prime minister Konoye Fumimaro, had also done.[2] Yet only days after Murayama left Beijing, the Chinese People's Liberation Army (PLA) undertook a major nuclear test, in close proximity to the fiftieth anniversary of the Hiroshima nuclear bombing. Chinese president Jiang Zemin also met in the same year with Korean president Kim Young-sam, to commemorate Tokyo's wartime defeat with a ringing denunciation of Japan.

Japanese relations with South Korea stabilized with the coming of Kim Dae-jung to the Korean presidency in early 1998. In a historic visit to Tokyo at mid-year, undertaken in the shadow of the Asian financial crisis, Kim indicated a clear willingness to forgive, and to forgo further apologies from Japan, in return for serious Japanese expressions of contrition for wartime transgressions. Japanese prime minister Obuchi Keizo reciprocated in the same conciliatory spirit as Kim, and relations between Seoul and Tokyo improved markedly. The North Korean missile shot of August 1998 deepened still further the sense of solidarity between those two "spokes" in the traditionally "hub-centric" San Francisco system's wheel.

Japanese relations with China, by contrast, did not improve, and indeed continued their deterioration. Jiang Zemin's 1998 Tokyo visit, coming on the heels of Korean president Kim Dae-jung's conciliatory triumph, was an abject failure, marred by bitter Chinese denunciations on Japanese soil of Japanese World War II behavior. Jiang's outspokenness and lack of delicacy, however understandable in view of his personal experiences,[3] hardened both Japanese elite and mass popular attitudes toward China. Taiwan's president Lee Teng-hui, a graduate of Kyoto University who proactively cultivated Japan, complicated Tokyo's relations with Beijing still further.

With the coming of Koizumi Junichiro to the Kantei in April 2001, and especially following his first Yasukuni Shrine visit that fall, Sino-Japanese political relations spiraled further downward. Koizumi's persistent annual visits between 2001 and 2006 to the Yasukuni Shrine, where since 1979 Class A war criminals have been enshrined, prevented any state visits at all between the two Asian giants during the last four years of Koizumi's tenure. In the absence of top-level communication, and with the provocative Chen Shui-bian leading Taiwan, broader Sino-Japanese relations deteriorated, contributing to the anti-Japanese riots convulsing China during the fall of 2004 and the spring of 2005.

Behind the marked deterioration in Sino-Japanese relations during the Koizumi years were not only leadership animosities and Chinese domestic-political factors, including Taiwan, but also three important structural changes in Japanese politics as well. Perhaps most important, the left-oriented Japanese opposition parties were collapsing, pushing the center of gravity in Japanese domestic politics sharply to the right, and giving Liberal Democratic Party (LDP) conservatives with confrontationist inclinations toward China more leverage in domestic politics than previously. In 1996 the socialists and the communists together held 14 percent of the seats in the powerful Lower House of the Diet. By 2005 that share had fallen to 4 percent, and to only 3 percent in early 2008.[4]

Internal changes within Japan's ruling LDP further complicated Sino-Japanese relations. Japanese ties to China had traditionally been brokered by the Tanaka faction of the LDP, long headed by former prime minister Tanaka Kakuei, who normalized long-disrupted relations with China in October 1972. Ever since the early 1970s, however, the Tanaka faction had been in deadly competition with that of Fukuda Takeo, Tanaka's rival for the prime ministership, who had maintained close ties with the United States and Taiwan.[5] Koizumi himself had personally served as private secretary to Prime Minister Fukuda, and was intent on destroying the political influence of the Tanaka faction. Disrupting the traditional Tanaka-faction brokerage role with China had been a major part of that effort.[6] Under Koizumi, such traditionally important Tanaka-faction politicians as former prime minister Hashimoto Ryutaro and former chief cabinet secretary Nonaka Hiromu had trouble playing effective brokerage roles in Sino-Japanese relations, given their political distance from Koizumi and his personal antagonism toward their pro-Beijing efforts.

A fourth and final complicating factor, which magnified the overall impact on Sino-Japan relations of the other factors (top-level tensions, weakening of the opposition, and Koizumi's efforts to marginalize the Tanaka faction) was generational change. As in China, the Japanese politicians, diplomats, and businessmen who had normalized relations with their counterparts across the East China Sea during the 1970s, and who felt a personal stake in positive bilateral relations, were steadily passing from the scene. The lack of state visits and other high-level bilateral interactions with China—potentially important lost networking opportunities—made it hard to replace those respected elders and their transnational networks. Sister-city ties and international expositions, like those in Nagoya (2006) and Shanghai (2010), as well as other subnational ties, could only, of course, provide a partial substitute.

Meanwhile, the U.S. and Japan were operationalizing joint missile defense, against the intense opposition of China. Japanese military forces were in Iraq and the Indian Ocean, collaborating with the United States in the struggle against terrorism. President George W. Bush and Prime Minister Koizumi Junichiro were on a first-name basis. And China and Japan were close to blows over conflicting energy claims in the East China Sea.[7]

To a greater degree than previously in modern history, the U.S.-Japan relationship was evolving into an authentic military alliance.[8] Tokyo and Washington, during the Koizumi years in particular, coordinated closely on a global basis. Yet that intimate cooperation with the global superpower came, for Tokyo, at a costly price. Japan grew increasingly distanced from Asia, even as continental Asia itself gained greater internal cohesion, and a hint of exclusivity vis-à-vis the broader world.

The atmosphere of Sino-Japanese relations improved markedly and surprisingly under Koizumi's successor, Abe Shinzo. Indeed, Abe—known for his nationalist views—visited Beijing (and also Seoul) within a month of his inauguration as prime minister in late 2006. China reciprocated with a fruitful visit by Chinese premier Wen Jiabao to Tokyo in April 2007, and Abe's successor, Fukuda Yasuo, held successful Beijing discussions in December 2007, as did Fukuda's successor, Aso Taro, in October 2008 and April 2009.

Sino-Japanese relations warmed further under the Democratic Party of Japan (DPJ) government that displaced the LDP in September 2009. The new DPJ Prime Minister, Hatoyama Yukio, visited Beijing within a month of his inauguration, while DPJ Secretary General Ozawa Ichiro took over 140 DPJ Diet members on his sixth annual Beijing policy visit, in December 2009, during which each member was accorded a personal photo opportunity with Chinese President Hu Jintao.

Fukuzawa's Dilemma Revisited

To understand the complex and contradictory forces that have so markedly transformed the triangular ties among Japan, the U.S., and Asia of late, thus shaping the profile of Japan's emerging relations with the nearby continent, one must consider both embedded history and the evolving interest-group structure of Japan itself. For Fukuzawa over a century ago, as we have seen, the burning domestic issue was whether Japan should stick with its traditional Eastern roots, and all that they meant for cultural continuity, or embrace the alien yet dynamic West. Asia, for Fukuzawa, was stagnant, and also traditional. The West, by contrast, was innovative, powerful, and clearly Japan's appropriate economic and cultural partner, he maintained.[9]

For half a century Japan finessed the issue of Asia versus the West through imperialism: adoption of Western technology, and development of Western-style military power, in order to achieve a dominion over neighboring continental Asia that would accord it great-power standing in Europe and the United States. Through that dominion, interdependence with Asia deepened, however perversely for many, to the extent that three-quarters of Japan's total worldwide trade was with Asia during the mid-1930s, as Table 9.1 suggests. Well over a third of that country's total was with Northeast Asia. China alone was a significantly larger market than the United States for prewar Japan, while both Korea/Taiwan and Southeast Asia were major supplementary sources of food and raw materials. After Pearl Harbor all these areas were merged into the Greater East Asia Co-Prosperity Sphere of wartime prime minister Tojo Hideki.

With empire and economic interdependence with the Northeast Asian continent came migration as well—often forced. By 1935, more than half a million Koreans lived in Japan. By 1945, under pressures of wartime, that number had nearly tripled, to 1.4 million. There were also significant numbers of Chinese, who had been part of the Japanese Empire, unwillingly, for two generations, although not nearly so many as Koreans.[10]

Japan's pattern of regional interdependence shifted abruptly and traumatically after 1945. As Table 9.1 points out, the economic pendulum swung to a pattern of deep economic links across the Pacific, and sharply limited relations with continental Northeast Asia. U.S.-Japan trade by 1955 had expanded to more than double the share of Japan's total trade that it had been only a decade earlier, while trade with China had shrunk to less than a quarter of its previous proportion. Trans-Pacific interdependence reached its high point near the end of the Reagan administration, with a full 34 percent of Japanese exports going to the United States in 1988, or roughly three times more than to Northeast Asia and ten times the amount flowing to China.[11]

TABLE 9.1

Changing Transwar Patterns of Interdependence in the Northeast Asian Political Economy

(Percent)

	Japanese Exports		Japanese Imports	
	1934–36	1956	1934–36	1956
United States	16	22	25	31
China	18	3	12	3
Korea/Taiwan	21	6	24	2
South/SE Asia	21	6	24	2

SOURCE: Original data from Ministry of International Trade and Industry, and adapted from Jerome B. Cohen, *Japan's Postwar Economy*, Bloomington: Indiana University Press, 1958, p. 153.

Demographically, the continental Northeast Asian profile also receded. Nearly two-thirds of the 1.4 million Koreans in Japan at war's end had returned to their homeland by 1947, and many of the Chinese, caught by their own ensuing civil war, were repatriated to Taiwan. Few Koreans or Chinese received Japanese citizenship, and both groups remained marginal in the Japanese political system until the 1990s, preoccupied mainly with ethnic education, repatriation issues, and economic support for their homelands.[12]

From the 1950s through the late 1980s, Japan focused on developing deep political-economic ties, predominantly with the United States and Southeast Asia. Since the dawn of the 1990s, however, this traditionally intimate and geopolitically propitious triangle has been complicated by an unsettling new current: the rise of Northeast Asia as an alternative market, raw material supplier, and source of labor. In 1990 slightly more than 8 percent of Japanese exports went to Korea and China combined, compared with 31.7 percent to the United States. Yet in little more than a decade that pattern had been sharply reversed. By 2006, almost the same amount of Japanese exports were flowing to Korea and China alone as to the entire U.S.[13] And in 2007 the total volume of Japanese trade with China surpassed that with the United States. In 2008, Japan's exports to China and Korea combined significantly surpassed its exports to the U.S, $184 billion versus $139 billion.[14]

Since the Asian financial crisis of the late 1990s, the heart of Japan's rising economic interdependence with Asia has increasingly been the Northeast quadrant of the continent—particularly China. Between 1980 and 1990, China's share of Japanese exports actually fell, from 4.3 to only 2.3 percent of Japan's overall total. In more recent years, however, Japan's exports to China rose sharply—from 6.3 percent of overall totals in 2000 to 16.0 percent in 2008. China's share of total

Japanese imports conversely rose from 14.5 in 2000 to 18.8 percent in 2008. Japanese trade with Southeast Asia expanded also, although not nearly so fast.[15]

The shift toward Northeast Asia in Japanese trading patterns is particularly striking in high-technology and consumer electronics, where regional-production networks are increasingly well developed. Some 59.4 percent of Japan's integrated-circuit exports in 2004, for example, went to South Korea, Hong Kong, or Taiwan, while 47.5 percent of its IC imports entered Japan from the same nearby countries. Japanese trade was also highly concentrated within Northeast Asia in the synthetic fiber, steel, and machine-tool sectors, where exports to the subregion constituted 65.1, 50.9, and 40.4 percent, respectively, of Japan's entire global totals.[16] And intraregional trade concentration for Japan in such vital industrial sectors continues to intensify steadily.

China's extraordinary growth surge has, to be sure, been a major driver of Japan's rising trade dependence on Northeast Asia. Yet the People's Republic of China's (PRC's) growth is *not*—it must be emphasized—the only factor at work, or even necessarily the most important one. A much broader regional dynamic is operating. In steel, for example, Japan's most important export destination in 2004 was not China but South Korea.[17] Similarly, Taiwan was by far Japan's most important source of ICs, and supplied more than four times the value of ICs to Japan that China did, with South Korea also a much larger supplier than the PRC.[18]

Trade among Japan, South Korea, Taiwan, and Mainland China was also interrelated, in complex, regionwide transnational production networks. Negative externalities, such as environmental pollution, pandemics, and organized crime, were also transnational. For Japan, something much more subtle than a mere Sino-Japanese symbiosis is at work. Indeed, economic forces—preeminently burgeoning transnational production networks—are driving Japan to press for broad regional policy arrangements that are substantial and much more extensive than a mere Sino-Japanese bilateral accommodation. Tokyo's support since the Asian financial crisis for a series of regionalist measures, increasingly Northeast Asia–centric and culminating in the December 2008 Fukuoka trilateral summit, are clear cases in point.[19]

A Mixed History: Japan and Region-Building

Previous chapters have stressed Korea's role as a hub and a catalyst for Northeast Asian regionalism, as well as China's rising support for intraregional multilateralism. Japan too has contributed positively to regional institution-building at times, albeit in less dynamic fashion than its two continental neighbors, over most of the past two decades. Unlike China, Japan has a fully democratic political system, within which veto players proliferate, emboldened by potential support from complex legislative processes, powerful intraparty factions, and influential mass media. Unlike Korea, another democratic state, however, it lacks a powerful chief executive. Its political structure thus renders Japan more reactive and hesitant in foreign-policy making than either of its neighbors, a tendency compounded by its geographical and cultural isolation, as a distinctive island nation on the rim of Asia.

Despite Japan's physical detachment from the continent, its commitment to Asian regionalism, of course, has a venerable heritage. During the first half-century after the Meiji Restoration, a variety of Japanese activists and intellectuals, including Saigo Takamori, Miyazaki Toten, and Kita Ikki, stressed the importance of deepened ties to Asia, in contrast to the pro-Westernism of Fukuzawa.[20] Asianism emerged as official policy, reinforced by the power of Japanese arms, with the birth of the New Order in East Asia (1938) and the Greater East Asia Co-Prosperity Sphere (1940). This pattern continued until Imperial Japan's overwhelming defeat in 1945.

For two decades after the war's end a chastened Japan, mindful of the bitter historical heritage, was reticent about promoting Asian regionalism, and structurally handicapped by its domestic political fragmentation in doing so. Yet during the 1960s, 1970s, and 1980s, Tokyo once again became more active in promoting the concept. Even the United States, concerned about the prospect of Chinese Cold War inroads elsewhere in Asia, was subtly supportive, as long as Japan did not pursue regional initiatives formally involving Communist Mainland China in a serious way.

During the early 1960s, for example, the Japanese Economic Research Center, led by Okita Saburo, became a forum for serious discussions of regional integration.[21] In 1966, the Japanese government took the initiative in establishing the Asian Development Bank (ADB), although it failed in determined efforts to locate the bank's headquarters in Tokyo, as it had originally hoped to do. Tokyo also proceeded with several formal initiatives, including the Ministerial Conference on Economic Development in Southeast Asia (MCEDSEA), in 1966, and the "Asian-Pacific Sphere of Cooperation" and Pacific Free Trade Area (PAFTA) proposals of 1967, although those government initiatives became defunct by the end of the Vietnam War in 1975.

Some cooperative Japanese regional initiatives, especially those involving partnering with Australia, were more successful.[22] The Pacific Basin Economic Council (PBEC), founded in the late 1960s at the initiative of the Japanese and Australian private sectors, and open to businessmen from a variety of Pacific and East

Asian states, has prospered, and currently involves more than four hundred firms. In 1980 Japanese prime minister Ohira Masayoshi teamed up with his Australian counterpart Malcolm Fraser to establish the Pacific Economic Cooperation Conference (PECC), which has also continued to be active. Building on the accomplishments of PECC, and using it as a political base, Australia's prime minister, Robert Hawke, collaborated with the Japanese, the Koreans, and ultimately the United States to found Asia-Pacific Economic Cooperation (APEC), the important international policy forum, in November 1989.

Beginning in the early 1990s, Japan grew somewhat less active in initiating and supporting Asian regional organization. Despite strong entreaties from Malaysian prime minister Mahathir Mohammed, it failed to back Mahathir's proposed East Asian Economic Caucus (EAEC), under strong counterpressure from the United States. Some senior Japanese bureaucrats, such as former Ministry of Finance vice minister for international affairs Sakakibara Eisuke, early proponent of the Asian Monetary Fund (AMF) concept, were supportive of regionalist initiatives. So were political leaders such as Foreign Minister (and subsequently Prime Minister) Obuchi Keizo, and longtime LDP secretary general Kato Koichi. Yet the regionalists for many years lacked sufficient domestic support, in the face of U.S. ambivalence, for Japan as a whole to emerge as a proactive force in region-building. As in so many areas of foreign policy, it remained a "reactive state," despite its massive economic scale.[23] It took growing interdependence with China and Korea, a gradual structural transformation of domestic interests, and critical junctures, such as the 1997 and 2008 global financial crises, to deepen Japan's receptivity to the Making of Northeast Asia.

Regionalism and the Emerging Profile of Japanese Domestic Political Interests

To understand Japan's ambivalent current and prospective future response to Fukuzawa's dilemma, as economic interdependence with Asia inexorably rises, it is useful to take a brief look at the profile of Japanese domestic interests engaged, and at how those interests are changing. While interests do not translate neatly into policy in the fragmented Japanese state, where change tends to occur reactively amid crises at critical junctures, those interests have been highly influential in determining the general disposition of policy in Tokyo. Either as constraints or increasingly also as supportive forces, these domestic interests profoundly affect long-term political-economic outcomes in Japan, including the evolution of Japanese approaches to interdependence with Asia.

It is also important to keep in mind the distinctive structural features of Japan's tortuous public-policy process. Unlike China, Japan is a full-fledged democracy, where grassroots as well as business interests and mass media have substantial sway. Unlike Korea—another democracy—Japan lacks a strong chief executive, and suffers from a more complex legislative process. Japan's decision-making thus tends to be slower and more reactive, to both domestic and international interests, than is typical in either of its neighbors.

The Japanese legislative process, in particular, is replete with obstacles that can be unobtrusively used by veto players, who thus have unusual ability to slow or stop legislative action.[24] The National Diet, for example, actually sits for an average of only 80 working days annually, compared with an average of 150 in Britain, the United States, and Italy. It is bicameral, unlike Korea, introducing further complexity. Like the U.S. (and unlike Korea and most of Europe), Japan has a committee system, creating additional hurdles for legislation. Yet unlike the United States, Japan has an unusual tradition of short sessions, whereby the legislative agenda is normally wiped clean several times annually, compared with once every two years in the U.S. It is thus typically much harder to translate underlying interests in particular legislation—such as treaties or free-trade agreements—through the Japanese Diet than in legislatures elsewhere, such as in Korea.

Understanding the history of past Japanese initiatives toward Asia, however, reveals much about the lines of domestic political cleavage that affect policy dispositions toward regionalism today. The Fukuda-Abe-Koizumi wing (Seiwa Kai) of the long-dominant Liberal Democratic Party, for example, descends from METI and Finance Ministry bureaucrats heavily involved in creating and administering the Greater East Asia Co-Prosperity Sphere of World War II. The recent Prime Minister Fukuda Yasuo, to cite one example, is the son of former prime minister Fukuda Takeo, financial advisor, as a young Ministry of Finance (MOF) bureaucrat, to the Nanjing collaborator government during World War II. His immediate predecessor, Abe Shinzo, is the grandson of former prime minister Kishi Nobusuke, who was the mastermind of wartime Manchurian economic development, before becoming Tojo's minister of munitions.

Given its wartime heritage, the Fukuda-Koizumi faction long experienced difficulty in dealing with continental Northeast Asia, especially Mainland China. Conversely, its members have tended to get along well with Taiwan and the United States. They have often also typically taken a special interest in the Korean peninsula, with varying degrees of success in bilateral relations, and have likewise valued informal entente with the Russians, and the Soviet Union before its collapse at the end of 1991. Members of this faction have also had strong personal networks in Southeast Asia, especially Indonesia.[25] Thus, their shift to priority on ties with China, from the fall of 2006, had a major catalytic impact on the Making of Northeast Asia, by undermining the influence in Tokyo of their erstwhile Russian and Southeast Asian friends.

Even during its long tenure (1955–93 and 1994–2009), the Liberal Democratic Party was by no means the only political group with influence on Japanese policies toward Asia generally, or toward Asian regionalism in particular. During the 1990s, the Japan Socialist Party (JSP) was quite important, especially while it served as a member of the ruling coalition from 1994 to 1998, with its leader, Murayama Tomiichi, occupying the prime minister's post during 1994–96. The party, historically antimilitary in orientation, pressed strongly for reconciliation with China since shortly after the 1949 revolution, and has traditionally enjoyed rather good relations with the PRC.

The waning strength of the Hashimoto/Tanaka faction of the LDP complicated Japanese relations with China and Korea in the early years of the twenty-first century. The rising role of the Komeito, or Clean Government Party, conversely, helped to stabilize those ties. Komeito, closely aligned with the peace-oriented Soka Gakkai religious movement, tended historically to align with the dovish, populist Hashimoto/Tanaka line on policy toward Asia, finding itself for many years markedly closer to the Chinese than to the Koreans. Yet it developed relatively positive relations with South Korea as well, especially following Seoul's democratization of the late 1980s. As a member of the ruling coalition from 1998 to 2009, Komeito generally served as a brake on pressures from the right wing of the LDP for more aggressive defense policies, a stance that has typically been welcomed by other Northeast Asians.

The Democratic Party of Japan's overwhelming August 2009 general-election victory arguably intensified the "pro–Northeast Asia" bias of Japan's political world,[26] in ways likely to have long-term consequences, barring external political-military shocks. Although the DPJ's membership includes a variety of views on Asia policy, the dominant current within the party advocates closer ties with China and Russia, albeit without sacrificing the U.S.-Japan alliance. The DPJ's early coalition partners, especially the Social Democratic Party of Japan, also advocated closer ties with mainland Asia, and an even more critical look at the military side of the existing U.S.-Japan relationship. Komeito also supported a "pro-Asia" line.

Japanese Northeast Asia policies, of course, are ultimately the product of more than shifting national political coalitions. They have their roots in history, and also in the institutional inclinations of Japanese ministries, local governments, and civil society. To gain a full basic understanding, and to assess the implications for Northeast Asian regionalism, it is important to review each of the major sub-national actors, as well as their policy orientations.

Bureaucracy and Regionalism

Within the Japanese bureaucracy, the three key ministries on Asian regional policies are the Ministry of Foreign Affairs (MOFA), the Ministry of Economics, Trade and Industry (METI), and the Ministry of Finance (MOF), while a few other ministries affect policy on important specialized matters, such as transportation. Generally speaking, MOFA is the most U.S.-centric of the major ministries, sometimes being known as the "Kasumigaseki branch of Foggy Bottom." Its America hands are often appointed to key posts in the Asia Bureau of MOFA, creating a built-in institutional ambivalence toward Asian regionalism in Japanese diplomacy.

METI is configured differently, and often has a contrasting orientation. Its North America specialists are by no means as internally dominant in ministerial affairs as at MOFA. METI's institutional concerns are more economic than strategic, and it is a traditional bureaucratic rival on trade-policy matters of MOFA as well. As such, METI has often been tempted to diverge, either subtly or otherwise, from MOFA's Washington-centric line. Certainly that was the case during the early 1970s, when Tanaka Kakuei was trade minister, and METI's predecessor MITI masterminded deeper relations with Mainland China.[27] METI's Northeast Asia Section, more insulated from Washington's pressures than its MOFA counterpart, has also been more pragmatic on issues of Asian regional integration.

Perhaps the most enthusiastic of the Japanese bureaucracies about Asian regionalism is the Ministry of Finance (MOF). MOF was the driving force behind the Asian Monetary Fund (AMF) proposal in 1996–97, and the Chiang Mai currency-swap agreement of May 2000, both of which were important milestones in Japan's evolution away from abject bilateralist dependence on Washington. MOF has also pioneered some of the most innovative recent policy steps toward Asian regionalism, such as creation of the Yen Bond Fund, and the Asian regional mortgage-insurance facility.

Behind MOF's relative enthusiasm about regionalism is an enduring memory of the Asian financial crisis. Japan's powerful standing as one of the world's foremost creditors, and the frustration that MOF's own initiatives for stabilizing the financial circumstances of Asia were stalled by resistance from nations, preeminently the United States, with less financial firepower at their disposal, still lingers among many. MOF officials tend to see little reason for the world's largest debtor to dictate to the major creditors, particularly when the outcomes of such suasion undermine the basic interests of the creditors themselves.

The Japanese central government, especially MOFA, has been hampered in its dealings on Northeast Asian regional questions by the complex territorial and historical issues that in different ways estrange Japan from each of its immediate neighbors. In the East China Sea, disputed ownership of the Senkaku (Diaoyutai) Islands, and conflicting criteria for determining maritime boundaries—with Japan using the median line and China the continental shelf criterion—estranged those two regional giants from each other. Between Japan and Korea there is the Tokdo (Takeshima) Island disputed-ownership problem, while between Japan and Russia lies the Northern Territories issue. These territorial questions were created by the breakup of the Japanese Empire in 1945, and left by the 1951 San Francisco Peace Treaty to fester.[28] To this day territorial conflicts inhibit proactive regional diplomatic initiatives by the Japanese government, compounded by endemic institutional fragmentation and the embedded influence of pressure groups in Kasumigaseki.[29]

These diplomatic and national-level political complexities, however, do not seem to affect Japanese local governments. As has been noted in Chapter 5, local-government ties with the Northeast Asian continent, such as sister-city relations, have been vigorous and expanding, even as national diplomatic ties have in many cases stagnated. This has been especially true since the mid-1990s, as continental Northeast Asia has begun to grow rapidly and to become more economically liberal. Local governments have pioneered not only cultural exchanges, in such areas as education, but also transnational plans for economic cooperation. Indeed, local governments such as those of Niigata and Toyama prefectures on the Japan Sea coast, and of Fukuoka City in Kyushu on the East China Sea, have been among the most effective and proactive government bodies in Japan at promoting regional integration.

Like local governments, semigovernmental think tanks can forge substantive and strategic relations with counterparts elsewhere, while finessing the diplomatic complications that pervade the region. This the Japanese think tanks very energetically do. The National Institute for Research Advancement (NIRA), for example, collaborates closely with the Korean Institute for Economic Policy (KIEP), and the development research center of the State Council (DRC) in China, as the analytical secretariat for the trilateral leaders' meetings among Japan, China, and South Korea. These summit sessions took place annually on the periphery of the ASEAN plus Three Summit conference from 1998 to 2008, and now operate independently from ASEAN entirely. NIRA has done extensive research on the modalities and implications of both a bilateral Japanese free trade agreement (FTA) with South Korea, and also of a trilateral FTA among Japan, Korea, and China, as well as regional energy-sharing agreements and cooperative infrastructural development. Its work takes place at the cutting edge of Asian regionalist agenda-setting.[30]

Country-Specific Interests

Substantial post–World War II Japanese political-economic relations with the Northeast Asian continent, and the interest groups supporting them, were relatively slow to develop, compared with ties to the United States and Southeast Asia. Yet a surprisingly well defined set of country-specific interest groups, articulating the concerns of Japan's neighbors and helping to mediate relations with them, has nevertheless emerged, particularly since the late 1950s. The profile of these lobbies has been shaped by a mixture of economic and security concerns—most of them embedded in early post–World War II history.

Economic ties with China began recovering with the Liao-Takasaki agreement of 1962, which institutionalized Sino-Japanese trade relations, although formal diplomatic relations were not established until 1972. Japanese economic ties with South Korea did not begin developing until after their bilateral diplomatic normalization in 1965. There was, to be sure, a substantial intensification of technological transfer, component exports, and Japanese investment in Korea during the late 1960s and the early 1970s. Yet these economic ties began to wane across the 1970s and the 1980s, as Korea became an increasingly formidable economic competitor.

Northeast Asian ethnic populations in Japan have also been substantial, as noted earlier, since the mobilization for war with China in the 1930s. The basis for deeper political ties with an ethnic dimension was laid in the 1950s, beginning with Taiwan.[31] Yoshida Shigeru, who had been consul general in Shenyang before World War II, wanted to normalize after the Chinese Revolution with Mainland China, as Britain did, and only reluctantly established diplomatic ties with Taiwan in 1952, under diplomatic pressure from John Foster Dulles and the U.S. Congress. Yet Kishi Nobusuke, former economic czar in Japanese-occupied Manchukuo, was much more enthusiastic, and served as the key political backer of Chiang Kai-shek and his political heirs for more than thirty years. One key early attraction of Taiwan for Japanese politicians was its export of bananas, a delicacy in early postwar Japan, allocated within Japan through politically negotiated quotas. Another, less pecuniary motive was gratitude to Chiang for having facilitated the smooth repatriation of Japanese expatriates in China to their homeland in the turbulent aftermath of World War II.

As Japan's foreign trade liberalized and the Cold War waned during the 1960s and the 1970s, the Taiwan lobby became primarily a defensive organization, attempting to freeze the early postwar status quo, and complicate Japan's rapprochement with Mainland China. It was galvanized by Tanaka Kakuei's recognition of Beijing in 1972, which provoked creation of the right-wing Blue Wave

Society (Seirankai), and the Japan-Taiwan Diet Members' Dialogue Committee (Nika Giin Kondankai), in 1973. Both strove mightily to block the 1974 Japan-China Aviation Agreement. In 1996 leaders of the lobby such as Kajiyama Seiroku supported Taiwan rhetorically in the missile crisis, and agitated for U.S.-Japan defense guidelines to protect Taiwan. Yet over time the lobby gradually aged and grew less influential. Dramatic evidence of its declining influence came in October 2006, when Abe Shinzo, grandson of Taiwan lobby stalwart Kishi Nobusuke, made his first overseas visit as prime minister to Beijing, conspicuously affronting Taipei.

As in Korea and China, the formation in Japan of both institutions and interest groups supportive of stronger intra-Asian interaction was intensified by the political-economic crisis of 1997–98. This crisis initially led to a sharp initial cutback in Japanese private loans to the region, but that was rapidly offset by a huge expansion in public-sector aid. As the crisis waned, Japanese investment largely returned to the region, with the renewed regional economic stakes that such investment implied. Yet the distribution shifted sharply northward toward China, less affected by the crisis, and away from Southeast Asia. Economic forces thus generated pressures for a gradual shift in Japanese policy emphasis toward Northeast Asia, even though Tokyo has clearly continued to see the strategic value of Southeast Asia as a counterweight—albeit a weakening force in relative terms—to areas further north. Japan has been less proactive than Korea, in particular, in pressing for Northeast Asia–centric institutional formats, in an effort to sustain ASEAN's diplomatic influence, but it has increasingly seen their practical value in the emerging, multitiered international system of the Twenty First Century.

The substantial structural transformation induced elsewhere in Asia by the 1997 crisis was muted in Japan itself, as compared with the continent, by Japan's massive economic scale, and the relatively low ratios of trade and foreign investment to GDP that prevail there. Size provided Japan, for better or worse, with a certain degree of insulation from the crisis that Korea, in particular, could not enjoy. As a consequence, Japan in the immediate aftermath of the crisis proved somewhat less open to foreign investment than Korea, especially to intra-Asian investment, although it did accept large volumes of imports from the continent.

The most powerful domestic political lobby in Japan pressing for deeper ties with Northeast Asia has, since the AFC, definitely been that of South Korea, although the political ascent of the Republic of Korea (ROK) within Japan began a few years earlier. In 1991, third-generation Korean residents of Japan (*zainichi*), truly immersed in Japanese life, were given permanent alien status. In 1995, the Seoul-oriented Korean residents' association, Mindan, began a campaign for the franchise in local elections.[32] In 1997, Yokohama became the first Japanese municipality to allow foreigners to be hired as municipal employees. The Korean lobby, primarily Seoul-oriented, was also energized in the early 1990s by the provision of permanent residence status to third-generation Koreans, and by the advent in 1995 of the local-government franchise movement—together with the decline of its rival, Chosen Soren, affiliated with the Democratic People's Republic of Korea (DPRK)—as North Korea itself became an ever less attractive option for *zainichi.*[33]

Koreans have the potential to exercise significant influence in the Japanese political economy. They are relatively numerous locally, and they have financial backing from influential Japan-based Korean multinational firms such as Lotte Corporation.[34] Since the late 1990s, the *zainichi,* increasingly unified under the auspices of Mindan, have also enjoyed rising support from the ROK government, as well as influential Japanese political parties such as Komeito, and are beginning to exercise their new-found influence within Japan in the interest of broader regional detente. Their rising role in local-level Japanese politics, supported strongly by the new DPJ government, and by Komeito, should amply their overall political influence in Japan even further.

There is an elaborate structure of seven Sino-Japanese friendship organizations, mediating ties between the two giants of Northeast Asia.[35] The PRC has long been somewhat weaker in Japanese interest-group politics than Korea, however, partly because of the embedded strength of the Taiwan lobby, which enjoys a long-established network, and operates at cross-purposes. Immigrants from Mainland China are relatively few and recent, while there are few affluent Mainland-related businesses. Beijing's growing political support within Japan comes largely from Japanese firms and local governments, leveraged by astute Chinese grassroots diplomacy, as with the Sino-Japanese Friendship Halls.[36] Together, these allied groups are a formidable combination, especially as the Taiwan lobby wanes and itself grows more conciliatory toward Beijing.

The Japanese public appears to remain ambivalent about relations with Northeast Asia as a whole. Increasingly favorable attitudes toward South Korea are juxtaposed to greater skepticism of China, mirroring the relative strength of existing political lobbies and a lingering sense of geopolitical threat, strongly evident during the Koizumi years (2001–6). As indicated in Figure 9.1, the Japanese public became more favorably disposed toward South Korea during the five years after Kim Dae-jung's dramatic and welcome 1998 assertion as Korean president that no future apologies from Japan were needed. Japanese views of Korea also improved further under Korean president Lee Myung-bak, inaugurated in February 2008, who also has indicated a desire to avoid becoming enmeshed in "apology politics." The conciliatory policies of Chinese president Hu Jintao, coupled with the

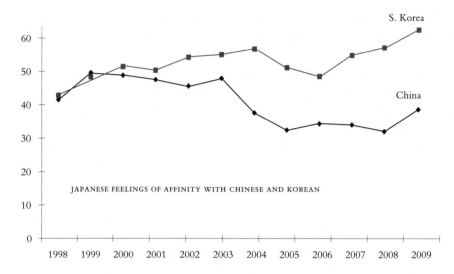

FIG. 9.1. Shifting Japanese Public Sentiments toward China and Korea. Source: Cabinet Office, Government of Japan website, http:// www8.cao.go.jp/survey/index-gai.html.

masterful elite confidence-building of Chinese ambassadors to Tokyo like Wang Yi (2004–7) and Cheng Yonghua (2010–) seem to be gradually transforming Japanese attitudes toward the PRC as well,[37] with positive sentiments toward China jumping sharply in 2009.[38]

The Key Role of Japanese Business

Japanese business dealings with Asia rapidly deepened during the Koizumi years, intermittent political frictions at the national level notwithstanding. They did so, interestingly, through a pattern strongly contrasting to the evolution of Japanese public opinion. Popular sentiments toward China, as noted earlier, sharply deteriorated during the 1998–2006 period. Yet Sino-Japanese economic ties grew ever tighter, and more important to Japanese firms. Indeed, China in 2008 accounted for fully 16 percent of Japan's exports, and 19 percent of its imports, compared with only 6.3 and 14.5 percent in 2000, just before Koizumi took office.[39]

As Japanese business dependence on Chinese and other Asian markets rises, in its many dimensions, Japanese firms naturally acquire new stakes in regional integration. They also become increasingly interested in articulation and lobbying, in order to safeguard those stakes. The major general trading companies (*sogo shosha*), configured to engage efficiently in resource-development and infrastructure projects, are one particularly concerned and proactive set of interests. Since the *sogo shosha* engage in both export and import, as well as direct investment and trade-financing transactions, they have special strengths in dealing with nonmarket and transitional economies. Their unique, transaction-oriented structure gives them special interest in China, the Russian Far East, and potentially North Korea, because of the enormous trade that the opening of those areas to the world could potentially generate.

Japanese consumer-goods producers, especially automobile manufacturers, are also becoming extremely interested in continental Northeast Asia. China, in particular, is seen as an enormous potential market for autos and electronics, as levels of personal affluence there steadily continue to rise. Honda, of course, has been an important player in China's automobile market since the 1990s. Toyota, although a relative latecomer in China, has grown significantly in recent years.

Since the 1950s, the Japanese economy has developed a broad and increasingly powerful range of institutions for both deepening ties with the Northeast Asian continent and lobbying for supportive policies that would aid it in doing so. Indeed, it has been business groups more than any other interest that have driven Japan's deepening ties with Northeast Asia, particularly China. The Japan-China Economic Association (Nichu Keizai Kyokai) both holds seminars and debriefings and also publishes books on policy issues. Keidanren, the Federation of Economic Organizations for Japan as a whole, likewise plays an active, powerful role, with recent Keidanren presidents hailing from Toyota and Canon having large and growing personal interests in China, just as Nippon Steel's Inayama Yoshihiro did a generation previously, in the early days of China's Four Modernizations.[40] Influential segments of the Japanese media, particularly the *Nihon Keizai Shimbun*, and the *Asahi Shimbun*, have also backed deepening economic ties with China, the Russian Far East, and South Korea, while *Sankei* has generally supported Taiwan.

Opponents of Closer Regional Ties

The Japanese private sector does not uniformly welcome deepened economic and political ties with continental Northeast Asia. Agriculture, in particular, is openly hostile. It cannot easily compete with continental Asian producers who have both more ample land at their disposal and lower labor costs. Its apprehensions were a major factor behind the 2001 "tatami war" between Japan and China. During that short but bitter bilateral trade conflict, the Japanese government, under severe Diet pressure, suddenly imposed stiff punitive quotas on imports of tatami mats, onions, and selected other agricultural goods from China, provoking even more draconian Chinese retaliation against autos and other competitive Japanese manufactures in return.

Differences over agricultural policy also led to collapse of the Japan-Korea bilateral free-trade talks in 2002. Japanese farmers and fishermen feared, in particular, imports of lower-cost seaweed, vegetables, and fishery products from the ROK. Combined with the challenge from China described above, agriculture—particularly opposition by Japanese farmers—has no doubt been the strongest single reason that trilateral FTA talks among Japan, the ROK, and the PRC, which have strong macroeconomic logic, have not progressed further.

It is not inevitable, however, that agriculture will be forever an insurmountable obstacle to Northeast Asian regional integration. In Japan, at least, there are substantial forces for agricultural liberalization that are growing progressively stronger. Keidanren and METI, for example, enthusiastically back significant change, on economic grounds. And the new DPJ-led government, in particular, could well ultimately back substantial liberalization on political grounds, as a means for undermining the structure of conservative dominance, even in the countryside as well. Its proposed direct subsidies to farmers, bypassing protectionist agricultural cooperatives, could well be a first start, although that prospect is far from certain. Japanese agricultural policy is thus truly a critical uncertainty, currently biased against change, that could open much more dynamic prospects for integration when it is liberalized, as seems increasingly likely.

Japanese small business, which constitutes nearly 60 percent of aggregate employment in Japan, is also ambivalent about deepened relations with continental Northeast Asia, on grounds similar to the logic in agriculture. Japanese small business simply cannot compete with the lower labor costs—and often higher efficiency as well—that prevail in China and the ROK. As Japanese multinationals, such as the major auto producers, invest ever more actively in China, and collaborate with Korea, they stir misgivings and antagonism among their small parts affiliates at home, especially among employees who work for such firms.

Fear of "industrial hollowing out" has been especially strong in areas such as Aichi Prefecture, where extensive auto and auto-parts manufacturing operations have traditionally been concentrated. In recent years, however, small Japanese firms themselves have begun to invest heavily in China, often in response to relocation decisions by parent companies. In 2002, more than 48 percent of Japanese small and medium firms were either investing or planning to invest in China, according to a JETRO survey.[41] As Chapter 5 suggests, since 1997 the number of Japanese investments in China has grown much more rapidly than that in the United States, with investments by small firms occupying the major share of new commitments.

In Conclusion

Seen in the aggregate, Japanese domestic interest groups are divided and ambivalent on matters of Northeast Asian regionalism—probably to a greater degree than is true of their counterparts in South Korea or China. That is probably not surprising, given that Japan has a higher per-capita income level than its neighbors, and a pronounced dual-structure economy. Japanese agriculture and some small businesses experience a palpable sense of threat from their neighbors, albeit one that is intensified by intermediate interest groups, such as the Central Federation of Agricultural Cooperatives (Zennoh), whose role is politically contingent, and could potentially be reduced by domestic political transformation within Japan. That parochial sense of threat led, in November 2004, to collapse of the Japan–South Korea FTA negotiations.[42] For multinationals, especially for consumer-goods producers such as the automobile and electronics industries, however, regional integration presents important new commercial opportunities, especially in China, encouraging big-business lobbies like Keidanren to defend the regional integration process against overt protectionist pressures.

Proactive steps toward regionalism, however, have been less forthcoming from Japan than from Korea, in the absence of crisis and critical juncture, despite the strength of big-business interests. Japanese consumer groups are not well organized, with such groups as do exist subverted by protectionist "health and safety" pressures. Japan, as has been noted, lacks a strong chief executive, capable of resisting particularistic interests. Local government has generally lacked the entrepreneurial drive that its counterparts manifest in China. Political parties and bureaucratic organization are also fragmented, making proactive steps difficult in the absence of compelling pressures, generally from outside.

In a market-oriented regional economy, the large, mobile Japanese manufacturers and general trading companies like Matsushita, Canon, and Mitsui can to some extent move quietly on their own to the continent, as they see fit, in the absence of major trade or investment-policy changes facilitating regionalism within Japan itself. Nonpolitical, market-oriented production networks, linking the home operations of large Japanese manufacturers with their burgeoning offshore activities in Dalian, Shanghai, and Zhejiang, as well as materials suppliers in Seoul or Busan, are rapidly proliferating, as we have seen. And these increasingly institutionalized transnational business ties are steadily deepening the stakes of Japanese industry and its political allies within Japan in stability across the East China Sea, making big business supportive of crisis-generated innovations in regional institutions, even as industry remains passive as long as business conditions are stable.

History is not a trivial political-economic issue in Northeast Asia. Patriotic education in all the nations compounds these tendencies. The specter of political backlash in China against Japanese investment, fueled by populist resentment of an affluent and historically aggressive neighbor, was made all too real by the widespread riots in Chengdu, Beijing, and Shanghai during late 2004 and the spring of 2005. Parallel developments could potentially occur in Korea. Hostility to Prime Minister Koizumi's persistent visits to Yasukuni Shrine also enflamed relations with both China and Korea well into 2006.

Throughout the Koizumi years, there was thus a persistent tension within Japan between the powerful, deepening logic of Northeast Asian economic interdependence and recurring political tensions, many of them related to wartime history. Abe Shinzo altered that equation somewhat with his successful September 2006 visits to Beijing and Seoul. Abe's later failure to recognize the wartime Japanese government's role in operating the system of comfort women, however, coupled with its emphasis on the North Korean abductee issue, and the Roh administration's impulse to bait Japan for political reasons, impeded regional normalization.

Political support in Tokyo for deepened ties with China and Korea increased sharply from late 2007, however. Two major domestic Japanese factors were at work. First of all, there was the changing orientation of the Japanese opposition on regional issues, and its rising Diet strength. DPJ leader Ozawa Ichiro, traditionally a hawk on China issues, shifted stances, and developed stronger ties with Beijing, making major policy trips to China annually from 2004 onward. And in July 2007, the DPJ and its allies gained control of the upper house of the Diet, through a sweeping electoral victory, en route to a decisive August 2009 victory in the lower house. As mentioned before, Ozawa took over 140 DPJ Diet members to Beijing for his annual visit in December 2009.

Support for Northeast Asian regional rapprochement continued to increase in Japan throughout 2008 and 2009. Following the Great Szechuan Earthquake of May 2008, Japanese Ministry of Self-Defense Force (MSDF) vessels were for the first time since World War II allowed into China to deliver emergency supplies, amid expressions of gratitude for Japanese support, which pleased many Japanese.[43] Democratic Party of Japan leader Hatoyama Yukio made his first official overseas trip as party leader to Seoul in May 2009, declaring a strong DPJ emphasis on relations with Asia,[44] and strengthened that orientation later that year as prime minister. After a major speech at the United Nations, and a G-20 summit meeting in Pittsburgh, his first two overseas diplomatic overtures were to Seoul and Beijing. These Japanese initiatives, and the positive Chinese and Korean responses with which they were met, helped to accelerate the gradual waning of historical animosities that have been for close to a century the principal obstacle to stable, productive ties between Japan and its Northeast Asian neighbors.

10

The United States and Northeast Asian Regionalism

For America's future, most observers would agree, Northeast Asia is inevitably a region of fateful importance. It is, after all, a strategically crucial fulcrum of the broader Pacific, where the American presence has been enduring. As George W. Bush noted early in his presidency, "America, like Japan, is a Pacific nation, drawn by trade and values and history to be part of Asia's future."[1] And as Obama's defense secretary Robert Gates concurred on Asian soil seven years later, "America is a resident power."[2] Its involvement with Northeast Asia is the central and highly strategic part of that.

With a fifth of global GNP, 30 percent of world savings, and a third of the world's industrial manpower, the economic scale and potential of Northeast Asia are clear. That reality cannot be lost on a global superpower like the United States. In geopolitical terms, stable relations with China, Japan, and Korea are indispensable as the "Far Eastern anchor" of America's worldwide strategy.[3]

Rising cohesion within Northeast Asia is also itself highly consequential to American interests. Since the days of the clipper ships over two centuries ago, the United States has generally regarded the region from afar, in broadly dispassionate terms, and often enhanced its influence through the divisions in the region, and America's ability to serve variously as a guarantor or an honest broker in conflicts among local interests. At times it has used these structural advantages of detachment, distance, and global power as a substitute for concrete strategy. Gradually, however, the United States has established an important forward-deployed military presence in Japan and Korea themselves,[4] while also developing increasingly important trade and investment ties, and rendering detachment a less felicitous approach than it at times was in past years.

The Making of Northeast Asia could profoundly affect all of those stakes, for either good or for ill. The response of the United States to the historic changes underway in ties among Japan, Korea, China, and across the Taiwan Straits will also critically affect how the trans-Pacific relationship itself—and indeed, the global political economy as a whole—ultimately evolve. Historically, Washington's resistance has no doubt often inhibited exclusivist East Asian regionalism, as during the 1980s and 1990s, when the U.S. enjoyed global hegemonic power. Yet U.S. leverage is waning, with Northeast Asian foreign-exchange reserves reaching two-thirds of global totals, and America's military preoccupied with the Islamic world. Asian trade dependence on U.S. markets has been slowly but surely declining, for close to a decade.

Going forward, Northeast Asian regional integration will likely grow even less contingent on American support. Yet the U.S. will retain a vital interest in the outcome, even as its ability to shape events through vague and general offshore suasion steadily declines. Confrontation within the region could provoke accelerated arms spending and escalating Sino-Japanese tensions that could indirectly threaten America. Proactive effort to ease Northeast Asia's integration into the broader global system, and to encourage its acceptance of international norms, could conversely help stabilize trans-Pacific relations. Yet the U.S. will need a clearer and more proactive strategy, based on concrete national interests, to achieve these important outcomes.

Northeast Asia's Importance to the United States

The strategic significance of Northeast Asia becomes crystal clear when one postulates, as a Hegelian thought experiment, its alienation from the United States. Japan and China together—not to mention Korea—constitute the one geopolitical mass in the world, apart from Russia and traditional American allies in Western Europe, with the scale to oppose or counterbalance Washington. The Making of Northeast Asia, in an adversarial form, could rank as a grave challenge to American security, although benign manifestations could conversely be an invaluable contribution to global peace and prosperity. Fortunately, a Moderate Center supportive of a nonconfrontational course appears to be emerging in the United States, as a result of demographic changes, a "Sunbelt Shift," and the rising influence of multinational firms in the domestic U.S. political economy, we argue. This Moderate Center, however, cannot effectively make the case for interdependence without evidence to support it. Pragmatic, flexible policies are needed on both sides of the Pacific, as well as in the cooperative interaction of Northeast Asia's constituent parts themselves.

For Northeast Asia's own future, the key issue is the extent to which broader Pacific structures will be a continuation of the past. Peter Katzenstein has recently argued that "ours is a world of regions, embedded deeply in an American imperium."[5] Yet in the East Asian case, at least, that assertion needs to be heavily qualified. Large parts of Northeast Asia, in particular, including the People's Republic of China (PRC), the Russian Far East, and North Korea, remain decisively *outside* the American imperium, and have *never* been part of it. Furthermore, Japan's current influence is limited also. These long-peripheral areas on the continent are exerting an ever-stronger political-economic pull on their more U.S.-centric neighbors, because of their rapid growth or resource potential. And the overall influence of the United States in the Northeast Asian region, such as it is, has been rooted not only in economic scale and military capability but also on divisions within Asia itself, as noted above, such as those across the DMZ, the Taiwan Straits, and the East China Sea. In the wake of the 1997 Asian financial crisis, the 2000 Pyongyang Summit, the 2006 retirement of Koizumi Junichiro, and the 2008 Taiwanese elections, most of those traditional lines of regional cleavage have palpably begun to dissipate.

While American influence may be relatively pronounced in Japan, dominance is too strong and categorical a term. Whatever American influence in Japan may be, it is decidedly more limited elsewhere in the region. And even in Japan, that influence is palpably declining, in the face of lessened trans-Pacific trade interdependence, rising nationalism, and domestic political transformation, as epitomized in the decisive August, 2009 defeat of the pro-U.S. Liberal Democratic Party, which had held power almost continuously for over half a century.

The mechanism of subordinate integration for East Asia within international affairs was for many years indeed a hub and spokes bilateralism, with the hub emphatically lodged in Washington, D.C. In this configuration the spokes of the wheel were firmly linked to the hub, but did not interact directly with one another. Not even a child's letter could pass across the DMZ, although vast torrents of trade and communication routinely flowed between Seoul and Washington, Tokyo and Washington, and even Beijing and Washington.

Growing trade and financial interdependence across borders long fraught with tension are bringing that bitter era of mutual isolation among the nations of Northeast Asia to an end, as we have seen. The mutual trade and cross-investment with one another of nations throughout Asia is now growing much faster than that across the Pacific—with intra–Northeast Asian flows, such as those between China and South Korea, at the cutting edge. The impending question, for both

America and the region, is what broader geopolitical consequences and institutional changes will flow from this new intimacy within Northeast Asia itself.

The cutting edge of political-economic change in Asia—and one most invested with geopolitical import—is clearly in the Northeast corner of the region, as we have seen. Japan, Korea, Mainland China, Taiwan, and indeed Far Eastern Russia, all have strong economic complementarities with one another, particularly with regard to energy and agriculture. Their levels of both economic and technological sophistication are much higher than in most of Asia to the south and west. Yet the Cold War has, until very recently, estranged these otherwise potent partners. Relaxation of tensions on and around the Taiwan Straits, with the Korean peninsula a future prospect, is making it possible at last to exploit those underlying complementarities, with both economic and geopolitical implications that remain to be fully explored.

The United States will without question be critically affected by the Making of Northeast Asia, as it steadily unfolds. Interest rates will be higher, domestic stock and housing prices will rise less rapidly, and Americans will feel less affluent if and when Asians turn to one another rather than across the Pacific to the United States. New security issues will also arise, including the future of U.S. bases, albeit within a multitiered world of interdependence in which it will be difficult for any nation to think in narrowly geostrategic terms.

Many of the plausible scenarios accompanying the Making of Northeast Asia, such as deepening U.S. domestic-credit crises, and stock-market instabilities as Japan, China, and Korea progressively redeploy their financial surpluses to local ends, would not be comfortable for Americans to entertain. Such developments could seriously intensify the turmoil of transition to a less U.S.-centric global political-economic order that the subprime mortgage crisis of 2007–8 has already begun to set in motion. Yet sudden, destabilizing shifts in existing parameters are not inevitable. With mutual understanding and forethought, brokered by the Moderate Center, inevitable transition can be made more symmetrical, and more gradual.

The economic approach of the United States to Asia itself, and its willingness to engage politically, will in turn critically influence the sort of regionalism within Asia that ultimately emerges. American national interest urgently requires understanding the rapid pace of Northeast Asian political-economic integration, and helping to shape it to mutually stabilizing ends, while proactively reinforcing existing trans-Pacific links. That accommodation with an increasingly cohesive Northeast Asia will need to be done on mutually acceptable terms, rather than through dictate. Fortunately the signs are that America's own political economy is gradually changing in ways that facilitate a softer landing for all concerned than appeared likely even a decade ago.

America's Early Absence from Northeast Asia

To understand the American approach to emerging regional integration in Northeast Asia, both in past and prospectively even in future, it is useful to revisit the unusual political-economic origins and character of the early U.S. role in the region. From the days of the China Clipper ships at the very dawn of the American Republic, Yankee merchants fancied that there were great fortunes to be made in Asia—particularly in China. In the 1890s Brooks Adams exulted that "Eastern Asia is the prize for which all the energetic nations are grasping."[6] In the aftermath of the Russo-Japanese War, Averill Harriman moved to clutch a portion, negotiating seriously for a half interest in the South Manchurian Railway.[7]

In contrast to Europe, Latin America, the Middle East, or even Southeast Asia, however, the United States never actually established a dominant economic or political presence in Northeast Asia prior to 1945, allowing it the luxury of relative detachment from the region's Byzantine intraregional struggles. Korea and Taiwan became Japanese colonies, largely isolated from American consciousness, and from trade interaction with the United States. In China, American influence was generally eclipsed by that of the European powers. American investment, with a few exceptions such as the AIG insurance firm in China and, ironically, the U.S. auto industry in Japan, was quite limited in this region.[8] The bulk of U.S. economic involvement in Northeast Asia, such as it was, concentrated in Japan.[9] Indeed, it was precisely the limited nature of American economic stakes in Northeast Asia, and the manifest desire of the State Department to avoid being enmeshed in such business interest-group politics as were emerging in late-nineteenth-century America, that led so easily to advocacy of the Open Door.[10]

The historic American presence, and U.S. attention, such as it was, tended to be concentrated in more idealistic spheres. There were thousands of American missionaries in China, Korea, and Japan.[11] They and other Americans played a key role in developing the educational systems of the region. Americans also provided technical advice on everything from rectifying Japan's unequal treaties with the West to building Seoul's first subway.[12] Yet Yankees neither colonized Northeast Asian nations nor invested heavily in them, by and large. Those delicate and controversial ventures, heavily embedded in turbulent local politics, they left largely to the Russians and the Japanese.

There was one fateful period of American involvement around the dawn of the twentieth century that left an enduring imprint on both Northeast Asia and trans-Pacific relations. As Meiji Japan prepared for war with czarist Russia in 1904, American investment bankers led by Jacob Schiff of Kuhn Loeb played a key role in financing the Japanese war effort, driven in substantial part by outrage at the ongoing czarist pogroms.[13] Following Russia's subsequent naval defeat in the Tsushima Straits, U.S. president Theodore Roosevelt brokered the peace, through the Treaty of Portsmouth. And following that settlement, Secretary of State William Howard Taft acquiesced in Japan's preeminent position in Korea through the controversial Taft-Katsura agreement.[14] America thus indirectly facilitated both Japan's rising imperial role in Northeast Asian affairs vis-à-vis Russia, and its related subjugation of Korea, even though the United States left no physical imprint on the ground. This unwitting American role, however, many Koreans have not forgotten to this day.

Not surprisingly, the American public was somewhat detached about Northeast Asia until the 1930s, and not particularly knowledgeable or concerned about day-to-day developments there. It could afford to be. In contrast to the multifaceted concerns of the Japanese and the Europeans, U.S. economic and geopolitical interests were only mildly engaged. Most Americans could afford idealism, and even a bit of naivety, about a truly distant corner of the world that rarely intruded much into their fundamental calculations of interest, or even into their consciousness.

Then the United States was blindsided from the region: twice within the bloody 1941–51 decade—first at Pearl Harbor and then in the Korean conflict. As the smoke began to settle, the United States still lacked transcendent economic interests in a decimated Northeast Asia, although its banks and oil companies established a foothold in Japan during the postwar U.S. occupation. Korea was both war ravaged and intently mercantilist, while China and the Russian Far East remained off-limits because of the Cold War for nearly four decades. Despite a lack of economic access, however, the United States gained, through its jarring military involvement with the region, a hard-won and deeply felt set of security stakes, reinforced by the deepening Cold War.[15]

Limited economic consciousness and a high military profile—this distinctive, historically grounded configuration to the U.S. presence and American policies in Northeast Asia—was institutionalized in the San Francisco Peace Treaty of September 1951, formally ending World War II in the Pacific. Indeed, the set of political-economic relationships embodied in the treaty and related documents—which provided the United States with Cold War allies and bases on the rim of Asia, and Asians with open American markets—has proven to be remarkably enduring. One can thus realistically speak of a "San Francisco System" of trans-Pacific relations as the defining paradigm for U.S. association with this tumultuous Northeast Asian region, persisting to this very day.[16]

Key Traits of the Classic San Francisco System

Constructed as the Korean War was raging, in an effort to integrate Japan systematically within a broader network of U.S. Pacific alliances, the San Francisco System embedded important American military and economic interests, especially those of the Pentagon and multinational business communities, structurally into trans-Pacific relations. The system had five basic features:

1. *Bilateral,* highly asymmetric U.S. *security alliances* with key nations of the Pacific, including Japan, South Korea, the Philippines, Taiwan, and Australia/New Zealand. These alliances, still mostly intact, generally obligate the United States to the defense of the local partner, with only limited converse obligations;

2. *American military bases* in most nations with whom the United States concluded bilateral security treaties, including initially Japan, South Korea, Taiwan, the ANZUS nations, and the Philippines;

3. *Asymmetrical economic arrangements* that opened U.S. markets to American security partners without commensurate foreign access for American firms;

4. *Selective exclusion* of American military adversaries—chiefly Mainland China and the Soviet Union—from the web of asymmetrical and reinforcing political-economic relationships between the United States and its allies;

5. *Little multilateral security or economic architecture.* Europe has developed a rich institutional fabric of both security and economic institutions, ranging from the North Atlantic Treaty Organization (NATO) to the European Union. The Western Hemisphere has the Organization of American States, Africa has the Organization of African Unity, the Middle East has the Arab League, and Southeast Asia has had the Southeast Asian Treaty Organization and the Association of Southeast Asian Nations (ASEAN). Yet Northeast Asia has never developed any significant formal regional institutions of its own.

Apart from their lack of institutional vehicles for mediating mutual relations, the nations of Northeast Asia found it immensely difficult even to communicate with one another. Japan and South Korea, although both anticommunist allies of the United States, were deeply suspicious of each other, given vividly bitter memories of the past. They did not even normalize their own bilateral relations until 1965. Japan failed to recognize the Soviet Union until 1956 and Mainland China until 1972. South Korea was even slower: it did not establish formal ties with the Soviet Union until 1990, or the PRC until 1992. And Seoul did not even speak publicly to North Korea, only a few miles across the DMZ, until the dramatic Pyongyang Summit of June 2000. Similarly, Beijing never dealt directly with Taipei until the early 1990s, and then only intermittently, until Ma Ying-jeou took power in 2008.

During the early 1950s, even John Foster Dulles was enthusiastic about an Asian regional security body; it was Japan's Yoshida Shigeru and South Korea's Rhee Syng-man who were opposed.[17] To say that the United States consistently opted for bilateralism at the outset in Asia, in contrast to a multilateral bias in Europe, is historically myopic, given Washington's active exploration of the Pacific Pact and other multilateral concepts in the late 1940s and the early 1950s. Despite the formidable regional supremacy of the United States in the early Cold War years, however, it was unable to forge an Asian equivalent to NATO, as we saw in Chapter 3, despite some initial interest in doing so.

Throughout the 1950s and 1960s, the U.S. worked actively to enhance multilateralism in the Western Pacific. In 1954 Dulles engineered the Southeast Asia Treaty Organization (SEATO), and in 1967 Washington actively supported the establishment of ASEAN. The United States also tried to strengthen trilateral ties among the U.S., Japan, and South Korea, playing a key role in inspiring Seoul and Tokyo's mutual-recognition agreement of 1965.

Yet by the early 1990s the United States had come to appreciate the geopolitical advantages of the San Francisco System's "hub-and-spokes" architecture. The spokes, after all, radiated out from Washington, in a network of asymmetrical ties that reinforced American dominance. U.S. leaders of the 1980s and early 1990s such as George H. W. Bush and James Baker saw little need for supplementary multilateral frameworks in Northeast Asia.[18] And they did little to further intra-Asian bilateral relationships in the region, save for some marginal encouragement of enhanced dialogue between Tokyo and Seoul.

America's Changing Geopolitical Stakes

It has been traditional to assume American dominance in the Asia-Pacific region, and hence that U.S. preferences would determine outcomes in trans-Pacific affairs. It has also recently been fashionable to assume Washington's dominance to rest on the role of Japan as a "regional core state," analogous to Germany in Europe, that is both a consistent supporter of the United States and central to regional politics.[19] Such conceptions may well indeed have been part of John Foster Dulles's original strategic design in creating the San Francisco System.[20]

Given America's traditional lack of powerful political-economic stakes in Northeast Asia, however, and its long-standing lack of detailed familiarity with regional developments, it would be dangerous to confidently infer consistent U.S. dominance of regional outcomes. That would be true even if Japan were the central determinant of regional affairs. And it would be true even if the "hub-and-spokes" structure really continued to prevail.

As the foregoing pages have suggested, however, both assumptions are now dangerously out of date. Traditional forms of American dominance, based on the "hub-and-spokes" precepts of the San Francisco System, are being sharply eroded by the rapid development of direct, mutually cooperative economic, cultural, and political ties among the "spokes states" that do not necessarily involve Washington at all. And Japan's role as an American surrogate is rapidly losing plausibility within Asia, as China rises in regional political-economic prominence while Japan conversely continues to stagnate. Even the United States is arguably broadening its own strategic conception of regional affairs, to include China in a more substantial and cooperative role as well.

In considering the changing character of U.S. influence in Northeast Asia, it is important to examine closely just what that influence entails in concrete political and economic situations. When key decision-makers within the United States have had strong personal command of issues on the trans-Pacific agenda, and been firmly intent on shaping their outcome, they have had a powerful impact on outcomes. Such influence was clear on Cold War security issues, where the United States often played a determining role, especially on the Korean peninsula, from World War II up to the very recent past.

A central U.S. role in Korean issues has been embedded since 1950 by the presence of large American military forces stationed in South Korea, and by the existence of the Combined Forces Command (CFC), placing South Korean forces also under the wartime command of a U.S. four-star general. This preeminent American role was also for many years reinforced by the division of the Korean peninsula, the hair-trigger "cold peace" along the DMZ, and the inability of Seoul and Pyongyang to communicate directly with each other.[21]

U.S. geopolitical leverage in Korea, ever more dependent on intra-Korean estrangement as Seoul's political-economic influence in Asia began to rise, was dramatically undermined in June 2000 by the Pyongyang Summit and the subsequent North-South détente.[22] The deepening subsequent tensions over North Korean nukes, culminating in Pyongyang's 2006 nuclear test, however, stimulated renewed American activism on Northeast Asian security issues, in the more collegial and less hierarchical setting of the so-called Six-Party Talks. Significantly, the nuclear issue, in the hands of former envoy to South Korea Christopher Hill, later assistant secretary of state for East Asia and Pacific Affairs, as well as chief U.S. delegate to the Six-Party Talks, became a vehicle for harnessing American influence at last to the cause of institution-building in Northeast Asia.

Throughout the history of the Six-Party Talks, and indeed back to the 1994 Korean nuclear crisis or even before, U.S. diplomacy in Northeast Asia has been confronted by an increasingly painful structural problem: a deepening divergence in the military and political-economic interests of its two major allies in the region—Japan and South Korea. For Japan, as North Korea gains nuclear capability and more accurate intermediate-range ballistic missiles (IRBMs), even as it holds an unknown number of Japanese citizens hostage, the strategic priority in multilateral talks must be arms control, with strict verification, and the immediate political priority must be return of the hostages. For South Korea, conversely, given proximity, its domestic difficulties, and Seoul's expectations of ultimate reunification, there is a much higher priority placed on stability itself. The United Sates is caught in the middle—a position that has often proven to be painful.

The Six-Party process began moving forward, from the fall of 2005, on the basis of broad multilateral cooperation, with the aforementioned difficulties largely obscured. To enhance Chinese cooperation, which he deemed vital to his overall enterprise, Hill agreed to Beijing as an ongoing venue for the talks. In September 2005, through both multilateral talks and informal U.S. direct discussions with North Korea, an agreement was reached by which North Korea in principle agreed to ultimately relinquish nuclear weapons. In this effort the American diplomatic role was that of low-profile catalyst, even as the U.S. engaged in subtle coercive diplomacy, in the background. Additional B-2 bombers were dispatched from the U.S. mainland to Guam in the fall of 2005, and American MIA search missions were recalled from North Korea. After North Korea actually tested in late 2006, the U.S. and Japan moved rapidly to censure North Korea for its nuclear tests at the United Nations. On the positive side, America broached the possibility of U.S. diplomatic representation in Pyongyang, and taking North Korea off the list of state sponsors of terrorism, thus prospectively facilitating Pyongyang's access to loans from multilateral financial institutions.

In February 2007, after intensive negotiations, Assistant Secretary Hill announced a breakthrough agreement for North Korea to close and ultimately disable the Yongbyon nuclear facility, in return for fuel oil and other assistance from the participants in the Six-Party process. Removal of North Korea from antiterrorism sanctions was apparently considered, bringing strong, albeit veiled, resistance from Japan. In July 2007, North Korea actually closed the facility, initiated a provisional disablement, and invited IAEA inspectors in to verify its actions. In 2008, citing various pretexts, North Korea reneged on its previous agreements, and in early 2009 conducted further missile and nuclear tests. As of this writing, the status of multilateral talks regarding North Korean weapons programs is thus unclear. Should the nuclear crisis be defused, however, one thing is certain: Russia, China, and South Korea—not to mention the United States—would all find it easier to deepen mutual ties, given the North's geographical centrality in the region.

When the U.S. has given priority to Northeast Asian issues, as during the 1994 Korean nuclear crisis, and as in the Six-Party process of 2005–8, and in dealing with renewed North Korean provocations during 2009, that activism has had a substantial impact on outcomes, although it has also aggravated differences of interest and perspective between America's twin allies, South Korea and Japan. When American policy-makers are not conscious of key issues for resolution, or domestically constrained to press U.S.-centric solutions, however, as has often been true on economic issues, the notion of "imperium" has much less credibility, and Washington gets caught in painful cross-fires. Agendas are then set, by default, elsewhere in the Pacific.

Patterns of implementation have likewise often been determined in Asia, rather than the United States, America's formidable military power notwithstanding, because of the deeper knowledge and interest in the problems at hand that America's Northeast Asian allies manifest. Japan, South Korea, and greater China simply care and know much more about trans-Pacific relations than most of their interlocutors in Washington. Thus, at the actual working level, where subnational factors are determining, the notion of "imperium" is less plausible with respect to Northeast Asian questions than it appears in the abstract. Gradually, when it works effectively, the role of the United States in noncrisis situations has morphed from proactive dictation into more of a brokerage function, such as Christopher Hill played in the Six-Party process, operating primarily out of Beijing, during 2005–8. Yet even there, as the differences among Tokyo, Seoul, and Washington, followed by more North Korean weapons tests, suggest, the mediating role of the United States is not an easy one.

Actual political influence within Asia itself depends profoundly on three inter-related phenomena with little direct relation to conventional military or economic power: *information*, *attention*, and *interpersonal networks*. As we have seen in previous chapters, Northeast Asians themselves were deficient along all three dimensions in their mutual relationships from the Korean War until the mid-1990s. Following the critical junctures of the 1997 AFC and—within Korea—the 1994–95 nuclear crisis, however, mutual consciousness and networks began to emerge, markedly strengthening intraregional ties and conversely weakening Washington's leverage.

The United States has, to be sure, been blessed with some brilliant and politi-cally gifted East Asian specialists over the years, including some, such as Joseph Grew, Edwin O. Reischauer, and Mike Mansfield, with substantial experience of diplomatic life. Yet Americans typically have not appreciated—or have felt only minimal need—for elaborate interpersonal tools in dealing with Northeast Asia, relying instead on the asymmetric advantages of the embedded "hub-and-spokes" system. Yet as the "spokes" come into ever-deepening mutual interaction with one another, and as the relative leverage of Asia with the United States continues to grow, Americans will need to grow significantly more knowledgeable, attentive, and connected than they have historically been, both intellectually and personally, in dealing with Northeast Asia. As they grow more engaged, and enhance their personal networks in Asia, their real interests will come to matter in new, more dynamic ways on the ground, across the Pacific.

America's Own Transformation

The United States itself is steadily changing, in ways that are making it progressively more open, more accepting of cultural involvement with Asia, and more interested in playing a stabilizing role in the Western Pacific—the waning of the Cold War notwithstanding. The United States is growing more diverse, more cosmopolitan, and more service-trade oriented. These domestic transformations do not necessarily make the country more knowledgeable or more strategic about Asia, nor do they themselves deepen national understanding of Asian regionalism. Yet they may well make America more open to the possibility of a redefined, less hierarchical relationship with Asia, especially when universalistic U.S. concerns are engaged, as on the Korean nuclear issue. And local cooperation is critical to their realization. Mutuality and two-way dialogue with that dynamic continent may well have more of a chance, going forward, than has been true across most of the "hub-and-spokes" era prevailing across the past half-century.

Most important, perhaps, the United States is growing more diverse in ethnic terms, with a rising share of its population Asian-born. The nationwide census of the year 2000 found that more than 8.2 million American residents came personally from Asia.[23] This Asian-born figure constituted more than 3 percent of the U.S. population, and half again as many as were actually born in Europe.[24] By 2005 the Asian-American population had risen more than 22 percent further, compared with 2000.[25] A large share of America's Asian residents were from Northeast Asia—Chinese were the largest group, numbering over 2.7 million in 2007, while Koreans and Japanese ranked fourth and sixth.[26]

The share of U.S. residents who had emigrated from Asia during the 1990s outnumbered those from Europe by more than two to one.[27] Not only Hawaii, but also San Francisco, Los Angeles, Seattle, and even New York—America's major East and West Coast metropolitan centers—have major Asian-American populations, as suggested in Figure 10.1. The recent governor of Washington State, and subsequently U.S. secretary of commerce in the Obama administration, Gary Locke, was Chinese- American, while the current governor of Louisiana, Bobby Jindal, is of Indian origin. Twenty years ago such developments were unheard of.

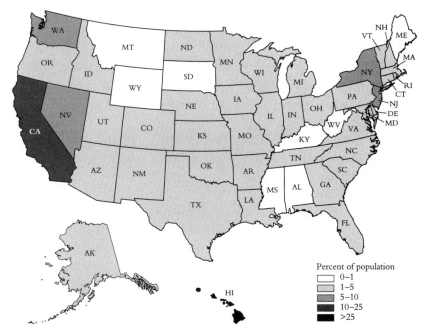

FIG. 10.1. Geographical Concentration of Asian Americans. Source: The East West Center, *Asia Matters for America*. See www.asiamattersforamerica.org.

Particularly important, from a political standpoint, are the rapidly rising number of Chinese and Korean Americans in the United States. From fewer than 500,000 in 1970, the number of Chinese in the United States had risen more than sixfold by 2006, to more than 3 million, while the number of Koreans nearly tripled, to almost 1.5 million, as indicated in Figure 10.2. Chinese, Koreans, and Japanese together constitute around 2 percent of America's population today, or roughly triple their relative share less than two generations ago. Asian Americans in total, including second- and third-generation residents, are approaching 5 percent of the U.S. population, or around 13 million people.[28]

The rapid increase in the number of U.S. residents of Northeast Asian origin is especially pronounced in the populous state of California, where more than 12 percent of the entire U.S. population now resides.[29] Chinese Americans are especially numerous in Northern California around San Francisco and Silicon Valley, while Japanese Americans are numerous in the Central Valley also. Koreans are increasing rapidly in number in the southern part of the state, in and around Los Angeles, which now has one of the largest ethnic Korean urban populations in the world. Between 1990 and 2000, the Korean population in Los Angeles increased 28.1 percent, rising from 145,431 to 186,350.[30] Within California as a whole, Asian

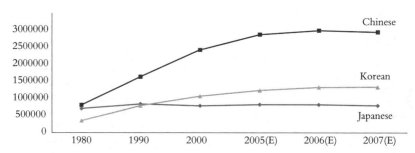

FIG. 10.2. Northeast Asian Population in the United States. Source: Original data are from the U.S. Census Bureau, www.census.gov.

Americans make up 12 percent of the total population, or about four times the average for the United States in general.

Demographic shifts have particular weight in national politics, because a rising share of national leaders are from California, especially within the Democratic Party. In 2010, House of Representatives speaker Nancy Pelosi hailed from a Northern California district, including a substantial part of San Francisco's Chinatown, that was over 30 percent Asian American, with that ratio having doubled over the previous generation.[31] California, with its one-eighth Asian-American population, is also crucial in presidential politics, holding more than one-fifth of the electoral votes required to elect a president of the United States.[32]

Cultural interaction with Asia is also increasing, creating ever deepening trans-Pacific networks. Some 6,331,080 Americans traveled to Asia in 2006, up 47.5 percent from only five years before.[33] In 2006, 66,605 were studying Japanese, while 51,582 Americans were studying Chinese in college.[34] A 2000 study by the U.S. Department of Education found that about 51,000 high school students were also studying Japanese.[35] In 2008, there were more than 10,000 U.S. college students studying in China, up fivefold from a decade before.[36] At the societal level, the United States is thus clearly more exposed to Northeast Asian culture than before, with so many young Americans learning Japanese and Chinese at school and traveling across the Pacific.

American academic institutions play an important, albeit still inadequate, role in promoting trans-Pacific understanding. Well over 200,000 Northeast Asian students are studying in the U.S.,[37] including more than 165,000 in American universities.[38] The top three countries sending students and visiting scholars to the United States—and five of the top ten suppliers of foreign students—are *all* in Northeast Asia.[39] In terms of F (student) and J (visiting scholar) visas, South Korea, the PRC, and Japan were the three largest suppliers of foreign students and visiting scholars to the United States, as indicated in Figure 10.3, ahead of Great

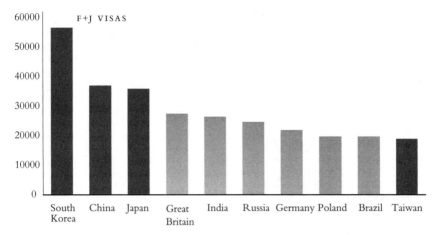

FIG. 10.3. Foreign Students and Visiting Scholars in the United States (2005). The "F" visa is a nonimmigrant, full-time student visa that allows foreigners to pursue education in the United States. "J" visas are issued to exchange scholars participating in programs in the United States that promote cultural exchange. Source: U.S. Department of State, *Report of Visa Office 2005: Non-Immigrant Visas Issued*, fiscal year 2005, http://travel.state. gov/pdf/FY05tableXVII.pdf.

Britain and India. Taiwan, with less than one-third the population of even the ROK, also made it to the top-ten list, with 18,987 U.S. cultural visas (F+J) issued in that year.

Among the prominent alumni of American universities in Asian leadership positions are Singapore's prime minister Lee Hsien Loong and Hong Kong governor Donald Tsang. There is also a large and important community of expatriates from China, totaling more than 50,000, who gained permanent residence after the 1989 Tiananmen massacres and have remained for a full generation to teach, do research, and pursue other occupations in the U.S.

All these deepening personal ties across the Pacific create at least the potential for American influence.[40] Two additional points, however, need to be made. First, effective transformation of networks into influence is by no means automatic; it requires both strategy and effort, points on which we will elaborate in the concluding chapter. Secondly, there are particular problems in translating trans-Pacific networks into influence inside Northeast Asia itself. The nations there are larger, more affluent, and in many ways more cohesive than farther south, or in the non-Western world more generally. And Northeast Asia, despite its dynamism and generally stable ties with the United States, tends to be culturally more closed to the West, with less developed English-language skills and a less prominent tradition of overseas undergraduate study (especially in Japan and China) than other

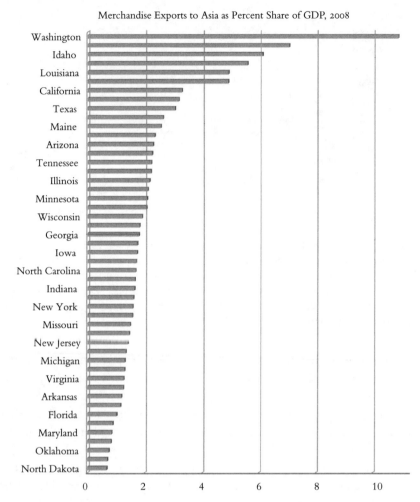

Merchandise Exports to Asia as Percent Share of GDP, 2008

FIG. 10.4. America's Exports to Asia. Source: The East West Center, *Asia Matters for America*. See www.asiamattersforamerica.org.

parts of the non-Western world, including India and Southeast Asia. Trans-Pacific networks, to repeat, do not translate automatically into U.S. influence on intra-Asian matters, especially in Northeast Asia, although the possibility, given serious American on-the-ground effort, is definitely there.

In broader political-economic terms, however, U.S. regions and interests inter-twined with Asia are growing stronger and stronger, reshaping the incentives of Americans themselves. Exports, for example, have become very substantial for some key American states such as Washington and California, as indicated in

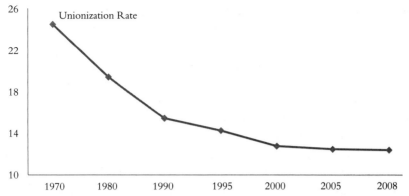

FIG. 10.5. America's Declining Unionization Rate (percentage). "Unionization rate" indicates share of total work force that holds membership in a labor union. Source: U.S. Department of Labor, *Union Membership Statistics*, various years.

Figure 10.4, and have been rising rapidly in recent years. In dynamic Silicon Valley, half of the CEOs of recent start-up firms were born either in China or India. Across the Sunbelt, there is not a single major steel mill or auto plant, with even a cooperative GM-Toyota joint venture plant in Fremont, California, recently closed.[41] And the Sunbelt, stretching from California across the Southwest to Texas to Florida, has produced every elected president of the United States except one since John F. Kennedy.[42]

America's industrial heartland—the so-called Rustbelt of Pennsylvania, Ohio, Michigan, and Indiana—has traditionally competed head-to-head with Northeast Asia, in sectors ranging from steel and autos to machine tools. Such regions are generally declining in relative national political influence. And they are simultaneously growing more politically and socially pluralistic within. Foreign investment is rising, even in these depressed regions, and labor union organization ratios are declining. Across the United States as a whole, the unionization rate has fallen steadily, as indicated in Figure 10.5—from 24.6 percent of the U.S. labor force in 1970 to only 12.4 percent in 2008.[43]

Deepening Corporate Stakes in Stable Trans-Pacific Relations

For the first quarter-century after World War II, the Atlantic was the clear locus of America's global foreign-economic relationships. Over the past thirty-five years, however, that picture has radically changed, with Northeast Asia becoming one of America's largest markets and destinations for foreign investment. In 2008, the United States did $784 billion in trade with Japan, the PRC, the ROK, Hong

Kong, and Taiwan, and in 2007 had more than $220 billion invested there.[44] The huge magnitude of these commitments naturally gave U.S. firms, like their trading partners, important collective stakes in the stability of trans-Pacific relations.

At the sectoral level, distributors have particularly deep economic interests in, and consequent incentives to stabilize, the trans-Pacific relationship between the United States and Northeast Asia. Walmart, for which Secretary of State Hillary Clinton served as a board member for many years (1986–92), alone imported more than $18 billion worth of goods from China in 2005, up substantially over the previous decade.[45] If Walmart were an individual economy, that single firm would, in 2004, have been the eighth-largest trading partner of China. More than 5,000 Chinese companies have set up steady supply alliances with Walmart.[46] On the other side of the Pacific, Walmart's extensive procurement in China has gained the company a positive corporate reputation that in turn aids its overall global commercial efforts. In 2006, Walmart had fifty-six stores in China with about 30,000 employees, and it expanded its network by another third during 2007 alone.[47] By 2009, there were already 146 Walmart stores in 89 cities in China, with more than 70,000 employees and forming roughly 20,000 supply alliances in the PRC.[48]

Boeing, Motorola, AIG, Eastman Kodak, General Electric, and a large number of other U.S. multinational firms also have major interests that give them strong incentives to help stabilize Sino-American relations. Boeing, for example, has dominated the Asian market for jet aircraft, with Asia expected to be the biggest growth market for aircraft in the world. In China alone, 2,000 new aircraft will likely be needed during the 2002–22 period. Boeing expects to be the major beneficiary of this future market expansion, just as it has benefited greatly from Northeast Asia's past growth.[49]

Motorola is another firm with deep stakes in China, and in stable U.S.-China relations. In 2001 it had already established eighteen R&D centers in China, and ranked as the PRC's number one cell-phone brand. By 2005, Motorola exported nearly $10 billion in merchandise from China, sold nearly an additional $10 billion there, and occupied 20 percent of the PRC's entire mobile-phone market.[50] China-based production thus accounted for around half of Motorola's $37 billion in global sales.[51]

Many other U.S. multinationals are also highly committed, through their business activities, to stable economic relationships with China. Cisco Systems entered China in 1994 and is set to make long-term investments. In 2006, China Telecom selected Cisco as the primary supplier for its rapidly expanding business network, and 400 Cisco 12416 routers were used in the expansion. The network, called CN2, covered nearly 200 cities in Mainland China.[52] Another major multinational,

General Electric, opened its largest training facility worldwide in Shanghai during 2005.

Among the most powerful supporters in the United States of stable, responsive relations with Northeast Asia are America's financial institutions—most notably its investment banks. These firms, prominent in Japan since the early postwar Occupation, and in China since before the 1949 revolution, also became deeply involved in Korea following the 1997 Asian Financial Crisis (AFC). Over the past decade, U.S. investment banks such as Goldman Sachs and Morgan Stanley have played a key role in privatizing the Chinese economy, and realigning its corporate governance structure, gaining enormous financial stakes in its transformation during that process.[53] These firms have played parallel, although less extensive, roles in Japan and Korea since the AFC. The influence of the powerful personal networks surrounding them, and the role of that influence in stabilizing trans-Pacific relations, is illustrated by the genesis of the U.S.-China Strategic Economic Dialogue (SED), initiated by Bush administration treasury secretary Hank Paulson, who had previously been deeply involved in U.S.-China financial relations while chairman of Goldman Sachs.

The Overall Profile of U.S. Interests and Northeast Asia's Future

Clearly the United States has powerful embedded stakes in the stability of trans-Pacific relations, and especially in ties with industrially and technologically sophisticated China, Japan, and Korea. The asymmetries of the prevailing political-economic order, including huge persistent trade imbalances across the Pacific, give U.S. diplomats and defense officials leverage with Northeast Asian nations that they would otherwise lack. Yet the cost to the broader trans-Pacific relationship of those parochial tools is rapidly rising, even as their utility progressively declines. The time has come for a reassessment, sensitive to the Making of Northeast Asia described in the preceding pages, albeit within the context of a multitiered system in which the United States looms large in some dimensions, including finance and security.

The "hub-and-spokes" system of bilateral alliances across the Pacific has long allowed the United States to capitalize on its relative size, and the manifest inabilities of the "spokes" to dialogue with one another. Both advantages are declining, however, as Asian growth steadily outpaces that of the United States, and Asians simultaneously deepen their intraregional ties. Exchange-rate shifts across the Pacific—especially a long-term revaluation of the Chinese renminbi and other Northeast Asian currencies against the dollar—are gradually accelerating the incentives in Seoul, Shanghai, Taipei, and even Tokyo toward intraregional integration, by magnifying the scale and attractiveness of nearby Asian markets for Asian producers, relative to trans-Pacific transactions. The global financial crisis of 2008, from which Asia began emerging more rapidly than Europe or most other regions, arguably has intensified the incentives for even deeper regional cohesion within Northeast Asia.

To the extent that the San Francisco System generates tangible stability dividends—as through the U.S.-Japan alliance—America's interests dictate that such a system should remain, and indeed be strengthened.[54] There is nothing wrong, from a U.S. standpoint, with using embedded history to self-advantage, as long as it does not trigger markedly perverse outcomes. Indeed, the United States would be foolish not to do so—a course it all too often tacitly pursues, through lack of active trans-Pacific engagement.

Yet the costs for the United States of clinging stubbornly to the "hub-and-spokes" system in its current anachronistic form are rising. They lie particularly in the deepening resentment that playing Asian nations against one another provokes within continental Asia. In some countries, particularly Korea and China, there is also resentment of U.S. ambivalence about local national integration. More broadly, relying on an asymmetric, archaic, balkanizing system for political-economic influence impedes development of the balanced communication and understanding that needs to lie at the heart of future trans-Pacific relations.

The polar alternative of an autarkic Northeast Asia, divorced from trans-Pacific interdependence, and estranged from the United States, is also obviously unrealistic and unacceptable, both in Washington and in global markets. Northeast Asia is among the most consequential of global regions; without its trade and capital flows, the American economy simply cannot function. Geopolitically, a Sino-Japanese entente, excluding the United States, or reducing it to a marginal role in triangular relations, would be among the most alarming challenges to American security that the United States could possibly confront. Korean accession to that entente would only compound the dangers. Such an occurrence is unlikely, but lack of engagement, or obliviousness to deeply held Asian concerns, could potentially produce it.

Multilateralism has been roundly condemned within the United States as subversive of U.S. interests in the Pacific, although it has functioned reasonably well in the Atlantic context. Clearly, bilateralism was effective, and perhaps crucial, in reassuring both Japan and its wartime antagonists in the aftermath of World War II, when alternative frameworks were infeasible. The U.S.-Japan security alliance, to be sure, remains fundamental to the long-term stability of the Pacific. Yet the emerging problems of Northeast Asia—the future of Korea foremost among them—are not well adapted to bilateral solutions alone. To the contrary, many aspects of those problems, such as energy and environmental challenges, are best confronted in a multilateral context, as broad recent support for the six-party framework, or narrower minilateral arrangements in the North Korean nuclear negotiations, suggest. A multitiered regional architecture with active U.S. engagement, which has both bilateral and, increasingly, multilateral dimensions, will need to be the order of the day. How this might be accomplished, and the specific issues that a more fully developed multilateral structure might consider, with American involvement, will be a major subject of our concluding chapter.

In Conclusion

The United States, as the preceding pages make clear, has a distinctive heritage to its relations with Northeast Asia—very different from its ties to Europe, Latin America, or even Southeast Asia—that profoundly colors its relations with that region, to this very day. Americans, as individuals, played an important role in opening Northeast Asia to the broader world—as missionaries, educators, adventurers, and technical specialists. Yet the United States as a nation never assumed colonial dominion or amassed really substantial economic presence on the ground. This early detachment produced a combination of idealism, naivety, and psychological aloofness, enhanced by geographical distance, that has persistently colored trans-Pacific relations across the years.

The congenial days of Perry, Clark, the Underwoods, and the Yenching Institute were succeeded, of course, by war and Occupation. America's diplomatic presence, symbolized by Dulles and MacArthur, came to loom large across the region. For three-quarters of a century, across three wars and many crises in Asia, national security has also grown to be a major U.S. concern, enhanced as Asia's economic and technological power rises, shaping much of the concrete agenda of American policy.

Apart from the embedded bias imbued by history, we have identified four other structural factors that shape the policy approach of the United States to Northeast Asia. First of all, ethnic ties, traditionally weak, are strengthening, as the number of Asian Americans—particularly those from China and Korea—grows rapidly. Secondly, unionization rates across the U.S. are declining. Thirdly, Asian involvement in broader American politics and social life is rising. And finally, American corporate interests in Northeast Asia are deepening.

Together, these structural changes provide the basis for deeper, more selective, and more realistic U.S. involvement in the region than heretofore. Stronger American interests, particularly human networks, may allow the United States to break through its curious socioeconomic isolation, and the heavy political-military cast that has dominated modern trans-Pacific relations. Yet as the recent experience of U.S.–Northeast Asian diplomacy suggests, this assertion takes effort, outstanding individuals, and often the outbreak of crisis.

In the final analysis, the Making of Northeast Asia is a gradual but inexorable and historic transformation, as the embedded political-economic barriers that mutually estranged China, Korea, and Japan from one another for so long are steadily dismantled, and as bitter historical memories fade. This gradual reconciliation process, aided by the passing of generations and the rising stakes of interdependence, is moving steadily forward. Fortunately, U.S. interests and sentiments themselves appear to be growing more congruent with the newly interdependent realities of Northeast Asia, although the United States generally remains too detached and oblivious to the latest on-the-ground trends across the Pacific.

The days of "American imperium" may be waning, as Asian political-economic power rises, Northeast Asian nations grow more mutually interdependent, and the United States itself grows more diverse within. Yet what will follow remains unclear. Economically and culturally, Northeast Asia seems headed for greater cohesion. Whether that will exclude the West, politically and socially, depends critically on how proactive the West proves to be, in asserting a desire to engage, and how adroit its diplomacy becomes in realizing that objective.

In the new postimperial Northeast Asia now emerging, the United States can still play a prospectively important role. It can be a stabilizer, a reassurer, and at times a broker, in a region where major geopolitical tensions remain, and where American geographical detachment increases U.S. credibility, provided that Washington's political-military commitment is credible. The United States can, in particular, reassure Japan, as that nation's complex geopolitical environment continues to change. It can likewise help to stabilize Japan's delicate relations with China, as cross-Straits interdependence rises. The United States can also help to safeguard the autonomy of Korea, which well understands the perils of being a "shrimp among whales." Indeed, Washington can capitalize on distinctive institutional strengths of Korean decision-makers, and their traditionally decisive temperament, to create a beachhead for U.S. interests in Northeast Asia. That, in turn, can help to enhance American influence across the broader region, provided that both nations are subtly respectful of each other's interests, as well as the market mechanism. Ratifying the Korea and U.S.(KORUS) economic agreement is a needed first step, from a U.S. standpoint.

Americans should be able to reconcile themselves to the Making of Northeast Asia in its socioeconomic dimensions, insofar as that process is not explicitly anti-American, and offers prospective scope for U.S. involvement. Americans are, after all, growing rapidly more linked to Asia—in both cultural and political-economic terms, than has ever been true in the past. And Northeast Asia is the emerging growth pole and technological locus of the broader region. The synergistic economic dynamism of Japan, China, and Korea could be attractive for American firms, while Northeast Asia's ongoing, if fitful transition to democracy and prosperity could be inspiring to the American public as well. Yet a systematic, long-term U.S. policy involvement in Northeast Asia—however fateful it may be in influencing the region's future—is by no means ensured.

The process of linking American political-economic interests to the Making of Northeast Asia, without stirring a backlash against the Pacific's inexorable tide toward Asian reassertion, will be a complex one. In a world beyond the "hub-and-spokes," where U.S. leverage grows weaker, even as intra-Asian ties continue to deepen, Americans will need to be more attentive, connected, and informed than heretofore of the historic trends flowing from across the Pacific. Americans must be strategic in defending their own core interests, as a "resident power" in the North Pacific. A proactive stance in engaging Asian regionalism, and claiming a substantive role for the United States, will be imperative. Yet Asians will also need to be more understanding of America's own dilemmas, not to mention the difficulties of transition from imperium to partnership. In particular, Asians will need to transcend local populist sentiment to give Americans tangible, sometimes material incentives for active involvement across the Pacific. And they must invoke idealism as well.

IN CONCLUSION

11

Summing Up

Over the past few years, there has been an outpouring of literature on Asian regionalism, as we have seen. Most of it has looked broadly at East Asia as a whole, from Hokkaido in the Northeast to Myanmar in the Southwest. It has been pre-occupied with explaining why regional integration European-style, with elaborate formal institutions and clear-cut legal frameworks, has not occurred. Presuming Asian institutional patterns to be largely static, it has assumed that since regionalism in the European sense does not currently exist in Asia, and since it has never done so, the future prospects are likewise limited.

A few recent publications, to be sure, have conceded the existence of some dynamic regionalization trends in East Asia, and even illustrated them.[1] Some of the emerging patterns that they consider—deepening economic interdependence and intensifying social exchanges, for example—are also highlighted in this book. Yet these recent works remain focused almost exclusively on East Asia as a whole, and hence overlook critically important subregional changes and shifts in the relative distribution of intraregional power and influence, particularly since the 1997 financial crisis.

The classical paradigm fails to reflect some crucial emerging realities. Most important among these changes are the increasingly intense and profound economic and social interactions within Northeast Asia itself. Since 2006 these socioeconomic dynamics have turned political as well, as clearly evidenced in the rapprochement of several Japanese prime ministers with China (September 2006–); improved Korean ties with Japan (February 2008–); and the substantially more relaxed cross–Taiwan Straits situation since Ma Ying-jeou's election (March 2008–).

Many have speculated that recent military developments in North Korea and the Taiwan Straits might well exacerbate intraregional political divisions, and return Northeast Asia to past configurations. As tensions have intensified over a succession of North Korean nuclear and missile tests, and a continuing missile buildup between China and Taiwan, however, cooperative dynamics have also been set in motion among those potentially affected. The spokes of the once Washington-centric wheel have been interacting vigorously with one another, as well as with Washington, through emergent institutions such as the Six-Party Talks. Crisis, as we have seen, in fact inspires cohesion among many actors in managing the challenge, although North Korea and Taiwanese conservatives may not be party to the cooperative steps. In a region of both deepening economic interdependence and persistent security tensions, economics appears to "trump" security; dangers of political-military conflict engender determined efforts to neutralize rather than exacerbate threatening security situations, leading to generally deeper, albeit not universal, regional cooperation.

Based on a counterintuitive understanding of how military tension relates to political-economic interdependence in today's Asia, this book departs from the conventional wisdom and comes to a much more optimistic assessment of regional integration prospects than is common in the United States. It focuses on Northeast Asia, historically the most divided part of the Asian region over the past half-century, and one characterized traditionally by a distinct "organization gap," as we have noted. We have directed less attention to developments south of China, including the evolution of the Association of Southeast Asian Nations (ASEAN), other than to note their positive historical impact on broader regional-integration dynamics. While noting ASEAN's early, constructive role in fostering Asian integration, particularly during the late Cold War, we have argued that the more crucial questions regarding Asia's communal future lie increasingly in the Northeast, the most consequential part of Asia in economic, military, and technological terms. There the most pronounced new movement toward Asian regional integration has taken place over the past decade, albeit from a low and precarious base. And we argue that a counterintuitive pattern of explicit political-economic cooperation, much of it intergovernmental, and more ambitious than the informal nongovernmental "network power" described a decade ago by Katzenstein and Shiraishi, is fitfully beginning to emerge in Northeast Asia.[2]

Northeast Asia's Quiet Yet Fateful Transformation

The Northeast will clearly be the driver of Asia's future, we maintain, for four basic reasons. First, that quadrant is decidedly the economic and political-military heart of the continent as a whole. Roughly 90 percent of total East Asian regional GDP, and more than 70 percent of military manpower, are concentrated in the three Northeast Asian nations: Japan, China, and Korea. Secondly, that political-economic heart is gaining more cohesion, as historic tensions among Japan, China, and their neighbors, as well as differences across the Taiwan Straits, continue to fade. Taiwan's deepening role, within both Greater China and Northeast Asia more generally, is one particularly potent new political-economic catalyst. Thirdly, foreign investment—by all the major global powers—has shifted from the southeast to the northeast quadrant of Asia since the 1997 financial crisis, and appears likely to concentrate predominantly there in future. And finally, levels of capital formation and technological progress are much higher in Northeast Asia than elsewhere on the continent. Among the business community of that region, transnational production networks involving Japanese, Koreans, Taiwanese, and Mainland Chinese business people in complementary roles are rapidly emerging, with Japanese firms increasingly focused on technology development, Chinese corporations on both sides of the Straits engaged in labor-intensive manufacturing, Taiwanese firms on specialized IT applications, and Korean companies positioning themselves eclectically in this regional synergy.

We have noted, in contrast to the conventional wisdom, that Northeast Asia already has considerable subregional cohesion, the traditional organization gap notwithstanding. Intricate, albeit low-profile political-economic networks that have developed robustly amid the regional tensions of the past decade have played key roles in fostering that deepened sense of community, which is at its most dynamic across the Taiwan Straits. They are complemented by newly emerging political-military networks—including even air and naval hotlines between Seoul and Beijing—that are building mutual confidence within a volatile region, and calming long-divisive memories of a bitter past.

A variety of summit conferences, unimagined before the Asian financial crisis of the late 1990s, now routinely bring regional leaders together, driven by deepening economic and political incentives. Epistemic communities, such as the Network of East Asian Think Tanks (NEAT), likewise align policy advisors in Beijing, Seoul, and Tokyo, generating creative new regional policy agendas on energy, telecommunications, and financial questions. Swap-quota agreements create contingency arrangements in the event of financial crisis, while coordinated stockpiles cushion the potential impact of future energy shocks. Track II regional gatherings, such as the periodic Boao and Jeju forums, network business and government leaders with one another, giving them a chance to exchange ideas systematically. Many of these networks involve participants from South and Southeast Asia, to be sure, but their fulcrum is increasingly the powerful Northeast Asian quadrant of the region.

Our analysis makes us relatively optimistic about future prospects, for both Northeast Asian economic interdependence and for deepening regional policy integration. Indeed, we have contended that the world will ever more clearly see the Making of Northeast Asia, as the ASEAN "figleaf" drops away, albeit in the context of a multitiered regional system where Southeast Asia—especially dynamic, proactive states like Singapore—retains a meaningful role. Strong underlying macroeconomic complementarities among capital-intensive Japan, labor-intensive China, and entrepreneurial Korea, reinforced by deepening transnational production and distribution networks at the microlevel, and with Taiwan as an intriguing new catalyst, clearly facilitate interdependence. Embedded Cold War political constraints on the operation of those economic complementarities—in areas from energy and finance to manufacturing—are steadily weakening, most dramatically across the Taiwan Straits, as local politicians grow increasingly pragmatic in their approach to history, and more personally familiar with one another. Transnational networks across the region, which link people together and help them to think collectively, are rapidly growing stronger—ironically aided by the apprehensions of just how explosive the flickering shadows of the past can be.

North Korea, to be sure, remains the one part of the region still largely isolated from an integration dynamic that now deeply involves even Taiwan. Yet given the pervasiveness of pressures toward interdependence and social pluralism elsewhere, it seems unlikely that North Korea can indefinitely remain an exception. Its stable integration into regional affairs, on a non-nuclear basis, would potentially accelerate Northeast Asian regional integration, even beyond dynamic recent trajectories. South Korea, after all, is at present effectively a geostrategic island, restrained from more substantial intercourse with the Asian continent by tensions across the DMZ. As those tensions relax, however, and especially if reunification proceeds, Korean interaction with China's Northeast, Russia's Far East, and even Japan could become much more intense than at present. Yet given the dynamism in long-hostile relationships elsewhere in the region, especially in cross-Straits and Sino-Japanese relations, Northeast Asian political-economic cohesion will likely advance beyond current levels, regardless of developments on the Korean peninsula.

Each of the three major nations of Northeast Asia—China, Japan, and Korea—today has significant and growing domestic reasons to acclaim the "making" of their subregion, as we have suggested in the three preceding Northeast Asian country chapters. Korea, Taiwan, and the South China coast, because of their geographical centrality, may stand to benefit most in economic terms. And South Korean domestic politics—with the waning of military influence and the political rise of nongovernmental organizations (NGOs) and depressed regions with stakes in broader regional ties—is increasingly configured to support regionalism.

Korea has, indeed, consistently played a catalytic role in the Making of Northeast Asia since the 1997 financial crisis, although the nuances of that role have varied substantially across the successive administrations of presidents Kim, Roh, and Lee. The ASEAN Plus Three (APT) process and the East Asian Vision Group (EAVG) were both regionalist institutions, first proposed by Kim Dae-jung in the late 1990s. Both government-affiliated and nongovernmental organizations in Seoul have been actively networking with their counterparts in Beijing and Tokyo ever since that time. Korean companies, while investing intensively in China, are likewise seeking strategic partnerships with leading Japanese firms.

China, because of its sheer size, sees Northeast Asian regionalism, within the context of a multitiered global system, as attractive in geopolitical terms. It is well placed to dominate regional arrangements and thereby leverage its broader international role. The People's Republic of China's (PRC's) interest has recently also been intensified by deepening prospects for rapprochement with Taiwan. Yet the PRC's political relationships with its two large neighbors to the east have long been complicated by Japan's wartime history, as well as the Korean War, and potential economic uncertainties generated by China's rapid economic rise, as well as Beijing's deepening cross-Straits relations with Taiwan.

Chinese strategists thus perceive that regionalism, in which China harnesses its explosive economic growth to the PRC's diplomatic objectives, including the recovery of Taiwan, is an attractive approach to dealing with Beijing's complex strategic environment. Northeast Asian regionalism, as a result of the Taiwan issue and the importance of neutralizing Japanese opposition in that context, has particular importance in connection with such PRC objectives. Moreover, Chinese economic actors and the PRC's epistemic communities are increasingly enmeshed in transnational networks with their Japanese and Korean counterparts. Greater integration in the Northeast Asian subregion brings advanced technology and capital that China needs, both to accelerate its domestic development and to enhance its international competitiveness, although the PRC is also eager to retain broader global ties as well. Rapprochement with Taiwan and the imperatives of reviving the Rustbelt of its northeastern provinces provide attractive rationales domestically for pursuing these priorities.

Japan, traditionally ambivalent about a claustrophobic Northeast Asian embrace, now sees greater attraction in Asian regional ties than previously, for both economic and political reasons. The growing long-term strength of the renminbi and the won, which magnifies the relative economic scale of China and Korea, together with the extraordinary dynamism of the Chinese market and new synergies among Japan, Korea, Taiwan, and Mainland China in both information technology and electronics, all make deeper ties across the Japan and East China seas more attractive in Tokyo than heretofore. For the Democratic Party of Japan (DPJ) government in Tokyo, inaugurated in September 2009, Asian regional ties also provide a lever for enhancing Japan's options beyond the intimate, and to some Japanese eyes claustrophobic, trans-Pacific embrace of recent years.

Western multinationals, to be sure, remain the primary business counterparts of Japan's powerful and sophisticated global enterprises. Yet a significant marginal deepening of Northeast Asian corporate ties has begun to occur. Indeed, between 2002 and 2008, Japanese firms substantially deepened their strategic alliances with Chinese and Korean counterparts, political tensions notwithstanding. Although Chinese and Korean firms are much smaller and often less technologically advanced than Western enterprises that are the current alternative for Japan, strategic partnerships with Taiwanese, Korean, and Mainland Chinese companies allow Japanese electronics giants to cut costs, expand sales, and strategically focus on their technologically sophisticated units so that they can compete more effectively in the global market beyond Northeast Asia itself. The steady growth of transnational production networks with those countries over the past decade makes at least stability in mutual relations indispensable. Sanyo, Matsushita, SONY, and Samsung are four important cases of such transnational synergies at work, in product lines ranging from washing machines to fuel cells.[3]

The Political Dimension

The overtures since late 2006 of both the ruling party in Japan and its opposition toward China and South Korea on issues ranging from energy to finance and information technology have been substantial. These new initiatives suggest clearly that Tokyo's long-time reluctance to engage its Northeast Asian neighbors politically is at an end. These important new policy shifts, likely to be intensified by a new generation of leadership in Tokyo, have been reciprocated by political leaders in both Beijing and Seoul. To a degree unprecedented in three-quarters of a century, all the major governments of Northeast Asia have grown enthusiastic about deepening political-economic interdependence, particularly since the advent of the Lee Myung-bak administration in Seoul (February 2008); that of Ma Ying-jeou in Taipei (March 2008); and that of the DPJ in Tokyo (September 2009).

Painful embedded history, and the institutional constraints it inevitably fosters, has long inhibited the Making of Northeast Asia. Our analysis has shown that those venerable constraints are largely waning in importance within the region, although they ironically continue to have substantial traction in U.S. domestic politics, far across the Pacific, as the 2007 evolution of the comfort-women issue on both sides of the Pacific demonstrated.[4] Economic, political, and global-system dynamics are all at work.

The "hub-and-spokes" structure of international relations in the Pacific is waning, however, as both America's economy and its dollar decline in influence relative to Asian alternatives; and as the "spokes" in the Pacific policy wheel begin interacting more often with one another, in both formal and informal settings. Japanese and South Korean trade dependence on the United States has been declining since 1986, and that of the PRC since 2002, as has been noted, with intraregional Asian mutual reliance conversely rising. The existence of a multitiered international system, in which the World Trade Organization (WTO), the United Nations, the East Asia Summit, Asia-Pacific Economic Cooperation (APEC), and other transcendent institutions coexist with narrower regional bodies, also make Northeast Asia–specific affiliations less threatening and embarrassing for their members, especially for Japan.[5] The Cold War days of black and white unidimensional affiliations are receding into the past.

Embedded history that has for so long estranged the nations of Northeast Asia continues to complicate their interaction in two still contentious settings within the region: Korea and the Taiwan Straits. Our analysis, while realistic about the considerable physical dangers involved, suggests that the potential volatility of the second, at least, is waning, under the impact of steadily deepening regional economic interdependence. Some 10 percent of Taiwan's labor force now works in the People's Republic of China, which takes more than 40 percent of Taiwan's exports—substantially more than the United States and Japan combined—even as the number of missiles implanted on both sides of the Taiwan Straits continues to spiral unabated.[6]

Our analysis has suggested that Northeast Asia's political-economic realities are by no means static. Indeed, we have found there to be a powerful engine of transformation—critical juncture (CJ)—that from time to time discontinuously reshapes the landscape of regional affairs, forging policy and institutional adjustment to long term geopolitical and geoeconomic trends. In the first modern manifestation of critical juncture in operation—the Korean War—an early, promising multilateral framework, the Pacific Pact, was discarded; communist and noncommunist Asia were torn asunder by embargo; and the bilateralist "hub-and-spokes" system was born.[7] In a series of subsequent critical junctures—most conspicuously the 1997 and 2008 financial crises, as well as various confrontations with North Korea—a host of new policy networks, as well as a soft institutionalism opening fateful new multilateralist prospects, were born.

To be sure, critical uncertainties remain. Korea across the DMZ, as well as China across the Taiwan Straits, both involve a delicate combination of economic

interdependence and military brinkmanship, and it is not categorically clear that
the peaceful logic of interdependence will prevail. Yet Japan and China have powerful economic incentives to set aside their long-standing geostrategic rivalry, and
numerous confidence-building steps are proceeding across the region. Although
underlying geopolitical rivalries themselves continue, and the ultimate degree and
form of mutual accommodation among longtime opponents remain painfully
uncertain, politics and economics, in their interaction, are creating new cooperative realities within Northeast Asia that will be ever more difficult to reverse in
future years.

What Is New in This Analysis

This book is distinctive in the literature on Asian regionalism for its focus
on Northeast Asia. Most other major works have used the broader East Asian
region, including Southeast Asia, as their unit of analysis,[8] or focused exclusively
on China.[9] There are, however, substantial reasons for formulating the geographic
parameters of analysis somewhat differently. ASEAN has been a central catalyst
heretofore, for various geopolitical and historical reasons, but its leverage and
legitimacy in that role, while still constructive, are declining. Northeast Asia, after
all, is substantially larger, more powerful, and generally more rapidly growing
outside of Japan, especially since the Asian financial crisis. It is also, as Southeast
Asia was three decades ago, the site of the most immediate threats to peace and
security in the region, and it is transforming itself along globally important new
lines that merit serious exploration. The issue, however, as we have seen, is not so
much China alone, or China and ASEAN, but China, Japan, and Korea in their
mutual interactions, responding to dynamic changes across the Taiwan Straits and
elsewhere.

This book is also unusual in its attention to the domestic-political determinants
of foreign policy, which provide the "supply" of regionalism, as Mattli points out.[10]
We consider in detail the internal shifts, such as the rise of labor and the declining
role of the military in South Korean politics, that help drive changing approaches
to regionalism in the nations of the region. The book also notes the importance
of key national leaders with inevitable domestic concerns, such as Kim Dae-jung,
in driving the integration process forward. They are especially central in times
of political-economic crisis, and especially when their institutional positions—as
with the Korean president early in his five-year term—are strong.

Regarding China, the book emphasizes the regional role of Chinese bureaucrats, entrepreneurs, and scholars who have become markedly more active in
regional policy dialogues since 1997. These Chinese domestic actors critically

redefined policy preferences toward Asian regionalism for Beijing political leaders. They also offered important economic and strategic rationales within Chinese domestic politics in support of a broader, cooperative approach to regionalist policy-making.[11] The advent of Hu Jintao's presidency in 2003 was a critical catalyst in initiating intra–Northeast Asian cooperation, in part due to the way it altered priorities in Chinese domestic politics. Two of President Hu's grand strategies: "peaceful rising" and "regionally balanced development," focusing on northeastern rejuvenation, together with a concern for national reunification with Taiwan, naturally led the PRC under Hu's leadership toward a growing role in the Making of Northeast Asia, reinforced by active steps by provincial leaders.

In Japan, erosion in the traditional dominance of the Liberal Democratic Party (LDP) forced that party's leaders to broaden the social basis of their organization, especially toward urban areas. Ongoing LDP transformation, coupled with rising competitive strength of urban-based opposition parties, also deepened consumer orientation and Asia focus. And the end of LDP dominance in late 2009, providing opportunities for younger, more Asia oriented political figures, further accelerated such processes. These recent historic changes in Japan, whose implications for regionalism remain largely unreported, have supported the Making of Northeast Asia.

This volume is distinctive, finally, in its attention to theory-building. It starts by considering the unusual collective-action problem of the "organization gap" that Northeast Asia confronts, contrasting it with the embedded historical circumstances of other world regions. The book inquires into the origins of that distinctive gap, and identifies the central role of critical junctures in creating and shaping its profile. Our work then explores the nature of critical junctures themselves, elucidating a critical-juncture concept that is a principal contribution of the work as a whole to political-science theory.

Across this volume we have identified three full-fledged critical junctures—the Korean War, the 1997–8 Asian financial crisis, and the 2008–9 global financial crisis. Two of these were primarily financial in nature, and the first a security critical juncture. Additionally, four security crises in the region since the mid-1990s—the 1994 North Korean missile crisis; the 1996 Taiwan Straits crisis; the 2006 North Korean nuclear-test crisis; and the 2009 North Korean nuclear and missile-test crisis—were catalytic/regional developments with important critical-juncture characteristics but more limited in geographic and political-economic scope.

Evidence from the critical junctures examined here suggests that security-related critical junctures tend historically to generate more pronounced and more rapidly manifest institutional consequences for regionalism than do predominantly financial critical junctures. Security CJs, after all, are matters of war and peace, with potentially sweeping existential consequences. The pre-existing policy networks for coping with them also tend to be well developed. Financial CJs appear to operate through a different and less established dynamic. In the 1997 AFC, for example, there was a pronounced lag between the initial CJ decision-making (1997–98) and implementation of institutional changes (1999–2000), resulting from the absence of transnational networks and bureaucratic procedures for dealing with the initial external shock. Key decision-makers—most critically in Japan and China—simply did not know one another. This lag between CJ decision-making and bureaucratic implementation in the financial sphere was shorter in 2008, however, as transnational networks capable of supporting policy definition and implementation had become significantly more substantial.

The consequences of both security and financial CJs for regional integration are also shaped by the degree of economic interdependence that prevails among the nations involved in a given set of crises. Where interdependence is high—especially interdependence with the geopolitically influential United States—CJs tend to generate more pronounced and more rapid institution-building consequences, as was true in the 2008–9 financial crisis, compared with that of 1997. Domestic political transitions in key nations—from Bush to Obama in the United States, or away from Koizumi in Japan—can also generate differences in national responses to CJs, although the central importance of CJs in the Making of Northeast Asia, and in regionalist evolution more generally, is a commonality across the cases examined here.

The critical-juncture concept is an important potential contribution to political-economic analysis, because it provides a parsimonious explanation not only for when and why political and institutional changes occur, but also for the configuration of such changes themselves. CJ helps us understand, in short, why systems move from point A to point B, and why policy and institutions at point B take the form that they do. It provides, with respect to the topic at hand, an explanation for the "supply of regionalism" that does not necessarily rely on the volition of a hegemonic leader nation. In our study here, critical juncture has provided detailed explanations both for why the organization gap emerged in Northeast Asia during the Korean War, and for why it abruptly began to close following the 1997 Asian financial crisis. In both cases, process was crucial, and in neither instance was hegemonic power determining. The critical-juncture concept also generates the provocative, falsifiable prediction that political-economic crisis, related to regime change in North Korea, could be fatefully important in enhancing the long-term institutional profile of Northeast Asian regionalism.

Our analysis here also helps provide a new and broadened understanding of the role of sociopolitical networks in regional integration. Katzenstein and

Shiraishi, in their edited volume *Network Power* (1997), suggested the importance of economic networks in the East Asian political economy, to be sure.[12] Their conception of networks, as exclusively commercial relationships embodied in the Japanese *keiretsu* and ethnic Chinese business *guanxi,* is very different, however, from our approach to that important socioeconomic phenomenon. The commercial networks on which they focus attention—*keiretsu, chaebol,* and *guanxi*—operate largely outside the political realm, with relatively little direct impact on government policy-making.

We concern ourselves here with more comprehensive Northeast Asian transnational networks, which incorporate bureaucracies, corporations, epistemic communities, and even military actors within their embrace. Such intraregional policy networks, relatively underdeveloped as late as the mid-1990s, have come to play significant—even decisive—policy roles since the 1997–98 Asian financial crisis. Some have included Southeast as well as Northeast Asian participation, but effective leadership even in those cases has increasingly concentrated in the Northeast. Autonomous China-Japan-Korea policy networks have also been evolving—first in the environmental area, but increasingly in finance, transportation, energy, and strategic affairs, progressing to the highest levels of national decision as well. In contrast to earlier views, we see such networks as both dynamic and policy-directed—concerned primarily with mediating the challenges of rising regional interdependence, rather than pursuing commercial gain. They are steadily evolving from mere talk shops toward serious policy-making relevance. Northeast Asians, in short, are beginning to forge distinctive communal policies of their own.

The empirical chapters in this book have explored concretely the policy roles played by these new networks, particularly in agenda-setting and political brokerage. The research and proposals generated by these dynamic policy networks are profoundly transforming regional policy-making across Northeast Asia, we have found. The emerging Asian bond market, in which Japan has been influential, was the product of such transnational, mixed public-private policy networks in operation, born of political crisis.[13] Similarly, the Six-Party Talks process, emerging amid the North Korean nuclear crisis, has similarly been nourished and enhanced by these complex transnational networks. The support provided by such networks for regional cooperation in energy and finance is eliciting growing and simultaneous backing from political leaders in China, Japan, and Korea. Regional policy networks within Northeast Asia itself also help to defuse tensions among this strategic triad, such as those relating to North Korean contingencies, which could otherwise easily disrupt their mutual relationships.

The three critical junctures that we describe in Chapters 3 and 4 demonstrate a crucial analytical point: that policy networks are typically forged during critical junctures, yet endure and influence policy for long periods thereafter. The first critical juncture that we consider—the Korean War—created deep, extensive bilateral ties between the United States and its Asian allies. At the individual, institutional, and national levels, bilateral policy networks across the Pacific became, as a consequence of that conflict and the ensuing Cold War, substantially more consequential than alternative intra-Asian regional networks alone. The security character of the critical juncture clearly seems to have reinforced the globalist, yet discriminatory, character of these networks, clearly favoring allies over Cold War adversaries.

In coping with the 1997–98 Asian financial crisis, however, intra-Asian, transnational policy networks were created, beginning in the financial sector itself, that in turn generated broader, multilevel linkages across a tortured Northeast Asian subregion that had long suffered from an organization gap. The financial character of this critical juncture seems to have fostered inclusive patterns of regional organization, as a result of the inclusive, systemic character of the assurances and public goods provided. This emerging web of regional policy networks created a more cooperative environment within the region, centering on crucial sectors such as finance and energy. The cooperative network in turn allowed member nations both to express common interests and to actually act on their cooperative commitments to an unprecedented degree, in a broadening range of issue areas.

The insights developed here into how policy networks form, how they are endowed with functional significance, and how their operation can in turn affect the politics of economic interdependence, should be useful to analysis far beyond the Northeast Asian political-economic context.[14] Such insights could be useful in predicting and assessing emerging profiles of regional integration elsewhere in the world, especially in developing regions such as the Southern Cone of South America or the Gulf Coordination Council nations of the Persian Gulf.[15] These insights could also help to explain emerging patterns of diaspora politics in poor, economically isolated, and chaotic nations, such as China in the 1970s, Latin America in the 1980s, or Russia and India in the 1990s.

Transnational networks, on which this research casts significant light, seem destined to grow more powerful, relative to domestic competitors, and thus to become increasingly important features of international affairs. In the context of deepening globalization, transnational networks are likely to rise in importance for three concrete reasons. First of all, they provide more realistic, actionable intelligence regarding the outside world than is available to domestically oriented competitors, thus affording correspondingly greater legitimacy to their members in domestic policy debates. Second, transnational networks have greater financial and intellectual resources at their disposal than do exclusively domestic competitors, due precisely to their global, transnational character. Transnational networks are therefore more effective in lobbying local governments than more domestically based groups. Transnational networks, finally, also tend to have close ties with multinational corporations, and can hence serve as valuable channels of economic communication across national boundaries. Understanding such networks and their political-economic roles must clearly be a rising priority of policy-oriented social science in coming years. It is hoped that this research casts light on such important questions.

A third theoretical contribution of this analysis, in addition to the critical-juncture concept and an expanded notion of policy-network formation, is a new paradigm of regionalism itself. Existing literature—Katzenstein and Shiraishi (1997) and Lincoln (2004), for example—emphasizes the fundamental dichotomy between a legalistic European paradigm, with clearly defined formal institutions, on the one hand, and a highly informal East Asian model, with no functioning transnational policy institutions, and coordinated within only by informal, apolitical business networks.[16] Our analysis here clearly suggests a soft-institutionalist halfway house. There policy-oriented yet informal epistemic networks perform important and increasingly substantive regional-governance functions, with important systemic implications. This sort of governance is, as we have pointed out, becoming remarkably effective in mediating deepening economic relations among political entities with ambiguous diplomatic relationships to one another, such as North and South Korea, Japan, Taiwan, and the PRC. Networks are thus dynamically assisting the Making of Northeast Asia in ways that state-to-state understandings have not so far done, and could not easily do.

The new regionalism paradigm emerging in Northeast Asia also differs from conventional characterizations of East Asian regionalism as involving the expansion of a dominant national policy model.[17] Our analysis suggests that this nation-centric paradigm has steadily declining relevance to Northeast Asia's future, whatever importance it may have had in the region's past. American dominance of international relations in Northeast Asia is declining, as trade and financial interdependence between the region and the United States continue to fall, even as intraregional ties among China, Japan, and Korea grow increasingly dense. Particularly given the rise of China, the paradigm of American dominance in Northeast Asia, and of Asia more generally, through influence over Japan appears increasingly implausible. Meanwhile, the concept of a more autonomous Northeast Asian core, with its components coordinated through soft-institutionalist networks among the spokes of the Pacific wheel, approaches more closely the emerging regional reality, given recent trade, financial, and even geopolitical trends as China rises, cross-Straits relations improve, and American hegemony wanes.

This eclectic emerging synthesis by no means represents, in any straightforward way, the regional expansion of any particular national power, although China no doubt benefits at the margin.[18] Japan is still the largest economic power in Asia, in nominal GDP terms, with the most sophisticated civilian technological base, and numerous world-class multinational firms that have active productive networks extending throughout Northeast Asia and beyond.[19] In the political-economic dimension, China's growing regional influence lies embedded in, and constrained by, the growing involvement of its elites in the dynamic transnational governance now emerging in the region. This increasing salience of transnational networks in Northeast Asian regional governance limits the dominance of individual nations. It suggests a more subtle ascendancy of the networks themselves as a new sort of governance mechanism, albeit one in which Beijing plays a rising role. Nye and Keohane, without considering intra-Asian politics specifically, of course, suggested the importance of "complex interdependence" in shaping international relations as early as the 1970s.[20] Their observations regarding how interdependence affects governmental institutions and private actors helps inform our observations regarding the increasing soft-institutional coherence of Northeast Asia.

Our analysis highlights, finally, the critical role of small yet strategic "middle powers" as catalysts for integration among their larger neighbors.[21] In highlighting their role, it suggests an alternative path toward regionalism, distinct from the leader-driven, hegemonically determined pattern emphasized by some scholars.[22] The PRC, to be sure, is playing an increasingly positive role in Northeast Asian regionalism, driven partly, no doubt, by its desire for reconciliation with Taiwan. Yet that role is still substantially more hesitant than Germany's powerful role in supporting European integration during the 1950s. South Korea, situated between the giants of the region, China and Japan, however, has also played an often important and catalytic role since the Asian financial crisis in helping to formulate and promote new regionalist options, despite its relatively modest scale. It may, in short, be Northeast Asia's Benelux. Kim Dae-jung, in particular, was the driving force behind establishment of the ASEAN Plus Three process, and the East Asian Vision Group a decade ago. His immediate successor, Roh Moo-hyun, dissipated some of Korea's credibility as a broker through rhetoric about "balancing" and confrontationist gestures, but more subtle triangular diplomacy was revived under Lee Myung-bak in early 2008, culminating in the Fukuoka Summit of December 2008. At the nongovernmental level, the Jeju Forum in South Korea, convened biannually, and the annual Boao Forum on China's Hainan Island, have also brought together government officials, corporate representatives, and epistemic communities from throughout Northeast Asia and the United States, usefully deepening North Pacific Track II networks.

Implications for the Broader World

The Making of Northeast Asia, a phenomenon more profound and consequential even than the rise of China, is still remarkably unappreciated in global political-economic analysis. Yet it has fateful implications for the underlying structure of international affairs worldwide. If China, Japan, and Korea come together in a substantially more cooperative relationship than at present, they would constitute a political-economic mass nearly equivalent to either North America or Europe in scale, with both nuclear weapons and other advanced technology, as well as a huge population and formidable organizational capabilities. Their influence would also be magnified by the dissipation of the bitter conflicts that have estranged these huge and dynamic nations from one another for most of the past century. Northeast Asia, as a unit, could very well, in short, be one of the few serious challengers to U.S. global preeminence. The world clearly needs to know such a prospective adversary or challenger.

Some argue that Northeast Asia's recent pattern of growing amity and interdependence is easily reversible. We do not dispute that possibility, but point to the strong underlying economic complementarities, shared regional interests, and deepening transactional—yet Northeast Asia–centric—networks, as well as the growing chronological distance from the painful years of conflict among them. History shows that the logic of economic cooperation is rarely—albeit occasionally—reversed by political conflict, and that geopolitical conflict has grown markedly more muted across Asia over the past two generations.

It is vitally important for outside powers—preeminently the United States—to engage with this important new development in world affairs, so as to prospectively influence its fateful yet still uncertain course. While it seems strongly probable, in our view, that a more cohesive Northeast Asia will be emerging, and that it will be technologically and industrially powerful, it is harder to be sure about its military capabilities and intentions, or what the region's general orientation toward the outside world might be. Northeast Asia has a long history of humiliation at the hands of the West, and is sensitive to past injustice, while also confident about future capabilities, and insistent on a respected future role. Belligerent or confrontational treatment could be counterproductive, just as naive optimism or overconfidence could also be.

U.S. engagement with Northeast Asia, we have found, does not necessarily come easily. The United States, until after World War II, did not historically experience the sort of intimate relationship with Northeast Asia that it did with Southeast Asia, since Japan was the dominant colonial power, and American economic and cultural involvement was minimal. There are all too few embedded institutions in America with a stake in Northeast Asia's future. Through more than a decade of warfare and occupation between 1941 and 1953, America did, to be sure, gain a firsthand appreciation of Japanese and Korean political-military realities, and began an intimate interaction with the region through forward military deployment. Yet on-the-ground engagement with the region's rising economies was much slower to come. U.S. investment played a much smaller role in Northeast Asian development than was true in Europe, Latin America, or even Southeast Asia, right down to the Asian financial crisis of 1997.

American financial involvement with China—especially through investment banking—has probably been the most important recent U.S. economic incentive for sustained involvement with Northeast Asia.[23] And even that has emerged only since the 1993–96 period, when the privatization of Chinese public enterprise, and related initial public offerings, began to take place. Compared with Europe, U.S. business dealings and financial interdependence with Northeast Asia remain remarkably limited, like America's cultural understanding of Asia as a whole. The United States should clearly be involved more proactively with Northeast Asia—both for strategic reasons and to benefit economically from its prosperity. Yet American domestic incentives for this dialogue to take place are sadly all too weak, and must be enhanced.

U.S. interest in Northeast Asian stability and security has clearly revived since 2005, and especially since October 2006, when North Korea detonated its first nuclear device. This renewed attention is most welcome. Ultimately, constructive U.S. involvement in the Making of Northeast Asia through both bilateral and minilateral engagement, is profoundly in the interest of both the United States and Northeast Asia, given America's embedded involvement as a "resident power," and the transcendent interest of both sides in political-economic stability for its own sake, from an increasingly important global perspective.

The prevailing rationale for American involvement in Northeast Asia is a worthy one, but hardly the sort of enduring foundation on which to build the structure of sustained engagement that in the final analysis is so profoundly necessary. Washington's current rationale, of course, is nuclear nonproliferation: North Korea has tested several nuclear devices, has tested sophisticated missile systems, and could potentially supply nuclear materials to terrorists. In order to roll back the North Korean military nuclear program, the United States needs to play a leading and constructive role in regional political-military talks, while carefully weighing other options as well. How substantial U.S. involvement in continental Northeast Asia would actually be in the absence of this global political-military imperative is open to question, although the importance of sustained U.S. involvement in Northeast Asian affairs—both to ensure North Korean abandonment of its nuclear program and to ensure broader long-term regional stability—is clear.

Stronger and more institutionalized U.S. capabilities to systematically understand and respond to a changing Northeast Asia are an urgent necessity. Fortunately, the United States has some of the world's best and most cosmopolitan universities, which can serve as an efficient base. They need better funding for Northeast Asian studies, including less dramatic and visible—yet still fundamental—disciplines such as anthropology, and less-often studied areas such as Taiwan and Japan.

University support, of course, is not enough. Think tanks and other policy research bodies need to direct more systematic attention to Northeast Asia. The Brookings Institution's Center for Northeast Asian Studies, which brings well-connected fellows from each of the nations of Northeast Asia to Washington, DC, and cultivates an ongoing network in the region, is a good model to emulate. Government analysis also needs to be expanded and strengthened, especially in its socioeconomic dimensions.

Specific prescriptions for future U.S. policy in Northeast Asia are difficult, given the vexing uncertainties surrounding the region's future course. Two imperatives, however, are clear. The United States must maintain its basic security alliances in the region—with Japan and South Korea—while reinforcing their political credibility through broad, win-win interdependence on the economic and cultural front.[24] Secondly, the United States also needs to participate actively in multilateralist efforts, such as the Six-Party Talks, to stabilize the region and to deal with lingering collective-security threats.

The Korean peninsula presents some of the most serious challenges, demanding the most active cooperative attention. Major problems looming on the Korean peninsula, beyond the urgent matter of North Korean nuclear weapons, include:

1. Reconstruction finance on a massive scale—many estimates of the cost of North Korean reconstruction are upward of $600 billion.[25]

2. Refugee problems, in the event of a sudden collapse of North Korea, or other sudden political transition in the region.

3. Planning for regional energy development, including transnational gas pipelines.

4. Environmental issues, including acid rain, deforestation, and disposal of poisonous and radioactive wastes.

5. Strategic dialogue, including mutual, balanced force reductions. Reduction of tensions on the Korean peninsula, where there are currently nearly 3 million men under arms, in the wake of a resolution to the North Korean nuclear problem, would make such talks imperative.

All of the foregoing problems share with the ongoing nuclear talks a common trait: they are most smoothly addressed in a *multilateral* context.[26] The rising salience of nationalism in the domestic politics of major nations across the region enhances the regional utility of multilateralism still further. The era of mutual deterrence, so salient during the Cold War, and for which bilateral security structures were so well suited, has not fully disappeared. Yet it could well be entering its twilight years. A serious resolution to the North Korean nuclear problem could accelerate that process of transition to a more peaceful order, although important uncertainties in Sino-Japanese relations remain.

There is also a constructive role in Northeast Asian architecture for minilateralism, which is organizationally simple, and a good vehicle for efficiently focusing policy efforts. Two especially recommendable variants, from an American standpoint, come to mind. One is the U.S.-Japan-ROK trilateral, which proved to be a constructive vehicle in the Clinton and Obama years in focusing opposition to North Korean nuclear tests. Such a minilateral could focus on hard security matters, as the three are all treaty allies, and also on improved cultural communication. A second priority needs to be the U.S.-Japan-China trilateral, which has particular value on soft-security matters such as energy and environmental protection. In support of such a mechanism, there should also be detailed working-level U.S.-Japan cooperation in support of Chinese developmental initiatives, and efforts to build conformity with international regimes in areas such as intellectual property.

Bilateral dialogues and understandings between the United States and each of the three individual nations of Northeast Asia are useful, especially since such interaction tends to be effective in deepening the top-level personal networks that are so important in dealing with Asian societies. The U.S.-China Strategic Economic Dialogue (SED) is the most developed, and should be continued. The United States must not, however, slight its allies, and more vigorous bilateral dialogue with both Japan and South Korea is in order. In support of such dialogue, long-range analytical capabilities should be fostered, through bilateral "Wisemen's Groups" such as the Carter administration employed in U.S.-Japan relations. Alliance ties also need broadening in both cases, to include cooperation with respect to trade, energy, and finance. The Korea-U.S. (KORUS) free-trade agreement with Korea, and a parallel economic cooperation agreement with Japan, are also urgent priorities.

The United States likewise needs more intensive representation on the ground in Northeast Asia, especially in the nonmilitary sphere, to deepen what has historically been a profoundly limited presence, which contributes importantly to American naivety concerning the region. More consulates, more American Centers, and more university-exchange programs are in order. Language study, on both sides of the Pacific, also needs to be a priority; national defense foreign language program (NDFL) funding should be available for all three Northeast Asian national languages, rather than just Chinese and Korean.

Northeast Asians need to realize the domestic political importance in the United States of *tangible incentives* encouraging Americans to support, and be actively involved in sustaining, multilateralism in the North Pacific region, beyond the current nuclear crisis. Multilateralism could prospectively be a useful means of providing "soft security" in such areas as energy and environmental protection—one argument that could potentially have some political-economic resonance in the United States. Ideally, a multilateral approach to such questions would include some support for the activities of U.S. business operating in the region. As noted earlier in this chapter, Americans historically have not had a major commercial presence in continental Northeast Asia, and hence little embedded economic stake in being active there. That lack of embedded economic interest has skewed U.S. policy to a heavy military emphasis, and has perversely reduced American commitment to a healthy, multilateral North Pacific regionalism involving the United States, that could otherwise productively evolve.

The contrasting analogy to European integration two generations ago, when an America whose multinationals stood to gain strongly backed the process, suggests the logic of this Asian support for a vigorous local U.S. economic role. European governments provided significant incentives, both direct and indirect, to foreign investment when the European Economic Community (EEC) was founded in 1957. American multinationals responded to this innovation eagerly, with vigorous investment in the new community. This capital provided both economic stimulus and also political-economic support for the new entity, enormously increasing Europe's credibility on Capitol Hill. Systematic local policies of support for multinational firms in China, Korea, and Japan could have a similarly positive impact in American politics that would help keep the United States engaged, in a positive way, in the Making of Northeast Asia. Conversely, Northeast Asian policies discriminating against multinationals could well complicate active American commitments to a region where U.S. economic interests have been historically weak.

One negative prescription that seems definitely in order is to refrain from exploiting Northeast Asia's traditionally deep intraregional tensions over history. World War II reputedly killed more than 30 million people across the region, and the Korean War 4 million more. For half a century from 1895, much of the region suffered under Japanese colonialism. Although the roles of Imperial Japan and North Korea as aggressors are broadly established, the magnitude of destruction, suffering, and culpability are still debated. For the United States to be directly and formally involved in judging these subjective issues would be both resented and counterproductive to its most constructive role as a guarantor of stability for the region as a whole. It is thus better for the United States to encourage Track II historical dialogues, or mediation by neutral middle powers such as Canada or Germany.

The imperative not to provoke historical tensions is especially important for Japan. Its early-twentieth-century motivations were complex and not easily understood. Whatever the normative case for self-justification might be, it is politically unsustainable outside Japan. The political dangers for Japan of pressing nationalistic interpretations of history are growing even in the United States, where the ethnic balance, among Asian minorities, is sharply and rapidly shifting, as we saw in Chapter 10. Today, Japanese Americans—traditionally the largest Asian minority in the United States—are outnumbered by Chinese Americans by nearly ten to four, an environment that should give Japanese nationalists pause on prudential grounds at least.

Northeast Asia, we have found, is a fascinating laboratory for testing propositions about how international affairs are changing, and what underlying forces drive those interactions. It is especially fascinating because it is so swathed in paradox. As we noted at the very beginning of this book, Northeast Asia ranks among the most dangerous areas on earth, plagued by security problems of global importance, including nuclear and missile proliferation. Despite its insecurity, however, the region has continued to be the most rapidly growing on earth, for more than five decades.

American power was, for many years, a central reason why Northeast Asia could appear so threatened, and yet rest so secure. Yet this dynamic region cannot live forever beneath the eagle's wings. Indeed, the very force of its explosive yet sustained economic growth—first for two double-digit decades in Japan, and now for even longer in China—is quietly but surely creating a world where U.S. dominion in the classic sense is no longer possible. And that must inevitably lead, in the truest sense, to the Making—it is hoped, on a more tolerant, inclusive basis than in past years—of Northeast Asia, coupled with a deepened and more balanced American involvement as well.

REFERENCE MATTER

Notes

Flashback

1. For factual corroboration, see http://homepage2.nifty.com/dk_tabi/annai.html. accessed July 24, 2009; as well as Yashiro Shunichiro (ed.), *Nihon Tetsudo Ryoko Chizu Cho: Manchu/Karafuto* [A Compendium of Japanese Railway Travel Maps: Manchuria and Sakhalin], Tokyo: Shinchosha, November, 2009.

Chapter 1

1. See, for example, T. J. Pempel (ed.), *Remapping East Asia: The Construction of a Region*, Ithaca, NY: Cornell University Press, 2005; and Mark Beeson, *Regionalism & Globalization in East Asia*, New York: Palgrave Macmillan, 2007. Ellen Frost expands the discussion of regionalism still further, to include both Russia and India. See *Asia's New Regionalism*, Boulder: Lynne Rienner, 2008.

2. See Kent E. Calder, "China and Japan's Simmering Rivalry," *Foreign Affairs*, March/April 2006, pp. 129–39.

3. See also Mia Oba, "Regional Arrangements for Trade in Northeast Asia: Cooperation and Competition between China and Japan"; and Min Ye, "Security Institutions in Northeast Asia: Multilateral Responses to Structural Changes," in Vinod Aggarwal and Min Gyo Koo (eds.), *Asia's New Institutional Architecture: Evolving Structures for Managing Trade, Financial, and Security Relations*, New York: Springer, 2008, pp. 121–50.

4. David Lampton, *The Three Faces of Chinese Power: Might, Money, and Minds*, Berkeley: University of California, 2008; David Kang, *China Rising: Peace, Power, and Order in East Asia*, New York: Columbia University Press; and Barry Naughton, *Greater China: Economics and Electronics in the PRC, Taiwan, and Hong Kong*, Washington, DC: Brookings Institution Press, 1997.

5. These statistics have been compiled by the authors, based on the annual data provided by the International Monetary Fund, *Direction of Trade*: 1980–2009.

6. Ibid., various editions.

7. International Monetary Fund, *Direction of Trade*. In 2007 only 13 percent of South Korea's, and 20 percent of Japan's, exports went to the United States, compared with 40 and 39 percent, respectively, in 1987.

8. See "Why Taiwan Matters?" *Business Week*, May 16, 2005. It should be noted that there are substantial cross-Straits differences in the accounting of Taiwanese investment on the Mainland, especially for investments made before 2008. Taiwanese figures suggested a stock in 2007 of $150 billion in such investment, as indicated at: http://www.winklerpartners.com/a/comment/taiwanese-investment-in-china.php. The stock of Taiwan's investment in the Mainland was only $40.1 billion in 2007, according to Chinese sources, however. See "Taiwan's Investment Exceeded $46 billion in Twenty Year," *Xinhua News*, April 10, 2008, http://tga2.mofcom.gov.cn/aarticle/workaffair/200804/20080405470069.html. The statistical difference may be due to substantial Taiwanese investment flowing to the Mainland through overseas subsidiaries in Hong Kong, the Cayman Islands, and Mauritius.

9. Related to these rising stakes, Toyota chairman Okuda Hiroshi played an important informal role in helping to mediate serious tensions between China and the Japanese government of Prime Minister Koizumi Junichiro during 2005–6.

10. See "Shanghai Volkswagen, Beijing Hyundai Compete for Taxi Market [Shanghai dazhong, Beijing xiandai qiangduo chuzuche shichang]," *Beijing Youth Newspaper* [Beijing qingnian bao], August 25, 2004; see also "Beijing Hyundai's Past Glory [Beijing xiandai de guoqu huihuang]," http://auto.ce.cn/main/xwzx/qyzx/200711/16/t20071116_13621404.shtml.

11. See, for example, "Beijing Hyundai March in Liu City's Taxi Market [Beijing xiandai jinjun liushi chuzuche shichang]," http://www.pcauto.com.cn/news/changshang/0507/320431.html. See also "Beijing Hyundai Surge in Hangzhou Taxi Market [Beijing xiandai zhanling Hangzhou chuzuche shichang]," http://news.chinacars.com/newsfiles/200507/117311.htm. Since 2007, however, Beijing Hyundai's performance in China has declined.

12. See http://www.pacificepoch.com/newsstories/31719_0_5_0_M/, accessed July 22, 2007.

13. See http://english.etnews.co.kr/news/detail.html?id=200707180007, accessed July 22, 2007.

14. See "As Chinese Businesses Blossom, They Buy Slumping Neighbor's Firms," *Washington Post*, February 6, 2003; and "Shanghai Electric Support Capital Infusion at Ikegai," *Nikkei Weekly*, August 9, 2004.

15. See "Sanyo-Haier Alliance Offers Lucrative Footholds," *Nikkei Weekly*, January 15, 2002.

16. See "Sanyo Eyes 30% Cost Cut with Fridge Tie-Up," *Nikkei Weekly*, November 6, 2006; and "Sanyo Sells Factory Stake to Haier," *Nation*, July 17, 2007.

17. "Sanyo Eyes 30% Cost Cut with Fridge Tie-Up."

18. See "Japan's Unfinished Business in China," *Asia Times*, April 23, 2005, http://www.atimes.com/atimes/Japan/GD23Dh03.html.

19. Kazuo Ogura, "Toward a New Concept of Asia," *International Politics*, Vol. 8, No. 4, Winter 2007, p. 42.

20. The book is entitled *The Contemporary and Modern History of Three East Asian*

Countries, and deals in a collaborative way with a range of contentious issues, including Japanese colonial occupations and World War II.

21. See "Visa Easing Lure Well-off Chinese," *Nikkei Weekly,* July 13, 2009; and *China's Statistical Yearbook* [*zhongguo tongji nianjian*], 2009 edition.

22. *South China Morning Post,* November 20, 2006.

23. See "The Prodigal Son Has Returned to Be Groomed for Supreme Leadership," *Times* (London), August 28, 2007.

24. Li Wen, *Dongya hezuo de wenhua chengyin* [*Cultural Roots of East Asian Cooperation*], Beijing: World Knowledge Press [shijie zhishi chubanshe], 2005, pp. 183–84.

25. Ishii Kenichiro, *Higashi Ajia ni okeru Nihon no Popu Bunka* [*Japanese Pop Culture in East Asia*], Tokyo: Sousou Sha, 2001, pp. 39, 77.

26. Chua Beng Huat and Koichi Iwabuchi, *East Asia Pop Culture: Analyzing the Korean Wave,* Hong Kong: Hong Kong University Press, 2008; and *Korea Herald* (ed.), *Korean Wave,* Seoul: Jimoondang, 2008.

27. See "Male Celebrities Just Latest Twist in Asia-Wide Craze," *Washington Post,* August 31, 2006.

28. *Chunichi Shimbun,* August 17, 2000.

29. *International Herald Tribune,* January 28, 2006.

30. *Newsweek,* May 9, 2005.

31. World Bank, *World Development Report,* 2000 edition.

32. See the World Trade Organization Regional Trade Agreements dataset, as of 2009, http://rtais.wto.org/UI/PublicSearchByCr aspx.

33. David Zweig and Bi Jianhai, "China's Global Hunt for Energy," *Foreign Affairs,* Vol. 84, No. 5, September/October 2005.

34. On Korea's pronounced energy vulnerabilities, see Calder, *Korea's Energy Insecurities: Comparative and Regional Perspectives,* Washington, DC: Korean Economic Institute, 2005; and Makoto Kanagawa and Toshihiko Nakata, "Analysis of the Impact of Electricity Grid Interconnection between Korea and Japan," *Energy Policy,* Vol. 34, 2006, pp. 1015–25.

35. Wu Kang, "Energy Demand and Supply in Northeast Asia," paper presented at the U.S.-China-Japan Trilateral Conference, Pacific Forum, Hawaii, August 15–17, 2005; and Calder, "Sino-Japanese Energy Relations: Prospects for Deepening Strategic Competition," paper presented at Conference on Japan's Contemporary Challenges, Yale University, March 9–10, 2007.

36. See Calder, *China's Energy Diplomacy and Its Geo-strategic Implications,* Washington, DC: Reischauer Center for East Asian Studies, 2005.

37. Wu Kang, "Energy Demand and Supply in Northeast Asia," p. 13.

38. Graciela Kaminsky and Carmen Reinhart, "The Twin Crises: The Causes of Banking and Balance-of-Payments Problems," *American Economic Review,* Vol. 89, June 1999, p. 3.

39. See IMF data on current foreign exchange reserves of reporting countries, as of December 2009.

40. Kwan Chi-hung, "The Economics of a Yen Bloc," Washington, DC: Brookings Institution and Nomura Research Institute, June 2000.

41. From August 2000 to August 2001, spanning the approval period, there were 1,000 articles regarding "Japan/textbooks" on Nexus-Lexus, compared with 699 for a comparable period in 2005, and only 34 in 2009.

42. See "More Cross-Strait Flights Added for Chinese New Year," *South China Morning Post,* January 2010.

43. Some 91,294 Mainlanders visited. See "Taiwan Sees Surge in Mainland Visitor Arrivals," *BBC Monitoring Asia Pacific,* March 11, 2009.

44. Ibid. The press conference in question was on March 10, 2009.

45. From March 13 to March 21, 2009, some 16,121 Mainland tourists visited Taiwan. See "Chinese Tourists Reach New Record," *China Post,* March 23, 2009.

46. "China's Taiwan Affairs Chief, Commerce Minister Review Cross-Straits Work in 09," *BBC World Monitoring Asia Pacific,* January 3, 2010.

47. Reported on Chinese Central Television. Also available at http://space.tv.cctv.com/video/VIDE1239972960810673.

48. Chen was also formally acting as chairman of the PRC Association for Relations across the Taiwan Strait (ARATS). The first ARATS chairman had been Wang Daohan, who conducted talks with Taiwan in Hong Kong and Singapore in the early 1990s. His counterpart at Taiwan's SEF was Koo Chen-fu. The 1992 Wang-Koo meeting in Hong Kong produced the first major breakthrough in the cross-Straits relationship—namely, the '92 Consensus.

49. Three "direct links" refer to postal services, sea, and air travel. Before July 2008, all these three links had to pass through a third party, such as Hong Kong, adding tremendous inconvenience and transaction costs to cross-Straits exchanges. See "Cheng Yunlin and Chiang Pin-kung Signed Four Agreements," www.xinhuanet.com, November 14, 2008.

50. See "Cheng and Chiang Met Again in Nanjing," www.sina.com.cn, April 28, 2009.

51. See "China Urges Mainland Investment in Taiwan," *Associated Press,* May 18, 2009.

52. See "North Korea's Nuclear Launch and Its Implications," *Korean Herald,* March 25, 2009.

53. "Rajin-Sonbong: A Strategic Choice for China in its Relations with Pyongyang," *China Brief,* April 1, 2010.

54. See www.xinhua.net, May 4, 2008; http://news.ifeng.com/world/200904/0411_16_1102291.shtml.

55. In addition to their previous swap agreements under the Chiang Mai framework, at this meeting the Japanese-Korean swap arrangement was increased to $20 billion and the Chinese-Korean swap to $28 billion. Furthermore, the currency swaps were based on the currencies of the countries in question, in contrast to previous U.S. dollar dominance under the Chiang Mai framework. See "China, Japan, and South Korea's Currency Swaps," *Investor Journal* [Touzizhe bao], December 28, 2009, http://www.investorchina.com.cn/ywpl/news/2008/12/29/125543.shtml; and "China, Japan, and South Korea Finance Ministers' Meeting in Washington," http://news.sina.com.cn/c/2008-11-15/235216661023.shtml.

56. See "China, Japan, and South Korea Joint Statement on Financial and Economic Cooperation [zhong ri han jinrong jingji hezuo lianhe shengmin]," *People's Daily* [*Renmin ribao*], December 13, 2009, http://politics.people.com.cn/GB/1024/8513643.html.

57. China, Japan, and South Korea Joint Press Conference of December 13, 2008, http://www.kantei.go.jp/foreign/asospeech/2008/12/12kaiken_e.html.

58. "East Asian Heads Eye Closer Trade Ties," *Daily Yomiuri,* October 12, 2009

59. Regionalism refers, in our terminology, to state-driven, top-down policy-making, while regionalization is defined as a society-driven, bottom-up process.

60. Gilbert Rozman, *Northeast Asia's Stunted Regionalism,* New York: Cambridge

University Press, 2004. Recent publications on broader East Asian regionalism do note the deepening regionalization trends in East Asia, yet they do not typically discuss the further prospects for Northeast Asian integration, or they are skeptical of future integration in this subregion. See Peter J. Katzenstein and Takashi Shiraishi (eds.), *Beyond Japan: The Dynamics of East Asian Regionalism*, Ithaca, NY: Cornell University Press, 2006; and Pempel (ed.), *Remapping East Asia*.

61. Rozman, *Northeast Asia's Stunted Regionalism*; Katzenstein and Shiraishi (eds.), *Network Power*, Ithaca, NY: Cornell University Press, 1997; and Aaron Friedberg, "Europe's Past: Asia's Future?" *Survival*, Vol. 142, No. 3, Autumn 2000, pp. 147–59.

62. Friedberg, "Ripe for Rivalry: Prospects for Peace in Multipolar Asia," *International Security*, Vol. 18, No. 3, 1993, pp. 5–33; and Friedberg, "Europe's Past: Asia's Future?" pp. 147–59.

63. Edward Lincoln, *East Asian Economic Regionalism*, Washington, DC: Brookings Institution Press, 2004.

64. Katzenstein, "Regionalism in Comparative Perspective," *Cooperation and Conflict,* Vol. 31, 1996; and Katzenstein and Shiraishi (eds.), *Network Power*.

65. Christopher W. Hughes, *Japan's Security Agenda,* Boulder, CO: Lynne Rienner Publishers, 2004, and *Japanese Re-emergence as a "Normal" Military Power*, London: Oxford University Press, November 2004.

66. Robert Gates address at the Shangri La Dialogue, Singapore, May 30, 2009. See Institute for International Security Studies, "The Shangri La Dialogue," *Defense News*, May 30, 2009, http://www.iiss.org/whats-new/iiss-in-the-press/may 2009/shangri-la-opens-with-concerns-over-north-korea/.

67. Calder, "Japanese Foreign Economic Policy Formation: Explaining the Reactive State," *World Politics*, Vol. 40, No. 4, July 1988, pp. 517–41.

68. See, for example, David Capie and Paul Evans, *The Asia-Pacific Security Lexicon*, Singapore: ISEAS Press, 2002, pp. 14–27; Amitav Acharya, "Ideas, Identity, and Institution-Building: From the ASEAN Way to the Asia-Pacific Way?" *Pacific Review*, Vol. 10, No. 3, 1997, pp. 319–30; and Alastair Iain Johnston, "The Myth of the ASEAN Way? Explaining the Evolution of the ASEAN Regional Forum," in Helga Haftendorn, Robert Keohane, and Celeste Wallander (eds.), *Imperfect Unions: Security Institutions over Time and Space,* New York: Oxford University Press, 1999, pp.287–338.

Chapter 2

1. Sixty years ago, of course, all of Northeast Asia was unhappily consolidated, as part of Japan's Greater East Asia Co-Prosperity Sphere. Following Japan's defeat, efforts to establish formal institutions, by contrast, have been largely a series of false starts and failures. After a half-century and more, the memory of brutal Japanese colonial rule still haunts Northeast Asia, from the leadership level down to the grassroots. Cooperation has been incessantly plagued by mutual mistrust and animosity among Japan, China, and South Korea.

2. For an overview, see Michael Schulz, Frederik Soderbaum, and Joakim Ojendal (eds.), *Regionalization in a Globalizing World: Perspectives on Form, Actors, and Processes,* London: Zed Books, 2001. See also Peter Haas, *Saving the Mediterranean,* New York: Columbia University Press, 1990; and Joseph Nye, *Pan-Africanism and East African Integration,* Cambridge: Harvard University Press, 1965.

3. Some of the best such comparative literature includes the so-called New Regionalism

works by European authors, works that are intent on moving away from the European Union model and that consider the multilevel dynamics of regionalism across a number of areas, including East Asia. These works include Shaun Breslin et al., *New Regionalisms in the Global Political Economy,* New York: Routledge, 2002; Kanishka Jayasuriya, *Governing Asia-Pacific: Beyond the New Regionalism,* Hampshire, RG: Palgrave Macmillan, 2004; Mary Farell et al., *Global Politics of Regionalism,* London: Pluto Press, 2005; Andrew Gamble and Anthony Payne, *Regionalism and World Order,* New York: St. Martin's Press, 1996; Glenn Hook and Ian Kearn, *Sub-Regionalism and World Order,* New York: Macmillan Press, 1999; Bertrand Fort and Douglass Webber (eds.), *Regional Integration in Europe and East Asia,* New York: Routledge, 2006; and Andrew Cooper et al., *Regionalization and Global Governance,* New York: Routledge, 2008.

4. Walter Mattli's 1999 book reviewed two main explanations for European integration: neofunctionalism, which stresses the spillover effect of supranational agencies; and intergovernmentalism, which focuses on bargaining among state leaders. See *The Logic of Regional Integration: Europe and Beyond,* Cambridge, UK: Cambridge University Press, 1999.

5. On the idea of institutionalized norms and culture, see Peter Katzenstein, *The Culture of National Security,* New York: Columbia University Press, 1996; and Stephen Krasner (ed.), *International Regimes,* Ithaca, NY: Cornell University Press, 1983.

6. Gilbert Rozman, "Flawed Regionalism: Reconceptualizing Northeast Asia in the 1990s," *Pacific Review,* Vol. 11, No. 1, 1998, pp. 1–27.

7. Aaron Friedberg, "Will Europe's Past Be Asia's Future?" *Survival,* Vol. 142, No. 3, Autumn 2000, pp. 147–39.

8. A similar power distribution was based on the power gap between the region and the United States. As Donald Crone has pointed out, while the United States was dominant in the Atlantic, power differentiation was never that great, and it was therefore never able to dictate. The relative power of the United States in the Pacific, however, was far greater. See Crone, "Does Hegemony Matter? The Regionalization of the Pacific Economy," *World Politics,* Vol. 45, No. 4, 1993, p. 503.

9. On the constitutional-hegemony concept, see John Ikenberry, *After Victory,* Princeton: Princeton University Press, 2001.

10. Mattli, *The Logic of Regional Integration,* p. 56.

11. On this point, which is to some degree empirically debatable, see Christopher Hemmer and Katzenstein, "Why Is There No NATO in Asia?" *International Organization,* Vol. 53, No. 3, Summer 2002: 575–607.

12. Rozman, "Flawed Regionalism," pp. 1–27.

13. At the end of 2006, the Russian Federation held proved natural gas reserves of 47.65 trillion cubic meters, or 26.3 percent of the global total. See *British Petroleum Statistical Review of World Energy,* 2007 edition. See www.bp.com.

14. See Raymond Vernon, *Sovereignty at Bay,* New York: Basic Books, 1971.

15. Bruce Cumings, "The Origins and Development of the Northeast Asian Political Economy: Industrial Sectors, Product Cycles, and Political Consequences," *International Organization,* Vol. 38, No. 1, 1984, pp. 1–40.

16. Mitchell Bernard and John Ravenhill, "Beyond Product Cycles and Flying Geese: Regionalization, Hierarchy, and the Industrialization of East Asia," *World Politics,* Vol. 47, No. 2, 1995, p. 171.

17. See, for example, Michael Borrus, Dieter Ernst, and Stephan Haggard (eds.), *International Production Networks in Asia: Rivalry or Riches*, London: Routledge, 2000.

18. Leonard Binder et al., *Crises and Sequences in Political Development*, Princeton: Princeton University Press, 1971, p. 308.

19. Katzenstein and Takashi Shiraishi (eds.), *Network Power*, Ithaca, NY: Cornell University Press, 1997.

20. Ibid., p. 21.

21. Ibid.

22. Katzenstein and Shiraishi, *Beyond Japan: The Dynamics of East Asian Regionalism*, Ithaca, NY: Cornell University Press, 2006.

23. Ibid., pp. 1–33.

24. Ibid.

25. T. J. Pempel (ed.), *Remapping East Asia: The Construction of a Region*, Ithaca, NY: Cornell University Press, 2005, p. 2.

26. Schulz, Soderbaum, and Ojendal (eds.), *Regionalization in a Globalizing World*.

27. Mattli, *The Logic of Regional Integration*, pp. 11–12.

28. The Zollvereign, or German Customs Union, was a coalition of German states formed to manage customs and economic policies within their territories. Established in 1818, it operated until rendered redundant by German unification in 1871.

29. Mattli, *The Logic of Regional Integration*, pp. 68–127.

30. Andrew Moravcsik, *The Choice for Europe*, Ithaca, NY: Cornell University Press, 1998.

31. Stefan Schirm, *Globalization and the New Regionalism*, Cambridge: Polity, 2002.

32. Schulz, Soderbaum, and Ojendal (eds.), *Regionalization in a Globalizing World*.

33. Mattli, *The Logic of Regional Integration*, p. 77.

34. Ibid., pp. 77–78.

35. Ibid., pp. 140–78.

36. Schirm, *Globalization and the New Regionalism*, p. 103.

37. Andrew Hurrell, "An Emerging Security Community in South America?" in Emanuel Adler and Michael Barnett (eds.), *Security Communities*, Cambridge: Cambridge University Press, 1998, p. 249.

38. Schirm, *Globalization and the New Regionalism*, pp. 104–5.

39 Ibid., p. 237.

40. Ibid., p. 172.

41. Mattli, *The Logic of Regional Integration*, pp. 11–12.

42. Ibid., pp. 13–14.

43. See, for example, ibid., p. 14.

44. This tendency may well be intensified by the 2006 accession of Venezuela, led by Hugo Chavez, as geoeconomic and ideological motives within MERCOSUR for autonomy from the United States assume greater prominence.

45. Mattli, *The Logic of Regional Integration*, pp. 11–12.

46. Theda Skocpol and Paul Pierson, "Historical Institutionalism in Contemporary Political Science," in Ira Katznelson and Helen Milner (eds.), *Political Science: State of the Discipline*, NY: W. W. Norton & Company, 2002, p. 720.

47. Binder et al., *Crises and Sequences in Political Development;* Krasner, "Approaches to

the State: Alternative Conceptions and Historical Dynamics," *Comparative Politics*, Vol. 16, No. 2, January 1984, pp. 223–46; Nelson Polsby, *Political Innovation in America: The Politics of Policy Innovation*, New Haven: Yale University Press, 1984; Peter Gourevitch, *Politics in Hard Times*, Ithaca, NY: Cornell University Press, 1986; Stephen Skowronek, *Building a New American State: The Expansion of National Administrative Capacities*, Cambridge, UK: Cambridge University Press, 1982; and Kent E. Calder, *Crisis and Compensation*, Princeton: Princeton University Press, 1988.

48. Binder et al., *Crises and Sequences*, p. 308.

49. Krasner, "Approaches to the State," pp. 223–46.

50. Skowronek, *Building a New American State*, p. 10.

51. See Seymour Lipset and Stein Rokkan, "Cleavage Structure, Party Systems, and Voter Alignments: An Introduction," in Seymour Lipset and Stein Rokkan (eds.), *Party System and Voter Alignments: Cross National Perspectives*, New York: Free Press, 1968, pp. 1–63.

52. Gourevitch, *Politics in Hard Times*, p. 35.

53. Calder, *Crisis and Compensation*, p. 28.

54. Graham Allison and Philip Zelikow, *Essence of Decision,* 2nd ed., New York: Longman, 1999.

55. A recent volume, Andrew MacIntyre, T. J. Pempel, and John Ravenhill (eds.), *Crisis as Catalyst: Asia's Dynamic Political Economy,* Ithaca, NY: Cornell University Press, 2008, is an exception. The book demonstrates that the AFC led to major changes in regional and national policies in a variety of issue areas, even long after the immediate impacts of crisis were over.

56. Vinod K. Aggarwal and Charles Morrison, *Asian Pacific Crossroads,* New York: St. Martin's Press, 1998, p. 26.

57. Ibid., p. 36.

58. Allison and Zelikow, *Essence of Decision*.

59. Ibid., p. 162.

60. For the concept of SOPs and its impact on decision-making, see ibid.

61. See ibid., p. 127.

62. Allison and Zelikow, *Essence of Decision*.

63. Ibid., p. 310.

64. See "Introduction to the Second Edition," in James March and Herbert Simon, *Organizations*, 2nd ed., Cambridge: Blackwell Publishers, 1993, p. 8.

65. Jack Levy, "Organizational Routines and the Causes of War," *International Studies Quarterly*, Vol. 30, 1986, p. 219.

66. Allison and Zelikow, *Essence of Decision*, p. 295.

67. Yoichi Nemoto, *An Unexpected Outcome of the Asian Financial Crisis*, Princeton: Princeton University Program on U.S.-Japan Relations Occasional Paper, June 2003.

68. Mattli, *The Logic of Regional Integration*, pp. 11–12.

69. Mancur Olson, *The Logic of Collective Actions*, New York: Schocken Books, 1965.

70. Katzenstein and Shiraishi (eds.), *Network Power*.

71. On how this makes crisis decision-making salient in Japanese domestic policy change, see Calder, *Crisis and Compensation*, p. 40.

72. Allison and Zelikow, *Essence of Decision*.

73. In China the relevance would be at the microlevel, for major banks and certain

heavy-industrial enterprises. On the forces at work in such "debt-driven industrialization," clearly salient in South Korea, and in parts of China and Japan, see Jeffrey Frieden, *Debt, Development, and Democracy,* Princeton, NJ: Princeton University Press, 1992.

74. Japanese government gross financial liabilities in 2009 were 170.3 percent of nominal GDP, compared with 69.8 percent in the United States and 52.3 percent in Britain. This relatively heavy Japanese public debt is often cited as a reason why Japan has not established a sovereign wealth fund (SWF). On Japan's relatively heavy public-debt burden, see Keizai Koho Center, *Japan: An International Comparison,* Tokyo: Keizai Koho Center, 2009, p. 68.

75. Japan and China were not directly ravaged by the AFC. Yet as later chapters explain, the crisis was perceived in 1997–98 as severe in China, and to a lesser extent in Japan. South Korea, of course, was devastated by the crisis. Hong Kong, which had just reverted to China in July 1997, was also heavily affected, shaping Beijing's perception of and response to the crisis in general.

Chapter 3

1. Milton Walton Meyer, *A Diplomatic History of the Philippine Republic,* Honolulu: University of Hawaii Press, 1965, pp. 142–43.

2. Meyer, *A Diplomatic History.*

3. On this concept and its relationship to broader international relations theory, see Kent E. Calder, "The San Francisco System in Comparative Perspective," *Pacific Review,* Vol. 17, No. 1, January 2004, pp. 135–57.

4. Akira Iriye, *The Cold War in Asia: A Historical Introduction,* Englewood Cliffs, NJ: Prentice-Hall, 1974, pp. 93–97.

5. See John W. Dower, *Embracing Defeat,* New York: W. W. Norton & Co., 1999; and Dower, *War without Mercy: Race and Power in the Pacific War,* New York: Pantheon Books, 1986.

6. Iriye, *The Cold War in Asia,* pp. 142–44.

7. Ibid., p. 172.

8. The transliteration of Chinese words and names is presented according to the pinyin system, with the exception of Mao Tse-tung, Chiang Kai-shek, and other such names that have had conventional transliterations in English writing.

9. See Chen Jian, *Mao's China and the Cold War,* Chapel Hill: University of North Carolina Press, 2001, pp. 46–48.

10. It is noteworthy that this treaty negotiation process involved a three-week deadlock, during which Stalin balked at signing an alliance treaty at all. Differences were finally resolved by Zhou Enlai, and the treaty was fittingly signed on Valentine's Day, February 14, 1950. See ibid., p. 52.

11. The United States recognized potential Sino-Soviet frictions as early as 1953, yet because of the two countries' deep animosity, accumulated during the Korean War, U.S. policy-makers failed to adopt conciliatory policies toward Communist China, being afraid that such gestures would be perceived as U.S. strategic weakness in both domestic and international settings. See Zhang Shuguang, *American Economic Embargo against China and the Soviet-China Alliance,* Stanford: Stanford University Press, 2002.

12. See Sergei N. Goncharov, John W. Lewis, and Xue Litai, *Uncertain Partners: Stalin, Mao, and the Korean War,* Stanford: Stanford University Press, 1993, ch. 5.

13. Meyer, *A Diplomatic History*, p. 143.

14. Robert T. Oliver, *Syngman Rhee and American Involvement in Korea, 1942–1960*, Seoul: Panmun Book Co., Ltd., 1978, p. 255.

15. Meyer, *A Diplomatic History*, p. 147.

16. Oliver, *Syngman Rhee and American Involvement in Korea,* p. 233.

17. Meyer, *A Diplomatic History,* p. 151.

18. The participants, apart from the Philippines, were Australia, Pakistan, India, Ceylon, Thailand, and Indonesia. South Korea and Taiwan were also, as indicated earlier, highly supportive of regional cooperation, including that in the security sphere. See ibid., p. 153.

19. Steven Hugh Lee, *The Korean War*, London: Longman, 2001, p. 45.

20. U.S. Department of State, *Foreign Relations of the United States, East Asia and the Pacific*, Vol. VII, Part I, 1951.

21. U.S. Department of State, *FRUS: East Asia and the Pacific*, 1951, p. 137.

22. David Langsam, "An Empire Coming Apart at the SEAMs: Confidential Papers Just Released from the Archives of Australia and Britain Throw Light on the Events of 30 Years Ago," *Sydney Morning Herald*, January 1, 1987.

23. On this trauma, see David Halberstam, *The Coldest Winter: America and the Korean War*, New York: Hyperion Books, 2007, pp. 395–502. The book as a whole eloquently presents the Korean War in its broader political, social, and human-relations contexts.

24. Glenn Paige, *The Korean Decision*, New York: Free Press, 1968, p. 45.

25. David McCullough, *Truman*, New York: Simon & Schuster, 1992, p. 814.

26. James McGovern, *To the Yalu: From the Chinese Invasion of Korea to MacArthur's Dismissal*, New York: William Morrow, 1972, p. 141.

27. Lee, *The Korean War*, p. 52.

28. Halberstam, *The Coldest Winter*, pp. 404–502.

29. U.S. Department of State, *FRUS*.

30. Ibid.

31. Lee, *The Korean War*, p. 53.

32. Halberstam, *The Coldest Winter*, pp. 404–536.

33. Lee, *The Korean War*, p. 102.

34. Lee, *The Korean War*.

35. Dean Acheson, *Present at the Creation: My Years at the State Department*, London: Hamish Hamilton, 1969, p. 426.

36. Ibid., pp. 428–29.

37. David Washington, "War Plan that Spawned ANZUS," *Advertiser*, July 17, 1990.

38. Langsam, "An Empire Coming Apart at the SEAMs."

39. Ibid.

40. Walter Mattli, among others, stresses the presence of strong nation-state leaders in driving regionalism, but the Korean War case shows that even the behavior of hegemonic leaders is profoundly shaped by process during CJs. See *The Logic of Regional Integration: Europe and Beyond,* Cambridge: Cambridge University Press, 1999, pp. 14–15.

41. See Robert Jervis, "The Impact of the Korean War on the Cold War," *Journal of Conflict Resolution*, Vol. 24, No. 4, December 1980, pp. 563–92.

42. Lee, *The Korean War*, p. 43.

43. See Thomas Christensen, *Useful Adversary: Grand Strategy, Domestic Mobilization, and Sino-American Conflict, 1947–1958*, Princeton: Princeton University Press, 1996, pp. 138–93.

44. For the idea of indeterminate prediction of regional institutions, see Steve Weber, "Shaping the Postwar Balance of Power," *International Organization*, Vol. 46, No. 3, Summer 1992, pp. 633–80.

45. U.S. Department of State, *FRUS*, 1951, pp. 143–44.

46. See George Jan, "Japan's Trade with Communist China," *Asian Survey*, Vol. 9, No. 12, 1969, pp. 900–918.

47. Ibid., p. 905.

48. Zhang, *American Embargo against China*, p. 152.

49. Ibid., pp. 82–83.

50. Christensen, *Useful Adversaries*, pp. 194–201.

51. See John W. Garver, *The Sino-American Alliance: Nationalist China and America's Cold War Strategy in Asia,* Armonk, NY: M. E. Sharpe, 1997.

52. Ibid.

53. Christopher Hemmer and Peter J. Katzenstein, "Why Is There No NATO in Asia? Collective Identity, Regionalism, and the Origin of Multilateralism," *International Organization*, Vol. 56, No. 3, Summer 2002, pp. 575–607.

54. See World Bank, *Key Development Data & Statistics*, www.worldbank.org.

55. In 2007, Northeast Asia's global GDP share was 15.7 percent, compared with the EU's 22.5 percent. See ibid.

56. Mark Valencia, "Engaging North Korea in Regional Cooperation," *Business Times* (Singapore), December 25, 1993.

57. Ibid.

58. See "Time to Reconsider the Case for a Northeast Asia ADB," *Korea Herald*, May 5, 2007.

59. Masato Ishizawa, "Development Bank Urged for Northeast Asian Region," *Nikkei Weekly*, August 3, 1998.

60. Ibid.

61. See "Northeast Asia Development Bank Will Advance S–N Economic Cooperation," *Korea Times*, October 14, 2000.

62. See "Kim Positive on NE Asian Bank," *Korea Herald*, September 24, 2001.

63. See "Development Bank Urged for Northeast Asian Region," *Nikkei Weekly*, August 3, 1998.

64. See "Time to Reconsider the Case for a Northeast ADB," *Korea Herald*, May 5, 2007.

Chapter 4

1. As Walter Mattli observes, "most integration projects in the Americas and in Asia were triggered by external events that threatened prosperity." See *The Logic of Regional Integration: Europe and Beyond*, Cambridge: Cambridge University Press, 1999, p. 16.

2. See Kevin Cai, "Is a Free Trade Zone Emerging in Northeast Asia in the Wake of the Asian Financial Crisis?" *Pacific Affairs*, Vol. 74, No. 1, Spring 2001, p. 11.

3. Japan did, however, play a key role in the organization and sustenance of the ADB, traditionally providing its president and much of its capitalization.

4. Peter J. Katzenstein and Takashi Shiraishi (eds.), *Network Power*, Ithaca, NY: Cornell University Press, 1997.

5. Stephan Haggard, "Thinking about Regionalism: The Politics of Minilateralism in

Asia and the Americas," paper presented at the annual meeting of the APSA, New York, September 1–4, 1994.

6. Donald Crone, "Does Hegemony Matter? The Reorganization of the Pacific Political Economy," *World Politics*, Vol. 45, No. 4, 1993, pp. 501–25.

7. The so-called Pacific Business Forum, formed in 1994 to represent regional business interests, meets routinely, for example, before APEC summit meetings to prepare road maps designed to guide APEC toward free trade. Since 1995 business interests have also been represented in the APEC Business Advisory Council (ABAC). They have pushed for such measures as common product standards, harmonized customs procedures, common rules on the protection of intellectual property, and an APEC business visa. See Mattli, *The Logic of Regional Integration*, pp. 171–72.

8. In 1994, for example, the APEC leaders' summit at Bogor, Indonesia, set an ambitious target of zero tariffs throughout the Pacific by 2020, with economically advanced APEC members admonished to meet this target by 2010. By 1996, however, the momentum embodied in the Bogor Declaration had disappeared.

9. See "The Prospect of an East Asia Free Trade Area Agreement," www.mier.org.my/drhafalsh30_11_2002.pdf.

10. The ASEAN Plus Three framework developed in the wake of the financial crisis of 1997 shares some of the regionalist vision expressed in the EAEG, yet its realization, in contrast to the failure of EAEG, tests the proposition that a crisis-driven critical juncture is important for institution-building in Asia.

11. Roughly a year before the onset of the Asian financial crisis, following the U.S. Mexican bailout, the AMF idea had been promoted informally on various occasions by Japanese economists and former policy-makers, such as Toyoo Gyohten of IIMA. On the details, see Philip Y. Lipscy, "Japan's Monetary Fund Proposal," *Stanford Journal of East Asian Affairs*, Vol. 3, No. 1, Spring 2003, pp. 93–104.

12. Ibid., pp. 95–96.

13. Ibid.

14. Eric Altbach, "The Asian Monetary Fund Proposal: A Case Study of Japanese Regional Leadership," *Japanese Economic Institute Report*, Vol. 47a, No. 19, December 1997, p. 10.

15. On this earlier deepening Southeast Asian cohesion resulting from Vietnam, see Michael Leifer, *Singapore's Foreign Policy: Coping with Vulnerability*, London: Routledge, 2000.

16. This important minilateral body involved the United States, Japan, and the ROK, as well as North Korea. On the birth and early evolution of KEDO, the Korean Peninsula Energy Development Organization, see Joel Wit, Daniel Poneman, and Robert Gallucci, *Going Critical: The First North Korean Nuclear Crisis*, Washington, DC: Brookings Institution, 2004, pp. 265–396.

17. TCOG refers to Trilateral Coordination and Oversight Group.

18. James Schoff, Charles Perry, and Jacquelyn Davis, *Nuclear Matters in North Korea: Building a Multilateral Response for Future Stability in Northeast Asia*, Washington, DC: Potomac Books, 2008.

19. Robert Garran, *Tigers Tamed: The End of the Asian Miracle*, St. Leonard's, Australia: Allen and Unwin, 1998, p. 176.

20. Mattli, *The Logic of Regional Organization*, pp. 11–12.

21. Indonesia and South Korea also contributed $500 million each, while the IMF added $4 billion, and multilateral banks $2.7 billion. See Kawai Masahiro, "Exchange Rate Arrangements in East Asia: Lessons from the 1997–98 Currency Crisis," *Monetary and Economic Studies*, December 2002, pp. 167–214.

22. A major reason for this political unwillingness may have been underestimation of how serious the crisis might be. President Bill Clinton, when asked about aid for Thailand amid the crisis, is said to have dismissed the collapse of the baht as "a few glitches in the road" to economic prosperity. See Joseph E. Stiglitz, *Globalization and Its Discontents*, New York: W. W. Norton, 2002, p. 93.

23. In 1999, Asia took 37.3 percent of Japan's exports, compared with 30.7 percent going to the United States. See Asahi Shimbun Sha, *Japan Almanac*, 2003 edition, Tokyo: Asahi Shimbun Sha, 2002, p. 90.

24. Yoichi Nemoto, *An Unexpected Outcome of the Asian Financial Crisis*, Princeton: Princeton University Program on U.S.-Japan Relations Occasional Paper, June 2003, p. 14.

25. Guan Jian, "Dongnanya jinrong weiji tantao guandian zongshu" ["Analyzing the Southeast Asian Financial Crisis"], *Dongnanya yanjiu* [*Southeast Asian Studies*], Vol. 6, 1998, pp. 22–24.

26. The New York Dow Jones average fell by 7.2 percent—the largest ever in terms of absolute points, but only 7.2 percent, as opposed to a 22.6 percent fall on October 19, 1987, in response to the U.S.-German financial dispute.

27. James Laurenceson, "External Financial Liberalization and Foreign Debt in China," Discussion paper No. 304, School of Economics, University of Queensland, Australia, 2002.

28. Huang Dehong and Jiu Tianjin, "Yazhou jinrong weiji toushi ji xiangyin duice" ["The Asian Financial Crisis and China's Response"], *Dongnanya yanjiu* [*Southeast Asian Studies*], Vol. 2, 1998, pp. 4–5.

29. World Bank chief economist Joseph Stiglitz, for example, visited Beidaihe in the summer of 1998 and stressed his support of Chinese policies in discussions with Chinese leaders while there. See his *Globalization and Its Discontents*, pp. 125–26.

30. See Nemoto, *An Unexpected Outcome of the Asian Financial Crisis*, p. 14.

31. Cao Yunhua, "Jinrong weiji yu dongnanya diqu guoji guanxi de xinbianhua" ["The Financial Crisis and the Change of International Relations in Southeast Asia"], *Dongnanya yianjiu* [*Southeast Asian Studies*], Vol. 2, 2001, pp. 4–10.

32. Edward Graham, *Reforming Korea's Industrial Conglomerates*, Washington, DC: Institute of International Economics, 2003, p. 111.

33. The PRC's reserves rose 104.7 percent between 1997 and 2002, according to *People's Daily*, March 10, 2003.

34. Ibid.

35. See "China Foreign Exchange Reserves Surpass $1 Trillion," ibid., January 16, 2007.

36. Hong Kong Special Administrative Region (SAR) and IMF estimates.

37. Assif Shameen and Claire MacDonald, "Boosting the Market," *Asiaweek*, May 28, 1999, accessed from www.asiaweek.com, September 4, 2003.

38. Mohamad Mahathir, 1999, "Asian Financial Crisis Not Over," accessed from www. southcentre.org/info/southbulletin/bulletin20/bulletin20.htm, July 22, 2003.

39. On the Chiang Mai agreement, see William Grimes, *Currency and Contest in East Asia*, Ithaca, NY: Cornell University Press, 2008.

40. The ASEAN Plus Three (APT) members did agree, however, that 10 percent of the swaps could be implemented without an agreement with the IMF. See Randall Henning, *East Asian Financial Cooperation*, Washington, DC: Institute for International Economics, 2002, pp. 17–18.

41. See "Uneasy Collaborators," *Business Week*, August 14, 2000.

42. See "Why Taiwan Matters," *Business Week*, May 16, 2005.

43. See "Chinese, Japanese Scholars on Hu Jintao's Visit to Japan," *BBC Monitoring Asia Pacific*, May 17, 2008.

44. See www.people.net.cn.

45. The first was held on Jeju Island, Korea, during June 2007; the second in June 2008 in Tokyo; and the third in September 2008 in Beijing. See the Ministry of Foreign Affairs of PRC website, http://www.fmprc.gov.cn/eng/wjb/wjbz/2467/.

46. See *Mainichi Shimbun,* August 30, 1998.

47. See "Hu Calls for Resuming Six Party Talks," *China Daily*, March 20, 2009; "Outrage over North Korean Nuclear and Missile Tests," *Straits Times*, May 26, 2009.

48. See "N.E. Asia Cooperation Key to $80B Fund," *Korea Herald*, October 7, 2008.

49. See "Recession Could Force a Further 50 Million Out of Work Worldwide," *Times* (London), January 29, 2009.

50. See "South Korea, Japan Agree to Closer Financial Crisis Cooperation," *BBC Monitoring Asia Pacific*, October 24, 2008.

51. See "Korea, China, Japan, to Set Up Financial Body," *Korea Herald*, October 23, 2008.

52. Ibid.

53. The forum consists of major national financial authorities such as finance ministries, central bankers, and international financial bodies. It was founded by the G-7 in 1999 to promote international financial stability.

54. Ibid.

55. See "Zhongrihan jinrong hezuo shengming" ["Joint Statement of China, Japan, and Korea Financial Cooperation"], http://politics.people.com.cn/GB/1024/8513643.html.

56. See "China, Japan, and Korea Reached Agreement on Contribution Ratio of Regional Reserve Pool," Xinhua Net, May 3, 2009, http://news.xinhuanet.com/english/2009-05/03/content_11302829.htm.

57. See "Zhongrihan huoban guanxi lianhe shengming" ["China, Japan, and Korea Joint Statement on Partnership"], http://politics.people.com.cn/GB/1026/8513641.html.

58. See "Pursue Shared Interests via Regular Dialogues," *Daily Yomiuri,* December 14, 2008.

59. See "Zhongrihan ziran zaihai lianhe shengming" ["China, Japan, and Korea Joint Statement on Natural Disaster Relief"], http://politics.people.com.cn/GB/1024/8513642.html.

60. One initial option considered by advisors was a bilateral accord between China and South Korea, which could be extended later to Japan as well. See "Fukuoka Summit Signals Maturity," *Business Times,* December 16, 2008.

61. Mancur Olson, *The Logic of Collective Action*, New York: Schocken Books, 1965.

62. The phrase is that of U.S. secretary of defense Robert Gates, at the 2009 Shangri La Dialogue, in Singapore.

63. The ASEAN Regional Forum (ARF) may be an exception to this. It draws together

twenty-three countries that have a bearing on the security of the Asia-Pacific region. The forum's main operating mechanism is dialogue. It has played a role in confidence-building among ASEAN members, yet its impact on preventive diplomacy or conflict resolution across Asia in general is thus far minimal. ARF has still less impact on Northeast Asian security matters.

Chapter 5

1. The early pan-Asianism—of Sun Yat-sen's day and before, which was centered heavily on relations within Northeast Asia—provides a "regional cognitive prior," in Acharya's parlance, for relations within the region that could well shape the trajectory of future regional institutions. See Amitav Acharya, *Whose Ideas Matter?: Agency and Power in Asian Regionalism*, Ithaca, NY: Cornell University Press, 2009, p. 145.

2. Edwin Reischauer and John K. Fairbanks, *East Asia: The Great Tradition: A History of East Asian Civilization*, Vol. I, Boston: Houghton Mifflin, 1960, p. 3.

3. On this Asian intraregional dialogue, and its analogue in the Islamic world, see Cemil Aydin, *The Politics of Anti-Westernism in Asia*, New York: Columbia University Press, 2007, pp. 71–92.

4. Stephen Hay, *Asian Ideas of East and West: Tagore and His Critics in Japan, China, and India*, Cambridge: Harvard University Press, 1970, p. 312.

5. On the broad historical evolution of pre–World War II Japanese pan-Asianism, see Yukie Yoshikawa, *Japan's Asianism, 1868–1945: Dilemmas of Modernization*, Washington, DC: Reischauer Center for East Asian Studies, 2010.

6. Sugita Teiichi, "Koa Saku" ["Methods for Reconstructing Asia"], in Zoga Hakuai (ed.), *Sugita Junzan o Den*, Tokyo: Junzan Kai, 1928, p. 552. Also discussed in Wen Li, *Dongya hezuo de wenhua chengyin* [*Cultural Roots of East Asian Cooperation*], Beijing: World Knowledge Press, 2005, pp. 119–30.

7. Tarui Tokichi, *Daito Gappo Ron* [*Recommendations to Incorporate Japan and Korea*], Tokyo. 1893. Also presented in Kageyama Masaharu, *Kageyama Masaharu Zenshu* [*The Complete Works of Kageyama Masaharu*], Tokyo: Kageyama Masaharu Zenshu Kankokai, 1992, pp. 12–13. Discussed in Li, *Dongya hezuo de wenhua chengyin* [*Cultural Roots of East Asian Cooperation*], pp. 119–30.

8. On the thought of Naito Konan, see Naito Torajiro (ed.), *Naito Konan Zenshu* [*The Collected Works of Naito Konan*], Vols. I–V, Tokyo: Chikuma Shobo, 1972. Also Naito Konan, "Konan Naito's East Asian History," in Chengyou Song and Chongnan Tang (eds.), *Asian Regional Identity and Peaceful Development*, Chengdu: Sichuan University Press, 2001.

9. Okakura Tenshin, "Ideas of Asia," in Chengyou Song and Chongnan Tang (eds.), *Asian Regional Identity and Peaceful Development*, Chengdu: Sichuan University Press, 2001.

10. Miwa Kimitada, "Japanese Policies and Concepts for a Regional Order in Asia, 1938–1940," in James White, Michio Umegaki, and Thomas Havens (eds.), *The Ambivalence of Nationalism: Modern Japan between East and West*, Lanham, MD: University Press of America, 1990, p. 140.

11. See, for example, Rōyama Masamichi, "Toa Kyodotai no Rironteki Kozo" ["The Theoretical Structure of East Asian Community"] (1939), in Rōyama (ed.), *Tōa to Sekai: Shin Chitsujo e no Ronsaku* [*East Asia and the World: Toward a Theoretical Understanding of the New Order*], Tokyo: Kaizōsha, 1941, p. 158. Also Miki Kiyoshi, *Miki Kiyoshi Zenshu* [*The Collected Works of Miki Kiyoshi*], 15 Vols., Tokyo: Iwanami, 1967; and Ozaki Hotsumi, *Ozaki*

Hotsumi Jihyoshu [*Ozaki Hotsumi's Selection of Contemporary Critics*], Tokyo: Heibonsha, 2004.

12. William Henry Chamberlin, *Japan over Asia,* Boston: Little Brown, 1937, p. 22.

13. Among the numerous anti–Japanese invasion scholars, the most vocal and best known was Liang Qichao. Prior to Japan's aggression against China, however, Liang studied and lived in Japan for an extended period and was a strong advocate for pan-Asianism when he returned to China.

14. Sun, *China and Japan: Natural Friends and Unnatural Enemies,* Tang Leangli (ed.), Shanghai: United Press, 1941, p. xiv.

15. Ibid., p. xiv.

16. Sun Yat-sen's historic speech in Kobe, Japan, on November 28, 1924.

17. Sun, *China and Japan,* p. 151.

18. Ibid., pp. 147–49, 158; and He Baogang, "East Asian Ideas of Regionalism: A Normative Critique," *Australian Journal of International Affairs,*Vol. 58, No. 1, 2004, pp. 105–25.

19. Li, *Dongya hezuo de wenhua chengyin* [*Cultural Roots of East Asian Integration*], Beijing: World Knowledge Press, 2005, p. 131.

20. The Triple Intervention was a diplomatic maneuver by Russia, Germany, and France on April 23, 1895, over the terms of the Treaty of Shimonoseki, previously signed between Japan and Qing dynasty China, which ended the First Sino-Japanese War. Japan was forced to return the Liaotung peninsula and other major spoils of victory in the Sino-Japanese War, only to see many of those spoils subsequently ceded to other imperialists, particularly czarist Russia. See Mark Borthwick, *Pacific Century,* Boulder, CO: Westview Press, 1998, pp. 40–55.

21. *Zhang Taiyan zhengzhi sixiang xuanji* [*Collection of Zhang Taiyan's Political Thoughts*], Beijing: Chinese Publisher, 1977, p. 6.

22. Li, *Dongya hezuo de wenhua chengyin* [*Cultural Roots of East Asian Cooperation*], p. 140.

23. Gilbert Rozman, *Northeast Asia's Stunted Regionalism,* New York: Cambridge University Press, 2004, pp. 82–84.

24. Yotaro Kobayashi, "Nihon: Sai Ajia-ka" ["The Re-Asianization of Japan"], *Foresight,* April 1991, p. 144.

25. Walter Hatch and Kozo Yamamura, *Asia in Japan's Embrace: Building a Regional Production Alliance,* Cambridge, UK: Cambridge University Press, 1996, pp. 19–121.

26. Hatch, "Globalization versus Regionalization: A Study of Japanese Identity from a Neo-Gramscian Perspective," paper presented at the Conference on Asian Values, National University of Singapore, October 5–6, 2001.

27. *Business Week,* April 10, 1989, p. 44.

28. Muhamad Mahathir and Ishihara Shintaro, *Voice of Asia: Two Leaders Discuss the Coming Century,* Tokyo: Kodansha International, 1995, p. 41.

29. Ibid.

30. Mahathir and Ishihara, *Voice of Asia.*

31. The "Asianist nationalism" in Japan during the 1990s was counterbalanced between 2001 and 2006 by the even greater popularity of the pro-American prime minister Koizumi Junichiro, who also embraced nationalist symbols, such as the Yasukuni Shrine. Yet he was succeeded by clearly nationalist politicians with somewhat greater ambivalence toward the United States, such as Abe Shinzo. At the turn of the twenty-first century, Japanese nationalism clearly flowed in a variety of streams, as will be discussed later.

32. Following a surge of Asianist sentiment around the time of the Russo-Japanese War, a second wave crested around 1990, led by Malaysia's Mohammed Mahathir.

33. East Asian Vision Group, "Toward an East Asian Community: Region of Peace, Prosperity, and Progress," report adopted at the ASEAN Plus Three Summit, Cambodia, November 2002.

34. See ASEAN+3 Summit, *East Asia Vision Group Report,* Phnom Penh, Cambodia: ASEAN+3 Summit Secretariat, 2002.

35. He Baogang, "East Asian Ideas of Regionalism," *Australian Journal of International Affairs,* Vol. 58, No. 1, March 2004, pp. 105–25.

36. See Ma Licheng, "Zhongrihan zimaoqu: yazhou zhenghe de xumu" ["China, Japan, and South Korea Free Trade Area Opens Pathway to Regional Integration"], *Zhongguo qiyejia* [*Chinese Entrepreneurs*], No. 9, 2003, p. 1.

37. Ma Licheng, "Duiri guanxi xin siwei" ["New Perspectives on the Sino-Japanese Relationship"], *Zhanglue yu guanli* [*Strategy and Management*], No. 6, 2002.

38. Lee Chang-jae, "Northeast Asian Economic Cooperation: The Need for a New Approach," *NIRA Review,* Autumn 2000, pp. 5–10.

39. Jeong Kap-young and Choe Kwan-kyoo, "Northeast Asian Economic Regionalism: A Korean View," *Global Economic Review,* Vol. 30, No. 1, 2001, p. 111.

40. Ogawa Yuhei, "Dongya dizhonghai ziyou maoyiqu xingcheng de kenengxing" ["On the Possibility of Forming East Asia Mediterranean Sea Free Trade Zone"], *Dongbeiya luntan* [*Northeast Asia Forum*], No. 4, November 2000.

41. Ibid.

42. Ibid.

43. Ibid.

44. Ibid.

45. BBC News, October 20, 2000; see also http://www.mutantfrog.com/2007/01/09/the-japan-korea-tunnel-gets-revisited/.

46. Shioya Takafusa, "The Grand Design of Northeast Asia," speech at the "International Conference on Revitalizing Northeast China and Promoting Regional Cooperation in Northeast Asia," Dalian, China, 2004, http://www.nira.or.jp/past/newse/paper/gdna/report.html.

47. See "Tokyo Dreams of Rail Link to London," *Times* (London), October 24, 2000.

48. See "Northeast Asia Economic Forum Issues Shenyang Declaration," *BBC Monitoring Asia Pacific,* September 21, 2005.

49. See "Trilateral TV Programs Urged," *Daily Yomiuri,* September 29, 2007.

50. Zha Daojiong, "Ditai jingji" ["Low Carbon Dioxide Economy"], speech at the NEAT Annual Conference, 2007, www.neat.org.ch.

51. Gao Haihong, "Dongya meiyuan benwei he quyu jiejue fangan" ["Dependence on U.S. Dollars in East Asia and the Regional Response"], speech at the NEAT Annual Conference, 2007, www.neat.org.cn.

52. Zhang Yunling, *Dongbeiya jingji hezuo* [*Northeast Asian Economic Cooperation*], Beijing: World Affairs Publisher, 2004; "Dongbohui qiandong dongbeiya keji jingmao hezuo" ["Northeast Asian High-Tech Trade Fair Promotes Northeast Asian High-Tech Cooperation"], *Zhongguo gaige bao* [*China's Reform*], September 21, 2007, p. 7.

53. See "Liaoning yu rihan kaizhan quyu nongye hezuo wenti tanxi" ["Research on Liaoning's Agricultural Cooperation with Japan and Korea"], *Nongye jingji* [*Agricultural*

Economy], November 2007, pp. 79–80; "Wei dongbeiya jingrong hezuo pulu jiaqiao" ["Work for Financial Collaboration in Northeast Asia"], *Jingji ribao* [*Economics Daily*], April 1, 2005, p. 7; "Shenhua jiaoliu hezuo, cujin dongbeiya nengyuan anquan" ("Deepen Cooperation to Promote Northeast Asian Energy Security"), *Guoji shiyou jingji* [*International Petroleum Economics*], October 2007, pp. 10–23; "Dongbeiya zhongxiao qiye guoji hezuo yu fazhan" ["Development and Cooperation of Small- and Medium-firms in Northeast Asia"], *Hebei ribao* [*Hebei Daily*], May 19, 2006, p. 1; "Dongbeiya mingren hui" ["Meeting of Luminaries in Northeast Asia"], *Xinhua Daily*, April 17, 2007, p. 5.

54. These excerpts are from the Trilateral Meeting of the Foreign Ministers of Japan, the People's Republic of China, and the Republic of Korea, November 27, 2004, www.mofa.go.jp.

55. Ibid.

56. See "China, Japan, and South Korea Held Seventh Leaders' Meeting in Philippines," *BBC Monitoring Asia Pacific*, January 16, 2007.

57. Ibid.

58. *China Daily,* June 5, 2007, chinadaily.com.cn.

59. See "China, Japan, and South Korea Hold Trilateral Talks in Beijing," *BBC Monitoring Asia Pacific,* May 19, 2007.

60. See "Northeast Asia Initiatives," *Korea Herald,* June 5, 2007.

61. See "Asian Cooperation Dialogue Calls for Narrowing Internet Gap," *BBC Monitoring Asia Pacific*, June 5, 2007.

62. See "Convergence, Creativity and Cooperation for the Future of Internet," *Korea Herald,* June 18, 2008.

63. See "Roh Proposes Northeast Asia Economic Bloc," *Korea Times,* June 22, 2007.

64. See "Roh to Hold China, Japan Summits Today," *Korea Times*, November 19, 2007.

65. See "Beijing Forges New Diplomacy with Neighbors," *South China Morning Post,* November 24, 2007.

66. See "Will the Helsinki Process Work in Northeast Asia?" *Korea Herald*, January 10, 2008.

67. See "Chinese, Japanese, and Korean Foreign Ministers Meeting in Tokyo," *BBC Monitoring Asia Pacific,* June 14, 2008.

68. See "Korea, China, Japan to Set Up Financial Body," *Korea Herald,* October 23, 2008.

69. Influential South Korean leaders, led by former prime minister Nam Duck-woo, were also pushing for a Northeast Asian Development Bank that would help direct the massive capital surpluses of the region to region-specific developmental projects.

70. See "Northeast Asian Cooperation Key to $80 Billion Fund," *Korea Herald,* October 7, 2008.

71. See "New Era for Korea, China, Japan Cooperation: Three Nations Hold First Independent Summit, to Establish Future-Oriented Relations," ibid., December 12, 2008.

72. Ibid.

73. Ibid.

74. See "Pursue Shared Interests via Regular Dialogues," *Daily Yomiuri,* December 14, 2008.

75. See "China, Japan, and South Korea to Enhance Cooperation," *BBC Monitoring Asia Pacific,* December 12, 2008.

76. See "Korea, Japan, and China to Strengthen Financial Ties," *Korea Herald*, April 11, 2009.

77. Ibid.

78. Korea's financial supervisory service senior deputy governor, Lee Jang-yung; China's vice chairman of the Banking Regulatory Commission, Wang Zhaoxing; and Japan's Financial Service Agency deputy commissioner of international affairs, Yamazaki Tatsuo, were the top delegates. See ibid.

79. See "China, South Korea, and Japan Vow to Cement Cultural Ties," *BBC Monitoring Asia Pacific*, December 25, 2008.

80. See "China, Japan, and South Korea Agree on Water Cooperation," *BBC Monitoring Asia Pacific*, March 20, 2009.

81. "Joint Statement of the Second Trilateral Summit," www.fmprc.gov.cn/chn/pds/siliao/1179/t619525.

82. Shi Yinhong, "Zhongri jiejin yu waijiao geming" ["China-Japan Rapprochement and China's Diplomatic Revolution"], *Zhanlue yu guanli* [*Strategy and Management*], No. 2, 2003, pp. 71–75; Ma Licheng, "Zhongri xin siwei" ("New Perspectives on Sino-Japan Relations—Worrisome Nationalism"), *Zhanlue yu guanli* [*Strategy and Management*], No. 6, 2002, pp. 41–47; Ye Zicheng, "Zhongguo de heping jueqi yu dongbeiya hezuo" ["China's Peaceful Rise and Northeast Asian Cooperation"], Beijing University working paper, 2004; and Hu Angang, *Zhongguo da zhanlue* [*The Grand Strategy of China*], Hangzhou: Zhejiang People's Publisher, 2003.

83. See Frank-Jurgen Richter and Pamela Mar, *Recreating Asia*, New York: Wiley, 2002.

84. This view in China is represented by the Ministry of Commerce, notably Vice Minister Long Yongtu, and the Center of Chinese Economic Studies at Beijing University, notably longtime director Justin Lin, named in early 2008 as chief economist of the World Bank.

85. Acharya, "Ideas, Identity, and Institution-Building," *Pacific Review*, Vol. 10, No. 3, 1997, pp. 319–46, 328–30.

86. Kenzaburo Oe, "Aimai-na Nihon no Watashi" ["Japan, the Ambiguous, and Myself"], in *Aimai-na Nihon no Watashi* [*Japan, the Ambiguous, and Myself*], Tokyo: Iwanami Shinsho, 1995, pp. 1–17. The English original is available as "Japan, the Ambiguous, and Myself," Stockholm: Nobel Foundation, 1994, http://nobelprize.org/literature/aureates/1994/oe-lecture.html.

87. Li, *Dongya hezuo de wenhua chengyin* [*Cultural Roots of East Asian Cooperation*].

88. Kazuhiko Togo, *Japan's Foreign Policy: 1945–2003*, Boston: Brill Academic Publishers, 2005.

89. This included India, Australia, and New Zealand, with Russia as an observer, in addition to ASEAN Plus Three.

90. Ma Licheng, "Duiri xin siwei" ("New Perspectives on Sino-Japan Relationship"), *Zhanlue yu guanli* [*Strategy and Management*], No. 6, 2002.

91. Tang Shiping, "2010–2015 Zhongguo zhoubian anquan huanjing" ["China's Regional Security in 2010–2015"], *Zhanlue yu guanli* [*Strategy and Management*], No. 5, 2002.

92. Shi Yinhong, "zhongguo jinqi zhuyao duiwai zhanlue wenti" ["China's Main Strategic Problems in the Near Term"], *Zhanlue yu guanli* [*Strategy and Management*], No. 6, 2003.

93. Shi Yinhong, "Meiguo quanshi, zhongguo jueqi, yu shijie zhixu" ["American Power, the Rise of China, and the World Order"], *Guoji wenti yanjiu* [*Study of International Relations*], No. 3, 2007.

94. See "Chinese Premier Stresses Cooperation among China, Japan, and South Korea," *BBC Monitoring Asia Pacific*, December 13, 2008.

95. See "Shounao huiyi: sheji dongbeiya quyu hezuo xin shinian" ["Summits: Design Northeast Asian Cooperation in the Next Ten Years"], *Changchun ribao* [*Changchun Daily*], September 2, 2006, p. 2.

96. See David Kang, "Getting Asia Wrong: The Need for a New Analytical Framework," *International Security*, Vol. 24, No. 4, Summer 2003, pp. 57–85; Li, *Dongya hezuo de wenhua chengyin* [*Cultural Roots of East Asian Cooperation*], pp. 91–115; and Kang, *China Rising: Peace, Power, and Order in East Asia*, New York: Columbia University Press, 2007.

97. Kang, *China Rising*.

98. On the key elements, especially the Chinese emperor's practice of according tributary states more favors than he received from them, as a reward for fealty, see Eric Teo, "Asia's Security and the Reemergence of China's Tributary System," *China Brief*, Jamestown Foundation, October 24, 2004; and David Kang, "Getting Asia Wrong," *International Security*, 27:4, Summer, 2003, pp. 57–85.

99. Ma Licheng, "Duiri guanxi xin siwei" ["New Perspectives on Sino-Japan Relationship"], *Zhanlue yu guanli* [*Strategy and Management*], No. 6, 2002, p. 47.

100. Acharya, "Will Asia's Past Be Its Future?" *International Security*, Vol. 28, No. 3, Winter 2003/4, pp. 149–64.

101. See "Northeast Asian Ties," *Korea Herald,* June 17, 2008.

102. See Roger Altman, "The Great Crash, 2008: The Geopolitical Setback for the West," *Foreign Affairs,* Vol. 88, No. 1, January/February, 2009, pp. 2–15.

103. On the distinguished career of Wang Yi, so important to the making of Northeast Asia, see Zhang Shuo, "New Young Boss of State Council Taiwan Affairs Office Assumes Office," *BBC Monitoring Asia Pacific,* June 5, 2008.

104. Each Diet member had an individual photo taken with Chinese President Hu Jintao. See "Ozawa-led Group Welcomed in China; Hu, DPT Officials Look Forward to Better Relations While Skirting Thorny Issues," *Daily Yomiuri,* December 12, 2009.

105. See Kent Calder, "Regionalism and Alliance: Can Korea Be Northeast Asia's Benelux?" paper presented at the American Political Science Association Annual Convention, September 1–4, 2005, Washington, DC; and Stefan Schirm, *Globalization and the New Regionalism*, Cambridge, UK: Polity, 2002.

106. Kang, *China Rising*, p. 106.

107. ASEAN, for example, often solicits China's proactive involvement in the region and simultaneously encourages the perception in the United States that "China is eating America's lunch." ASEAN is also strategic in energizing Japan-ASEAN trade negotiations competitive with China's initiatives.

108. Kang, *China Rising*, pp. 104–25.

109. See, for example, "Northeast Asian Ties," *Korea Herald,* June 17, 2008.

110. See "Zhang yunling fangwen neimenggu" ["Visiting Mongolia during July 4–9, 2005"], news article, Chinese Academy of Social Science, www.cass.net.cn.

111. More than 34,000 Mongolians, or more than 1.2 percent of the total population, are currently living in the ROK, remitting $200 million annually to their homeland, and

Korea is also the most prominent overseas educational destination for Mongolians. Korea is known to the Mongolians as Solongos, or "Land of Rainbows." See *Korea Herald* (ed.), *Korean Wave,* Seoul: Jimoondang, 2008, pp. 110–11.

112. See "Two Koreas Discuss the Timing for the Next Talks on the Joint Industrial Park," *BBC Monitoring Asia Pacific,* May 5, 2009.

113. "North Korea Opens Border; Again Calls for U.S. Treaty," *New York Times,* September 2, 2009.

Chapter 6

1. It is useful for our purposes to distinguish regionalization from regionalism. *Regionalization* is defined here as a bottom-up, private-initiated process. *Regionalism* conversely implies a top-down, governmental effort. See Shaun Breslin, "Decentralization, Globalization, and China's Partial Re-engagement with the Global Economy," *New Political Economy,* Vol. 5, 2000.

2. Peter J. Katzenstein and Takashi Shiraishi (eds.), *Network Power,* Ithaca, NY: Cornell University Press, 1997.

3. For a discussion of the regional development connection, see Bruce Cumings, "The Origins and Development of the Northeast Asian Political Economy: Industrial Sectors, Product Cycles, and Political Consequences," *International Organizations,* Vol. 38, No. 1, Winter 1984, pp. 1–40; and Chalmers Johnson, "Political Institutions and Economic Performance: The Government-Business Relationship in Japan, South Korea, and Taiwan," in John Ravenhill (ed.), *Japan,* Brookfield, VT: Elgar, 1995.

4. Trade volume is a standard measure of interdependence. See, for example, Bruce Russett and John Oneal, "The Classical Liberals Were Right: Democracy, Interdependence, Conflict, 1950–1985," *International Studies Quarterly,* Vol. 41, June 1997, pp. 267–94. Northeast Asia here includes Japan, the PRC, Taiwan, Hong Kong, and South Korea.

5. In 1997, for example, Japan's trade with China totaled about $60 billion, and that with South Korea $40 billion, while Japanese trade with the United States was close to $200 billion. See IMF, *Direction of Trade Statistics,* 1998 edition.

6. Ibid., 2007–9 editions.

7. The boundary of "Greater China" is fluid in the literature. It can be narrowly defined as southern China plus Taiwan, Hong Kong, and Macao. It also has been defined as China plus Taiwan, Hong Kong, and Macao, as well as the immense area including Mainland China, Taiwan, Hong Kong, Macao, and Southeast Asia.

8. See "More Cross-Strait Flights Added for Chinese New Year," *South China Morning Post,* January 4, 2010.

9. For Taiwan's trade statistics, see the ROC, Bureau of International Trade. The other trade statistics are from IMF, *Direction of Trade,* various editions.

10. Edward Lincoln, *Economic Integration in East Asia,* Washington, DC: Brookings Institution Press, 2004.

11. John Ravenhill, Rick Doner, and Gregory Noble, *Industrial Competitiveness of the Auto Parts Industries in Four Large Asian Countries: The Role of Government Policy in a Challenging International Environment,* Washington, DC: World Bank Policy Research Working Paper, WPS 4106, December 2006.

12. The data for 2003 is from Korea International Trade Association, KOTIS data.

13. Data is from ibid.

14. On the emergence of Japanese production networks in electronics, see Gene Gregory, *Japanese Electronics Technology: Enterprise and Innovation*, Tokyo: *Japan Times*, 1985.

15. JETRO, *Balance of Payment Statistics,* 2009 edition.

16. Korean Exim Bank, Foreign Direct Investment Statistics, 2007, www.koreaexim.go.kr.

17. See CIA, *World Factbook*, available https://www.cia.gov/library/publications/the-world-factbook/.

18. Ravenhill, "The Growth of the Chinese Automotive Industry and Its Impact on Production Networks in East Asia," unpublished working paper, Australia National University, 2005.

19. The operations of Acer, now one of the world's top personal-computer makers, are a case in point. See Ashlee Vance, "Acer's Everywhere. How Did that Happen?" *New York Times,* June 28, 2009.

20. Mitsuhiro Seki, "Dynamism of the East Asian Economic Zone and the Small and Medium sized Enterprises," unpublished paper presented at the 6th APEC Meeting on special economic zones (SEZs), 2006.

21. On the concept of natural economic territories (NETs), see Robert Scalapino, "Northeast Asia Today: An Overview," working paper, University of California, Berkeley, 2002. Also available at http://gsti.miis.edu/CEAS-PUB/200202Scalapino.pdf.

22. Interviews by Yanbo Wang, in Kunshan, China, summer 2006.

23. Source: development research center of the State Council (DRC) Database.

24. Kim So-young, "Korean Investment in China Rises Sharply," *Korean Herald,* January 26, 2005, www.ipr.co.kr.

25. Kwan Chi-hung, "Why Korea Does Not Perceive China as a Threat?" *China in Transition,* April 18, 2005, www.rieti.go.jp.

26. Ravenhill, "The Growth of China's Automotive Industry," working paper, Australia National University, 2005.

27. China's share in Japan's exports of auto parts more than doubled between 2000 and 2003, reaching 8 percent of Japan's total in 2003.

28. Ibid.

29. See "China May Be the Bailout Global Car Industry Seeks," *Straits Times* (Singapore), April 16, 2009.

30. The case was based on the author's interview and field research at Xinkai Inc., July 2006.

31. Paul Krugman, *Geography and Trade,* Cambridge: MIT Press, 1991.

32. Michael E. Porter, *The Competitive Advantage of Nations,* New York: Free Press, 1990.

33. JBIC, *Survey on Overseas Investment,* 2008 edition, http://www.jbic.go.jp/en/research/report/index.html.

34. Fred Bergsten, Bates Gill, Nicholas Lardy, and Dereck Mitchell, *China: The Balance Sheet,* Washington, DC: CSIS, 2006, p. 106.

35. Jason Dean, "The Laptop Trail," *Wall Street Journal,* June 9, 2005.

36. At the end of March 2009, Acer had a global market share of over 11 percent in PCs, compared with 13 percent for Dell Computer. See Vance, "Acer's Everywhere." Also see Yadong Luo, *Strategy, Structure, and Performance of MNCs in China*, Westport, Conn.: Quorum Books, 2001.

37. *Shanghai Statistics Yearbook*, 2009 edition.

38. Peng Dajin, "Invisible Linkages: A Regional Perspective of East Asian Political Economy," *International Studies Quarterly*, Vol. 46, 2002, p. 438.

39. In 2007, for example, Hong Kong's share of Beijing's FDI was 19 percent, Japan's 15 percent, and South Korea's 8 percent. See *Beijing Statistical Yearbook*, 2008.

40. The Sino-Korean agreement allowed Korean fishermen to increase productivity more than W300 billion annually. See "Korea, China Reach Fishing Accord," *Korea Times*, April 6, 2001.

41. From the Ministry of Foreign Affairs of the PRC.

42. From the Ministry of Foreign Affairs of the PRC, "Zhongguo tong riben de guanxi" ["Sino-Japan Relationship"], January 2009.

43. Ravenhill, "A Three Bloc World? The New East Asian Regionalism," *International Relations of the Asia-Pacific*, Vol. 2, No. 2, 2002, pp. 167–95.

44. Jennifer Amyx, "A Regional Bond Market for East Asia: Evolving Political Dynamics of Regional Financial Cooperation," paper presented at Australia National University, March 9, 2004, http://apseg.anu.edu.au/pdf/apseg_seminar/ap02_amyx.ppt#1.

45. See "Asia: 10 Years after the Crisis," *Nation*, June 24, 2007.

46. For a broad analysis of integration trends in Asian regional finance, stressing the obstacles still remaining, see William W. Grimes, *Currency and Contest in East Asia,* Ithaca, NY: Cornell University Press, 2008.

47. Lee Chang-jae, *Joint Study on a China-Japan-South Korea FTA*, Seoul: KIEP Policy Analyses, December 30, 2004; and Inkyo Cheong, *Study on a China-Japan-South Korea FTA,* Seoul: KIEP Policy Analyses, February 20, 2003.

48. For example, in 2005, Chinese commerce minister Bo Xilai proposed the establishment of a bilateral FTA to South Korea. In 2007, South Korean president Roh Moo-hyun also proposed a Northeast Asian economic bloc.

49. The three types of institutions represent three layers of policy networks in Northeast Asia. APT is a governmental process in which heads of the states meet to discuss a variety of issues. The BFA is a nongovernmental, Track II framework in which heads of state, major economic bureaucracies, and private sector representatives attend informally to exchange views and formulate a cooperation agenda. Subnational policy networks are also vibrant, including both think tanks and local governments.

50. ASEAN Meeting Calendar, 2008, *APT Cooperation Database on Cooperation Progressing in the ASEAN Plus Three and ASEAN Plus One Frameworks*, available http://www.neat.org. cn/uploadfiles/20080317020233316.pdf, p. 10.

51. Ibid., p. 12.

52. Ibid.

53. Interview with the Secretary General of the BFA, Beijing, July 2006.

54. Zhang Xiang is China's deputy minister of commerce. Long Yongtu has been a chief negotiator at the Ministry of Commerce and also served as chief negotiator in Geneva, preparing the way for China's WTO entry.

55. China's Peaceful Rise strategy and northeastern rejuvenation were introduced at the Boao Forum in 2003. In 2006, when PRC relations with Taiwan and Japan were difficult, Chinese vice president Zeng Qinghong met Vincent Siew, chairman of the Taiwan-based Cross-Straits Common Market Foundation, and Toshihiro Nikai, the two-time Japanese trade minister.

56. See "Leaders to Seek Asian Values to Tackle Global Financial Crisis," *Xinhua News*, April 17, 2009, http://ca.china-embassy.org/eng/xwdt/t557880.htm.

57. Ibid.

58. See www.internationalonline.com, April 21, 2005.

59. Interview with the general secretary of BFA, Beijing, July 2006.

60. See www.xinhua.net, November 4, 2003.

61. For a discussion of the epistemic community's role in international policy-making, see Peter Haas, "Epistemic Community and International Policy Coordination," *International Organization*, Vol. 46, No. 1, 1992, pp. 1–35.

62. The Pacific Basin Economic Cooperation group (PBEC), a Track II organization, preceded the establishment of APEC, while the Council for Security Cooperation in Asia Pacific (CSCAP) preceded establishment of the ARF. See Paul Evans, "Between Regionalism and Regionalization," in T. J. Pempel (ed.), *Remapping East Asia: The Construction of a Region*, Ithaca, NY: Cornell University Press, 2005.

63. This observation is based on the co-author's own interviews with Chinese scholars and officials regarding the APT process.

64. See the article collection at the Institute of Asian Pacific Studies, CASS, http://iaps.cass.cn/english/Articles/Articles.asp.

65. See http://www.sis.pku.edu.cn/web/Browse.aspx?id=623.

66. Ibid.

67. See "South Korea Mulling Cutting Military Ties with Japan," *Korea Times*, September 5, 2008. This disputed islet is known to the Japanese as Takeshima.

68. See "South Korea, the U.S., and Japan to Start Military Dialogue," *BBC Monitoring Asia Pacific*, March 12, 2008.

69. See "Defense Minister Lee to Visit Japan," *Korea Times*, April 20, 2009.

70. For details underlying the following narrative, see sina.com.cn news, www.sina.com.cn; CCTV News, www.news.cctv.com/world; Xinhua Net News, www.news.xinhuanet.com; People's News, www.military.people.com.cn; and China News.com, www.chinanews.com.cn.

71. The most recent previous visit of a Chinese defense minister to Japan had been in February 1998, just before President Jiang Zemin's state visit to Tokyo.

72. The Korean War Casualties Statistics, http://www.centurychina.com/history/krwarcost.html.

73. See "South Korea, China Defense Ministers' Talk," *Korea Times*, August 27, 1999; "ROK Defense Minister Calls for China's Cooperation on NK Missile Program," *Korea Times*, August 23, 1999.

74. See "Visit by Chinese Defense Minister," Ibid., January 17, 2000.

75. See "Chinese Warships at Inchon for First-time ever Call to South Korea," *Korea Herald*, May 9, 2002.

76. See "Chinese Defense Minister and Korea Air Force Chief Staff Discuss Ties," *BBC Monitoring Asia Pacific*, July 18, 2005.

77. See "Chinese Defense Minister Vows to Boost Military Ties with South Korea," Ibid., December 18, 2008.

78. See "China and South Korea Agreed to Further Military Ties," Ibid., April 29, 2009.

79. Jung Sun-ki, "South Korea and China Open Military Hot Lines," *Defense News*, November 24, 2008.

80. Dennis Tachiki, "Between Foreign Direct Investment and Regionalism: The Role of Japanese Production Networks," in T. J. Pempel (ed.), *Remapping East Asia*.

81. Zhang Yunling, *Dongbeiya quyu jinji hezuo* [*Northeast Asian Economic Cooperation*], Beijing: World Affairs Press, 2005.

82. Council for Local Authorities for International Relations (CLAIR), www.clair. or.jp, 2005.

83. See the Foreign Affairs Bureau, Beijing Municipality.

Part Four

1. This approach usually refers to the relatively venerable functionalist tradition. See Ernst Haas, "The Challenge of Regionalism," *International Organization*, Vol. 12, No. 4, Autumn 1958; Karl Deutsch et al., *Political Community and the North Atlantic Area,* Princeton: Princeton University Press, 1957; David Mitrany, *A Working Peace System,* Chicago: Quadrangle Books, 1961.

2. Paul Pierson, "The Path to European Integration: A Historical Institutionalist Analysis," *Comparative Political Studies,* Vol. 29, No. 2, 1996, pp. 126–63; and Peter J. Katzenstein and Takashi Shiraishi (eds.), *Network Power*, Ithaca, NY: Cornell University Press, 1997.

3. This view is advocated in the new regionalism literature. See, for example, Helen Milner and Edward Mansfield, *The Political Economy of Regionalism,* New York: Columbia University Press, 1997.

Chapter 7

1. Edward Steinfeld also observed, referring to the PRC's new embrace of capitalist reform since the AFC, that China "both escaped the immediate impact of the 1998 regional collapse and experienced the greatest transformation" in the region. See "The Capitalist Embrace: China Ten Years After," in Andrew MacIntyre, T. J. Pempel, and John Ravenhill (eds.), *Crisis as Catalyst: Asia's Dynamic Political Economy,* Ithaca, NY: Cornell University Press, 2008.

2. See *Zhongguo duiwai jingji tongji daquan 1979–1991* [*China's Statistics on Foreign Trade and Investment 1979–1991*], Beijing: Zhongguo Tongji Xinxi Zhixun Fuwu Chubanshe, pp. 401–7.

3. CCP Archival Compilation Commission, *Deng Xiaoping wenxuan* [*Selected Works of Deng Xiaoping*], Vol. Three, Beijing: Renmin Publishers, 1993, p. 347.

4. China signed FTA treaties with ASEAN in 2004 and 2008 and with Singapore separately in 2009.

5. Shao Feng, "Chaohe weiji de weilai yu dongbeiya anquan jizhi" ["The Future of North Korean Crisis and Construction of NEA Security Institutions"], *Shijie jingji yu zhengzhi* [*World Economics & Politics*], No. 9, 2007.

6. See "Harmony through East Asian Friendship," www.chinadaily.com.cn, November 19, 2007.

7. See "Shounao huiyi: sheji dongbeiya quyu hezuo xin shinian" ["Summit: Design Northeast Asian Integration in the Next Ten Years"], *Changchun ribao* [*Changchun Daily*], September 2, 2006, p. 2.

8. "Dongbeiya jingji hezuo luntan kaimu" ["Northeast Asia Economic Cooperation Forum Opens"], *Jilin ribao* [*Jilin Daily*], September 3, 2006, p. 1; and "Wuyi dui dongbeiya

quyu jingji hezuo tichu sandian jianyi" ["Wu Yi Proposed Three Suggestions for Northeast Asian Economic Cooperation"], *Zhongguo jingji shibao* [*China Economic Times*], September 5, 2006, p. 1.

9. See "Dongbeiya jingmao hezuo gaoceng luntan huo guowuyuan pizhun" ["Northeast Asian High-Level Forum Was Authorized by China's State Council"], *Tumenjiang bao*, August 1, 2007, p. 1.

10. See Thomas Christensen, "Old Problems Trump New Thinking: China's Security Relations with Taiwan, North Korea, and Japan," *China Leadership Monitor*, No. 14, Summer 2005.

11. The first talk by ARATS and SEF was held in 1992 and resulted in a broad 1992 consensus. In 1993 and 1998, the talks were held again, yet no significant agreements were reached.

12. *Sing Tao Daily*, August 2, 2009, p. A3. The Chinese official source puts the total number of tourists to Taiwan in 2009 at 603,000. See "China's Taiwan Affairs Chief, Commerce Minister Review Cross-Strait Work in 2009," *BBC Monitoring Asia Pacific*, January 3, 2010.

13. See "Premier Says He Would Crawl to Get to Taiwan," *South China Morning Post*, March 14, 2009.

14. Alan Romberg, "Cross-Straits Relations: First the Easy, Now the Hard," *China Leadership Monitor*, No. 28, Spring 2009.

15. Philip Sanders and Scott Kastner, "Is a China-Taiwan Peace Deal in the Cards?" *Foreign Policy*, July 27, 2009.

16. Romberg, "Cross-Straits Relations."

17. Jiang consolidated his power in 1995, when he took charge also over the military. Before 1995, Deng Xiaoping played a very important role from behind the scene.

18. See "Boao Forum Participants Debated on China's Peaceful Rise," *BBC Monitoring Asia Pacific*, April 26, 2004.

19. Zheng Bijian, "China's Peaceful Rise to Great Power Status," *Foreign Affairs*, September/October, 2005.

20. See "Wang Yi tan xinshiqi waijiao gongzuo" ["Wang Yi Interviewed on New Diplomacy in the New Era"], *Shijie zhishi* [*World Knowledge*], No. 11, 2003.

21. Yan Xuetong and Shi Yinhong, "Zhongguo jueqi yu taiwan wenti" ["Rise of China and Taiwan"], *Lingdao wencui* [*Selection for Leaders*], No. 11, 2002.

22. Hu Angang, "Quyuhuo zhanlue: jianli zhongguo, xianggang, riben, hanguo sanguo sifang ziyou maoyiqu de shexiang" ("Regionalist Strategy: Building Free Trade Area among China, Japan, Korea, and Hong Kong"), in *Zhongguo da zhanlue* [*The Grand Strategy of China*], Hangzhou: Zhejiang Remin Publisher, 2003, p. 146.

23. Christensen, "The Party Transition: Will It Bring a New Maturity in China's Security Policy?" *China Leadership Monitor*, No. 5, Winter 2003; and "Optimistic Trends and Near Term Challenges," *China Leadership Monitor*, No. 6, Spring 2003.

24. See "Xunqiu hezuo yu wending de dongbeiya" ["Northeast Asia Seeks Cooperation and Stability"], *People's Daily*, December 4, 2006, p. 8.

25. Robert Suettinger, "China's Foreign Policy Leadership: Testing Times," *China Leadership Monitor*, No. 12, Winter 2004.

26. In response to these critiques, Chinese leaders dropped the term "peaceful rise" and instead used "peaceful development." The two terms, however, are identical in substance, and "peaceful rise" remains more popular in policy discussions. See also Bonnie Glaser

and Evan Medeiros, "The Changing Ecology of Chinese Foreign Policy Making: The Ascension and Demise of Peaceful Rise Theory," *China Quarterly*, No. 190, June 2007, pp. 291–310.

27. See "Wang Yi: Being Appointed at a Difficult Time," *Nanfang zhoumo* [*Southern China Weekend*], December 30, 2004.

28. See "Harmony through East Asia Friendship," chinadaily.com.cn, November 19, 2007.

29. See ibid.

30. See "Chinese Agency Profiles New Taiwan Affairs Office Director Wang Yi," *BBC Monitoring Asia Pacific*, June 8, 2008.

31. Wang Yi was engaged in meetings with these actors within months of his appointment.

32. See "Cross-Straits Interactions and Exchanges," available at the State Council Taiwan Affairs Office website, www.gwytb.gov.cn.

33. Bo Xilai's press conference on the Sino-Japan relationship was widely reported in China. See *Guoji shangbao* [*International Business*], April 23, 2005, and *People's Daily*, April 23, 2005.

34. See "Bo Xilai's Speech at the 2005 China-ROK Economic Cooperation Forum," *Zhongguo jingji daobao*, June 21, 2005.

35. Barry Naughton, "The Emergence of Wen Jiabo," *China Leadership Monitor*, No. 6, Spring 2003; and Cheng Li, "The Emergence of Fifth Generation in Provincial Leadership," *China Leadership Monitor*, No. 6, Spring 2003

36. Central Committee small leading groups are strategic, informal bodies formed to advise the party politburo on policies and to coordinate the implementation of policy decisions made by the politburo.

37. Northeastern China, or Manchuria, was part of the Japanese colonial empire, and served as a main source of raw materials and heavy industrial production.

38. See Min Ye, "How Did China Join the Capitalist World through Foreign Direct Investment?" in Joseph Fewsmith (ed.), *China's Economic Reform at Thirty and the Way Ahead*, Lanham, MD: Rowman and Littlefield.

39. Itochu received the title of "friendly trading company" from Beijing, the first Japanese general trading company to receive such a designation. See www.itochu.co.jp.

40. The Chinese First Auto Works was headquartered in Jilin. It has maintained a strategic and long-term partnership with Toyota since 1996, and it formed another joint venture with Mazda in 2005.

41. See "Itochu Gets Involved in SOE Reform in NER," *Caijing shibao* [*Finance and Economics*], October 18, 2003.

42. See *Zhongguo zhengquan bao* [*Chinese Stock Market*], March 15, 2001.

43. Bo promoted the idea of developing Liaoning as well as northeastern China as a new growth pole to senior officials attending the APEC senior officials' meeting in Dalian in 2001. See "Bo Xilao Met Senior Officials at APEC," *Liaoning ribao* [*Liaoning Daily*], August 27, 2001.

44. Other officials in Liaoning were resentful of Bo Xilai's gaining preferential treatment for Dalian without facilitating development in the province in general. However, Bo Xilai's father was able to get him a seat in Shanxi Province, his native province.

45. Provincial-level municipalities—in Chinese, *zhixiashi*—are the highest level classifi-

cation for cities used by Chinese governments, with a status equal to that of the provinces.

46. See "Bo Xilai: Zhonghan jingmao hezuo jiangyou gengda fazhan" [There Will Be Major Developments in the Sino-Korean Trade"], *Zhongguo guomen shibao* [*China's Door*], April 5, 2004.

47. See *People's Daily*, April 23, 2005.

48. Ibid., June 22, 2005.

49. Li Cheng, "China's Northeast: From Largest Rust Belt to Fourth Economic Engine?" *China Leadership Monitor*, No. 9, Winter 2004.

50. There are four vice premiers in the State Council. Li Keqiang is ranked the first among the four, after only Premier Wen Jiabao.

51. Qi Wenhai et al., *Dongbeiya jingmao hezuo quanfangwei yanjiu* [*Northeast Asian Economic Cooperation*], Beijing: Social Science Publisher, 2006.

52. Wu Dawei, "Gongchuang dongbeiya hezuo xinshidai" ["Jointly Build the New Era of Northeast Asian Cooperation"], speech at the Convention of Rebuilding Northeastern China and Northeast Asian Cooperation," September 28, 2004; Li Hui, speech at the Convention Local Governments' Cooperation in Northeast Asia, September 21, 2004, www.sina.com.

53. See "Zhongguo yu dongbeiy quyu jingji hezuo qianjing guangkuo" ["Prospects for Economic Cooperation between China and Northeast Asian Neighbors"], *Guoji shangbao* [*International Business*], September 1, 2005, p. 7; "Dongbei zhenxing yu dongbeiya hezuo" ["Northeastern Rejuvenation and Northeast Asian Cooperation"], *Zhongguo maoyi bao* [*Chinese Trade*], September 16, 2008, p. 3

54. See "Liaoning canyu dongbeiya quyu hezuo de tujing yanjiu," *Touzi yu licai* [*Investment and Money Management*], http://www.enki.net; and "Dongbei Zhengxin guochengzhong de duiwai kaifang: zhongmeng hezuo" ["China and Mongolian Cooperation in the Process of Developing Northeastern China"], *Dongbeiya luntan* [*Northeast Asia Forum*], No. 5, Vol. 16, September 2007, pp. 47–49.

55. Peng Yonglin, "Dazhao jilin duiwai touzi hezuo xin pingtai" ["Develop a New Platform for Jilin's Overseas Investment"], *Jingji shijiao* [*Economic Perspective*], No. 10, 2007, pp. 12–14; "Dongbohui qiandong dongbeiya keji jingmao hezuo" ["Northeast Asian Trade Fairs Emphasize High-Tech Trade and Investment in Northeast Asia"], *Zhongguo gaige bao* [*Chinese Reform*], September 21, 2007, pp. 7–8.

56. See "Dongbei zhengxing yu dongbeiya hezuo" ["Northeastern Rejuvenation and the Cooperation in Northeast Asia"], *Zhongguo maoyi bao* [*China Trade*], September 16, 2008.

57. Li Cheng, "A Pivotal Stepping Stone: Provincial Leaders' Representation at the 17th Party Congress," *China Leadership Monitor*, No. 23, Winter 2008.

Chapter 8

1. Robert Keohane, "The Big Influence of Small Allies," *Foreign Policy*, Vol. 2, 1971, pp. 161–82.

2. Kent E. Calder, "Regionalism, Alliance, and Domestic Politics: The Benelux Model and Northeast Asian Cooperation," *International Journal of Korean Unification Studies*, Vol. 15, No. 1, 2006, pp. 1–29.

3. See, for example, Mohammed Mahathir and Shintaro Ishihara, *Voice of Asia: Two Leaders Discuss the Coming Century*, Tokyo: Kodansha International, 1995; and Bridget

NOTES TO CHAPTER 8

Welsh (ed.), *Reflections: The Mahathir Years,* Washington, DC: Johns Hopkins University SAIS Southeast Asian Studies, 2004.

4. The Chiang Mai swap arrangements were concluded in May 2000, while the first East Asia Summit was held in Kuala Lumpur, in December 2005.

5. On obstacles to the effectiveness of ASEAN in dealing with Asian security issues beyond Southeast Asia itself, see Shaun Narine, "ASEAN and the Management of Regional Security," *Pacific Affairs,* Vol. 71, No. 2, Summer 1998, pp. 195–214. Narine sees increasingly diverse interests within ASEAN, as its membership expands, coupled with divergences between Southeast Asian and Great Power interests in the post–Cold War world, as being the principal factors limiting ASEAN's diplomatic influence outside Southeast Asia.

6. High-growth Vietnam is a partial exception to this pattern, but the relative importance of Indonesia and most other ASEAN nations, apart from Vietnam, in spurring East Asian prosperity has definitely declined.

7. For an articulate Korean view of this issue, see Bae Kichan, *Korea at the Crossroads: The History and Future of East Asia,* Seoul: Happy Reading Books, 2007, esp., pp. 437–68.

8. See Charles K. Armstrong, Gilbert Rozman, Samuel S. Kim, and Stephen Kotkin (eds.), *Korea at the Center: Dynamics of Regionalism in Northeast Asia,* Armonk, NY: M. E. Sharpe, 2006, pp. 42–45.

9. The Taft-Katsura agreement between U.S. secretary of war William Howard Taft, soon to become president, and Japanese prime minister Katsura Taro is recalled bitterly by many Koreans as providing U.S. acceptance of a Japanese preeminence in Korea that led rapidly thereafter to harsh colonial rule.

10. Bruce Cumings, *Korea's Place in the Sun: A Modern History,* New York: W. W. Norton, 1997, p. 147.

11. Ibid., p. 155.

12. Ibid., pp. 175–77.

13. Ibid., pp. 177–79.

14. Ibid., p. 183.

15. South Korea's current president, Lee Myung-bak, inaugurated in February 2008, was one of the conspicuous participants. Lee was imprisoned for six months for his role.

16. Cumings, *Korea's Place in the Sun,* pp. 387–88.

17. The actual increase was 64 percent. See ibid., p. 388.

18. South Korea was able to do so by convincing the Taiwanese to join as "Chinese Taipeh" in November 1991, together with the PRC and Hong Kong. See Donald Crone, "The Politics of Emerging Pacific Cooperation," *Pacific Affairs,* Vol. 65, No. 1, Spring 1992, pp. 78–79.

19. Moon Chung-in and Kim Taehwan, "South Korea's International Relations: Challenges to Developmental Realism?" in Samuel S. Kim (ed.), *The International Relations of Northeast Asia,* Lanham, MD: Rowman and Littlefield, 2004, p. 263.

20. On the details, see Joel Wit, Daniel Poneman, and Robert Gallucci et al., *Going Critical: The First North Korean Nuclear Crisis,* Washington, DC: Brookings Institution Press, 2004.

21. See U.S.-ASEAN Business Council, *ASEAN+3,* at http://www.us-asean.org/ASEANOverview/asean+3.asp, accessed September 10, 2005.

22. Calder, "The New Face of Northeast Asia," *Foreign Affairs,* March/April 2001, pp. 106–23.

23. For the text, see *Korea Times,* February 26, 2008. Lee made no negative comments about North Korea at all, despite its nuclear testing and other recent confrontationist behavior, and stressed a willingness to aid the DPRK in attaining a $3,000 per capita GDP over ten years, provided that the nuclear issue was resolved.

24. Japanese prime minister Fukuda Yasuo and Russian premier Viktor Zubkov both attended his inauguration. See *Korea Herald,* February 26, 2008.

25. See "Toward a Peaceful and Prosperous Northeast Asia," www.nabh.go.kr, accessed September 15, 2005.

26. On the activities of the presidential committee, see Presidential Committee on Northeast Asian Cooperation Initiative, *Toward a Peaceful and Prosperous Northeast Asia,* Seoul: Office of the President, Republic of Korea, 2004.

27. Ibid.

28. Korean International Trade Association, http://global.kita.net./marketing/main/staticsIndex.jsp. On the remarkable transformation in the ROK's relations with China over the past quarter-century, see Jae-ho Chung, "South Korea between Eagle and Dragon: Perceptual Ambivalence and Strategic Dilemma," *Asian Survey,* Vol. 41, No. 5, September–October 2001, pp. 777–96; and Jae-ho Chung, *Between Ally and Partner: Korea-China Relations and the United States,* New York: Columbia University Press, 2006.

29. Statistics are from the Korea International Trade Association.

30. June Sun-ki, "South Korea, China Open Military Hot Lines," *Defense News,* November 24, 2008.

31. Personal interviews at Republic of Korea Fair Trade Commission, Seoul, February 2008.

32. See www.xinhua.net.

33. Chung Jae-ho, "South Korea between Eagle and Dragon," *Asian Survey,* September–October 2001, p. 783.

34. See "China Attracts Most ROK Visitors," www.china.org.cn, August 21, 2002, accessed September 13, 2005.

35. See "Nation Enjoys Soaring Overseas Visitors," *China Daily,* April 27, 2005, www2.chinadaily.com.cn, accessed September 13, 2005.

36. See China's Ministry of Foreign Affairs, Sino-South Korea Relations, http://www.fmprc.gov.cn/chn/pds/gjhdq/gj/yz/1206_12/sbgx/.

37. See "FKI Proposes to Establish Chinatown in Seoul," *Maeil Daily News,* May 7, 2008.

38. See "Russia-Korea Trade Ties Look Beyond Energy," *RT Business,* September 30, 2008.

39. Calder, *Korea's Energy Insecurities,* Washington, DC: Korea Economic Institute, 2005.

40. See "Russia, Korea Cement Economic, Political Ties," www.texcom.com.

41. See www.mofat.go.kr.

42. See IMF, *Direction of Trade Statistics,* various years.

43. *Korea Herald* (ed.), *Korean Wave,* Seoul: Jimoondang, 2008, p. 110.

44. Ibid.

45. High-level Korean business leaders, for example, accompanied President Lee Myung-bak on a major April 2008 visit to Tokyo for a Business Summit Round, focusing on component and materials-industry cooperation. See *Maeil Daily News,* April 29, 2008.

46. In that tragic case 269 Koreans and several foreigners, including a sitting U.S. con-

gressman, were killed in the crash of their Korean Airlines plane, shot down by a Soviet fighter pilot in one of the bloodiest nonwartime incidents of the Cold War.

47. See Paik Keun-wook, *Gas and Oil in Northeast Asia: Politics, Projects, and Prospects,* London: Royal Institute of International Affairs, 1995.

48. In January 2009, for example, some fifty top leaders of Japanese and Korean business met in Seoul to discuss establishment of an independent Asian financial center, and other responses to the subprime financial crisis, including a Korea-Japan economic partnership agreement. Japanese prime minister Aso Taro also spoke. See *Maeil Daily News,* January 11, 2009.

49. Lee indicated an energy-diplomacy priority clearly in his inaugural address. See *JoongAng Daily,* February 26, 2008.

50. See Joel Wit et al., *Going Critical.* Washington, DC: Brookings Institution Press, 2004.

51. See Donald Kirk, *The Korean Crisis: Unraveling the Miracle in the IMF Era,* Palgrave Macmillan, 2000.

52. The ABF is being structured in response to a proposal from EMEAP-member central banks. The ABF portfolio will be invested in a basket of liquid U.S. dollar bonds issued in major Asian economies (excluding Australia, Japan, and New Zealand), and its initial size will be approximately $1 billion. EMEAP (Executives' Meeting of East Asia and Pacific Central Banks and Monetary Authorities) comprises representatives of eleven Asian economies: Australia, China, Hong Kong SAR, Indonesia, Japan, Korea, Malaysia, New Zealand, the Philippines, Singapore, and Thailand. See William W. Grimes, *Currency and Contest in East Asia,* Ithaca, NY: Cornell University Press, 2009, pp. 177–84.

53. This term refers to activists in their thirties, educated in the 1980s, and born in the 1960s, who were the driving force in Korean progressive politics under presidents Kim Dae-jung and Roh Moo-hyun (1998–2008).

54. See, for example, the plea of FKI chairman Cho Suk-rae for an East Asian economic union centered on China and Korea, at the 4th Korea-China Business Leaders' Conference, only two months after Lee's inauguration, as reported in *Maeil Daily News,* April 29, 2009.

55. Kim Hak-joon subsequently served for many years as president of the Dong A Ilbo, one of Korea's preeminent newspaper chains.

56. The TCOG originated in response to the North Korean missile test over Japan in August 1998. Highly active from 1998 to 2001, TCOG was revived again following the advent of the Lee administration in Korea, after five dormant years during 2003–8.

57. Lee's first prime minister, Han Seung-soo (February 2008–September 2009), had spent extended time in Japan, as visiting professor at Tokyo's Graduate Research Institute for Policy Studies (GRIPS), while his foreign minister, Yu Myung-hwan, had been serving as ambassador to Japan when named to the principal foreign-policy post. See *JoongAng Daily,* February 25, 2008.

58. Korean Exim Bank, www.koreaexim.gov.kr.

Chapter 9

1. See Fukuzawa Yukichi, *The Autobiography of Fukuzawa Yukichi* (rev. translation by E. Kiyooka), New York: Columbia University Press, 1966.

2. Konoye was Japanese prime minister when Imperial Army troops stormed across the Marco Polo Bridge in July 1937, to start the Sino-Japanese War.

3. Jiang had particularly bitter personal memories of the war with Japan, having grown up in Jiangsu province under Japanese occupation as a teenager, and having had an uncle killed by the invading Japanese army. See Bruce Gilley, *Tiger on the Brink: Jiang Zemin and China's New Elite,* Berkeley: University of California Press, 1998.

4. This figure represents the share of the combined seats by the Social Democratic Party (7) and the Japanese Communist Party (9), among the 480 total seats in the Lower House of the Diet, as of early 2008.

5. Tanaka defeated Fukuda for the prime ministership in mid-1972, serving until derailed by scandal in 1974, while Fukuda served in the same position during 1976–78. On the Tanaka-Fukuda rivalry, see Kent E. Calder, "Kanryo vs. Shomin: The Dynamics of Conservative Leadership in Postwar Japan," In Terry E. MacDougall (ed.), *Political Leadership in Contemporary Japan,* Ann Arbor: University of Michigan Occasional Papers in Japanese Studies No. 1, 1982, pp. 1–31.

6. On Koizumi's diplomatic activities, see Tomohito Shinoda, *Koizumi Diplomacy,* Seattle: University of Washington Press, 2007.

7. On the domestic and international changes underlying the deepening Sino-Japanese tensions, see Calder: "China and Japan's Simmering Rivalry," *Foreign Affairs,* March/April 2006, pp. 129–40.

8. The revision of the U.S.-Japan defense guidelines in 1997 was a crucial first step in a process thereafter continued under the George W. Bush administration. See Christopher Hughes, *Japan's Re-Emergence as a "Normal" Military Power,* London: International Institute for Strategic Studies, Adelphi Paper, 2005, pp. 368–69.

9. See Albert M. Craig, *Civilization and Enlightenment: The Early Thought of Fukuzawa Yukichi,* Cambridge: Harvard University Press, 2009; and Fukuzawa, *The Autobiography of Fukuzawa Yukichi.*

10. There were more than 30,000 forced laborers from China in wartime Japan. See "GHQ Documents Shed Light on Measures to Repatriate Chinese Forced Laborers," *Daily Yomiuri,* May 19, 1994.

11. In 1988, Japan's exports to the United States were 34 percent of its total worldwide exports, with 5.8 percent to South Korea, and 3.6 percent to China. See IMF, *Direction of Trade,* 1989.

12. North Korean sympathizers preoccupied themselves with repatriation (especially between 1955 and 1961), and economic support for the DPRK (especially from 1970 to 2006). South Korean sympathizers focused on education and, after Japan-Korea mutual recognition in 1965, welfare issues, such as health insurance and alien registration. See Kim Chan-jung, *Chosen Soren [The Korean General League],* Tokyo: Shincho Sha, 2004; and Mindan website, http://www.mindan.org/eng.

13. Some 22 percent of Japan's total exports went to China and Korea in 2006, but only 23 percent went to the entire United States. See IMF, *Direction of Trade Statistics,* 2007 edition; and JETRO website, http://www.jetro.go.jp/cgi-bin/nats/cgi-bin/search.cgi.

14. see IMF, *Direction of Trade Statistics,* 2009.

15. See IMF, *Direction of Trade Statistics,* various editions; and Asahi Shimbun, *Japan Almanac,* 2006 edition, Tokyo: Asahi Shimbun Sha, p. 130.

16. Asahi Shimbun, *Japan Almanac,* 2006 edition, pp. 132–33.

17. Some 21.3 percent of Japan's steel exports in 2004 went to South Korea, compared with 21.0 percent to China. See ibid., p. 132.

18. Some 23.4 percent of Japan's IC imports came from Taiwan in 2004, compared with 18.8 percent from Korea, and only 5.3 percent from the PRC. See ibid., p. 133.

19. Tripartite initiatives that Tokyo has clearly supported have included the Tripartite Environmental Ministers' Meetings (TEMM), initiated in 1999; the Three Party Committee, formed in 2004; and, of course, the trilateral summits, beginning in December 2008.

20. See Victor Koschmann, "Asianism's Ambivalent Legacy," in Peter Katzenstein and Takashi Shiraishi (eds.), *Network Power: Japan and Asia,* Ithaca, NY: Cornell University Press, 1997, pp. 83–100; and Yukie Yoshikawa, *Japan's Asianism, 1868–1945: Dilemmas of Modernization,* Washington, DC: Reischauer Center for East Asian Studies, 2009.

21. On Japanese initiatives during this period, see Katzenstein, "Asian Regionalism in Comparative Perspective," in Katzenstein and Shiraishi (eds.), *Network Power,* pp. 1–44; and Akiko Fukushima, *Japan and Multilateral Diplomacy,* New York: St. Martin's Press, 1999.

22. On postwar Japanese regionalist initiatives within Asia, see David Arase, *Buying Power: The Political Economy of Japanese Foreign Aid,* Boulder, CO: Lynne Rienner, 1995; Arase (ed.), *The Challenge of Change: East Asia in the New Millennium,* Berkeley, CA: Institute of East Asian Studies, 2003; Arase (ed.), *Japan's Foreign Aid: Old Continuities and New Directions,* London: Routledge, 2005; and Reinhard Drifte, *Japan's Quest for a Permanent Security Council Seat,* New York: St. Martin's Press, 1998.

23. Calder, "Japan as a Post-Reactive State?" *Orbis,* Fall 2003, pp. 605–16.

24. On the details, see Calder, *Japan's Stealth Reform: The Key Role of Political Process,* Washington, DC: Reischauer Center for East Asian Studies, 2005.

25. Former prime minister Fukuda Yasuo, for example, is the longtime chairman of the Japan-Indonesia Dietmen's League.

26. The DPJ garnered 308 seats out of 480 contested in the dominant Lower House, compared with the ruling LDP's 118, with the DPJ nearly tripling its strength and establishing itself as the likely ruling party until at least 2014. See *Asahi Shimbun,* August 31, 2009.

27. "MITI" stands for Ministry of International Trade and Industry, the predecessor of METI before macroeconomic analytical functions were added to MITI's responsibilities in 2001.

28. On this problem, see Calder, "Securing Security through Prosperity: The San Francisco System in Comparative Perspective," *Pacific Review,* Vol. 17, No. 1, January 2004, pp. 135–57.

29. Kasumigaseki is the section of central Tokyo in which major Japanese government ministries are concentrated.

30. See, for example, National Institute for Research Advancement, "A Grand Design for Northeast Asia: National Land Planning and Sectoral Development Strategies," *NIRA Research Output,* No. 0602, 2006. Available http://www.nira.or.jp/past/publ/routp/html/n00602.html.

31. On Japan's Taiwan Lobby, see Motozawa Jiro, *Taiwan Lobby,* Tokyo: Datahouse, 1998, and "Taiwan Lobby Seiken no Shidoko," http://journalist-net.com.

32. On this campaign, seen in comparative international perspective, see Mari M. Calder, *Achieving Power without Power? The Politics of Japanese Immigrant Policy in Comparative Perspective,* unpublished Harvard College senior thesis, 2002.

33. In 1959 roughly 445,000 Korean residents of Japan were affiliated with North Korea (and hence loosely with Chosen Soren), compared with 174,000 for the ROK (and

hence Mindan). By 1969 that ratio had shifted to 298,000/310,000, and by 2009 to around 100,000/600,000. See Mindan website, http://www.mindan/org/eng.

34. The Lotte conglomerate runs hotels, department stores, credit-card companies, recreation complexes, food-product companies, and restaurants in both Japan and Korea, while also sponsoring its own baseball teams in both countries.

35. These include two MOFA affiliates, one METI affiliate, a JETRO affiliate, two Diet-member leagues, and a cultural-exchange body, all headed by prominent Japanese politicians and business leaders.

36. This network, which manages hostels for Chinese foreign students across Japan that also serve as locales for binational celebrations, lectures, and other meetings, is affiliated with Japan's Ministry of Foreign Affairs, and was chaired in 2009 by Hayashi Yoshio, a prominent former politician and METI official.

37. Wang Yi gave more than a hundred lectures during his three years as Chinese ambassador to Japan, frequently dined with the chairman of the *Nihon Keizai Shimbun* one on one, and joined Japanese political and business celebrities to promote energy-conservation and CO_2 emissions reduction—popular causes in Japan. See *BBC Worldwide Monitoring Asia-Pacific,* June 5, 2008.

38. Interestingly, positive sentiment toward China in Japan was concentrated among the elderly (over 70), while that toward Korea was strongest among Japanese in their 20s and their 40s. See Government of Japan Cabinet Office website, http:///ww8.cao.go.jp/survey/index-gai.html.

39. JETRO website, http://www.jetro.go.jp/egi bin/nato/ogi bin/search.ogi.

40. Toyoda Shoichiro, chairman of Toyota Motor Corporation, served also as chairman of Keidanren from 1994 to 1998, while his successor at Toyota, Okuda Hiroshi, also succeeded him at Keidanren (1999–2005), followed by Mitarai Fujio of Canon (2006–10).

41. See 2003 JETRO Annual Public Survey, www.jetro.org.jp.

42. See the Japanese MOFA website, http://mofa.go.jp/mofaj/gaiko/fta/j_korea/genjo.html.

43. See "MSDF Ship Docks at Chinese Port," *Japan Times Online,* June 25, 2009, http://search.japantimes.co.jp.

44. *International Herald Tribune,* June 7, 2009.

Chapter 10

1. *New York Times,* February 19, 2002.

2. See the address of U.S. secretary of defense Robert Gates at the Shangri La Dialogue in Singapore, May 30, 2009, http://www.defenselink.mil/home/features/2009/0609_gates1/.

3. See Zbigniew Brzezinski, *The Grand Chessboard: American Primacy and Its Geostrategic Imperatives,* New York: Basic Books, 1997, pp. 151–93.

4. In September 2005, the United States deployed 33,871 troops in Japan, and 30,683 in South Korea on a permanent basis. See U.S. Department of Defense, *Worldwide Manpower Distribution by Geographical Area,* 2005 edition. These were the largest U.S. forward deployments in the world, except for Germany and the wartime deployments in Iraq and Afghanista.

5. Peter J. Katzenstein, *A World of Regions: Asia and Europe in the American Imperium,* Ithaca, NY: Cornell University Press, 2005, p. 1.

6. Akira Iriye, *Across the Pacific: An Inner History of American-East Asian Relations* (rev. ed.), Chicago: Imprint Publications, 1992, p. 77.

7. John G. Roberts, *Mitsui: Three Centuries of Japanese Business,* New York: Weatherhill, 1973, p. 164.

8. On the early history of Western investment in Northeast Asia, see G. C. Allen and Audrey Donnithorne, *Western Enterprise in Far Eastern Economic Development: China and Japan,* London: Allen and Unwin, 1962.

9. Several early U.S. ambassadors to Japan, it might be noted, did have experience or close personal ties to the mainstream American business community, however. W. Cameron Forbes (1930–32) was a director of American Telephone and Trust prior to being sent to Tokyo, while his successor, Joseph Clark Grew (1932–41), was a cousin of J. Pierpont Morgan. See Roberts, *Mitsui,* pp. 314–15.

10. Iriye, *Across the Pacific,* pp. 80–81.

11. John K. Fairbanks, *The United States and China* (4th ed.), Cambridge: Harvard University Press, 1979, pp. 307–35.

12. Bruce Cumings, *Korea's Place in the Sun: A Modern History*, New York: Norton, 1997, pp. 86–138.

13. In all, Schiff helped Japan sell Americans four bond issues totaling almost $350 million, or nearly half the cost of the entire war for Tokyo. See Walter LaFeber, *The Clash: US-Japan Relations throughout History,* New York: W. W. Norton, 1997, p. 81.

14. Ibid., pp. 85–86.

15. On how this economics and security dualism unfolded over time, see Kent E. Calder, "U.S. Foreign Policy in Northeast Asia," in Samuel S. Kim (ed.), *The International Relations of Northeast Asia*, Lanham, MD: Rowman and Littlefield, 2004, pp. 225–50.

16. Calder, "Securing Security through Prosperity: The San Francisco System in Comparative Perspective," *Pacific Review,* Vol. 17, No. 1, March 2004, pp. 135–57.

17. See Michael Schaller, *Altered States: The United States and Japan since the Occupation,* New York: Oxford University Press, 1997, p. 33.

18. See James Baker, "America in Asia," *Foreign Affairs,* Winter 1991–92, pp. 1–18.

19. Katzenstein, *A World of Regions,* pp. 1–3.

20. See Calder, "Securing Security through Prosperity," pp. 135–57.

21. On the evolution of U.S. policies toward North Korea, and the domestic politics within the United States of that evolution, see Calder, *The North Korean Nuclear Crisis and American Policy*, Washington, DC: Reischauer Center for East Asian Studies, Asia-Pacific Policy Paper No. 1, 2005.

22. See Calder, "The New Face of Northeast Asia," *Foreign Affairs*, March/April 2001, pp. 106–23.

23. U.S. Census Bureau, *American Community Survey*, 2005 edition.

24. Some 4,916,000 U.S. residents were born in Europe, according to the 2000 Census, versus 8,226,000 born in Asia. See ibid.

25. Ibid.

26. See East West Center, *Asia Matters for America*, Washington, DC, www.asiamattersforamerica.org.

27. There were a total of 3.5 million American residents during 2000 who came from Asia, as opposed to 1.6 million who had emigrated from Europe. See ibid.

28. For details on distribution by state, together with broader state-specific data on trans-Pacific relations, see the excellent East-West Center data collection, http://www. asiamattersforamerica.org/index.cfm?event=page.search.

29. U.S. Census Bureau, *State and County Quick Facts,* http://quickfacts.census.gov, accessed July 15, 2009.

30. Korean American Coalition, *Population Change by Race and Ethnicity, 1990–2000: USA, California, Southern California, LA County, Orange County, Koreatown,* Los Angeles, July 2, 2003.

31. The ratios of Chinese Americans to Japanese Americans has also been shifting sharply, with the ratio of Chinese to Japanese in San Francisco having grown from 3.6 to 1 to 12 to 1 since 1980. See U.S. Census Bureau, *Census of Population,* 1990 and 1980 editions, as well as U.S. Census Bureau, *American Community Survey,* 2005 edition.

32. California has 55 electoral votes, with 270 required to elect a president of the United States. Its Asian American population in 2003 was, as noted above, around 12 percent of the state's total. See Michael Barone and Richard E. Cohen, *The Almanac of American Politics,* 2008 edition, Washington, DC: National Journal Group, 2007, pp. 141–49.

33. Office of Travel and Tourism, "Tourism Industries Publication: Outbound Profile 2006," July 2007, http://tinet.ita.gov/cat/f-2006-101-001.html, accessed April 1, 2008.

34. Nelly Furman, David Goldberg, and Natalia Lusin, "Enrollment in Languages Other than English in U.S. Institutions of Higher Education, Fall 2006," Modern Foreign Language Association of America, 2007, http://www.mla.org/2006_flenrollmentsurvey, accessed April 1, 2008.

35. National Center for Education Statistics, "Enrollment in Foreign Language Courses Compared with Enrollment in Grades 9–12 in Public Secondary Schools: Selected Years, Fall 1948–Fall 2000," April 2002, http://nces.ed.gov/programs/digest/d07/tables/dt07_053.asp, accessed April 1, 2008.

36. Opendoors Online: Reports on International Educational Exchange, "Americans Studying Abroad at Record Levels—Up 8.5%," November 12, 2007, http://opendoors. iienetwork.org/?p=113744, accessed April 1, 2008.

37. U.S. Department of Education Institute of Educational Sciences, *Digest of Educational Statistics,* 2006 edition.

38. During the 2006–7 academic year, 67,723 students from China, 62,392 from South Korea, and 35,282 from Japan were attending U.S. universities, according to the Institute of International Education. See *Japan Times,* January 18, 2008.

39. U.S. Department of State Bureau of Consular Affairs, *Report of the Visa Office,* http:// travel.state.gov/visa/report.html.

40. On the potential relation of transnational networks to U.S. national interest, see Anne-Marie Slaughter, "America's Edge: Power in the Networked Century," *Foreign Affairs,* January/February 2009, pp. 94–114. Slaughter, previously dean of the Woodrow Wilson School at Princeton University, served as State Department director of policy planning in the Obama administration from early 2009.

41. The two opened their joint venture in 1984, being touted as a way for GM to learn the Japanese method of "lean" manufacturing, focused on just-in-time delivery. "GM to Stop Making Cars in California," *Los Angeles Times,* June 30, 2009; "Toyota Closing Plant in California," *Metal Bulletin Weekly,* August 28, 2009.

42. On the details, see Calder, "The Emerging Politics of the Trans-Pacific Economy,"

World Policy Journal, Vol. II, No. 4, Fall 1985, pp. 595–623. President Barack Obama, of course, is the exception, although he grew up in Hawaii, before going to school in the Northeast and representing Illinois in the Senate, after serving as a community organizer and state senator there.

43. U.S. Department of Labor Bureau of Labor Statistics, *Union Member Summary*, January 28, 2009, http://www.bls.gov/news.release/union2.nro.htm.

44. Original data are from the Office of the U.S. Trade Representative, http://www.ustr.gov/countries-regions.

45. *Financial Times*, April 18, 2006.

46. *China Daily*, November 29, 2004, http://www.chinadaily.com.cn/english/doc/2004-11/29/content_395728.htm.

47. Ibid., March 21, 2006, http://www.chinadaily.com.cn/bizchina/2006-03/21/content_548509.htm.

48. "Walmart Stores Open Fast, Occupying Second and Third Tiered Cities." See www.sun0769.com/news/finance/t20090915_546264.shtml

49. See www.smh.com.au.

50. *People's Daily*, April 13, 2001; and http://china.seekingalpha.com/article/13942.

51. These figures are for 2005. See *Financial Times*, April 18, 2006.

52. See newsroom.cisco.com, July 6, 2006.

53. Edward Steinfeld, "The Capitalist Embrace: China Ten Years After," in *Crisis as Catalyst: Asia's Dynamic Political Economy*, Ithaca, NY: Cornell University Press, 2008, pp. 183–205.

54. See Calder, *Pacific Alliance: Reviving U.S.-Japan Relations*, New Haven: Yale University Press, 2009.

Chapter 11

1. Peter Katzenstein and Takashi Shiraishi, *Beyond Japan: The Dynamics of East Asian Regionalism*, Ithaca, NY: Cornell University Press, 2006; T. J. Pempel (ed.), *Remapping East Asia: Construction of a Region*, Ithaca, NY: Cornell University Press, 2005; and Mark Beeson, *Regionalism & Globalization in East Asia*, New York: Palgrave Macmillan, 2007. On broader Asian regionalism, see Vinod Aggarwal and Min Gyo Koo (eds.), *Asia's New Institutional Architecture*, Springer, 2008; and Ellen Frost, *Asia's New Regionalism,* Boulder, CO: Lynne Rienner, 2008; as well as Andrew MacIntyre, Pempel, and John Ravenhill, *Crisis and Catalyst: Asia's Dynamic Political Economy*, Ithaca, NY: Cornell University Press, 2008.

2. Katzenstein and Shiraishi (eds.), *Network Power: Japan and Asia*, Ithaca, NY: Cornell University Press, 1997.

3. See, for example, "Sanyo-Haier Group Alliance Offers Lucrative Footholds," *Nikkei Weekly*, January 15, 2002; "Sanyo-Haier JV Boosting Sales," *Nikkei Weekly*, March 3, 2003; "Sanyo Eyes 30% Cost Cut after Fridge Tie-up," *Nikkei Weekly*, November 5, 2006; "Sanyo, Samsung Ally on Fuel Cell," *Asahi Shimbun*, January 12, 2002; "TCL Builds on Japanese Links; Toshiba and Sumitomo Take Stakes in Guangdong-based Consumer Electronics Firm," *South China Morning Post*, April 18, 2002; "Samsung Agrees to Cooperate with Mitsubishi on Washing Machines," *Business Korea*, March 22, 2002; and "SONY Courts Its Rival, Samsung," *International Herald Tribune*, July 26, 2005.

4. The U.S. House of Representatives passed a resolution of censure of Japanese prime minister Abe Shinzo's ill-considered remarks, while Chinese and South Korean

officials remained largely silent, despite their presumed outrage. See "Mistaken View of History Must Be Corrected," *Daily Yomiuri*, August 2, 2007; "Japan Should Ponder over U.S. Comfort Women Bill," *www.china.daily.cn*, August 7, 2007; "U.S. Lawmakers Condemn Japan 'Human Trafficking,'" *Korea Times*, September 15, 2006.

5. On the importance of multitiering in influencing the incentive structures of participants in regional integration, see Aggarwal and Charles Morrison (eds.), *Asia-Pacific Cross Roads: Regime Creation and the Future of APEC*, Palgrave Macmillan, 1998.

6. Kent E. Calder, *Stabilizing the U.S.-Japan-China Strategic Triangle*, Washington, DC: SAIS Reischauer Center for East Asian Studies, Asia-Pacific Policy Paper No. 4, 2005, p. 10.

7. The strategic embargo administered against Communist China and North Korea was much more comprehensive and strict than that in Europe. See J. Wilczynski, "Strategic Embargo in Perspective," *Soviet Studies*, Vol. 19, No. 1, July 1967, pp. 74–86; and Shu Zhang, *Economic Cold War: The American Embargo against China and the Sino-Soviet Alliance, 1949–1963*, Stanford University Press, 2002.

8. See Pempel (ed.), *Remapping East Asia;* Katzenstein and Shiraishi, *Network Power;* and Katzenstein and Shiraishi (eds.), *Beyond Japan*.

9. Barry Naughton, *Greater China: Economics and Electronics in PRC, Taiwan, and Hong Kong*, Washington, DC: Brookings Institution Press, 1997; David Lampton, *The Three Faces of Chinese Power: Might, Money, and Minds*, Berkeley: University of California, 2008; and Robert Ross and Feng Zhu, *China's Ascent: Power, Security, and the Future of International Politics*, Ithaca, NY: Cornell University Press.

10. Walter Mattli, *The Logic of Regional Integration: Europe and Beyond*, Cambridge: Cambridge University Press, 1999, p. 13.

11. For a discussion of how the stance of Chinese elites on regionalist issues began to change during the late 1990s, see Li Cheng, "China in 1999: Seeking Common Ground at a Time of Tension and Conflict," *Asian Survey*, Vol. 40, No. 2, 2000, pp. 111–22.

12. Katzenstein and Shiraishi, *Network Power.*

13. See "A Bond Market for East Asia? The Evolving Political Dynamics of Regional Financial Cooperation," *Pacific Economic Papers*, No. 342, Australia-Japan Research Centre, Australian National University, 2004; William Grimes, "East Asian Financial Regionalism and U.S. National Interest," E-Note, Foreign Policy Research Institute, April 2006, http://www.fpri.org/enotes/200604.asia.grimes.eastasianfinancialregionalism.html.

14. Giovanni Capoccia and Daniel Klemen, "The Study of Critical Junctures: Theory, Narrative, and Counterfactuals in Historical Institutionalism," *World Politics*, Vol. 59, No. 3, April 2007. On both theory and application in East Asia, see also our previous piece, Calder and Min Ye, "Critical Junctures and Comparative Regionalism," *Journal of East Asian Studies*, Vol. 4, 2004, pp. 191–226.

15. Stefan Schirm, *Globalization and the New Regionalism*, Cambridge: Polity, 2002.

16. See Katzenstein and Shiraishi, *Network Power;* and Edward Lincoln, *East Asian Economic Regionalism*, Washington, DC: Brookings Institution Press, 2004.

17. See Katzenstein and Shiraishi, *Beyond Japan.*

18. On this point, we differ to some extent from David Kang's pronounced emphasis on China's emerging centrality in Northeast Asia, especially in view of recent political changes in Korea. See David Kang, *China Rising: Peace, Power, and Order in East Asia*, New York: Columbia University Press, 2007; and Calder, "Small States as Catalysts in Regional

Integration: Can Korea Be Northeast Asia's Benelux?" Washington, DC: American Political Science Association Annual Convention, 2005.

19. In 2007, Japan's GDP in nominal terms was $4.3 trillion, compared with China's $3.2 trillion. In 2008, Japan's GDP had reached $4.8 trillion, and China's $4.22 trillion, according to CIA figures. See *CIA World Factbook*, 2009.

20. Robert Keohane and Joseph Nye, *Power and Interdependence*, Boston: Little Brown, 1977.

21. Calder, "Small States as Catalysts in Regional Integration."

22. See, for example, Mattli, *The Logic of Regional Integration,* p. 14.

23. The Japan-based carry trade, in which multinational institutions, especially hedge funds, borrow at low interest in Japanese yen and lend broadly at higher rates around the world, is also important, but volatile, episodic, and essentially unsystemic.

24. For details on how such broadening in the political foundations of alliance might be achieved, see Calder, *Pacific Alliance: Reviving U.S.-Japan Relations,* New Haven: Yale University Press, 2009.

25. Marcus Noland, *Avoiding the Apocalypse: The Future of the Two Koreas,* Washington, DC: Institute for International Economics, June 2000, p. 308.

26. On the prospective value of multilateralism in Northeast Asia, see Francis Fukuyama, "Re-Envisioning Asia," *Foreign Affairs,* January/February 2005, pp. 75–87; as well as Calder and Fukuyama (eds.), *East Asian Multilateralism,* Baltimore: Johns Hopkins University Press, 2008.

Bibliography

Acharya, Amitav. "Ideas, Identity, and Institution-Building: From the ASEAN Way to the Asia-Pacific Way?" *Pacific Review,* Vol. 10, No. 3, 1997, pp. 319–30.

———. *Whose Ideas Matter? Agency and Power in Asian Regionalism.* Ithaca, NY: Cornell University Press, 2009.

———. "Will Asia's Past Be Its Future?" *International Security,* Vol. 28, No. 3, Winter 2003/4, pp. 149–64.

Acharya, Amitav, and Alastair Iain Johnston. *Crafting Cooperation: Regional International Institutions in Comparative Perspective.* Cambridge: Cambridge University Press, 2007.

Acheson, Dean. *Present at the Creation: My Years at the State Department.* London: Hamish Hamilton, 1969.

Aggarwal, Vinod, and Min Gyo Koo (eds.). *Asia's New Institutional Architecture: Evolving Structures for Managing Trade, Financial, and Security Relations.* Springer, 2008.

Aggarwal, Vinod K., and Charles Morrison. *Asia Pacific Crossroads.* New York: St. Martin's Press, 1998.

Allen, G. C., and Audrey Donnithorne. *Western Enterprise in Far Eastern Economic Development: China and Japan.* London: Allen and Unwin, 1962.

Allison, Graham, and Philip Zelikow. *Essence of Decision,* 2d ed. New York: Longman, 1999.

Arase, David (ed.). *Japan's Foreign Aid: Old Continuities and New Directions.* London: Routledge, 2005.

Armstrong, Charles, Gilbert Rozman, Samuel Kim, and Stephen Kotkin (eds.). *Korea at the Center: Dynamics of Regionalism in Northeast Asia.* New York: M. E. Sharpe, 2006.

Asahi Shimbun Sha. *Japan Almanac,* 2003 ed. Tokyo: Asahi Shimbun Sha, 2002.

Asian Development Bank. *Emerging Asian Regionalism: A Partnership for Shared Prosperity.* Manila: Asian Development Bank, 2008.

Asian Development Bank, Japan Bank for International Cooperation, and World Bank. *Connecting East Asia: A New Framework for Infrastructure.* Manila: Asian Development Bank, 2005.

Aydin, Cemil. *The Politics of Anti-Westernism in Asia.* New York: Columbia University Press, 2007.

Bae, Kichan. *Korea at the Crossroads: The History and Future of East Asia.* Seoul: Happy Reading Books, 2007.

Baker, James. "America in Asia." *Foreign Affairs,* Winter 1991–92, pp. 1–18.

Bernard, Mitchell, and John Ravenhill. "Beyond Product Cycles and Flying Geese: Regionalization, Hierarchy, and the Industrialization of East Asia." *World Politics,* Vol. 47, No. 2, 1995.

Binder, Leonard, et al. *Crises and Sequences in Political Development.* Princeton: Princeton University Press, 1971.

Borrus, Michael, Dieter Ernst, and Stephan Haggard (eds.). *International Production Networks in Asia: Rivalry or Riches.* London: Routledge, 2000.

Bowles, Paul. "Asia's Post-Crisis Regionalism: Bringing the State Back In, Keeping the United States Out." *Review of International Political Economy,* Vol. 9, No. 2, May 2002, pp. 230–56.

Breslin, Shaun, et al. *New Regionalisms in the Global Political Economy.* New York: Routledge, 2002.

Brzezinski, Zbigniew. *The Grand Chessboard: American Primacy and Its Geostrategic Imperatives.* New York: Basic Books, 1997.

Cai, Kevin. "Is a Free Trade Zone Emerging in Northeast Asia in the Wake of the Asian Financial Crisis?" *Pacific Affairs,* Vol. 74, No. 1, Spring 2001.

Calder, Kent E. "China and Japan's Simmering Rivalry." *Foreign Affairs,* March/April 2006, pp. 129–39.

———. "Regionalism, Alliance, and Domestic Politics: The Benelux Model and Northeast Asian Cooperation." *International Journal of Korean Unification Studies,* Vol. 15, No. 1, 2006, pp. 1–29.

———. *Korea's Energy Insecurities: Comparative and International Perspectives.* Washington, DC: Korea Economic Institute, 2005.

———. *The North Korean Nuclear Crisis and American Policy.* Washington, DC: Reischauer Center for East Asian Studies, Asia-Pacific Policy Paper No. 1, 2005.

———. *Japan's Stealth Reform: The Key Role of Political Process.* Washington, DC: Reischauer Center for East Asian Studies, 2005.

———. "Securing Security through Prosperity: The San Francisco System in Comparative Perspective." *Pacific Review,* Vol. 17, No. 1, January 2004, pp. 135–57.

———. "Japan as a Post-Reactive State?" *Orbia,* Fall 2003, pp. 605–16.

———. "The New Face of Northeast Asia." *Foreign Affairs,* January/February 2001, pp. 106–23.

———. *Crisis and Compensation.* Princeton: Princeton University Press, 1988.

———. "Japanese Foreign Economic Policy Formation: Explaining the Reactive State." *World Politics,* Vol. 40, No. 4, July 1988, pp. 517–41.

———. "The Emerging Politics of the Trans-Pacific Economy." *World Policy Journal,* Vol. 2, No. 4, Fall 1985, pp. 595–623.

Calder, Kent E., and Francis Fukuyama (eds.). *East Asian Multilateralism.* Baltimore, MD: Johns Hopkins University Press, 2008.

Calder, Kent E., and Roy Hofheinz, Jr. *The Eastasia Edge.* New York: Basic Books, 1982.

Calder, Kent E., and Min Ye. "Critical Junctures and Comparative Regionalism." *Journal of East Asian Studies*, Vol. 4, 2004, pp. 191–226.

Calder, Mari M. *Achieving Power without Power? The Politics of Japanese Immigration Policy in Comparative Perspective*. Unpublished Harvard College Honors Thesis, 2002.

Camilleri, Joseph. *Regionalism in the New Asia-Pacific Order: Political Economy of the Asian Pacific Region*. Northampton: Edward Elgar, 2003.

Capoccia, Giovanni, and Daniel Klemen, "The Study of Critical Junctures: Theory, Narrative, and Counterfactuals in Historical Institutionalism." *World Politics*, Vol. 59, No. 3, April 2007.

Central Headquarters of the All Japan Association of Koreans [Zainihon Daikanmin Koku Mindan Chuo Honbu] (ed.). *Zuhyo de miru Kankoku Mindan 50 Nen no Ayumi* [A Visual 50 Year History of the Association of Korean People]. Tokyo: Satsuki Shobo, 1997.

Chamberlin, William Henry. *Japan over Asia*. Boston: Little Brown, 1937.

Chen, Jian. *Mao's China and the Cold War*. Chapel Hill: University of North Carolina Press, 2001.

Cho, Lee Jae (ed.). *A Vision for Economic Cooperation in East Asia: China, Japan, and Korea*. Seoul: Korea Development Institute, 2003.

Christensen, Thomas. "The Party Transition: Will It Bring a New Maturity in China's Security Policy?" *China Leadership Monitor*, Winter 2003, No. 5.

————. "Optimistic Trends and Near Term Challenges." *China Leadership Monitor*, Spring 2003, No. 6.

————. *Useful Adversary: Grand Strategy, Domestic Mobilization, and Sino-American Conflict, 1947–1958*. Princeton: Princeton University Press, 1996.

Chu, Shulong. "Lengzhan hou zhongguo zhanlue sixiang de fazhan" ["Development of China's Strategic Thinking after the Cold War"]. *Shijie jinji yu zhengzhi* [*World Economics and Politics*], No. 9, 1999, pp. 11–15.

Chung, Jae-ho. *Between Ally and Partner: Korea-China Relations and the United States*. New York: Columbia University Press, 2006.

————. "South Korea between Eagle and Dragon: Perceptual Ambivalence and Strategic Dilemma." *Asian Survey*, Vol. 41, No. 5, September–October 2001, pp. 777–96.

Chyon, Ingyo. *Nichukan FTA no Kanosei to Sankakoku no Taigai Tsusho Seisaku* [*The Possibility of a China-Japan-Korea FTA and the Foreign Commercial Policies of the Three Countries*]. Tokyo: Vista P.S., 2004.

Cohen, Stephen. "Mapping Asian Integration: Transnational Transactions in the Pacific Rim." *American Asian Review*, Vol. 20, No. 3, Fall 2002, pp. 1–30.

Cooper, Andrew et al. *Regionalization and Global Governance*. New York: Routledge, 2008.

Craig, Albert M. *Civilization and Enlightenment: The Early Thought of Fukuzawa Yukichi*. Cambridge: Harvard University Press, 2009.

Crone, Donald. "Does Hegemony Matter? The Regionalization of the Pacific Economy." *World Politics*, Vol. 45, No. 4, 1993.

Cronin, Richard. "Asian Financial Crisis: An Analysis of U.S. Foreign Policy Interests and Options." CRS Report to the Congress, January 28, 1998.

Cumings, Bruce. *Korea's Place in the Sun: A Modern History*. New York: W. W. Norton, 1997.

————. "The Origins and Development of the Northeast Asian Political Economy: Industrial Sectors, Product Cycles, and Political Consequences." *International Organization*, Vol. 38, No. 1, 1984.

Deng, Xiaoping. *Deng Xiaoping Wenxuan* [*Selected Works of Deng Xiaoping*]. Beijing: Xinhua Publisher, 1993.

Deutsch, Karl, et al. *Political Community and the North Atlantic Area*, Princeton: Princeton University Press, 1957.

Dower, John W. *Embracing Defeat*. New York: W. W. Norton/New Press, 1999.

———. *War without Mercy: Race and Power in the Pacific War.* New York: Pantheon Books, 1986.

Evans, Paul. "Regional Institutions, Regional Identities." In Colin Mackerras (ed.), *Eastern Asia: An Introductory History*. Melbourne, Australia: Longman, 2000.

Evans, Peter. *Embedded Autonomy.* Princeton: Princeton University Press, 1994.

Farell, Mary, et al. *Global Politics of Regionalism*. London: Pluto Press, 2005.

Feng, Shaokui, and Lin Xu. *Zhongri guanxi baogao* [*A Report on China-Japan Relationship*]. Beijing: Shishi Publisher, 2007.

Fort, Bertrand, and Douglass Webber (eds.). *Regional Integration in Europe and East Asia*. New York: Routledge, 2006.

Friedberg, Aaron. "Europe's Past: Asia's Future?" *Survival*, Vol. 42, No. 3, Autumn 2000, pp. 147–59.

———. "Ripe for Rivalry: Prospects for Peace in Multipolar Asia." *International Security*, Vol. 18, No. 3, 1993, pp. 5–33.

Frieden, Jeffrey. *Debt, Development and Democracy*. Princeton University Press, 1992.

Frost, Ellen. *Asia's New Regionalism*. Boulder, CO: Lynne Rienner, 2008.

Fukushima, Akiko. *Japan and Multilateral Diplomacy*. New York: St. Martin's Press, 1999.

Fukuyama, Francis. "Re-Envisioning Asia." *Foreign Affairs*, January/February 2005.

Fukuzawa, Yukichi. *The Autobiography of Fukuzawa Yukichi*. Revised translation by E. Kiyooka. New York: Columbia University Press, 1966.

Funabashi, Yoichi, "The Asianization of Asia." *Foreign Affairs*, Vol. 72, No. 5, November–December 1993.

Gamble, Andrew, and Anthony Payne. *Regionalism and World Order*. New York: St. Martin's Press, 1996.

Garran, Robert. *Tigers Tamed: The End of the Asian Miracle*. St Leonard's, Australia: Allen and Unwin, 1998.

Garver, John W. *The Sino-American Alliance: Nationalist China and America's Cold War Strategy in Asia*. Armonk, NY: M. E. Sharpe, 1997.

Glaser, Bonnie, and Evan Medeiros. "The Changing Ecology of Chinese Foreign Policy Making: The Ascension and Demise of Peaceful Rise Theory." *China Quarterly*, No. 190, 2007, pp. 291–310.

Godement, Francois. *The New Asian Renaissance: From Colonialism to the Post-Cold War*. London: Routledge, 1997.

Goncharov, Sergei, John W. Lewis, and Xue Litai. *Uncertain Partners: Stalin, Mao, and the Korean War,* Stanford: Stanford University Press, 1993.

Gourevitch, Peter. *Politics in Hard Times*. Ithaca, NY: Cornell University Press, 1986.

Graham, Edward. *Reforming Korea's Industrial Conglomerates*. Washington, DC: Institute of International Economics, 2003.

Green, Michael J., and Bates Gill (eds.). *Asia's New Multilateralism: Cooperation, Conflict, and the Search for Community*. New York: Columbia University Press, 2009.

Gregory, Gene. *Japanese Electronics Technology: Enterprise and Innovation.* Tokyo: Japan Times, 1985.

Grimes, William W. *Currency and Conflict in East Asia: The Great Power Politics of Financial Regionalism.* Ithaca, NY: Cornell University Press, 2009.

Guan, Jian. "Dongnanya jinrong weiji tantao guandian zongshu" ["Analyzing the Southeast Asian Financial Crisis"]. *Dongnanya yanjiu* [*Southeast Asian Studies*], Vol. 6, 1998, pp. 22–24.

Haas, Ernest. "The Challenge of Regionalism." *International Organization,* Vol. 12, No. 4, Autumn 1958, pp. 440–58.

Haas, Peter. "Epistemic Community and International Policy Coordination." *International Organization,* Vol. 46, No. 1, 1992: 1–35.

———. *Saving the Mediterranean.* New York: Columbia University Press, 1990.

Hachi Ichi San Saiban Kiroku Saikan Iinkai. *Wana* (Trap). Tokyo: Bansei Sha, 2006.

Haftendorn, Helga, Robert Keohane, and Celeste Wallander (eds.). *Imperfect Unions: Security Institutions over Time and Space.* New York: Oxford University Press, 1999.

Haggard, Stephan. *The Political Economy of the Asian Financial Crisis.* Washington, DC: Institute for International Economics, 2000.

———. "Thinking about Regionalism: The Politics of Minilateralism in Asia and the Americas." Paper presented at the annual meeting of the APSA, New York, September 1–4, 1994.

Halberstam, David. *The Coldest Winter: America and the Korean War.* New York: Hyperion Books, 2007.

Hatano, Masaru, and Shimizu Rei. *Yuko no Kakehashi o Yume Mite* [*Viewing a Dream Crossing the Bridge of Friendship*]. Tokyo: Gakuyo Shobou, 2004.

Hay, Stephen. *Asian Ideas of East and West: Tagore and His Critics in Japan, China, and India.* Cambridge: Harvard University Press, 1970.

He, Baogang. "East Asian Ideas of Regionalism: A Normative Critique." *Australian Journal of International Affairs,* Vol. 58, No. 1, 2004, pp. 105–25.

Helpman, Elhanan. "Imperfect Competition and International Trade." *Journal of Japanese and International Economics,* Vol. 1, 1987, pp. 62–81.

Helpman, E., and Paul Krugman. *Market Structure and Foreign Trade.* Cambridge: MIT Press, 1985.

Hemmer, Christopher, and Peter J. Katzenstein. "Why Is There No NATO in Asia? Collective Identity, Regionalism, and the Origin of Multilateralism." *International Organization,* Vol. 56, No. 3, Summer 2002, pp. 575–607.

Henning, Randall. *East Asian Financial Cooperation.* Washington, DC: Institute for International Economics, 2002.

Honzawa, Jiro. *Taiwan Lobby.* Tokyo: Data House, 1998.

Hook, Glenn, and Ian Kearn. *Sub-Regionalism and World Order.* New York: Macmillan Press, 1999.

Hu, Angang. *Wending yu fazhan* [*Stability and Development*]. Beijing: Renmin Publishers, 2005.

———. *Zhongguo da zhanlue* [*The Grand Strategy of China*]. Hangzhou: Zhejiang Remin Publisher, 2003.

Huang, Dehong, and Jiu Tianjin. "Yazhou jinrong weiji toushi ji xiangying duice" ["The

Asian Financial Crisis and China's Response"]. *Dongnanya yanjiu* [*Southeast Asian Studies*], Vol. 2, 1998, pp. 4–5.

Huang, Ping. "Dongbeiya diyuan zhengzhi tedian yu zhonghan jingmao guanxi" ["Geostrategic Features of Northeast Asia and Sino-Korean Economic Cooperation"]. *Renwen dili* [*Culture and Geography*], No. 1, 1997, pp. 29–33.

Ikenberry, John. *After Victory*. Princeton: Princeton University Press, 2001.

Ikenberry, John, and Chung-In Moon (eds.). *The United Sates and Northeast Asia: Debates, Issues, and New Order*. Lanham, MD: Rowman & Littlefield, 2008.

Iriye, Akira. *The Cold War in Asia: A Historical Introduction*. Englewood Cliffs, NJ: Prentice-Hall, 1974.

Ishii, Kenichiro. *Higashi Ajia ni okeru Nihon no Popu Bunka* [*Japanese Pop Culture in East Asia*]. Tokyo: Sousou Sha, 2001.

Jayasuriya, Kanishka. *Governing Asia-Pacific: Beyond the New Regionalism*. Hampshire, UK: Palgrave Macmillan, 2004.

Jeong, Kap-Young, and Kwan-Kyoo Choe. "Northeast Asian Economic Regionalism: A Korean View." *Global Economic Review*, Vol. 30, No. 1, 2001, pp. 103–19.

Jervis, Robert. "The Impact of the Korean War on the Cold War." *Journal of Conflict Resolution*, Vol. 24, No. 4, December 1980.

Johnson, Chalmers. *MITI and the Japanese Miracle*. Stanford: Stanford University Press, 1982.

Kaminsky, Graciela, and Carmen Reinhart. "The Twin Crises: The Causes of Banking and Balance-of-Payments Problems." *American Economic Review*, Vol. 89, No. 3, June 1999.

Kang, David. *China Rising: Peace, Power, and Order in East Asia*. New York: Columbia University Press, 2008.

———. "Getting Asia Wrong." *International Security*, Vol. 27, No. 4, Spring 2003, pp. 57–85.

Katzenstein, Peter. *A World of Regions: Asia and Europe in the American Imperium*. Ithaca, NY: Cornell University Press, 2005.

———. "Regionalism in Comparative Perspective." *Cooperation and Conflict*, Vol. 31, 1996.

———. *The Culture of National Security*. New York: Columbia University Press, 1996.

Katzenstein, Peter, and Takashi Shiraishi (eds.). *Beyond Japan: The Dynamics of East Asian Regionalism*. Ithaca, NY: Cornell University Press, 2006.

——— (eds.). *Network Power*. Ithaca, NY: Cornell University Press, 1997.

Kawai, Masahiro. "Exchange Rate Arrangements in East Asia: Lessons from the 1997–98 Currency Crisis." *Monetary and Economic Studies*, December 2002.

Keohane, Robert. *After Hegemony: Cooperation and Discord in the World Political Economy*. Princeton: Princeton University Press, 1984.

———. "The Big Influence of Small Allies." *Foreign Policy*, Vol. 2, 1971, pp. 161–82.

Kikuchi, Tsutomu. "East Asian Regionalism: A Look at the 'ASEAN plus Three' Framework." *Japan Review of International Affairs*, Spring 2002, pp. 1–23.

Kim, Chan-jung. *Chosen Soren* [*The General Association of Koreans*]. Tokyo: Shincho Sha, 2004.

Kim, Samuel S. (ed.). *The International Relations of Northeast Asia*. Lanham, MD: Rowman and Littlefield, 2004.

Kirk, Donald. *The Korean Crisis: Unraveling the Miracle in the IMF Era*. Palgrave Macmillan, 2000.

Kobayashi,Yotaro. "Nihon: Sai Ajia-ka" ["The Re-Asianization of Japan"]. *Foresight*, April 1991, pp. 44–46.

Kohara, Masahiro. *Higashi Ajia Kyodotai: Kyodaika suru Chugoku to Nihon no Senryaku [The East Asian Community: Growing Chinese Power and Japanese Strategy]*. Tokyo: Nihon Keizai Shimbun Sha, 2005.

Korea Herald (ed.). *Korean Wave*. Seoul: Jimoondang, 2008.

Korean Institute for International Economic Policy (ed.). *Financial Hub in Northeast Asia: Road to Prosperity and Cooperation*. Seoul: KIEP, 2006.

Krasner, Stephen. "Approaches to the State." *Comparative Politics*, January 1984, pp. 223–46.

——— (ed.). *International Regimes*. Ithaca, NY: Cornell University Press, 1983.

Krugman, Kathie, and Homi Karas (eds.). *East Asia Integrates: A Trade Policy Agenda for Shared Growth*. Washington, DC: World Bank, 2003.

Krugman, Paul. "Intra-Industry Specialization and Gains from Trade." *Journal of Political Economy*, Vol. 89, 1981, pp. 959–73.

Kurth, James. "The Pacific Basin versus the Atlantic Alliance." *Annals AAPSS*, Vol. 505, 1989.

Kwan, Chi-hung. "The Economics of a Yen Bloc." Washington, DC: Brookings Institution and Nomura Research Institute, June 2000.

LaFeber,Walter. *The Clash: US-Japan Relations throughout History*. New York: W. W. Norton, 1997.

Lampton, David (ed.). *The Three Faces of Chinese Power: Might, Money, and Minds*. Berkeley: University of California, 2008.

———. *The Making of Chinese Foreign and Security Policy in the Era of Reform, 1978–2000*. Stanford: Stanford University Press, 2001.

Lee, Chang-jae. "Northeast Asian Economic Cooperation: The Need for a New Approach." *NIRA Review*, Autumn 2000, pp. 5–10.

Lee, Steven Hugh. *The Korean War*. London: Longman, 2001.

Leifer, Michael. *Singapore's Foreign Policy: Coping with Vulnerability*. London: Routledge, 2000.

Levy, Jack. "Organizational Routines and the Causes of War." *International Studies Quarterly*, Vol. 30, 1986.

Li, Cheng. "A Pivotal Stepping Stone: Provincial Leaders' Representation at the 17th Party Congress." *China Leadership Monitor*, No. 23, Winter 2008.

———. "China in 1999: Seeking Common Ground at a Time of Tension and Conflict." *Asian Survey*, Vol. 40, No. 2, 2000, pp. 111–22.

Li, Wen. *Dongya hezuo de wenhua chengyin [Cultural Roots of East Asian Cooperation]*. Beijing: World Knowledge Press, 2005.

Lim, Hoa Shin, Hama Katsuhiko, and Shibutani Yu (eds.). *Ajia Keizai Hatten no Achilles Ken [The Achilles Heel of Asian Economic Development]*. Tokyo: Bunmeido, 2008.

Lincoln, Edward. *East Asian Economic Regionalism*. Washington, DC: Brookings Institution Press, 2004.

Lipscy, Phillip Y. "Japan's Asian Monetary Fund Proposal." *Stanford Journal of East Asian Affairs*, Vol. 3, No. 1, Spring 2003, pp. 93–104.

Liu, J. "Ziyou zhuyi yu gongzheng" ["Justice Is Embedded in a Market Distribution of Income"]. *Dangdai Zhongguo yanjiu [Contemporary China Studies]*, No. 4, 2000, pp. 50–67.

Liu, Liyun. "Ruhe kandai lengzhan hou yatai anquan ji zhongguo de yingxiang" ["How to Conceptualize Post-Cold War Asian Pacific Security and China"]. *Jiaoxue yu yanjiu* [*Teaching and Research*], No. 6, 2000, pp. 50–55.

Liu, Tao. *Zhongguo jueqi ce* [*China's Strategy of Rise*]. Beijing: Xinhua Publisher, 2007.

Liu, Yizhen, and Xie Chaoyang. "Dongya huobi hezuo yu renminbi huilu zhidu xuanze" ["East Asian Currency Cooperation and Choices for the RMB Exchange Rate System"]. *Management World*, Vol. 3, 2000.

Long, Guoqiang. "New Development in China's Regional Cooperative Policy: From APEC to CAFTA." *China's Public Policy Report,* Beijing, 2004.

Ma, Licheng, "Zhongri xin siwei" ["New Perspectives on Sino-Japan Relations—Worrisome Nationalism"]. *Zhanlue yu guanli* [*Strategy and Management*], No. 6, 2002, pp. 41–47.

MacIntyre, Andrew, T. J. Pempel, and John Ravenhill (eds.). *Crisis as Catalyst: Asia's Dynamic Political Economy.* Ithaca, NY: Cornell University Press, 2008.

Mackie, Jamie. *Bandung 1955: Non-Alignment and Afro-Asian Solidarity.* Singapore: Editions Didier Millet, 2005.

Mahathir, Muhamed, and Ishihara Shintaro. *The Voice of Asia: Two Leaders Discuss the Coming Century.* Tokyo: Kodansha, 1995.

Mann, Jim. *About Face: A History of America's Curious Relations with China, from Nixon to Clinton.* New York: Alfred Knopf, 1999.

March, James, and Herbert Simon. *Organizations,* 2d ed. Cambridge: Blackwell Publishers, 1993.

Marchand, Marianne. "Informal Regionalization in the Context of NAFTA: From Cross-Border Alliances to Cross-Border Identities?" Paper presented at the 4th International Congress of the Americas, Puebla, September 29–October 2, 1999.

Mattli, Walter. *The Logic of Regional Integration: Europe and Beyond.* Cambridge: Cambridge University Press, 1999.

McCullough, David. *Truman,* New York: Simon & Schuster, 1992.

McGovern, James. *To the Yalu: From the Chinese Invasion of Korea to MacArthur's Dismissal.* New York: William Morrow, 1972.

Meyer, Milton. *A Diplomatic History of the Philippine Republic.* Honolulu: University of Hawaii Press, 1965.

Milner, Helen, and E. Mansfield. *The Political Economy of Regionalism.* New York: Columbia University Press, 1997.

Milner, Robert S., and Diane K. Mauzy. *Malaysian Politics under Mahathir.* Routledge, 1999.

Mitrany, David. *A Working Peace System.* Chicago: Quadrangle Books, 1961.

Moravcsik, Andrew. *The Choice for Europe.* Ithaca, NY: Cornell University Press, 1998.

Motozawa, Jiro. *Taiwan Lobby.* Tokyo: Datahouse, 1998.

Naito, Konan. "Konan Naito's East Asian History." In Song Chengyou and Tang Chongnan (eds.), *Asian Regional Identity and Peaceful Development.* Chengdu: Sichuan University Press, 2001.

National Institute for Research Advancement (NIRA). *Grand Design for Stability and Prosperity in Northeast Asia.* Tokyo: KRI International Corporation, 2003.

Naughton, Barry. *Greater China: Economics and Electronics in PRC, Taiwan, and Hong Kong.* Brookings Institution Press, 1997.

Nemoto, Yoichi. *An Unexpected Outcome of Asian Financial Crisis.* Princeton: Princeton University Program on US-Japan Relations Occasional Paper, June 2003.

Noble, Gregory W., and John Ravenhill (eds.). *The Asian Financial Crisis and the Architecture of Global Finance.* Cambridge: Cambridge University Press, 2000.

Noland, Marcus. *Avoiding the Apocalypse: The Future of the Two Koreas.* Washington, DC: Institute for International Economics, June 2000.

Nye, Joseph. *Pan-Africanism and East African Integration.* Cambridge: Harvard University Press, 1965.

Ogura, Kazuo. "Toward a New Concept of Asia." *International Politics,* Vol. 8, No. 4, Winter 2007.

Okakura, Kakuzo. *The Awakening of Japan: The Book of Tea* [*Tenshin Zenshu*]. Kyoto: Sogensha, 1961.

Oliver, Robert T. *Syngman Rhee and American Involvement in Korea, 1942–1960.* Seoul: Panmun Book Company, 1978.

Olson, Mancur. *The Logic of Collective Action.* New York: Schocken Books, 1965.

Pai, Guohua, and Zhang Xizheng (eds.). *Dongya diqu hezuo yu hezuo jizhi* [*Regional Cooperation and Mechanism in East Asia*]. Beijing: Central Compliance and Translations Press, 2002.

Paige, Glenn. *The Korean Decision,* New York: Free Press, 1968

Paik, Keun-wook. *Gas and Oil in Northeast Asia: Politics, Projects, and Prospects.* London: Royal Institute of International Affairs, 1995.

Pempel, T. J. (ed.). *Remapping East Asia: The Construction of a Region.* Ithaca, NY: Cornell University Press, 2005.

———. (ed.). *The Politics of the Asian Financial Crisis.* Ithaca, NY: Cornell University Press, 1999.

Pempel, T. J., and Ellis Krauss (eds.). *Beyond Bilateralism: Japan-U.S. Relations in the New Asia-Pacific.* Stanford: Stanford University Press, 2003.

Peng Dajin. "Invisible Linkages: A Regional Perspective on East Asian Political Economy." *International Studies Quarterly,* Vol. 46, 2002.

Pierson, P. "The Path to European Integration: A Historical Institutionalist Analysis." *Comparative Political Studies,* Vol. 29, No. 2, 1996, pp. 126–63.

Polsby, Nelson. *Political Innovation in America: The Politics of Policy Innovation.* New Haven: Yale University Press, 1984.

Presidential Committee on Northeast Asian Cooperation Initiative. *Toward a Peaceful and Prosperous Northeast Asia.* Seoul: Office of the President, Republic of Korea, 2004.

Qi, Wenhai, et al. *Dongbeiya jingmao hezuo quanfangwei yanjiu* [*Northeast Asian Economic Cooperation*]. Beijing: Social Science Publisher, 2006.

Ravenhill, John. "The Growth of China's Automotive Industry and Its Impact on Production Networks in East Asia." Working Paper, Australia National University, 2005.

———. "A Three Bloc World? The New East Asian Regionalism." *International Relations of the Asia-Pacific,* Vol. 2, No. 2, 2002, pp. 167–95.

——— (ed.). *Japan.* Brookfield, VT: Elgar, 1995.

Ravenhill, John, Rick Doner, and Gregory Noble. *Industrial Competitiveness of the Auto Parts Industries in Four Large Asian Countries: The Role of Government Policy in a Challenging International Environment.* Washington, DC: World Bank Policy Research Working Paper, WPS 4106, December 2006.

Reischauer, Edwin O., and John K. Fairbank. *East Asia: The Great Tradition. A History of East Asian Civilization*, volume I. Boston: Houghton Mifflin, 1960.

Richter, F. J., and P. C. M. Mar (eds.). *Recreating Asia: Visions for a New Century*. Singapore: John Wiley and Sons, 2002.

Ross, Robert, and Feng Zhu. *China's Ascent: Power, Security, and the Future of International Politics*. Ithaca, NY: Cornell University Press.

Roberts, John G. *Mitsui: Three Centuries of Japanese Business*. New York: Weatherhill, 1973.

Royama, Masamichi. "Toa Kyodotai no Rironteki Kozo" ["The Theoretical Structure of East Asian Community"] (1939). In *Royama Toa to Sekai: Shin Chitsujo e no Ronsaku* [*East Asia and the World: Toward a Theoretical Understanding of the New Order*]. Tokyo: Kaizosha, 1941.

Rozman, Gilbert. *Northeast Asia's Stunted Regionalism*. Princeton: Princeton University Press, 2004.

———. "Flawed Regionalism: Reconceptualizing Northeast Asia in the 1990s." *Pacific Review*, Vol. 11, No. 1, 1998, pp. 1–27.

Ruggie, John. "International Regimes, Transactions, and Change: Embedded Liberalism in the Post-War Economic Order." *International Organization*, Vol. 36, No. 2, 1982, pp. 379–415.

Schaller, Michael. *Altered States: The United States and Japan since the Occupation*. New York: Oxford University Press, 1997.

Schirm, Stefan. *Globalization and the New Regionalism*. Cambridge: Polity, 2002.

Schulz, Michael, Frederik Soderbaum, and Joakim Ojendal (eds.). *Regionalization in a Globalizing World: Perspectives on Form, Actors, and Processes,* London: Zed Books, 2001.

Shambaugh, David (ed.). *Power Shift: China and Asia's New Dynamics*. Berkeley: University of California Press, 2005.

Shi, Yinhong. "Zhongri jiejin yu waijiao geming" ["China-Japan Rapprochement and China's Diplomatic Revolution"]. *Zhanlue yu guanli* [*Strategy and Management*], No. 2, 2003, pp. 71–75.

Shindo, Eiichi. *Higashi Ajia Kyodotai o dou tsukuru ka?* [*How to Build an East Asian Community?*]. Tokyo: Chikuma Shobo, 2007.

Shinoda, Tomohito. *Koizumi Diplomacy*. Seattle: University of Washington Press, 2007.

Skocpol, Theda, and Paul Pierson. "Historical Institutionalism in Contemporary Political Science." In *Political Science: State of the Discipline*, New York: W. W. Norton, 2002.

Skowronek, Stephen. *Building a New American State*. Cambridge: Cambridge University Press, 1982.

Solingen, Etel. "Mapping Internationalization: Domestic and Regional Impacts." *International Studies Quarterly,* Vol. 45, 2001, pp. 517–55.

———. "ASEAN, Quo Vadis? Domestic Coalitions and Regional Cooperation." *Contemporary Southeast Asia,* Vol. 21, No. 4, 1999, pp. 30–54.

Song, Chengyou, and Tang Chongnan (eds.). *Asian Regional Identity and Peaceful Development*. Chengdu: Sichuan University Press, 2001.

Stiglitz, Joseph E. *Globalization and Its Discontents*. New York: W. W. Norton, 2002.

Stubbs, Richard. "ASEAN plus Three: Emerging East Asian Regionalism?" *Asian Survey* Vol. 42, No. 3, 2002, pp. 440–55.

Suettinger, Robert. "China's Foreign Policy Leadership: Testing Times." *China Leadership Monitor*, No. 12, Winter 2004.

Sun, Yat-sen. *China and Japan: Natural Friends and Unnatural Enemies*. Edited by Leangli Tang. Shanghai: China United Press, 1941.

Takahara, Akio. "Japan and China: New Regionalism and the Emerging East Asian Order." In H. and G. H. Dobson (eds.), *Japan and Britain in the Contemporary World*. London: Routledge Curzon, 2003.

Tanaka, Hitoshi. *"21 Seiki Nihongaiko no Senryaku-teki Kadai"* ["Strategic Agenda for Japanese Diplomacy in the 21st Century"]. *Gaiko Forum*, No. 207, 2005, pp. 8–13.

Tanaka, Naoki. *Higashi Ajia Kyodotai Koso Jitsugen e no Kadai* [*Steps for Realizing the East Asia Community Plan*]. Tokyo: 21st Century Public Policy Institute, 2005.

Thompson, Williams. "The Regional Subsystem: A Conceptual Explanation and a Propositional Inventory." *International Studies Quarterly*, Vol. 13, 1973.

Tilton, Mark. "Seeds of an Asian E.U.? Regionalism as a Hedge against the U.S. on Telecommunications Technology in Japan and Germany." *Pacific Review*, Vol. 20, No. 3, September 2007, pp. 301–27.

Timmerman, Martina, and Jitsuo Tsuchiyama (eds.). *Institutionalizing Northeast Asia: Regional Steps toward Global Governance*. Tokyo: United Nations University Press, 2008.

Togo, Kazuhiko. *Japan's Foreign Policy: 1945–2003*. Boston: Brill Academic Publishers, 2005.

U.S. Department of State. *Foreign Relations of the United States: East Asia and the Pacific*, volume VII, part I, 1951.

Verdoorn, Petrus. "The Intra-Bloc Trade of Benelux." In E. A. G. Robinson (ed.), *Economic Consequence of the Size of the Nations*. London: Palgrave Macmillan, 1960.

Vernon, Raymond. *Sovereignty at Bay*. New York: Basic Books, 1971.

Watanabe, Toshio. *Nihon no Higashi Ajia Senryaku* [Japan's Strategy toward East Asian Economic Integration]. Tokyo: Toyo Keizai Shinpo Sha, 2005.

Weber, Steve. "Shaping the Postwar Balance of Power." *International Organization*, Vol. 46, No. 3, Summer 1992, pp. 633–80.

Wilczynski, J. "Strategic Embargo in Perspective." *Soviet Studies*, Vol. 19, No. 1, July 1967, pp. 74–86.

Wit, Joel, Daniel Poneman, and Robert Gallucci (eds.). *Going Critical: The First North Korean Nuclear Crisis*. Washington, DC: Brookings Institution Press, 2004.

Yamazawa, Ippei. "Comments." In Lee Jae Cho (ed.), *A Vision for Economic Cooperation in East Asia: China, Japan, and Korea*. Seoul: Korea Development Institute, 2003.

Yan, Xuetong, and Shi Yinhong. "Zhongguo jueqi yu taiwan wenti" ["Rise of China and Taiwan"]. *Lingdao wencui* [*Selection for Leaders*], No. 11, 2002.

Yao, Shumei. "Korea's FDI in China: Status and Perspective." KIEP Research Paper, 2003.

Yashiro, Shunichiro (ed.) *Nihon Tetsudo Ryoko Chizu Cho: Manchu/Karafuto* [*A Compendium of Japanese Railway Travel Maps: Manchuria and Sakhalin*], Tokyo: Shinchosha, November, 2009.

Ye, Min. "Developmental State—The Governmental Role in China's Electronics Industry." *Waseda Journal of Political Science and Economics*, No. 356, 2005.

Ye, Zicheng. "Zhongguo de heping jueqi yu dongbeiya hezuo" ["China's Peaceful Rise and Northeast Asian Cooperation"]. Beijing: Beijing University, Working Paper, 2004.

Yoshikawa, Yukie. *Japan's Asianism, 1868–1945: Dilemmas of Modernization*. Washington, DC: Edwin O. Reischauer Center for East Asian Studies, 2009.

Yoshimatsu, H. *Japan and East Asia in Transition: Trade Policy, Crisis and Evolution, and Regionalism*. New York: Palgrave Macmillan, 2003.

Zhang, Jianjin. *Zhongguo jueqi: tongxiang daguo zhilu de zhongguoce* [*Rise of China: China's Approach to Becoming a Big Power*]. Beijing: Xinhua Publishers, 2005.

Zhang, Shugang. *Economic Cold War: The American Embargo against China and the Sino-Soviet Alliance, 1949–1963*. Stanford: Stanford University Press, 2002.

Zhang, Taiyan. *Zhang taiyan zhengzhi sixiang xuanji* [*Collection of Zhang Taiyan's Political Thoughts*]. Beijing: Zhonghua Shuju, 1977.

Zhang, Yunling. *Northeast Asian Economic Cooperation*. Beijing: World Knowledge Publisher, 2004.

———. "Dongya hezuo de fazhan jiqi yiyi" ["The Development and Meaning of East Asian Cooperation"]. Beijing: Chinese Academy of Social Science Working Paper, 2003.

Zheng, Bijian. "China's Peaceful Rise to Great Power Status." *Foreign Affairs*, September/October 2005, pp. 18–24.

Zheng, Yongnian. *Globalization and State Transformation in China*. New York: Cambridge University Press, 2004.

Index

Studies in Asian Security

A SERIES SPONSORED BY THE EAST-WEST CENTER

Muthiah Alagappa, Chief Editor
Distinguished Senior Fellow, East-West Center

The Making of Northeast Asia. By Kent Calder and Min Ye. 2010

Islam and Nation: Separatist Rebellion in Aceh, Indonesia. By Edward Aspinall. 2009

Political Conflict and Economic Interdependence Across the Taiwan Strait and Beyond. By Scott L. Kastner. 2009

(Re)Negotiating East and Southeast Asia: Region, Regionalism, and the Association of Southeast Asian Nations. By Alice D. Ba. 2009

Normalizing Japan: Politics, Identity, and the Evolution of Security Practice. By Andrew L. Oros. 2008

Reluctant Restraint: The Evolution of China's Nonproliferation Policies and Practices, 1980–2004. By Evan S. Medeiros. 2007

Why Taiwan? Geostrategic Rationales for China's Territorial Integrity. By Alan M. Wachman. 2007

Beyond Compliance: China, International Organizations, and Global Security. By Ann Kent. 2007

Dangerous Deterrent: Nuclear Weapons Proliferation and Conflict in South Asia. By S. Paul Kapur. 2007

Minimum Deterrence and India's Nuclear Security. By Rajesh M. Basrur. 2006

Rising to the Challenge: China's Grand Strategy and International Security. By Avery Goldstein. 2005

Unifying China, Integrating with the World: Securing Chinese Sovereignty in the Reform Era. By Allen Carlson. 2005

Rethinking Security in East Asia: Identity, Power, and Efficiency. Edited by J. J. Suh, Peter J. Katzenstein, and Allen Carlson. 2004